Sri Saundarya Lahari
The Descent

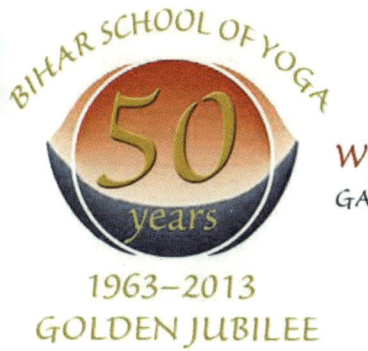

WORLD YOGA CONVENTION 2013
GANGA DARSHAN, MUNGER, BIHAR, INDIA
23rd–27th October 2013

Sri Saundarya Lahari
The Descent

Swami Satyasangananda Saraswati

Yoga Publications Trust, Munger, Bihar, India

© Bihar School of Yoga 2008

All rights reserved. No part of this publication may be reproduced, transmitted or stored in a retrieval system, in any form or by any means, without permission in writing from Yoga Publications Trust.

The terms Satyananda Yoga® and Bihar Yoga® are registered trademarks owned by International Yoga Fellowship Movement (IYFM). The use of the same in this book is with permission and should not in any way be taken as affecting the validity of the marks.

Published by Yoga Publications Trust
 First edition 2008
 Reprinted 2009, 2013

ISBN: 978-81-86336-70-0

Publisher and distributor: Yoga Publications Trust, Ganga Darshan, Munger, Bihar, India.

Website: www.biharyoga.net
 www.rikhiapeeth.net

Printed at Thomson Press (India) Limited, New Delhi, 110001

Dedication

*In humility we offer this dedication to
Swami Sivananda Saraswati, who initiated
Swami Satyananda Saraswati into the secrets of yoga.*

My Inspiration

गुरु गोविन्द दोऊ खड़े काकें लागूँ पाय ।
बलिहारी गुरु आपनो, जिन गोविन्द दियो मिलाय ॥
—कबीरदास

Contents

Swami Satyananda's Ashirvaad		xii
Author's Annotation		xiv
Swami Sivananda on Saundarya Lahari		xvi
Preface		xviii
Introduction		1

Mantras and Commentary:

1	Meditation on Shiva and Shakti	93
2	Meditation on Sri Devi's feet	102
3	Meditation on Devi in the mudra of granting what you desire	107
4	Meditation on Devi's full form in abhaya mudra (mudra of fearlessness) and vara mudra (mudra of granting boons)	111
5	Meditation on Devi's full form radiating light	114
6	Meditation on the divine and irresistible form of Devi	119
7	Meditation on Devi as a kanya with four hands holding a bow, arrows, noose and goad	122
8	Meditation on Devi at her abode made of gems, reclining on a bed made of Shiva, which is covered with a bedspread made of Paramashiva	126

9	Meditation on the chakras forming a pathway for kundalini's ascent	131
10	Meditation on the beautiful form of Devi seated on the lap of Shiva in close embrace	137
11	Meditation on Sri Chakra	141
12	Meditation on the beautiful form of Devi	147
13	Meditation on the compassionate form of Devi	151
14	Meditation on the primeval form of Devi as Prakriti, the cosmic nature	155
15	Meditation on Devi speaking	159
16	Meditation on the beautiful form of Devi bathed in the light of the sun, moon and fire	162
17	Meditation on Devi placing her hand on your head	165
18	Meditation on Devi in bhairavi mudra	167
19	Meditation on the bewitching glance of Devi	171
20	Meditation on Devi's form emitting rays of light	176
21	Meditation on Devi's glistening body in the form of lightning	180
22	Meditation on Devi sitting on a beautiful throne like an empress listening to the prayers of her worshippers	184
23	Meditation on the Ardhanarishwara (half woman and half man) form of Shakti	187
24	Meditation on Kali	190
25	Meditation on Devi being worshipped	193
26	Meditation on Shiva-Shakti in maithuna or union	196
27	Meditation on worship of Devi being done by you	199
28	Meditation on the exquisite form of Devi oozing nectar	202
29	Meditation on the Devi bedecked like a bride	204

30	Meditation on Devi seated regally amidst her divine attendants	206
31	Meditation on sound emanating from the form of Devi	209
32	Meditation on Devi as mantra, in the form of Sri Yantra in the heart centre	215
33	Meditation on Devi as mantra, in the form of Sri Yantra at the eyebrow centre	220
34	Meditation on Shiva-Shakti in maithuna	224
35	Meditation on the nirakara Shakti	227
36	Meditation on Shiva-Shakti at ajna	231
37	Meditation on Shiva-Shakti at vishuddhi	236
38	Meditation on Shiva-Shakti at anahata	239
39	Meditation on Shiva-Shakti in swadhisthana	243
40	Meditation on Shiva-Shakti at manipura	246
41	Meditation on Shiva-Shakti at mooladhara	249
42	Meditation on the crown of Devi	252
43	Meditation on the locks of Devi's hair	256
44	Meditation on the parting line of Devi's hair	258
45	Meditation on Devi's smile	260
46	Meditation on Devi's forehead	263
47	Meditation on the captivating eyes of Devi	266
48	Meditation on the three eyes of Devi	269
49	Meditation on the glories of Devi's eyes	271
50	Meditation on the allure of Devi's eyes	274
51	Meditation on Devi's glance	276
52	Meditation on Devi's seductive look	279
53	Meditation on Tri Devi, Kali, Lakshmi and Durga	281
54	Meditation on the convergence of Devi's three eyes	284
55	Meditation on Devi Aparna's eyes	288
56	Meditation on Devi's unblinking eyes	291
57	Meditation on Devi's compassionate eyes	294

58	Meditation on the sideways glance of Devi	297
59	Meditation on the erotic face of Devi	300
60	Meditation on Devi's sweet speech	302
61	Meditation on Devi's nose	305
62	Meditation on the redness of Devi's lips	308
63	Meditation on Devi's sweet smile	312
64	Meditation on the redness of Devi's tongue	314
65	Meditation on Devi's worship by the devas	317
66	Meditation on the sweetness of Devi's voice	321
67	Meditation on Devi's matchless chin	324
68	Meditation on Devi's graceful neck	326
69	Meditation on the three strands at Devi's throat	328
70	Meditation on Devi's protective arms	331
71	Meditation on the splendour of Devi's hands	334
72	Meditation on Devi's overflowing breasts	337
73	Meditation on the nectar of Devi's breasts	341
74	Meditation on the pearl necklace adorning Devi's breasts	345
75	Meditation on Devi's breast milk	349
76	Meditation on the navel of Devi	352
77	Meditation on Devi's slender waist	355
78	Meditation on the glory of Devi's yoni	358
79	Meditation on Devi before giving birth to creation	361
80	Meditation on Devi giving birth to creation	364
81	Meditation on Devi's expansive hips	366
82	Meditation on Devi's thighs and knees	368
83	Meditation on Devi's thighs and toenails	372
84	Meditation on the feet of Devi	375
85	Meditation on Devi in the mudra of granting happiness	379
86	Meditation on the kick of Devi's lotus foot	381
87	Meditation on the lotus of Devi's feet	385
88	Meditation on the feet of Devi	387

89	Meditation on the wish-fulfilling feet of Devi	389
90	Meditation on Devi as Saraswati	391
91	Meditation on Devi's graceful gait	394
92	Meditation on Devi Tripura Sundari	396
93	Meditation on Aruna Shakti	398
94	Meditation on the reflection of Shakti in the sun	400
95	Meditation on Devi in her mansion	402
96	Meditation on the most supreme Tripura Sundari in her inner apartment	404
97	Meditation on the unattainable Shakti above sahasrara	406
98	Meditation on Tripura Sundari	408
99	Meditation on the inconceivable and limitless power of Devi	411
100	Meditation on the full form of Devi	413
101	Meditation on Tripura Sundari blessing her devotee	415
102	Meditation on Devi's hidden treasures	416
103	Meditation on Devi as the source of this hymn	418
	Prayer to Shiva, the beloved of Shakti	420

Prayoga for Saundarya Lahari	423
Appendices	461
A: Sanskrit Text	463
B: Translation	478
Glossary	498
Index	508

Swami Satyananda's Ashirvaad

Suffering follows man like a shadow. Man faces distress, whether in the form of illness, financial crisis, loss of loved ones, attacks of enemies or severe emotional breakdowns. He encounters these in some way or the other throughout his life and they mar the little happiness that he may enjoy from time to time. Whether the distress is real or imaginary, he needs a solution to counteract it. Adi Sankara must have experienced this more than anyone else. Thus, out of his immense compassion, he has left behind a mantra shastra in which a remedy can be found for each and every affliction. Each sloka is a mantra which can bring a specific benefit through the blessing of Devi.

Feeling the need to present this shastra for the benefit of humanity, I inspired Swami Satyasangananda to take up the task of this monumental work after she completed her commentary on *Vijnana Bhairava Tantra*, which figured in a recent survey as an outstanding book on tantra and yoga, in terms of authenticity and popularity. I asked her to present this classical subject from the point of view of a non-classical person, so that the layman can grasp the relevance of this text in his day to day life.

In actual fact there was no need for another commentary as this sacred composition, *Saundarya Lahari*, has many commendable commentaries to its credit for scholars, which are academic, intellectual and most classical. Swami

Satyasangananda, however, has aimed her commentary towards the ordinary reader, a category which the majority falls under. Her sound analysis of tantric upasana, its immense benefits and efficacy in averting difficulties through anusthana of mantra, yantra and mandala caters to the layman, who is in dire need. Side by side it will also be of immense use to a sadhaka who wishes to expand the frontiers of his mind and discover that he is essentially Divine.

May the Goddess Tripura Sundari shower her blessings in abundance on the upasaka of *Saundarya Lahari*.

Swami Satyananda Saraswati
Rikhiapeeth
Ashwin Navaratri, 2008

Author's Annotation

Early one morning in 1986, two years before his departure from Bihar School of Yoga, Munger, Swami Satyananda called all the sannyasins to his kutir. Naturally, we were eager and excited, as we sat down before him. The room was full of sannyasins and he said, "From today, we will begin the chanting of *Saundarya Lahari* every morning at four am. Please be here on time each day." After that, each morning we all poured in and chanted the sacred mantras, many of us not familiar with the Sanskrit letters, and most of us unable to understand what we were reading. But that did not matter in the least, for the chanting of these mantras with Gurudev gave us so much *anandam*, bliss.

When we became proficient in chanting, Sri Swamiji asked us to do *likhit japa*, writing of the sacred hymns, as well as to draw the yantras related to each mantra. He pasted the yantras on a board each morning for all of us to see and copy in our drawing books. This was a fantastic experience, which every sannyasin who had the good fortune to be present must still be treasuring in the depth of his heart. It was truly unforgettable. Although we did not know it at that time, Sri Swamiji was giving each of his sannyasins the master key that would help to overcome any difficulties they might face in life, whether material or spiritual. In addition, he was revealing a way to peace, plenty and prosperity through Devi *aradhana*, worship.

Soon after that Sri Swamiji left Munger and all his sannyasin disciples, but not before he had given them an invaluable treasure. During those classes it was my duty to prepare the yantras each day on giant sized sheets of drawing paper for all to copy. I must have drawn all of those yantras at least a dozen times each. I found them truly fascinating and enjoyed every moment of it. Then I began to collect the usage of each mantra and yantra, and to see how it should be made effective. Naturally my interest deepened as I began to understand the immense importance of these hymns for each and every one of us. That is how this book was born.

Each time I read the text, or chanted the slokas, or practised the prayogas, or contemplated on them, the feeling I got was that I was diving into the deep and bottomless ocean. Just as you find new gems, new life, new treasures, every time you go deep sea diving, in the same way, each and every time I discovered something new about this amazing work of Adi Guru Sankaracharya. Just as the depth of the ocean can never be fathomed unless you are a very skilled diver and even then there are portions that you may never discover, in the same way, the depth of this work can only be fathomed by a person such as Adi Guru Sankaracharya.

The countless jewels that the reader can assimilate depends entirely on the grasp of his awareness. For those who are in tune there is no limit to their understanding. Nevertheless, the Devi will guide each one of us to understand it in the way that she knows is best for us. The understanding of this work is an ongoing process which is aided by the sadhana of Shakti worship. Thus, nothing that can be said on this magnificent work is final; there are always new ways of looking at it which the reader will experience the more he plunges into the depths of this sacred hymn, for *Saundarya Lahari* bathes the reader with the radiance of his own Self.

Swami Sivananda on Saundarya Lahari

Saundarya Lahari is an eminent text on tantra shastra, which describes the worship of *Parabrahman* or absolute consciousness in the form of upasana shakti, or Sri Vidya. It reveals the essence of Sri Vidya, which is the reason why maximum commentaries have been written on it.

This sacred hymn reflects Adi Guru Sankaracharya's heightened flight of imagination, the affectionate smooth flow of his devotion, and the unique poetic touch of his profound contemplation. It also provides an insight into the secrets of agama and tantra by giving a descriptive account of kundalini yoga, chakras and various topics on tantra.

This text is a compilation of beautiful stotras in praise of Devi or Tripura Sundari. These slokas are associated with many mantras and yantras through which the Devi can be worshipped for the acquisition of various *siddhis* or supernatural powers. Devi in the form of Sri Vidya is worshipped in two forms: intrinsic, for the highly evolved practitioners, and extrinsic, for the less evolved practitioners.

The intrinsic form of worship has neither ritual nor method. The form of Parabrahma Shiva along with Shakti is worshipped in the various energy centres or chakras within the human body. Those internal practitioners who believe in the unity of Shiva and Shakti can awaken their kundalini and raise it through the various chakras to sahasrara by worship and mantra japa. There the individual soul unites with the Supreme soul.

In the extrinsic form of worship, Sri Chakra is worshipped. The yantra of Sri Chakra is outlined on gold or any metal sheet. Then the yantra is worshipped by offering mudra, asana, arati, incense, light, naivedya and other offerings. Sri Chakra is the culmination of all yoga sadhana. One need not do any yoga practice once perfection is obtained in Sri Chakra.

Sri Chakra is made of forty-three triangles and comprises the palatial residence of the Devi. In the Sri Chakra palace, Vishnu resides between the seventeenth and eighteenth walls, Brahma between the sixteenth and seventeenth walls, and Indra and other guarding regents between the fourteenth and fifteenth walls. They all reside in their different places only for the worship of Devi. According to the *Devi Bhagavat Purana*, all the devas, including: Brahma, Indra, Varuna, Yama, Vayu, Agni, Kubera, Twasta, Poosha, Ashwins, Bhaga, Aditya, Vasu, Rudra, Vishvadeva and Marugan, meditate on the Devi, who is the cause, sustenance and dissolution of the entire creation.

By the worship of Devi, one can obtain wealth, learning, riches, success in special work, victory over the enemy, cure of chronic ailments, and so on. In order to obtain these, various yantras, bija mantras and oblations are utilized. Many people practise these slokas in order to please Devi for the fulfilment of worldly desires. The success depends on the faith and devotion of the sadhaka. If there is some delay in the fulfilment of the desired object, then the practice should be continued with devotion for a few more days. If one prays to the Mother for salvation through these slokas, one can even attain *mukti*, or liberation, the supreme goal of life.

According to the *Kurma Purana*: "Just as water has the inherent quality of putting out fire and sunlight wards off darkness, so in this Kali yuga, the name of Devi is verily capable of destroying all sins."

Preface

The worship of the Divine as Mother can be traced back to the most ancient times that predate even history. The Gayatri mantra and early vedic hymns in worship of Shakti, personified as Usha, the dawn, indicate the existence of Shakti worship from the earliest times. Of all the images of Shakti, perhaps the dawn, the exact moment when the sun comes up over the horizon, showering the earth with prana, is the most striking. This significant display of Shakti's splendour and power has been forever enshrined in the Vedas. Saraswati, Lakshmi and Durga also find a significant place in the vedic hymns.

In early times, the vedic culture was matriarchal, not patriarchal. It spoke of *matri bhoomi*, the Motherland, and not *pitri bhoomi*, the Fatherland. People conversed in their *matri bhasha*, mother language, not *pitri bhasha*, father language. Sons were addressed by their mother's name, and belonged to the mother, not the father. Krishna was called Yashodha nandan, son of Yashodha, and Devaki nandan, son of Devaki. Similarly, Arjuna was addressed as Kaunteya, belonging to Kunti. Such examples are found throughout the vedic literature.

The vedic culture was a progressive tradition. The women had an important role in society and entered all fields of life, whether warfare, governance, acquisition of wealth, romance, art, dance, literature, music or even the spiritual quest. As recorded in the *Brihadaranyaka Upanishad*, the great female rishi, Gargya, in the presence of a full court of intellectuals, openly asked Yajnavalkya, "What is that imperishable government that remains when everything else is vanquished?" To which he replied, "Yes, there is an imperishable government of the Self that exists even when the sun and moon cease to shine."

In the Satya yuga, the devas invoked the power of Devi before they entered into battle with the *daityas*, or demons. In the Treta yuga, Sri Rama performed the *Navaratra*, nine days worship of Devi, to invoke the power of Shakti before he set foot on Lanka. Later, in Dwapara yuga, Arjuna invoked Devi before entering the Mahabharata war. In the Kali yuga, Adi Guru Sankaracharya invoked Devi in his time of distress to avert an illness, so that he could accomplish his mission.

The deities of the Kali yuga are Devi and Ganesha. They are manifesting everywhere and have infiltrated our very lives. Ganesha represents good living, comfort, luxury, good food, good clothes, art, literature and music. Devi symbolizes immense wealth and unlimited power, coupled with beauty and glamour. Is that not what the whole world is mad about today? So this attraction for Shakti has filtered down through the ages to the present day, in spite of the overshadowing influence of other religions and cultures. India is the only land that addresses women as Devi. Whether mother, sister, daughter or wife, she is regarded as Devi.

Devi is a combination of Lakshmi, Parvati, Durga and Saraswati. All of her roles are sacred and enacted in every home, such is her immense influence on this land. Twice a year Devi is worshipped throughout India for nine days during Navaratri. This worship is conducted in Christianity also and is known as the Novena, nine days worship of Mary. Navaratri means the nine nights when the soul has to journey through immense darkness to experience the light. The nine nights represent the eight *apara prakriti*, which are the five tattwas, mind, buddhi and ahamkara, the symbols of darkness, and the one *para prakriti*, the symbol of illumination.

Significantly, both periods of Navaratri occur at specific times of the year when nature is in transition. The first occurs in March, when nature transits from winter to spring, and the second in October, when it transits from autumn to winter. At these times nature is in motion and vibrant with prana to facilitate this transition. The Navaratra worship is very special, because at these times Shakti comes alive. This gives immediate and immense benefits to the worshipper, which can range from the mundane to the sublime. Like Rama, Arjuna, and much later Sankara, we too are in dire need of help during times of distress. There are moments of crisis in our lives when we do need divine intervention, and in this lies the importance of *Saundarya Lahari*.

This invocation of the supreme Shakti by Sankara has been recorded by the tradition. Had the *stutis*, or songs of Rama and Arjuna praising God as Devi been recorded, perhaps we could have utilized them as well, but unfortunately that is not the case. Sankara's stuti is most relevant to us today, because it can help to alleviate the crises we face in our daily lives when we are poor, destitute and hungry, when we are struck with disease, grief and loss, or when we want to acquire name, fame and good fortune.

Saundarya Lahari can also alleviate mental conflicts such as fear, turmoil, insecurity, depression, disappointment, lack of self-confidence, despair, worry and anxiety. It can be utilized for the cure of diseases that are *adhidaivika* in nature, due to some unknown, mysterious causes that no medicines can heal. Most modern day ailments, which are not of an infectious nature, come under this category.

The tradition has given a detailed description of how to utilize these sacred mantras and the benefits that can be derived by the chanting of every *sloka*, or verse. This list is appended at the end of the book for the knowledge and use of the reader. However, to obtain their full efficacy, these mantras and yantras should be known through an adept or proficient guru.

These sacred mantras can also be recited daily as a form of worship. It is not necessary to chant the entire *Saundarya Lahari* every day. Daily chanting can even be done of three, six, nine, twelve (multiples of three) slokas, setting aside *ashtami*, or the eighth day of the moon, which is specific for Devi worship. On this day the entire *Saundarya Lahari* can be chanted.

Gradually, as you become proficient in chanting the mantras, you can start the practice of *likhit japa*, or writing the mantras, as well as drawing the yantras in your *Saundarya Lahari* notebook, which you should keep nicely at your place of worship. In the course of time, an entire sadhana will unfold before you. These mantras and yantras are a boon, and will allow you to awaken a very important source of strength within yourself.

Shakti has to be worshipped and revered if you are to experience her full benefits. Since she is present in everything, you will have to inculcate an attitude of reverence for all that you are, all that you have and all that you experience. A culture that regards Shakti as an energy to exploit, use and strip naked can never attain her full glory, which is of immense and unimaginable potential. From the day you were born, you have been surviving on her handouts. The air you breathe, the water you drink, the food you eat, the homes you live in are all the gifts she has bestowed upon this earth. The iron, steel, gold, silver, gems and wealth are all her creations. No creature has used nature for this sort of benefit, apart from man.

Shakti is abundant with prosperity which she reflects through her cosmic nature. She is always replenishing the creation which she has given birth to. So, if you wish to experience the full force of her benevolence, you will have to develop an attitude of reverence towards her, not arrogance. That is the secret key to release the great power of Shakti. Therefore, the mantras of *Saundarya Lahari* should always be chanted with reverence, as an act of worship and with due respect. It is this attitude of reverence and worship that will unlock the closed door of inner experience and unleash the full force of its magnitude.

This book provides a wonderful way to resolve the difficulties and distress faced in life, whether as a *grihastha*, householder, or a *sannyasin*, renunciate. It is a book of worship and prayer, which is the highest attitude the mind can assume. This attitude arises when the mind comes under the influence of the *atman*, or soul. The same gross mind constituted of the twenty-six tattwas, which is subject to time, space and object, is refined to the highest degree, and begins to act in conjunction with the heart and soul. Such a mind projects the higher traits of love, compassion, devotion, surrender, faith and belief, because these are qualities of the soul.

Worship requires a one-pointed mind and a pure heart. It also requires a disciplined body and the constant, unbroken attitude of surrender. In addition, the intellect must be balanced so that it does not disturb the mind by undue reasoning, which interrupts the worship. By performing *Saundarya Lahari* sadhana in this way, you are simultaneously practising raja yoga, bhakti yoga, hatha yoga, karma yoga and jnana yoga. Thus *Saundarya Lahari* sadhana is the culmination of yoga, intended to draw out your highest potential.

Nothing happens until something moves.

—Albert Einstein

Introduction

Human beings alone have the capacity to define God. All other beings, such as animals, birds, snakes, insects, plants and minerals, do not. We have been granted this ability by divine grace. Other life forms may understand, experience or see the creator, but they cannot convey that or elaborate upon it. Human birth has given us immense possibilities. We can discuss and define God, as well as experience Him directly. Ultimately, it is not the knowledge of God that transforms, but the experience.

In the midst of this tumultuous world, we can come face to face with the creator. Five thousand years ago Arjuna did just that on the battlefield of Kurukshetra. Amidst rockets and missiles, arrows and ammunition, Arjuna experienced the Godhead! This is why the human birth is most coveted, even amongst the devatas. Both Rama and Krishna, who have been revered since time immemorial as the incarnations of Vishnu, took birth as human beings.

Nothing can compare with the human existence. Even the saints and siddhas descend to the earthly plane to experience the wondrous creation of God! The cool breeze, the sparkling seas, the lustrous trees, the wondrous mountains, the amazing diversity of flora and fauna, all speak in silent testimony of the glory of the creator.

The animals and birds may have supernormal abilities to sense the creator, but they are unable to explore the existence of God. Man alone is capable of inquiring into the nature of God: How does God look? Is he fair or dark, tall or short? Does he have hair? Does he have many hands and legs, or two of each as we do? Does he have a beard? Is God male or female? Where does he dwell, up in the sky or down on earth? Does God get married and have children? After all, who the hell is God?

From time immemorial many rishis and munis, saints and sages, tapasvis and sannyasins have tried to answer these questions. One such person was Adi Guru Sankaracharya and the modern world owes much to him. Although born in a traditional Indian setting, Sankara had a universal flavour. Even today intellectuals, sannyasins, scholars, spiritualists, sadhakas, philosophers, religious heads and laymen the world over are grappling with the complexities of his teachings, which shed light on many questions about the nature of existence, whether macrocosmic or microcosmic, relative or absolute.

Life of Sankara

Sankara was born in his maternal home at Perawa, a village in Kerala. In the period when he lived, vedic thought had seen its decline. Buddhism had reached a zenith and was also starting to decline. The masses had turned away from the vedic lifestyle, denying many of its fundamental assertions. Described as a saviour of the vedic philosophy, Sankara's style of teaching and resurrecting the Sanatana tradition was inimitable. The ease and aplomb with which he resolved contentious issues between the Vaishnava and Shaivite sects, whose differences were deeply entrenched, was an achievement which only an enlightened visionary could accomplish.

Today, the high priest of the Vaishnava temple at Badrinath in the Himalayas is a Namboodri Brahmin Shaivite from South India, and the poojari of the famed Shiva temple at Rameshwaram at the southern tip of India is a Vaishnava from the Garhwal region of North India.

Can you ever conceive today of a Muslim conducting Rudra abhisheka at Mahakaleshwar in Ujjain, or a Hindu conducting namaz at the Dargah? This was Sankara's vision and contribution to national and spiritual cohesiveness. Only an evolved soul can integrate the minds of the people in such a fashion.

The Dashnami Order, to which all sannyasins today belong, was also Sankara's vision. Prior to the founding of this order, sannyasins had no platform through which they could be recognized, acknowledged or unified with a common aim. The Saraswati tradition with its peetha at Sringeri was founded by Sankara twelve hundred years ago. My guru, Swami Satyananda Saraswati, was initiated into this tradition in 1947 by Videhamukta Swami Sivananda Saraswati. Tripura Sundari, the Devi invoked by Sankara in *Saundarya Lahari*, is the *adhishthatri devi*, established deity, of Sringeri peetha and forever enshrined there. Sri Vidya upasana, another name for Sri Chakra pooja, is the worship that is performed at this most sacred peetha of the Sankara tradition.

Sankara formulated the sannyasa tradition, the akharas and maths, the tradition of Sankaracharyas and their democratic outline, for he recognized them to be the upholders of Vedic Dharma and essential for its sustenance. If the Vedic Dharma is still vibrant today, it is on account of the Dashnami sannyasins, who roam the length and breadth of India, saturating the people with vedic ideas, customs, beliefs, traditions and concepts. Sankara's *bhashyas,* or commentaries on Vedanta, stand unparalleled right up to this day, in the face of which Buddhism, a mighty doctrine, simply disappeared from the face of this land.

Sankara's invocation of Devi

Due to his strong appeal and influence, Sankara also made many enemies amongst the adherents of various traditions to whom he posed a threat. In those days certain sects practised forms of black magic and sorcery with the potential to destroy or annihilate others. Sankara fell victim to one such plan on account of the boldness of his ideas and beliefs, which were turning the minds of the people, as recounted in his famous *Digvijaya*, or conquest of Bharatavarsha.

One of Sankara's rivals thus plotted to terminate his life by transmitting a deadly disease into his body. At this time Sankara invoked the cosmic Shakti or Devi in order to avert the malefic influence. Where else can a child in deep distress turn but to the mother, for no one is more loving, caring, kind, beautiful and powerful than a mother. So Sankara turned to that divine power, which is the substratum of existence, before whom even the mightiest of the mighty are humbled.

The mere glance of Devi Ma can breathe energy and life into even lifeless dust particles, for she is the source from which all beings have emerged. As Sankara himself has proclaimed, "The attributeless Reality or *Paramataman*, which can assume many different foms for the benefit of the devoted, becomes most fit to be worshipped as the Mother, who has the power to endow the entire world with prosperity and auspiciousness in every sphere of life."

The outcome of this invocation was the rapturous mantras of *Ananda* and *Saundarya Lahari*, which have astounded even modern scholars by the nature of their content. Until this time, Sankara was essentially preaching the doctrine of Advaita Vedanta in which there is simply no room for worship of any form. This ultimately led some of the strongest supporters of his vedantic views to deny that that these exquisite verses were composed by the great vedantin, Sankaracharya. Unlike any of his other works, *Ananda* and *Saundarya Lahari* paid homage to the *roopa*, or form, of Devi. However, the basic tenets of Advaita Vedanta that Sankara practised and preached were of the formless reality, which has no gender, designation, shape or size.

In *Saundarya Lahari*, Sankara calls out in ecstasy to Devi and propitiates her form, which he describes in minute detail from the top of her head down to the tips of her toes. This kind of worship of Devi with a detailed description of the different parts of her body bewildered people, for Sankara was not under the influence of maya. There is a well known and interesting story about him in this regard.

Sankara performs an unusual feat

Once Sankara was pulled into a debate with Sharada, the wife of Mandan Mishra. In order to save her husband from defeat by the acharya, she had asked Sankara to answer some pertinent questions from the *Kama Shastra*, knowing fully well that the acharya had no knowledge or experience in this field. Thus she hoped he would admit defeat and her husband would not be humiliated. However, instead of accepting defeat, Sankara asked for three days grace, so that he could prepare his argument and win the debate.

The acharya then performed a rare feat known as *parkaya pravesh*, which literally means 'to enter the body of another'. First, he prepared a place for his body to rest in a cave under the watchful eye of a close disciple to whom he had given the necessary instructions. Then he directed his consciousness out of the body through yogic kriyas and went in search of a suitable person whom he could enter to have the experience of conjugal life.

He soon came across the recently deceased King Amruk, who was lying in state, being mourned by his kith and kin. Amongst the mourners was the beautiful wife of the king. So, Sankara decided to enter the dead king's body, upon which the king opened his eyes, as if he had simply been asleep, and resumed his life in the kingdom. Although the queen and all the subjects of the king were astonished by this miraculous event, they were too elated to even question how the king could have risen from the dead.

Sankara remained in the body of the deceased king for three days and nights, performing all the royal duties, one of which was marital relations with the queen. After that, he had to leave the kingdom and return to his own body, as the period of grace was drawing to an end and he had to resume the debate. His physical body, which was being closely guarded by the disciple, also had to be rejuvenated before the stipulated period of time elapsed.

Sankara returned to the debate, which he won with flying colours, much to the surprise of Sharada, the wife of Mandan Mishra. According to the stipulation of the debate, both husband and wife then had to accept Sankara as the final authority and become his disciples. The tradition in those days was that when defeated in *shastrartha*, intellectual debate on the scriptures, one had to accept the victor as one's master, guru and teacher.

Advaita or Dvaita?
Other than this episode, unparalled in history, where a saint entered the body of another to experience sexual intimacy, Sankara lived the life of a *tapasvi*, or ascetic, preaching the doctrines of the formless reality which exists within the individual and need not be sought outside. The four *Mahavakyas*, or great statements, of Vedanta: *Aham Brahmasmi*: I am Brahman, *Tat Twam Asi*: That thou art, *Ayamatma Brahma*: Atman is Brahman, and *Prajnanam Brahma*: Awareness is Brahman, formed the basis of his teachings.

So, where and how did the concept of Devi's form creep in, and how did the great acharya concede to the worship of Devi? Sankara said that the supreme reality cannot be confined to any form, gender, time, space or designation, because it is formless. Then what is the meaning of this contradiction in his beliefs, his critics argued. Needless to say, if one is in search of contradiction, it can easily be found, even where it does not exist.

Sankara was an exponent of Advaita Vedanta, a doctrine that firmly reiterates the oneness of existence. *Advaita*, or one, is the opposite of *dvaita*, or two. In Advaita, the individual and the supreme reality are one and the same; duality simply does not exist. However, the verses of *Saundarya Lahari* appear to describe the worship of Devi as the supreme godhead, existing as a separate entity somewhere in the stratosphere. Here the experiencer and object of experience are two, not one.

Had Sankara conceded to dvaita, as the poem suggests? At face value this may appear to be so, but upon closer examination, one may arrive at a different conclusion. The mantras of *Saundarya Lahari* suggest that Sankara was undergoing a unique experience within the framework of his mind and body. He was experiencing divinity in the form of Adi Shakti, the highest power, and she manifested before him to answer his fervent prayers. He saw her form and conversed with her, just as we see people around us and converse with them every day.

The only difference, although a significant one, was that his experience was internal and our experiences are external. The outer experience is composed of gross *tattwas*, elements or matter, and the inner experience is composed of subtle and higher tattwas: *satyam, shivam, sundaram*, or truth, effulgence and beauty. These are a potent combination of qualities which pave the way for higher experience. The brilliance of a person who can invoke such an experience will outshine every adversary, as Sankara did. Even today his teachings captivate the minds of sadhus, sannyasins, spiritual seekers, philosophers and intellectuals, as well as the general public.

Sankara's inner experiences endowed him with a divine hue. These experiences were not ordinary, but transcendental. He did not experience the Devi as an entity outside of himself; rather this experience took place in the depths of his consciousness. His vision, conversations, ecstasy and devotion were internal. He was in the raptures of samadhi. There was unity within and without. He had transcended the body and mind, and become the experience itself. Is that not *advaita bhava*, the experience of oneness? In fact, *Saundarya Lahari* establishes that the Shakta experience of this variety is not in opposition to Advaita.

Power of materialization

Even if one assumes that Sankara was seeing Devi as a separate entity and was conversing with her, as one would with someone who appears in front of him, that does not contradict the tenets of Vedanta. Vedanta does not oppose the idea of materialization of matter through the power of a mind that has attained transcendence of matter. Only the mind that has transcended matter can cause matter to manifest. Sankara had that rare quality of mind.

Once when he was living with his venerable guru, the great Govindapadacharya, on the banks of the Narmada, the river was in spate and rose until it was about to rush into the cave of his guru, who was deep in meditation. At that time, the young Sankara stood at the entrance of the cave with his *kamandala*, or water pot, so that the samadhi of his guru would not be disturbed, and the strong waves of the Narmada were swallowed up in his water pot by the power of his mind. The other disciples, who were there in the service of the guru, witnessed this unique phenomenon.

Sankara not only experienced Shakti, the divine manifestation of energy, he could also confer her grace on others. His *Kanakdhara Stotra* showered wealth on the poor woman, who readily gave him the last morsel of food in her house when he went there for alms. She did not refuse him, although she had many mouths to feed. After Sankara left her house, gold coins rained down upon her and she received wealth beyond her dreams. The *Sat Chandi Mahayajna*, held by Swami Satyananda at Rikhiapeeth for twelve years, is a contemporary example of how the divine energy of Shakti can confer grace and blessings on those who worship her with love and devotion.

During the five days of yajna, the cosmic energy is invoked within the nucleus, or *bindu*, of the *Devi vigraha*, or yantra of the cosmic Mother by the repetition of mantras. At the seat of Chandi in Rikhiapeeth, the body of Devi is *yantrasharira*, represented by yantra. Swami Satyananda's worship of Devi created this convergence of energy in the same way as Sankara created it, through worship in the form of mandala. Through the chanting of mantras and ritual worship of yajna, the energy invoked in the yantra vigraha of Devi then projects outward, conferring blessings upon the thousands of people who come into that energy field during the yajna.

In the same way the energy contained in the mantras of Sankara's *Saundarya Lahari* create an energy field, conferring blessings and boons of all kinds upon those who chant them in worship and with devotion. In order to create that energy field, the highly refined forces that are omnipresent within oneself and also in the atmosphere are awakened through powerful mantras and crystallized or merged in the receptacle of yantra or mandala to become a unified energy field.

Just as the radio receives sound waves, the yantra and mandala are efficient receptacles to attract and hold the energy that is gathered in the vicinity where mantras are chanted for any length of time. The energy can also be invoked in the appropriate manner, so that it resides permanently in that mandala or yantra and does not abandon it. This ritual is known as *pranapratishtha*. These are the awakened shrines or *siddhapeethas*, where the energy is on display and available to each and everyone.

During a yajna the cosmic energy is invoked, worshipped and displayed within a particular time frame, after which the worshipper bids farewell to the force field with proper rites and rituals. In the Sat Chandi Mahayajna the cosmic energy invoked in the yantra was encapsulated in the hearts of thousands of participants, who had *darshan*, a glimpse or vision, of Devi in her radiant splendour. Afterwards they took this highly potent capsule back to their homes and utilized it in their life, whether for progeny, wealth, name and fame, or to generate the experience of divinity within themselves, which is the highest aim of yajna.

Means and end

So, Advaita is the ideal or goal, and Dvaita is the means to reach it. If the supreme consciousness can manifest as man, then why does it seem impossible that it can manifest in other forms as well, such as Devi or Shakti? Dvaita is the systematic approach to the experience of oneness. When that goal is achieved, the concept of Dvaita naturally falls away, without any effort or struggle. Dvaita is a crutch or support for the vagrant tendencies of the mind, which needs a point of focus on which to converge. In external life the mind has many things to focus on: job, wealth, family, loved ones and oneself. But the mind which looks inwards encounters total darkness at first. To counteract that darkness, it needs an inward point of focus; otherwise it will enter the unconscious state and regress. The mandala or yantra acts as that point of focus.

Even if Dvaita were not considered to be a part of Sankara's ethos or teaching, still one could understand his need to reach out to the beliefs and level of awareness at that time. The people he was addressing were steeped in esoteric practices, which invoked the divine through the use of mantras, herbs and rites. Although Sankara formulated the tenets of Vedanta and was one of its fiercest defenders, he also showed the way to those who were not able to reach that goal directly.

One of the fundamental characteristics of Sanatana Dharma and the vedic tenets that Sankara preached, which other religions do not possess, is its way of adapting to the needs of different levels of people and society. Thus it was able to address the changing notions of mankind most effectively, for under this system God could be male or female, with attributes or without. If the trend of people was to pursue *nirguna upasana*, formless worship, then it was perfectly all right, but if instead they wished to perform *saguna upasana*, worship with form, then mantras, yantras and mandalas were made available, whereby they could develop their inner awareness through them.

You may believe in vegetarianism, but if you open a shop in a locality where everyone eats meat, you will carry meat as a commodity. The needs of people must be catered to in order to reach out to them, no matter what your personal beliefs may be. This applies most to a saint or mahatma, whose primary goal is to guide mankind towards the divine life and realization of oneness with the Supreme Self residing within. Each and every person is poised at a different level of evolution. A few people may perceive the reality as Absolute and One, but most need the support of duality to reach the godhead.

Swami Satyananda's tradition is also Vedanta, not yoga. But he preached yoga to the people, as that was the need of the hour. A visionary thinks not just of the present, but well into the future. Society is not static; there is constant change, development and degeneration of ideas, beliefs and understanding. Visionaries are more concerned with the shape that society will take in the course of man's evolution; what the understanding of people will be in two hundred or even two thousand years from today.

Therapeutic and divine properties of mantra

At the same time, one must remember that the immediate purpose of Sankara's worship was to alleviate the disease that had struck his body. He utilized the spiritual science and the rites and rituals propagated in tantra to influence the gross matter of the body. He availed himself of an extraordinary method to cure himself, which one could never imagine or conceive of.

When one is ill, does one ever think of chanting mantras to awaken and arouse the healing force of prana shakti? No, one rushes off to the doctor. Only when all the doctors have failed to cure the disease will this option be considered.

Sankara could also have gone to the *vaidya*, or doctor, but instead he appealed to the creatrix of matter from whom the *pancha mahabhutas*, five elements, emanate, permute and combine to create our bodies and all other forms, both animate and inanimate.

Saundarya Lahari designates the specific mantras and their yantras and mandalas for the cure of the three different types of afflictions: i) *adhibhautika*, physical disease, ii) *adhidaivika*, those afflictions caused by natural calamities, and iii) *adhyatmika*, or those ailments that have their root in some unknown cause. It also reveals the manner in which these mantras and yantras can be utilized to awaken the *moola prakriti*, or primal energy, which resides in the form of kundalini within the framework of the body. In this way one can generate a higher level of energy and awareness to influence the body or any form of matter and attain the aim which one seeks.

This enchanting composition of Sankara consists of 103 mantras. The first 41 mantras form the first section, known as *Ananda Lahari*, and the following 62 mantras form the second section, *Saundarya Lahari*. *Ananda Lahari* contains the mantras that describe the invocation of Devi by singing her praises, with reverence, devotion and surrender. They also depict her subsequent awakening in the temple of the body, where she resides as *kulakundalini*, primordial cosmic energy, and her ascent through the chakras up to sahasrara. There she unites with *akula*, Param Shiva, and enjoys her honeymoon. Afterwards, drenched in *amrita*, or nectar, she begins her descent back down the sushumna passage, irrigating, rejuvenating and awakening the entire structure of the body, mind, and emotions to the experience of *param ananda*, highest bliss and ecstasy. This time she is not alone; she is accompanied in her divine descent by her consort, Shiva.

The descending of the awakened kundalini results in a state of total intoxication in which the awareness is alert, aware and alive to the divinity within the body. Each and every pore, cell, nerve, tissue and membrane is divinized. This description of the entire process that generates ecstasy and bliss, or *ananda*, forms *Ananda Lahari*, which deals with the pancha mahabhutas, chakras and kundalini, and thus is related to kundalini yoga and mantra shastra. However, that is not the final experience, because then the Devi manifests in her full splendour and glory. Seeing that radiant form, Sankara burst into rapturous praise of her beauty and glory, which comprises the substance of *Saundarya Lahari*.

His mastery of verse and eloquence of expression, coupled with divine sentiment, gave rise to mantras that contained the power of the energy that converged within him at that time. *Saundarya Lahari* contains the most refined form of mantra energy. Sankara captured and concealed that energy in the *shabda*, or words, of the mantras. Anyone who chants those mantras can awaken the healing energy of Shakti, either as an experience of *advaita bhava*, or oneness with the Devi as in the case of Sankara, or *dvaita bhava*, the experience of seeing the Devi outside of oneself as a separate entity to behold, as Paramahamsa Ramakrishna did.

The dvaita experience
Advaita is a concept or belief, but one's daily experiences are of dvaita. Advaita is the ultimate experience, but dvaita is the reality one faces in day to day life. How can one ignore it? Although Sankara preached, believed in and had the experience of advaita, this does not mean that he had no knowledge or experience of dvaita. The *chandala*, or outcast, reminded him of his own teachings when he happened to pass by him on the road. Sankara saw the outer form of the chandala, which was of low caste, and hastily avoided him. Even though he had established that the Absolute was everywhere and in all beings, yet this action revealed that he saw the chandala as different from himself.

Every embodied jiva has to live within the gambit of the senses, subject to taste, touch, sound, smell and sight. Sankara was no exception, yet he was not bound to the world of matter and senses. He was able to transcend them with utmost ease and enter a different dimension of consciousness, known as *samadhi*, total oneness or absorption in the object of meditation. At once, he paid heed to the chandala's words and realizing his error, bowed down to touch his feet and embrace him.

In the *Nasadiya Sukta* of *Rig Veda*, where the seed of atheism is intricately woven, the rishis and munis raised some very pertinent questions. What existed before creation, when there was nothing? What was there before the sun, moon, stars, light and fire came into existence? And what was the cause of creation? Why did this creation manifest? Was it because the supreme consciousness felt alone and the desire arose to become many?

The Upanishads boldly declare that the supreme consciousness became many due to the desire to stand face to face with itself, to revel in its own glory, and to see its own reflection in creation, as if in a mirror. The absolute reality beholds itself in myriad forms in this wondrous creation, in all the sentient and insentient beings. That is the dvaita experience of the creator. If the creator can have the dvaita experience, then why is it absurd to think that the devotee also has the same experience?

Nature of Shakti

The power to manifest itself is inherent in the supreme consciousness, and that power is Shakti, energy in all forms: organic, physical, mental, emotional, spiritual, kinetic, electric and electromagnetic. *Shakti* literally signifies that which has the potential to create. When people create ideas out of thin air, they are revealing their Shakti. There are people who create empires, and they too are showing their Shakti. Anyone who exhibits talent and creativity puts their Shakti, or power to create, on display. Even the creation of a beautiful moment in someone's life is a glimpse of Shakti. Shakti is that force which can be known through her multifarious activities.

Shiva is omnipresent and thus it stands to reason that Shakti, who is none other than Shiva, is omnipresent too. There is no place where Shakti does not reside. Shakti is the pure, vibrant energy at the core of each and every object in the manifest and unmanifest creation. Shakti is inherent in all existence, seen and unseen, from the tiniest pebble to the mightiest galaxy. The air one breathes, the food one eats, the homes one lives in, the mountains, seas, forests, sun, moon and stars are all manifestations of Shakti.

Shakti is present even in an abstract thought or idea. Without Shakti, or energy, one could not think or have any plan or purpose. Every situation and event is also a display of Shakti. On account of the energy field inherent in an event, it can be transformed into waves and later recreated and produced on a television screen. One often perceives and responds to the energy fields in which one lives and works. These fields are subtle forms of Shakti created by the people who live and work in that place. One attracts different kinds of energy to the immediate environment by the nature of one's lifestyle, thoughts, actions and speech. The energy in an awakened shrine such as Tirupathi, Baidyanath Dham or Vaishnava Devi is very different to the energy in one's home and work place, where one spends most of one's life.

Shakti determines the birth, life and destiny of all manifest beings, but that does not restrict her role to the material world. Shakti is both *jada*, inert, as well as *chetana*, conscious. Shakti exists and also knows her existence. Both of these qualities are present in Shakti, as opposed to Shiva, who is only chetana, or consciousness. Shiva manifests into form through Shakti, so that he can perceive himself in order to know that he exists. This is the theory of tantra, which assumes that we are all manifestations of the Supreme Being, and the purpose here is to realize that.

Power of the mind

However, the majority of people are so ensnared in the glamour of Shakti's outward appearance that they are unable to transcend worldly experience. Perhaps the emerging theories of science will change all that, for now we are on the threshold of a new era. Scientists are talking about higher forms of energy which are not just physical and tangible, but mental, emotional and spiritual in nature. Moreover, they relate these forms of energy to the creation of matter. They say that man is just a bundle of thoughts. As he thinks, so he becomes. What he wishes for is what he gets.

These theories substantiate the claims of the tantric and vedic rishis, who spoke about mind over matter and the power of mind to materialize objects at will. What scientists are discovering today was already known thousands of years ago to the sages and seers who systematically recorded it in the tantric and vedic texts. The only difference is that in the present scenario, scientists require machines to create matter, whereas in ancient times, the original scientists known as *rishis* accomplished the same through a powerful mind.

Today it would be absolutely impossible for the average person to conceive of a higher force manifesting before his eyes in the form of devi or devata. But there have been and even today there are people who have had this experience of darshan. In previous eras materialization through the power of mind or mantra was commonplace. During the *Satya, Treta* and *Dwapara yugas*, thousands of years ago, there were many instances of such happenings. These were not mere tales told by grandmothers to amuse young children. They were events in history that were later recorded in the Puranas.

The word *purana* means 'old', and the *Puranas* speak of events that occurred once upon a time, long long ago. They are not mythology, but ancient history recorded and preserved in the garb of legend. In the Treta yuga, Sri

Rama invoked the most powerful *astras*, or weapons, ever known, through the power of mantras. The *brahmastra* and the *pasupatastra* were missiles of such high potency that they could dry up an ocean. Today, poised on the threshold of a new era, man is playing with the idea and possibilities of mind over matter, but he has lost the mental power necessary to make it happen. He may believe that it is possible, but he cannot experience it as his ancestors did in the past, without the immense power and potency of Shakti.

The pure, unadulterated force of Shakti makes things happen in a way nothing else can. The first and foremost step one has to take is to believe in the existence of this supreme Shakti, who is at the very root of all beings. If one succeeds in this first step, then half the battle is won. That is the most difficult step, but if one can take it, life will be transformed as one beholds the wonders of Shakti. The belief in Shakti should become inherent, just as you believe that you are a man or a woman. You do not need to be convinced of this; you just know it with the same quality of faith and conviction. There is no doubt, not even for a second, as the idea is not just superficial but deep rooted. Similarly, one has to believe in Shakti as the source of creation with the same grade of faith and conviction.

The ordinary awareness of man is too gross to perceive the play of Shakti at subtle levels. He remains stuck at the sensorial level in the enjoyment of form, smell, sound, touch and taste perceived by the gross senses. But the role of the senses is severely limited. With age or disease, they cease to function. Moreover, they are totally dependent on time, space and object, which are the categories of the mind. If any of these is absent, the mind does not function and cannot enjoy or experience anything.

However, when the refined awareness is developed or awakened, it does not depend on the senses for its source of experience; it can perceive in the absence of time, space and object. The refined awareness is able to experience subtle states of form, sound, taste, touch and smell, which have their source in higher dimensions of consciousness. In one's present state of mind it is difficult to conceive of this idea, as it is beyond the range of normal day to day experience. But one should not reject this possibility; rather one should draw inspiration from the illumined souls who have been blessed with the divine inner experience, which is darshan.

Sankara was one such luminary. He had the darshan of Devi and invoked her grace to retain the spark of life within him. He had no physical attachment to the body, but his mission was not fully accomplished. His devotion and surrender to that mighty, awesome power of Shakti did not go unheeded, and the Devi appeared before him. This experience resulted in the mantras of *Saundarya Lahari* in which he described each and every *anga*, or limb of Devi, from head to toe, without the least reserve. Critics and followers of the great Sankara, a renowned vedantin, were perplexed by his tremendous upsurge of Devi bhakti. The great believer in the formless reality was speaking of nothing else but form.

Sundara – beauty

The supreme reality, or *paramatman*, has time and again been described by the vedic and tantric seers as satyam, shivam, sundaram. The first two of these attributes: *satyam*, truth, and *shivam*, auspiciousness, are intangible and imperceptible, except in the form of experience. The third attribute, *sundaram*, or beauty, however, is the attribute that is tangible and perceptible, because beauty always relates to form. Can satyam, truth, or shivam, auspiciousness, be perceived? No, they can only be experienced, but sundaram, beauty, can be perceived as well as experienced. Therefore, the attribute of sundaram is most vital, as it is the one through which one can see, hear, touch, smell and taste the divine.

Why were these mantras called *Saundarya Lahari*? The word *saundarya* means 'beauty' and *lahari*, which has often been translated as waves, in actual fact means 'surge'. A surge of electricity alters and completely overrides the flow of electrical energy to the different gadgets that are plugged into it. In the same way, inner experiences can cause a surge or influx of high voltage energy to the dormant parts of the brain, which can completely transform the mundane awareness into an exalted state, where one can even experience the divinity within.

Thus, by the title *Saundarya Lahari*, which literally means 'surge of beauty', one can assume that the experience Sankara was undergoing was a surge of beauty in the form of Devi. So, one has to first define saundarya, or beauty, in order to understand the title given to these mantras. What is beauty? The sublime experience of the rishis, munis and seers in regard to the Supreme Being was described as satyam, shivam, sundaram, which is similar to *sat-chit-ananda*.

They said that the supreme consciousness is satyam or truth, which means pure, unadulterated and spotlessly clean. Being of the nature of truth, it is also known as shivam, or auspicious, which means that it is always accompanied by positive and creative vibrations. This leads to the third attribute of sundaram, or beauty, because that which is pristine and pure emits positive vibrations and gives happiness and joy. A type of ecstatic thrill and excitement arises that has to be beautiful.

Bliss, or *anandam*, is an indication of satyam, shivam, sundaram. Misery is an indication of their absence. Whenever some bliss is experienced, one should trust it and follow that direction. Then one will be moving towards the Supreme Self, because bliss is its fragrance. If one follows bliss, one will be following nature and will never go astray. When one is natural, blissful and relaxed, one can behold beauty and wisdom as it arises. Beauty cannot be experienced by an agitated mind. The mind must be calm and dispassionate in order to perceive beauty.

Without discrimination and dispassion, beauty is short-lived; it withers and dies. If one wants to experience undying beauty, one must develop dispassion, *vairagya*, and discrimination, *viveka*, along with devotion and reverence to the form of beauty. Only then will the form of beauty elevate and bring one closer to the divinity that resides within. If one is full of desire, lust and passion, the experience of beauty will diminish, leaving one unsatiated and dissatisfied, and giving rise to mental agitations of every kind.

There is beauty in restraint, self-control and silence. The saints, sages, tapasvis, sadhus, sannyasins, rishis and munis bear silent testimony to that. The grace, beauty and equipoise that they carry cannot be found elsewhere, even in the most fashionably dressed Miss Universe. There is beauty in balance, which is why nature is beautiful, because nature is the epitome of balance. The day is balanced by the night, the heat by the cold, the sun by the moon, the high mountains by the low land and the deep seas by the skies. If one wants to add beauty to life, one has to inculcate balance in each and every aspect.

This entire creation is an expression of beauty. There are waves of beauty wherever one looks: the mountains, oceans, trees, animals, birds, aquatic life, flora and fauna, sunrise and sunset, full moon and stars. Each and every speck of nature compels one to accept that this creation is a work of some master craftsman. In sharp contrast, the gadgets and objects made by man may titillate the senses, but they do not stir his soul. One derives peace of mind and tranquillity from the beauty of nature, as it helps one to connect with God and with the divinity abounding in the universe. Whenever one wants to connect with oneself, one can just take a walk in the woods or along the seashore. The creations of man, on the other hand, agitate the mind and disturb its serenity.

People are driven by some mad passion to possess all the things that money can buy, and even those that it cannot. The beauty one sees in man-made creations is only a shadow or reflection of the beauty of God's creation. It is said that beauty lies in the eyes of the beholder. To the average person the idea of beauty is limited to clothes, jewellery, cosmetics, cars, and other objects, but a highly aware and sensitive person would have a totally different concept of beauty. A smile or a glance can be beautiful; the innocence of children can move the sternest of hearts. Beauty is not only related to objects and people; even thoughts and ideas can be beautiful. An ugly looking person may have a beautiful mind. Even the most beautiful person will not hold your attention for long, if there is not a beautiful mind to go with it.

There is beauty in the rose as well as the thorn. Wit and intelligence are beautiful, but a simpleton or fool may also be beautiful. There is beauty in the fierce tiger and the venomous snake. Although they are wild, dangerous and frightening, they are perfect creations. Another name for beauty is also perfection. Beauty always sends a thrill through one's being because of its perfect nature. Beauty brings one very close to the experience of the divine.

In the *Bhagavad Gita*, Lord Krishna says that wherever there is *aishwarya*, beauty, perfection and accomplishment, one should at once recognize that as his *amsha*, or manifestation. One should feel that a part of him has intermingled in the DNA of that person, place or thing. In this way one imbibes the active DNA of God. All have inherited the DNA or coded blueprint of divinity, but the password to decode and activate it has not yet been found. Those persons who have *vibhooti*, divine power, have activated that DNA through God's grace.

Beauty carries a taste of the universal. It has no caste, creed or religion; neither is it restricted to gender or nationality. It is just beautiful! Beauty can be spotted anywhere, even in vast crowds. There are people who stand out, for they are blessed with that essence of beauty. It radiates from them, compelling others to look at them again and again, so that the beauty becomes imprinted on their mind. Beauty is ethereal and mysterious. It always has a surreal aura around it, which leaves the beholder wonderstruck and immensely moved.

Beauty in any form reminds one of God, because God is the storehouse of beauty. All beauty has emanated from that divine principle which is all pervasive and has been described in the *Vedas* as sundaram, most beautiful. One simply cannot forget beauty; it remains etched in the mind and one is able to recall it vividly, even if the experience is long gone. Beauty brings out the best in everyone. Poets burst into poetry, musicians into music, and artists into beautiful art forms.

Even an ordinary person is transported by beauty into a world of dreams, ecstasy, relaxation and relief. People spend a lot of money to remain locked up in a theatre for three hours to watch the latest beauties on screen! This gives them thrills and joys which they do not get elsewhere!

Grades of beauty

There are grades of beauty. Beauty can enchant the senses, captivate the mind, stimulate the intellect, tickle the heart or stir the soul. The beauty that is limited to the body, senses, mind and intellect is of a lower grade, because eventually it loses its hold on one. The beauty that touches the heart and soul is everlasting and can be regarded as true beauty, which is of an ephemeral and divine nature. This is the beauty that *Saundarya Lahari* depicts while describing the perfection of Devi.

Beauty is always enticing. Lower grades of beauty entice one towards passion and lust, which eventually leads to attachment and bondage, but divine beauty attracts one towards liberation, or *moksha*. The luminous beauty of Devi that Sankara describes has every element of worldly beauty magnified a thousandfold. The thrill and excitement of beholding Devi's beauty is not of the senses, but the delight or *spandan*, vibration, of consciousness, the sattwic vibrations that emanate from the experience of atman.

The definition of beauty is any form that attracts or overwhelms the mind, that compels one to look at it again and again, and that one does not want to take the eyes away from. Everyone wants to behold beauty. No one wants to look at ugliness. All forms are of three grades: beautiful, mediocre and ugly. Ugliness repels. Mediocrity may arouse temporary interest, but then the appeal wanes. Beauty is compelling. Whenever it comes within view, one does not want it to go away; one is absorbed by it and wants to see it again and again.

Attraction is the prime quality of beauty and repulsion of ugliness. Beauty draws one's total, undivided and unbroken attention. If a beautiful woman enters the room or appears on the television screen, at once one is captivated and immediately turns the attention to her, no matter what one is doing. Everything else can wait. Whenever the mind is captivated, one may consider that it is very close to the divine.

Form of beauty

When one thinks of beauty, what is the form that immediately captivates the mind? Is it the form of a dog, goat, elephant, mountain, river, sea, sky, plant or tree? Each of these is beautiful in its own right, but are any of them compelling enough to hold the unwavering attention for a length of time? For example, how long can one keep the gaze fixed on a dog, cat, tree or rose? These may generate some interest for a short period, but then the attraction wanes and the attention is distracted and diverted to something else. But the form of a beautiful woman can keep one transfixed! Even the diehards who speak against beauty pageants and obscene disclosure on television and in films, secretly find opportunities to look at the beauty of women.

The form of beauty exists within the realm of maya, but beauty is in all dimensions and at all levels, for beauty is a thing of joy forever. It exists at the level of maya in the glamour and glitter of the world, and also at the level of atma in a glimpse of the divine. If beauty is considered to be one of the attributes of God, then it is eternal. Just as truth and auspiciousness are eternal, concepts of beauty also never die. Beauty can be experienced in truth and auspiciousness, because beauty is truth and beauty is always auspicious. That is why intuitively one always has a craving for beautiful things!

The beauty that one beholds in matter has a limited lifespan. Over time it withers and dies, but nevertheless it is a reflection of the beauty of the atma. In fact, each and everything of this world has its origin in the atma, which is the seed of all creation. The atma has a *yoni*, or womb, just as the female form has a yoni for the purpose of creation. The atma has breasts too, just as the female form has breasts to nourish and suckle its newborn. The atma has hips and navel, a waist and a girdle, nails and hair, eyes and lips, each serving their own purpose, just as the human body parts serve their purpose. The atma has emotions too and a sexuality of its own, separate from the flesh.

Everything in this creation has a physical, mental, psychic and spiritual dimension. The human form has a yoni and lingam; in the spiritual form that would be the *atmalingam* and *atmayoni*, composed of the effulgent sattwic tattwas that bestow anandam in the form of beauty. That is the yoni of Devi, which Sankara worshipped, not the yoni which is related to in the physical form. The atmayoni and atmalingam are the source from which everything has sprung. The physical yoni gives a titillating, orgasmic experience, but the cosmic yoni of Devi confers liberation!

Similarly, atma has a mind, intellect and heart too. The human mind, intellect and heart are an extension of that supreme atma. One is closely connected to the cosmic heart and mind through the individual heart and mind. It is only possible to experience this connection by transcending the individuality in which one is rooted. Sankara transcended the individuality because of his purity and was able to experience the beauty, or saundarya, of the atma in its most glorious form, that of Devi.

Beauty and spirituality

In the tantric and vedic tradition, sex, spirituality and beauty, or saundarya, go together. Spirituality does not deny the beautiful and the sensuous. Beauty and purity also go hand in hand. An impure substance can never be beautiful. Beauty and simplicity too are synonymous. The most beautiful things in the world are always pure and simple. Another quality of beauty is truth; whatever is truthful is beautiful. The main criteria of spiritual life: truth, purity and simplicity, are the same as those of beauty. So how can spirituality ever be deprived of beauty?

However, there is a vast difference between material and spiritual beauty. Material beauty is only a shadow of the brilliance of spiritual beauty. They are poles apart, like the earth and sky. One keeps you in bondage and the other liberates you. One is finite and fades with time, the other infinite and eternal. One keeps you in the realm of *dvaita bhava*, duality and limited experience; the other leads to the experience of *advaita bhava*, the experience of oneness with the supreme atman.

Sankara was devoid of dvaita bhava and immersed in advaita bhava. He did not feel himself to be different from *paramatman*, the supreme self. He was able to experience total unity within and without. Therefore, he perceived the three attributes of paramatman: *satyam, sivam* and *sundaram*, and conveyed the magic of that experience to humanity through the splendid mantras of *Saundarya Lahari*. These mantras remain unparalled, because they convey and confer the same grace which Sankara experienced in a glimpse of the divine.

The form of the atma is sundara, or beautiful. The word saundarya also denotes form, because beauty is first seen and then experienced as pleasant, overwhelming, attractive, compelling or unique. But one cannot have that experience unless one sees it through the outer or inner eye. The experience of the outer eye is within the realm of the *gunas*, or qualities of nature, and the experience of the inner eye is *trigunatita*, beyond the gunas, consisting of pure, unadulterated consciousness.

Bondage and liberation

The same form of a beautiful woman, which evokes passion, lust and desire at the level of maya or dvaita, can also generate the experience of *moksha*, liberation, at the level of advaita, when maya has been transcended. Desire is not in the woman; it is in the mind. When the mind evolves to the level of advaita, the form of a woman can confer benediction and the highest level of experience. This is a most important claim of tantra, which should not be overlooked or underrated, because herein lies the seed of liberation! One does not have to deny anything; one simply has to evolve the mind to the extent that the object or form of bondage becomes the source of liberation.

When speaking on tantra, Swami Satyananda has often said that the rose one sees during the inner experience of meditation is actually a replica of the rose one sees outside. The outer rose is real and the inner rose is a *pratyaya*, or support for the mind. When the eyes are closed, the rose seen in the inner space is as authentic as the one that is seen outside with the eyes open. The only difference is in the quality of perception; one is made up of petals that can be touched, and the other is made up of consciousness that one can experience. In the same way, the form of a beautiful woman perceived outside with the eyes open is made up of flesh, blood, bones and marrow, which are subject to decay and death, whereas the beauty of Devi described in *Saundarya Lahari* is made up of consciousness, which is eternal and absolute. One confers bondage the other liberation!

Movement of awareness from dvaita to advaita

Even the objective experience that one has in daily life is on account of what is within. It is oneself that reflects in the outer world. The love one feels towards someone is a result of one's inner perception. The same is true for all emotions, such as hatred, compassion, guilt, anxiety, mercy and kindness. One's inner self is reflected through these emotions. The outer person to whom these emotions are directed is not the cause of the upsurge of emotions. The cause is inherent and one is projecting oneself or one's mind. If one is objective in every situation and remains analytical about oneself, one will come to the same conclusion.

This idea forms the basis of *mandala* or *murti pooja*, worship of an image. The three-dimensional mandala or murti, which is seen outside, becomes a receptacle for the projection of mental energy, which according to the nature and potency of the mandala comes back to one divinized and transformed. Through the ritual of mandala worship, when this energy re-enters one's inner space, on account of its purity it fuses with the consciousness, releasing *brahma granthi*, the psychic knot of creation, in mooladhara. At that moment total absorption is experienced in the form of the mandala on which one has been meditating.

This absorption, if sustained, leads to the release of *vishnu granthi*, the psychic knot symbolizing emotional attachment, in anahata. At that time the level of absorption in the mandala is transcended and one experiences the pure nature of consciousness. This is a state of non-duality, where the experiencer, the experience and the object of experience merge and become one experience of unity with the self or atman. However, this is only a momentary merger; the main merger takes place when *rudra granthi*, the psychic knot symbolizing attachment to manifest form, is pierced in ajna by maintaining the non-dual awareness for long periods.

In anahata, there is a movement from samprajnata to asamprajnata samadhi. But once the awareness ascends to ajna, the destination for the mega merger is sahasrara. The most important chakra for *Samaya tantra*, which is the basis of *Saundarya Lahari*, is sahasrara, not anahata or ajna. In ajna, the awareness experiences nirvikalpa samadhi and in sahasrara it experiences nirbija samadhi. This is the systematic movement of awareness from dvaita to advaita for those who are steeped in duality, which is the case for most of us. Only rarely does a Sankara appear, who is beyond duality from birth.

Projection of consciousness

The form which one worships outside is the projection of one's own consciousness. The atman projects itself outside on the form of the mandala made of stone or inside on the form of the mandala made of consciousness; both are real. When one opens the eyes the inner mandala disappears, and when one closes the eyes the outer one fades away. Similarly, Sankara's darshan of Devi was a projection of his own atman, which he perceived in the form of Devi. The atman has no gender; it is formless, attributeless and can assume any form.

The yogic and tantric texts stipulate that each being is comprised of a combination of three energies: positive, negative and neutral. These energies are also known as *ida*, *pingala* and *sushumna*. Ida relates to *chandra*, the moon, or mental energy and is negative or female. Pingala relates to *surya*, the sun, or physical energy and is positive or male. Sushumna relates with atman, the spirit, and is the neutral or spiritual energy. This means that each individual, regardless of gender, is a combination of male and female energies.

The concept of *Ardhanarishwara*, a form of Shiva-Shakti, which is half male and half female, illustrates this potentiality. The statue of Ardhanarishwara, a symbol of the Shiva-Shakti tattwa residing in each individual, is enshrined at the Elephanta Caves, on an island off Mumbai. The atman can thus assume any form, according to whatever the consciousness is attuned to. So, if the consciousness is attuned to beauty, or sundara, then it will manifest as a form of Devi.

The form of Devi is not just beautiful; it is bewitching and totally captivating. Even Vishnu assumed the form of Mohini in order to cast a spell over the danavas, or demons, during the historic *samudra manthan*, churning of the ocean. Vishnu could have assumed any form. Why did he choose that of a woman? Because he knew that the danavas would be so fascinated by this form that they would forget about the coveted *amrita*, or nectar, that could grant them immortality.

Devi, the supreme Shakti, is beautiful and beneficent, but she is terrifying and powerful too. Her glory is unlimited, as she governs the entire creation. Even her terrifying form is strikingly beautiful, attractive and appealing, because her terror is all merciful and intended for the benefit of mankind. She is the epitome of love and compassion for all living beings and the entire creation. She nurtures and nourishes everything out of this tremendous love that she embodies. It is her love and compassion that renders her the most beautiful of all. True beauty is reflected in Devi, who is a personification of love and compassion. Beauty without these qualities is just superficial and cannot hold the attention of anyone for long.

Although she is described as capable of putting down the mightiest of the mighty in texts such as *Devi Mahatmya* and *Srimad Devi Bhagvatam*, those who love her with devotion are rewarded with a glimpse of her beautiful form, radiating love and compassion. Even the most egotistic demon, Mahishasura, supported by a large army of brave soldiers, could not subdue her and had to admit defeat. With smiles and guiles, Devi is victorious in every situation, because her magnificent energy is the outcome of satyam, shivam, sundaram; truth, auspiciousness and beauty.

Tools of tantra

During Sankara's time, spiritual culture was in decline and the sacred rites and rituals of tantra were very popular because they could be used to achieve whatever goal one desired:

wealth, health, prosperity, power, revenge, virility, warding off evil, disease and death, obtaining beautiful women, progeny and property. These rites and rituals were being used to help others as well as to achieve devious ends. A weapon can be utilized to protect as well as to kill; it depends entirely on whose hands it falls into. As a result the use of black magic, occultism and sorcery was rampant in society.

Sankara tried to restore the sanctity of these important rites and rituals, which incorporated the use of yantras, mantras, mandalas and amulets. As a philosopher and visionary, he understood the value of tantric practice and how much it had degenerated. So he tried to bring back its true perspective by teaching its proper relevance, importance and utility in life. Thus, even though his tradition was Vedanta, in *Saundarya Lahari*, Sankara presented the mantras, yantras and mandalas that can be utilized to achieve all aims in human life, whether *dharma*, *artha*, *kama* or *moksha*, righteousness, material fulfilment, emotional fulfilment or liberation. Sankara had complete knowledge of the science of mantra, yantra and mandala, and every stanza of *Saundarya Lahari* is a testimony to this.

Sankara was a disciple of Govindapadacharya, a student of the revered Gaudapadacharya, author of the well known *Subhagodaya*, a treatise on tantric upasana that sings the glories of Tripura Sundari. She is the highest Shakti, who is none other than Parvati, the consort of Shiva, who manifests when kundalini awakens.

As Sankara belonged to the tradition of these two highly acclaimed acharyas, he was well acquainted with the principles of this work. He added his personal experience, as well as all that he must have learnt from his own guru to his composition of *Saundarya Lahari*, which became famous as a shastra of mantra, yantra and mandala, and can be regarded as an enlargement of Guru Gaudapadacharya's work. That Sankara was also a noted tantric teacher of the Tripura line is thus beyond doubt. Another important tantric text authored by him is *Prapanchasara*, which lends credence to this fact.

Although *Saundarya Lahari* is commended for its poetic excellence, the potency of each mantra to achieve a vast array of benefits is most remarkable. The efficacy lies in the fact that each stanza is composed of powerful mantras, which have corresponding yantras and mandalas. Together or singly these mantras, yantras and mandalas confer a vast array of benefits, which relate to one's daily life as well as spiritual aspirations.

Sankara worshipped Devi in order to avert the disease which he had developed while putting down the stalwarts of certain philosophical and religious beliefs. Quite naturally some of them tried to retaliate by casting a spell on him. In order to nullify their attack, Sankara stood in the waters of Narmada at Omkareshwar, the place where he had met his Guru, Govindapadacharya, and began an *anusthana*, intensive mantra meditation, for the worship of Devi, in her *shodashi roopa*, her complete form as Parvati, the daughter of Himalaya and the beloved of Shiva. The disease which had struck his body was eradicated by this ritual worship. However, a trace of it still remained in the form of a fistula, which later made him decide to leave his mortal body at the age of thirty-two, when the purpose of his birth had been fulfilled.

This is most significant, because the heritage that Sankara left for humanity was a treasure trove of invaluable techniques to ward off the afflictions and obstructions faced in the course of human life. Everyone faces afflictions and searches for remedies. One knocks on many doors. But Sankara says why search outside, when one has the power within to overcome all difficulties. There are techniques and tools available to protect oneself from all dangers and difficulties.

The valuable techniques of mantra, yantra and mandala, which are an integral part of tantric science, were handed down by Sankara in the form of a poem. Therein lies the importance of *Saundarya Lahari*. This poem is like a nuclear missile. One has to become the launching pad and aim the missile at the right target. Tantra has utilized the tools of yantra, mantra and mandala here in a unique manner to achieve the complex and complicated desires that obsess man in his life, as well as to confer divine blessings and supernatural powers.

According to *Lalita Sahasranam*, in which the thousand names of Devi are venerated, it is said that the form of Devi is not composed of flesh, blood, bones and marrow, but of mantra, yantra and mandala. Everyone is composed of sound, but that transcendental sound has been reduced to its grossest form in the physical body. In the case of Devi, the purity is retained. If the thousand names of Devi in *Lalita Sahasranam* were classified, one would discover that her auspicious form, or *swaroopa*, is described as *murtiswaroopa*, the three-dimensional mandala that adorns many homes, *mantrikswaroopa*, the mantra received from the guru, and *yantrikswaroopa*, the linear, geometrical designs within which the Devi resides, just as one rests within the confines of the body.

Sound produces waves. When these waves condense and converge, they constitute lines, which form circles, triangles or squares. This is how mantra is transformed into *yantra*, which literally means to restrain or centralize a strong force within the confines of something. Yantra is the subtle form of mantra, or transcendental sound, which assists the sadhaka in awakening an uncontrollable power or energy. Yantra focuses the mental energy of the sadhaka in such a way that it can align itself with the power of the mantra. Just as a focused awareness helps the sadhaka to perfect the mantra, in the same way, yantra helps to generate the experience of inner illumination through mantra. Yantra and mantra are both tools for awakening the enlightened consciousness.

According to the science of mantra, if one meditates on the meaning of any sound and simultaneously focuses or absorbs one's total awareness in that, the object on which one is meditating manifests before one. This three-dimensional object which manifests before one through the power of mantra is known as *mandala*. Together yantra, mantra and mandala are invaluable tools in this process of perfecting the inner awareness and expanding it throughout the body, which is the true aim of tantra.

The uniqueness of tantra lies in the fact that it is both a sublime philosophy and a practical science. It does not proclaim high sounding theories without giving ways for their practical and daily application. This is achieved through the highly evolved science of mantra, yantra and mandala, which is intricately woven into its philosophy. These three tools form the basis of *Saundarya Lahari*, thus shedding light on many aspects of both tantric upasana as well as yoga sadhana. Thus, in order to utilize this splendid work as a basis of sadhana, it is necessary to understand the mechanics of each of them.

Mechanics of mantra

The word mantra is composed of two syllables: *man*, which signifies 'contemplation', and *tra*, which means 'liberation'. As such, *mantra* literally means contemplation upon that which leads to liberation: *Mananaat trayate iti mantraha*. The possibility of a sound leading to liberation seems incredible, because the power of sound has been underestimated and related only to the gross sounds that are heard in everyday life. However, a particular decibel of sound has the capacity to shatter glass or even to start an avalanche. Sound also has an effect on plants, trees, birds and animals. Cows yield more milk if mantras and stotras are played in their vicinity. In fact, the cows at Rikhia refused to give milk on the day that the *Ramayana* was not played for them due to the absence of electricity! Such was the power and effect of the sound of the *Ramayana* mantras.

Sound has four frequencies, known as *para*, cosmic, *pashyanti*, mental, *madhyama*, subtle, and *vaikhari*, gross. In order to attain the right frequencies for liberating energy, one will have to attain the pashyanti and para frequencies. Vaikhari is audible sound, such as the spoken word. At this level one repeats the mantra aloud, intoning each sound. As one perfects the vaikhari stage, one gradually enters into the madhyama stage, where the sound of mantra is not audible, but repeated in a slight whisper, inbetween verbal and mental repetition.

In the pashyanti stage the repetition is purely mental, which heightens the frequency of the mantra. With that subtle vibration of sound energy, the mantra repetition becomes spontaneous and the consciousness begins to assume the form of the mantra. When this stage is perfected and the frequencies are intensified, one automatically enters the stage of para or transcendental experience of the mantra. The energy of the mantra creates an awakening and explosion within. There is expansion of the mind and liberation of the energy, allowing the consciousness to skip over the boundary of the finite mind, time and space, to experience what is beyond.

In the theories of creation, according to Tantra, Vedanta, Samkhya and other Indian philosophies, *nada*, or sound, is the first manifest form of creation. Even in the Bible one finds the statement: "In the beginning was the word and word was with God." The first word is *Aum*, which is described as the transcendental or cosmic sound. Constant repetition of the mantra *Aum* stimulates and expands the different levels of consciousness within. All mantras and sounds originate from *Aum*, which is the eternal nada, reverberating in the atmosphere. With the correct instruments one can listen to the sound of eternity in the surrounding space as well as within one's own being, and one will find striking similarities to the *Aum* sound, which is regarded as the *pranava* mantra.

Aum is the first mantra, but all mantras are forms of nada. In fact, the Sanskrit alphabet is composed of fifty-one *matras*, or letters, and each letter is a mantra in its own right and can be used as such. Each letter of the alphabet is called an *akshara*, which means imperishable, and relates to the eternal sound that is forever reverberating in the cosmos at extremely subtle frequencies. This is why merely reading Sanskrit stotras, such as *Saundarya Lahari*, alters the framework of the mind and consciousness, inducing heightened states of awareness. The Sanskrit akshara (letters) and *shabda* (words) are related to energy centres which are directly connected to the centres in the brain. Correct intonation causes pressure at those points which stimulates corresponding areas in the brain and alters the awareness.

Sound has both volume and frequency. But in relation to mantra, the most important aspect of sound is frequency. Volume has a limited range, confined to a certain area, where one is speaking or chanting. In order to increase that range and cross the unlimited borders of time and space, it is necessary to increase the frequency. Just as radio waves of high frequencies carry the news that is recorded thousands of miles away to one's home, similarly mantras, or transcendental sounds, operate through heightened frequencies. So, if one wants to penetrate the depths of consciousness, right up to the *karana sharira*, or causal body, where the samskaras and karmas are stored, one will have to raise the frequency of the mantra through regular and constant repetition.

Mantra and purification
Mantra is most important for spiritual evolution, because it speeds up the process very effectively. Tantra claims that the first requirement of spiritual sadhana is *shuddhi*, purification. Without shuddhi, one can remain stuck at the same point for a very long time. Tantra advocates asana and pranayama to purify the body, and the practices of antar mouna, ajapa japa, yoga nidra, tattwa shuddhi and kriya yoga to purify the mind. These methods effectively purify the *sthoola sharira*, gross body, and *sukshma sharira*, subtle body, but how is one to purify the *karana sharira*, causal body, where nothing can reach?

Purification at this level is most important if one wants to advance in meditation. The only force that can penetrate this deepest layer of one's being is nada, or transcendental sound. The karana sharira immediately responds to nada in the form of mantra. This response is similar to a person who has heard a melody in the womb of his mother or in his early childhood. Much later, when he happens to hear the same melody accidentally somewhere, he immediately feels drawn to that sound, although he may not consciously remember having heard it before.

The karana sharira is attuned to transcendental sounds of amazing frequencies, which are storehouses of shakti. These individual aksharas, or sound syllables, are called *matrikas*, which is synonymous with shakti. These are the most powerful form of mantra, called *bija*, or seed, mantra, which are the root sounds from which other mantras have arisen. A bija mantra is a concentrated form of energy, which is ascribed to a particular level of consciousness.

Mantras are not the name of God, as is often the misunderstanding. They are sound energy in seed form, which are sown in the depths of the consciousness where they cause a stir, bringing everything up to the surface. If one had to clean an abandoned house full of rubbish, first one would push everything out, then sweep, dust and clean away the cobwebs. After that one would bring any useful items back inside, arrange them nicely, and discard the rubbish. In the same way, the practice of mantra is a means to clean up and rearrange the entire psyche at the causal level.

According to tantra there are many specific and special energy centres or points located in the body. These centres, along with each part of the physical body, have a corresponding mantra by which they are influenced. These mantras are used in the tantric practice of *nyasa*, in which mantras are systematically placed at specific centres and parts of the body, to perfect the inner awareness, thus generating an awakening and subsequent illumination, which transforms the body into a receptacle for higher powers. The sound produced by the movement of the breath is also a mantra, which is known as *Soham*. This mantra is spontaneously repeated with each breath, 21,600 times a day, and is known as the *ajapa* mantra. The Upanishads say that contemplation on this mantra alone can arouse the kundalini and alter the awareness.

Mechanics of yantra

Mantra and yantra are totally inseparable, like two sides of the same coin. Every mantra has a corresponding yantra, which is utilized for focusing the consciousness when it is released from the matter of the body through the practice of mantra. If this is not done, the consciousness has no direction and begins to dissipate; it may even regress or enter into darkness. The word yantra is derived from the root *yam*, which means to stop, to control, to balance, to contain, to focalize a powerful energy at one point or place.

The molecules and atoms that compose matter can be conceived as yantras, because they are perfectly designed storehouses of nuclear energy. Within each atom there is endless energy and the aim of tantric sadhana is to awaken this dormant energy. The point where the energy is contained in atomic or molecular form, and where it manifests, is known as yantra. In that sense the chakra centres along the spinal column in the human body are also yantras. By focusing the awareness on these centres, one can attain great supernatural powers. For example, if one is successful in focusing the awareness on the centre which controls the eyesight, then one can have visions of far away events and places. In the same way, the *indriyas*, or senses are also yantras which can be expanded to release the inherent energy within them, so that one may taste, touch, see, hear or smell in the absence of objects.

There is a cosmic dance taking place within each and every atom which constitutes the body and all matter. The partners in the dance are Shiva and Shakti, but one is unaware of this phenomenon, because they are perfect dancers and never miss a step. So, one sways to their rhythm without knowing it. Even science is not fully aware of this cosmic phenomenon which exists in each and every part of one's being. Tantra says, why search outside, when the real source is lying within? One's whole body is a yantra in which the tremendous energy of the cosmic superpower resides.

Without the aid of yantra, it is impossible to focus and direct the awakened energy for higher purposes. A yantra is composed of a combination of geometrical shapes, such as line, square, triangle, circle and point, or bindu. The focal point of a yantra is always the bindu, which is the nucleus, representing the seed from which creation has sprung and into which it will return. In the scheme of evolution, according to Tantra and Samkhya, the interplay of nada, bindu and kala gives rise to creation. Bindu is the point from which a *spandan* or vibration gives rise to *nada*, sound, and *kala*, waves and particles of light. Just as nada gives rise to mantras, kala, which emanates as rays of light, gives rise to yantra. This world is a result of sound and light interacting upon each other. Science also says the same.

The visual concept of yantra, although symbolic, has vast significance in terms of spiritual experience. The internal consciousness that one tries to tap is a world of signs and symbols, not of words and logic. As the saying goes, one should use a thorn to remove a thorn. In the same way these esoteric and occult symbols relate to the inner being, which is also a world of symbols. This process may be difficult to understand with the conscious mind, but that is irrelevant because the process takes place anyway, even if one does not understand what is going on.

In French schools, yantras have been utilized to improve the memory, performance, intelligence and inherent potential of children from the ages of six to twelve. The yantras were placed on the walls of the classroom for a period of time. Sometimes the children were asked to copy the yantras in their drawing classes, but other than that, the conscious attention of the children was not drawn to the yantras. The subliminal influence was entering the children's brain, as the yantras were in their indirect view all the time. Those children who were exposed to yantras in the classroom showed significant improvement in their aptitude, behaviour, attention and memory. They became quiet, peaceful and happy, as opposed to the earlier restless and disturbed state which was blocking their learning potential.

Sri Yantra
Yantras influence the creative and intuitive intelligence, but their true purpose is the flowering of spiritual experience. This is accomplished through a gradual unfoldment of the multiplicity of layers that comprise one's entire being from gross to transcendental. Yantras can be made of sand, clay, silver, copper, bronze, gold, crystal or even drawn on paper, with each medium having its own efficacy. The most versatile and efficacious of all yantras is *Sri Yantra*, which is complete in itself, as it houses the entire energy of the *pindanda*, or microcosmos, and reveals the connection with *brahmanda*, the macrocosmos, as well. This yantra is the abode of the entire manifest universe, its creation, sustenance and dissolution, and also contains the missing link to its source, the unmanifest. Sri Vidya forms the basis of tantric worship according to Samaya tantra and its esoteric potential is revealed by Sankara in *Saundarya Lahari*.

Sri Yantra is constructed around the bindu at the centre, which is enclosed in forty-three triangles that are formed by the intersection of four upward facing triangles and five downward facing triangles. These intersecting triangles are further surrounded by three circles, the first of which has eight petals on its outer rim, the second has sixteen petals and the third has three rims. This entire complex structure of bindu, triangles, circles and petals is surrounded by an armoury or protective outer layer which has four gates or points of entry.

Sri Yantra represents the body of Shiva and Shakti. It is the place where they are eternally seated. It is a depiction of the totality of energy abounding in the universe in all its different forms, as well as its interrelation with consciousness. In this way it depicts both Shiva and Shakti. According to the *Shaktisutra*, an important tantric text by Rishi Agastya, this body is the Sri Chakra. Just as nine triangles or chakras enclose one bindu, in the same way, one bindu, located in sahasrara, is the central point of the six chakras located in the body.

Visualization
Although yantra and mantra play a significant role in *Saundarya Lahari*, the most important point revealed by Sankara is the importance of mandala. We have to remember that Sankara was not thinking, he was seeing. Thought and visualization are two entirely different processes. The first depends entirely on the mind and the second begins only when the mind is transcended. As long as the mind is active, one can think, but cannot visualize. Visualization begins when the mind slows down and the thoughts begin to cease.

Visualization is a highly creative process. A person who is able to visualize clearly will definitely have a superior level of perception, which is very useful for developing the inner experience in its entirety. Even the deadliest diseases can be cured through a process of visualization. In order to gain proficiency in visualization one must first learn how to reduce the flow of thoughts. Thoughts are dissipated energy, which prevent one from seeing within. If one is able to concentrate this dissipated energy which keeps arising in the form of millions of thoughts, then visualization occurs.

The process of seeing involves *roopa*, form, and thus the concept of mandala, which is essentially form, is the most prominent feature of *Saundarya Lahari*. Sankara was seeing the mandalas of Devi in a vast array of hypnotic and enchanting forms which were full of soul stirring beauty. He was not seeing yantras or hearing mantras, rather the form sprang forth in his moment of inner illumination. Although this may seem like an anticlimax to his staunchest followers, the vedantins, on the other hand, it shows the broadness of his vision and his capacity to resolve the contentious issue of *sakara* and *nirakara*, with and without form, in such a wonderful way.

What one sees depends on the quality of his mind. This is why *shuddhi*, or purification, is a prerequisite in all the traditions or systems of meditation. Otherwise, one will only see the demons and ghosts buried inside the Pandora's box of the mind. Sankara was pure, untainted and aware, so his vision was of the wondrous form of Devi. Moreover, it was not just a vision, but an experience which touched the depths of his being. Thus, he started conversing with Devi, just as one would with a beautiful woman who happened to enter the room. He praised her and described her beauty, grace and radiance, as well as each and every part of her body from head to toe. Mind you, he was not just seeing a woman; rather he was seeing his atman projected before him as the highest Shakti.

Power of Shakti

Sankara's worship of Devi was accepted, and he was able to awaken Adi Shakti, the root matrix of creation, the one who is responsible for human birth and evolution. She appeared in the depths of his sublime meditation to bless and redeem him from the effects of the disease that had attacked him due to the curse of his enemies. After all, who can correct the defects that arise in one's body and mind better than the force that created one? One's mother and father are simply the biological parents, but the atman, which is responsible for life and enters the foetus in the fourth month, is infused by a greater force, known as shakti. The parents may take all the credit for one's birth, but they are mere puppets in the hands of that force, and would not have the potency to produce a child without it.

Similarly, that force cures one of disease and despair, but the doctor takes the credit and collects the bill. All the greatest inventions in the field of medical science and technology are nothing compared to the power of Shakti. Whatever one has understood and known until today is due to that power, due to which one is able to perceive, think, cognize and discover. If that principle of intelligence and energy were to withdraw, one would be nothing more than a corpse.

Shakti alone can resolve any suffering that one undergoes on the physical, mental, emotional, psychic or spiritual levels. Shakti, not Shiva, is the source of the body, mind, psyche, and atman. The *jivatman*, or individual self, enters the body on account of its attraction for the prana shakti, in the form of kundalini that is hidden within its folds. Sankara understood that in order to fulfil his purpose, it was not Shiva whom he had to worship, but Parvati, who is none other than Shakti. Together they are the father and mother of the universe, but in order to influence the life process, it is mother Parvati who has to be invoked.

Mechanics of mandala

What Sankara saw was not yantra, but mandala, which he evoked through a process of deep, inner visualization. His ecstasy on seeing these beautiful mandalas of Devi resulted in the rapturous and most efficacious hymn of *Saundarya Lahari*. These mandalas or three-dimensional images of Devi are important tools of meditation, because they are the closest replica of living creatures that one can identify with. Sankara invoked the mandala of Devi because he wanted to exert a healing influence on his body by directing the energy from the different parts of Devi to the corresponding parts in his own body. The spiritual aspirant can also do the same.

Every mantra has a mandala. As the mantra gains frequency through repetition, it manifests in the form of mandala. Mantra may also manifest as yantra, the linear and geometrical representation, but yantra is abstract, not solid like matter. The manifestation of mandala through the potency of mantra has the appearance of matter. Imagine that, while repeating your mantra, someone appears before you and blesses you with *shaktipat*, transference of energy. That is what happened to Sankara. He was praying to the cosmic Shakti to bless him, and his prayer was of such a high frequency that Devi appeared before him, and he began to speak to her in verse and poetry. This is the ultimate culmination of prayer, worship and all sadhana, to be able to manifest the atman.

Tantra has a vast array of mandalas, depicting all the devis and devatas which are responsible for the rich imagery that is an integral part of tantra. These devis and devatas, presiding over everyone's destiny, do not exist as objective entities in any part of the stratosphere. However, it is necessary to conceptualize and depict divinity in human form in order to give a substratum and focal point to the gross awareness of the mind. In time the mandala acts as a vehicle to awaken the inner visions and allows the deeper layers of the mind to rise to the surface and manifest.

The mere act of sitting for hours with closed eyes does not guarantee inner experience. In the present state of mind, all the doors leading to inner experience are closed. It is not the higher mind, but the ordinary gross mind which is under the spell of the senses, ego and intellect. That lower mind experiences itself in the form of thoughts and visions, when one sits with the eyes closed in meditation. Although one mistakes it for the real stuff, it is just the tip of the iceberg.

Tantra says that in order to transcend the ordinary gross awareness in which the mind presently dwells and gain entry through the closed doors of the higher mind, a *pratyaya*, or support, will have to be introduced. This pratyaya should be one which spontaneously attracts the mind without the least effort. The tantric mandalas are unique because they fulfil this condition. As the awareness dwells on the pratyaya for long, unbroken periods, the inner experiences emerge from behind the closed doors to manifest as transcendental experience.

Tantra is concerned with developing the inner awareness to the stage of *dharana*, total concentration, so that *dhyana*, or meditation, can happen. For this purpose, the mandala is most useful because it acts on the subconscious and unconscious mind in such a way that it brings about transcendence. How can a person who cannot see within be able to visualize or grasp the formless reality? Most people cannot even witness their thoughts or hold onto a single thought for any length of time. The mind is always drifting and dissipating. The average mind needs the support of a symbol such as yantra or mandala to rest its wavering attention upon.

The mandala acts in two ways. Firstly, to draw the latent *vasanas*, desires, *samskaras*, archetypes, and *karmas*, residual impressions, to the surface of the mind in the form of dreams, visions and thoughts. In this way, purification of consciousness takes place without having to face the samskaras directly. They are dispensed with in meditation and dream, so they do not affect one's daily life. This is a way of bypassing the contents of the psyche, a terrible and fearsome enemy, for which one has no defence.

Secondly, mandala gives the mind a base to rest upon for as long as this is needed. Mandalas are able to direct the imagination and capture the mind, because they are visually arresting, aesthetically pleasing and perfectly conceptualized. Moreover, they were originally conceived by evolved and illumined people who had transcended the mind and awakened the inner eye. As such, they contain the potential to invoke an inner experience.

So the mandalas, representing the various forms of devis and devatas, developed an elaborate symbology based on the eternal, archetypal structure of man's collective unconscious. The great philosopher and psychoanalyst of the twentieth century, Carl Jung, who was greatly influenced by Eastern philosophy, spoke of mysterious, influential forces operating on the unconscious of man, which connected his psyche with profound symbolic levels of existence. He coined the word archetype for these forces and also stated that they existed in the collective unconscious.

The mandala symbolism is able to draw out the archetypes from within the deeper consciousness. The tantric mandalas are deeply related to what is stored in the unconscious, the world of symbols. Whether it be the terrifying mandala of Kali, standing naked on Shiva, with a garland of skulls around her neck, tongue lolling out, smeared with blood, or the powerful mandala of Durga, seated on a lion, bestowing boons, or the benign mandala of Lakshmi, radiant and glowing, one factor is common amongst them. They all compel one to look at them again and again and leave a strong imprint upon the psyche.

Mandala and dream

The first time I saw the mandala of Kali, I was transfixed. Although I was as terrified as a small child to behold her form, she never left my imagination. I wondered about her: how there could possibly be a form like hers or a person like her and why was she like that? If that mandala came to life, would I have the nerve to speak to her and what would I say? These thoughts were often in my mind, and then she appeared before me in a dream. All she did was laugh and laugh. Although at first I was amazed, gradually I began to laugh with her. Then we were both laughing, and as we laughed together, her terrible black form turned into a beautiful, dusky girl of my age.

She took my hand and we started walking towards the sun. The speed at which she walked was tremendous, and soon we were walking into the sun. The brightness and glare was absorbed into her body with such ease that I was not at all afraid. When we came out on the other side of the sun, I saw the moon, which came swimming towards her as she breathed in, and before my very eyes she swallowed it. As she swallowed the moon, a bolt of lightning struck us both, but instead of dropping dead, we began to fly and soared high. When I looked down, I saw beautiful blue waters with no trace of land; the sun and moon were on either side.

At that moment she looked straight into my eyes and said, "What you behold is me, and I reside in the lotus of your heart." As she said those words, a gigantic lotus began to fill the waters. As it opened, I saw a beautiful little girl. As I looked closer, I recognized her as the same girl who had walked with me, but much younger. I turned around to speak to my companion, but she had disappeared into thin air and I began to hear the mantra: *Hreem, Hreem, Hreem.* Much later, when I first met my guru, as I entered the room in which he was speaking to a few people, that was the first word I heard from his mouth. Although he uttered it to those people in a context which was unknown to me, the coincidence was amazing.

I had never tried to analyze this dream, as I was very young and did not have the capacity to do so at that time. But later, when I came to know of the symbolical significance of the sun and moon, as ida and pingala, and the lotus as the heart centre, I was taken aback at the importance of the dream and the effect that the mandala had had on me.

Circular movement of energy
Mandala is a Sanskrit word, which by inference signifies a continuous flow, having no beginning and no end, which is timeless and eternal. It is a sacred symbol of eternity, which can bring respite in this transient world. The word *mandal* means 'round', and the secret of mandala is that it lives and breathes within a circle. The dictionary translates mandala as 'a holy circle or magic wheel', thus implying that a mandala

always has some secret or hidden power which it can manifest. In fact, the circle is the most primordial symbol from which other symbols emerge. The formation of a mandala follows the same principle as that of light, as expounded by scientific theory. Light waves move in a curve, thus bending space and forming an arc or curvature. This circular aura is an essential feature of the mandala, as the arc or curve is what holds or contains the image or object, giving it a conception for all to behold.

The circular form of a mandala makes it efficacious, because a circle does not permit loss of energy in the form of waves due to its continuous circular motion. This keeps the form intact. A break in that continuity allows the energy to escape and thus leads to disintegration and subsequent disease and death. This applies to an object as well as to a person and other forms of animate life. The same rule also applies to an idea, no matter how creative and innovative it may be. Every experience is a mandala, which exists within the framework of time, space and object.

The concept of mandala was derived in tantra to combat the loss of energy that occurs when a person is meditating. Energy or shakti is essential for achieving higher states of mind. Without a high quantum of energy one simply cannot reach that goal. Shakti in the form of prana flows through the nadis to each and every cell of the body and brain. Meditation requires a greater influx of energy into the body and brain. For this reason, one of the main aims of yoga and tantra is to build up the prana in the individual. These traditions always emphasize conservation of energy through the practices of: *mouna*, silence, *ekanta*, solitude, *upavasa*, fasting, *pranayama*, elongation of the breath, *pratyahara*, isolation of the mind from the senses, and *dharana*, focusing the mind on a symbol, such as mandala.

The tantrics who followed yogic and tantric disciplines must have faced this problem of loss of energy. The building up of prana is one thing, but to conserve and maintain it in the body and mind is quite another. Prana in the form of the breath is sustained as long as the exhaled air remains within a distance of *dwadashanta*, or twelve fingers away from the nostrils. Within that distance the energy can be drawn back with the inhalation, but there is no return once it escapes beyond dwadashanta. The prana in the breath mingles with the prana in the atmosphere and is lost forever. This is why dwadashanta is an important aspect of breath management through pranayama.

Similarly, shakti is depleted all the time through speech, action and thought projection. Every time one projects anger, there is a severe depletion of shakti in the body. The same applies to anxiety, worry and fear. During sexual interaction, the greatest amount of energy is depleted, unless one knows how to reabsorb it through the methods of tantra. Most people waste their energy through nervous titillation for the sake of temporary pleasure. Mandalas are most effective in reversing this process. When utilized in the proper manner, the movement of energy creates a mandala, or circular effect, between the practitioner and the object of practice. This results in a build up of energy, as no energy is lost on account of the circular movement, so the awareness is able to penetrate into the deepest layers of one's being.

Connection with the divine

The mandalas of Devi are most effective for creating an intimate connection between you and the focus of your worship, simply because they are an exact replica of the human form. They depict the human form in a state of enlightenment, or satyam, shivam, sundaram. The process of identification with each and every part of the mandala is very natural and spontaneous, because it is exactly like you. The forehead, eyes, nose, mouth, lips, smile, waist, hips, ankles, toes and fingers of the mandala of Devi are just like your own.

As the gaze is fixed on the mandala, the spandan or vibration of energy contained within it is conveyed to you, which brings effulgence to your entire being, and you begin to glow with a divine lustre. That is the concept of beauty depicted in *Saundarya Lahari*. That beauty is not skin deep nor does it wither with time; it brings *kirti*, or everlasting remembrance. Sankara was a recipient of divine lustre bestowed on him by Devi, and that is why his kirti is growing all the time. Even today he is most revered and respected all over the world for the brilliance of his thought.

The ritual of mandala is also followed in the act of maithuna, which is an important part of *vama marga*, the left path of *Kaula tantra*. In that tradition the two opposite poles of energy, man and woman, unite to form a mandala, or circle of energy, which can lead to the awakening of the higher evolutionary centres. In Samaya tantra, which is advocated in *Saundarya Lahari*, the circular movement of energy is created within one's own body through the balance of ida and pingala, as well as the awakening of the chakras and sushumna. This can become an ongoing experience in which divinity and illumination are perceived in everything. All the energy that is projected outwards returns back a thousand-fold, because one has become a magnet of energy and attracts it to oneself. In this way one becomes *shaktiman*, the holder of Shakti, which is an epithet of Shiva.

When one worships the mandala and focuses on the different angas, or parts of Devi, the energy of Devi is transferred to those very parts in one's own body. This rejuvenates and awakens every *koshika*, or cell that comprises one's being. Tantra states that each cell in the body contains an entire replica of oneself; it has a head, heart and hands of its own. So, the energy of Devi has to awaken in each of those thousands of heads, hearts and hands that comprise one, even without one's knowledge.

Interplay of energy and consciousness

There are all kinds of mandalas. In fact, each and everything in creation is a mandala in the sense that every form is surrounded by or contained within a circle. The circular ripples in a lake spread outwards, becoming bigger and bigger; similarly, the ripples of energy spread outwards from each and everything. Every one is also emitting energy in this way at all times. In yoga and tantra, one learns to conserve this energy, so that it can be utilized to create an awakening within. This cannot be done directly by holding the energy inside. Rather, the energy that is flowing outwards has to converge at a point outside, so that it can rebound back on the practitioner without being dissipated or lost.

For an awakening, the mental energy needs to be directed towards a mandala of great potency, which will not allow it to escape or dissipate. The mandalas of Devi are most appropriate for this purpose, because Devi is Shakti, pure, unadulterated energy. Being the source of energy, she is able to generate the circular motion that continuously spreads towards and engulfs the practitioner's being. The constant interplay of energy and consciousness within that circle creates a momentum in the awakening of the evolutionary process of kundalini shakti, the reservoir of prana existing within the body.

Kavacha or protection

The mandala is a blueprint for life. Before any being becomes manifest in time and space, each and everything is conceived within a concise framework in order to be perfected in all aspects of its creation. Before coming into existence, one's blueprint was made somewhere in the unmanifest space, which later determined everything about one down to the last detail, such as the shape of the nose and size of the body. We are not just an accident; each and every one of us was planned and there is a definite scheme for our existence.

This mandala or blueprint is one's *kavacha*, or protection, which surrounds the body like an invisible shield. It enables one to face life in much the same way as the armour worn by a soldier protects him when he goes into battle. No harm or injury to the body or mind can take place unless one's mandala is damaged or destroyed during the ups and downs of life. The most deadly diseases, such as cancer, asthma and diabetes, invade the body when there is a break in this covering. This occurs on account of deep, emotional turbulence that penetrates into the recesses of the mind. Perhaps a person's only beloved son has died or a loved one has deserted him. A person discovers that his mother was not, in fact, his real mother but someone who picked him up from an orphanage, where his real mother abandoned him.

At that time the mandala is disturbed. A chink of something alien to one's being enters and invades the DNA structure, and it is altered. The mandalas of tantra are efficient mediums for repairing these disturbances in the molecular structure. They are not just iconographic statues or symbols created by an artist's vivid imagination, but the result of an insight into the evolution of sound into matter. They were realized by seers and sages in heightened states of meditation, when they appeared before their eyes, just as Devi appeared before Sankara.

Storehouse of energy
Mandala should not be considered the same as an icon or idol, which certain religions consider to be a part of pagan worship. In that case, one would denigrate a very useful tool for self-regeneration and evolution. Mandala immediately connects one with the benevolent and healing propensities abounding in the universe. Mandalas, like yantras, are storehouses of energy, which correspond to the archetypes stored in the individual as well as the collective unconscious. The individual unconscious is linked to the collective unconscious, and the mandala acts as a link between the

two, exploding areas of a person's being that may be totally unknown to him.

Mandala brings those unconscious areas to the surface and becomes a catalyst for eliminating the unnecessary impressions from the psyche. One carries a lot of garbage around from many incarnations and that has to be sorted, arranged and assigned a proper place. Mandalas enable one to dispense with the unnecessary memories and conditioning, and make one a fit and pure receptacle to receive the divine energies that will reshape one's life. With the aid of mandala, one can realize one's potential and attain *siddhi* or perfection in whatever one wishes to achieve in life

Mandalas also help to achieve immediate aims, such as resolution of disease, attainment of wealth, winning a lover, attainment of name, fame and status, and begetting progeny. Each of the mandalas in *Saundarya Lahari* has a distinct purpose or aim, which can be achieved through repetition of the mantras and worship of the yantra and mandala that it embodies. There are other mandalas which different traditions offer. Even the wondrous works of art handed down for centuries are mandalas. The buildings, temples, dargahs and churches are mandalas. But these are not potent mandalas for the transcendence of man's finite nature. Great works of art may generate elevated feelings, but they do not serve as tools for jumping over the mind.

Tantra is concerned with the mandalas that bring out and explode the universal potential in man. The tantric mandalas were realized by people who could materialize matter through the power of the mind. Thus they have the power to generate the same experience in the person who utilizes them for inner experience. Many of the tantric mandalas appear bizarre and completely illogical to the rational mind. But one should remember that the dimension one is trying to reach through sadhana is beyond the confines of the mind, intellect, rationale, logic and reasoning.

People often wonder why some mandalas of Devi are so grotesque and gruesome, such as Chinnamasta who holds her own severed head in her hand while a large stream of blood is gushing out of her slit neck. These mandalas signify states of consciousness that the awareness passes through on its journey from the gross to the transcendental. Such images are able to hold that awareness and act as stepping stones to higher states.

The earth we live on is round and can be called a mandala. The body is a mandala, as it forms a circle. Time, too, is perceived as circular, an eternal round of cycles within cycles. Past, present and future merge into one another in a marvellous unbroken chain that is hard to distinguish one from the other. Every object is a mandala, whether a tree, animal, house, chair, plane or car. The form of guru is an excellent mandala, as the divine energy reposes in him and is channelled to deserving disciples. Just as lightning drops on a good conductor or electricity passes through good conducting wires, in the same way, those persons who are good receptacles or mediums of energy become good mandalas.

Worship of the Dasa Mahavidyas

As the inner awareness develops and there is expansion of energy due to mandala sadhana, the consciousness that is entrapped in matter is liberated and becomes free to flow outwards in all directions. That is the turning point, when the barriers and obstacles that are psychic and esoteric in nature begin to arise. A sadhaka can even encounter a psychic attack, which may be very difficult to handle.

At that time, the *Dasa Mahavidyas*, ten forms of Shakti, come to the rescue, for they are the guardians of the ten directions of space: east, west, north, south, northeast, northwest, southeast, southwest, above and below. These are the ten directions through which the consciousness travels into boundless space, and there is a Mahavidya in every direction to block the exit until the sadhaka has fulfilled all the conditions. Any exit prior to that can be unjustified and even fatal for the sadhaka.

Thus, the worship of the Dasa Mahavidyas is included in all tantric sadhanas along with mandala. Sankara, too, must have worshipped the dasa mahavidyas during his anusthana of devi worship to combat his disease. These Mahavidyas are mainly related to Sati, the consort of Shiva, who immolated herself at the grand yajna of her father Daksha, and to Parvati into whom she reincarnated after her death by immolation, and once again reunited with Shiva. The story of Daksha Yajna is recorded in all tantric and vedic texts, as it is an event of considerable significance.

Once upon a time, the creators of this universe and all its galaxies were present together at a yajna. At that time Prajapati Daksha happened to drop by. On his arrival all the devatas and rishis stood up to greet him, except Shiva. This annoyed Daksha, who felt insulted by Shiva's behaviour and immediately cursed him never to be present at the sacred yajnas. Some time later, Daksha planned a great yajna to which he invited each and every devata and rishi of any significance, except Shiva and his wife Sati, who happened to be his own daughter.

As Sati was passing over the mountains where the yajna was taking place, she happened to see everyone gathered there. As the yajna was taking place at her father's home, Sati asked Shiva if she may join. When Shiva refused, Sati was at first very sad, and then she became enraged, as if she would destroy Shiva by the fire of her eyes. So, she left Shiva and went to join the yajna at her father's home. Until this point, all the texts tell a similar story, but after that there are a few differences.

The tantric texts include the birth of the Dasa Mahavidyas. Due to Shiva's refusal, Sati became so enraged that her body turned black from anger. She thus transformed herself into Kali, wearing a garland of skulls, with her tongue lolling out. On seeing her in this form, Shiva became so frightened that he began to flee. Sati pleaded with him not to be afraid of her because she was his own wife, but Shiva did not listen and tried to escape. Then Sati turned into the Dasa Mahavidyas and took her position in every direction of space to prevent Shiva from escaping her.

In sadhana, too, when the sadhaka is drawing near to the goal of realization or experience of cosmic consciousness, the Dasa Mahavidyas come to his aid by preventing Shiva from fleeing his experience. Shakti, through her Dasa Mahavidyas, contains Shiva within the uncharted space that the sadhaka traverses when nearing samadhi. This is why Shakti is the most important aspect of one's life, because she alone can give the experience of Shiva, as consciousness is attracted to energy. It is energy that holds consciousness within matter and saturates it with awareness. Without the assistance of Shakti, the sadhaka can never reach his goal.

This story explains the importance of Dasa Mahavidya worship in all tantric rituals. In fact, it relates to the journey of the individual soul from darkness to light. When the consciousness breaks free from the clutches of matter and begins to soar, it becomes free from the confines of the body. Inner awareness does not imply that one sees only within the body. The dimension of inner awareness is not limited to this body and mind. The heightened inner awareness is free to traverse boundaries that transcend time, space and object, linking it with the universal energy and consciousness, opening new dimensions of experience. At that time the sadhaka's present state of mind, intellect and ego cease to function. So, what or who will determine the direction in which it will travel, and prevent it from entering into a black hole or point of no return? Black holes are a reality in physics, and they are a reality in the life of a sadhaka too.

What are black holes?
The more gravity an object has, the faster one must fly to escape it. The gravitational pull of a black hole is so strong

that its escape velocity exceeds the speed of light. Nothing travels faster than light, so if light is not speedy enough to escape it, nothing else is either. The gravitational pull is like a bottomless hole from which there is no return. The hole cannot be seen since no light emerges, so it appears black.

In 1974, the physicist, Stephen Hawking, discovered that there was a way to escape black holes after all. The Hawking equations also suggest that the escaping particles seemed to contain hardly a trace of what made up the black hole. This is alarming, because in physics nothing is ever lost. If this page were tossed into a fire, physics says one could reconstruct every single detail of it, including the position of one's fingerprint on it, from the flicker of the flames, the way the air currents flow, the glow of the ashes, and a myriad other observations. In theory one could read the page by staring at the fire.

Yet, black holes violate the most basic tenet that the past and future are uniquely connected. Particles radiating out of a black hole carry virtually no information about what had fallen into the black hole. Once something disappears into a black hole, all knowledge and information about its contents is obliterated. Thus, the mystery of matching the future with the past is at stake. Black holes seem to make the most sacred laws of physics break down. However, the String theory, which describes all known forces, gives compelling evidence that this information is not lost. But where the information is and how it gets out is still a mystery.

Science may be trying to unravel this mystery, but tantra says that the sadhaka can prevent the escape of awareness when it is liberated from matter, so that he does not suffer the effects of falling into a black hole and forgetting his past on account of the Dasa Mahavidyas, who are the direct evolutes of the supreme energy, *Tripura Sundari*, and carry out all her orders. In meditation, when the consciousness is in ascent and reaches the higher centres, creating an awakening in ajna, it becomes uni-directional. Up to ajna, the supreme consciousness, coupled with energy, moves within the framework of ida, pingala and sushumna, piercing all the chakras. But after ajna, the energy encounters uncharted, open space.

At that time the Dasa Mahavidyas come to his protection and guard the eight quarters of space in order to prevent the consciousness from escaping into a black hole from which there is no return, or even if there is, all past information and knowledge would be lost. Many saints have been unable to avert this danger and despite heightened, inner experiences have lost total awareness of their body and personal identity after such an experience.

Role of the Mahavidyas
The energy contained within each of the Dasa Mahavidyas is complementary; thus they are able to connect perfectly with each other, creating a circular mandala in the open space of the sadhaka's consciousness. As they have evolved out of each other, there is a perfect synchronization and symphony of energy in motion, which prevents anything from escaping until it is transformed and ready for the exit. Apart from preventing the escape of consciousness and energy, the Dasa Mahavidyas also prevent the entry of any unwanted field of energy within the space of the sadhaka's consciousness. This helps in averting any psychic attack that may occur, for the sadhaka becomes highly vulnerable to such incidents at this time.

The Mahavidyas can be regarded as a protective shield that the sadhaka is endowed with due to his sincerity in sadhana. They carry out all their functions at the behest of Devi, or Adi Shakti, of whom they are direct evolutes, created out of her own sweet will. Shakti will decide the exact and correct moment for the sadhaka's union with Shiva, the cosmic consciousness. At that time the Dasa Mahavidyas will open the gates for the ascent of consciousness to sahasrara chakra, the thousand-petalled lotus at the crown of the head.

The Dasa Mahavidyas are known as: *Kali, Chinnamasta, Tara, Shodashi, Bhuvaneshwari, Tripura Bhairavi, Dhumravati, Bhagalamukhi, Matangi,* and *Kamala*. In terms of upasana, Kali is the foremost amongst these ten. They all arose as a consequence of her transformation from the terrible and frightening to the tender and benign Kali. The Dasa Mahavidyas represent that transformation process and although each has its own upasana, or form of worship, rite of initiation and mantras, they are all the same in essence.

When milk transforms into ghee, it appears different at each point of transformation, such as curd and butter, but in essence they are all milk. In the same way, although the Dasa Mahavidyas assumed their forms according to the transformation of Sati's mood, in essence they are all forms of that Mahashakti Sati. Her terrible forms are: Kali, Chinnamasta, Bhagalamukhi and Dhumravati; her benign and tender forms are: Tara, Bhuvaneshwari, Shodashi or Lalita, Tripura Bhairavi, Matangi and Kamala. The worship of the Dasa Mahavidyas is, in fact, the worship of Kali.

The Mahavidyas denote the process of dissolution and creation on both the microcosmic and macrocosmic levels. Kali stands for time and with her worship begins the destruction of individual time, space and object, along with the annihilation of ego. The process from Kali to Kamala leads to the experience of *Sadashiva*, which is none other than the highest Shakti, Bhuvaneshwari, reclining in embrace with Shiva or *Bhuvaneshwara*, on her couch, of which the four legs are Brahma, Vishnu, Rudra and Ishwara. Seven crore (seventy million) mantras emanate from them, resounding in the endless space in worship of Shiva and Shakti.

Sixty-four shaktipeethas

The story of Sati goes further. On reaching her father's yajna, Sati became even more furious because Daksha did not have the courtesy to offer her a seat or apologize for not inviting her husband Shiva and herself. Instead he deliberately ignored her and made it quite obvious that neither she nor Shiva were welcome in his house. At that point Sati assumed her most terrible form, breathing heavily with hissing sounds, her tongue lolling out, which terrified everyone. Then to the dismay of all present, she immolated herself in the yajna fire in front of their very eyes.

With the immolation of Sati, who was none other than Adi Shakti, the creatrix of this manifested world, everything began to disintegrate and the earth began to shake and fall apart. As soon as Shiva learned of this terrible incident, he too became enraged and left at once for the yajna. Pulling Sati's body out of the fire, he traversed the length and breadth of the world, holding her aloft in his hands. The earth shook, strong winds blew, the waters in the oceans swelled, and everything was in disorder because the very root of creation had abandoned the world. Seeing this and fearing the dissolution of the entire earth, Vishnu released his *sudarshana chakra*, or weapon, which dismembered the body of Sati,

The sixty-four different parts of Sati's body fell at different places on this earth and formed the sixty-four peethas where Shakti is venerated. Her eyes fell at Munger, her yoni at Kamakhya in Assam, and her heart at Deoghar, which is known as the *smashan*, or cremation ground, of Devi. So it can be said that Sati or Mahashakti died at Deoghar, because it is when the heart stops that a person is declared dead. In 1989, while doing chaturmas sadhana at Neel Parbat in Trayambakeshwar, Swami Satyananda was directed in meditation to make the smashan of Shakti his abode, after which he came to Rikhia, as the entire area is the cremation ground of Shakti. Swami Satyananda has said that the cremation ground of Sati will also be the place where Shakti will resurrect herself in the Kali yuga.

Even today, the shaktipeethas are centres of vibrant energy, affecting a positive transformation in the lives of all who come within their range. They are powerful and awakened centres that contain the supreme energy of Mahashakti from whom they were dismembered, and their influence prevails far and wide in all parts of the world. Just by remembrance of these peethas or chanting their names, one can connect with their especially refined energy and avail oneself of their blessings. Their energies are all pervasive and their influence is soul-deep, because together they recreate that Mahashakti. *Tantrachudamani*, a tantric text, describes these sixty-four peethas in connection with the tantric ritual known as *peethanyasa*, or consecration of the different parts of Devi's body.

In *Saundarya Lahari*, when Sankara venerates the different parts of Shakti, in actual fact he is performing this esoteric ritual of peethanyasa, to invoke the divine energy residing in the sixty-four peethas that together constitute her full form, (mantra 56). Ultimately, this worship of the sixty-four peethas or peethanyasa, which is a very important tantric ritual, is intended to divinize the body as one meditates on the different parts of the Devi, which fell at different points on this earth. In the *dakshina kaula marga*, or right hand path of tantra, this is done through external worship, either by visiting the shrines themselves, which are spread over the length and breadth of India, or by worshipping the *vigraha*, or mandala, of Devi through the external rites of pooja and worship.

In *vama kaula marga*, the left hand path of tantra, peethanyasa is done by worshipping the Devi in living form. This is a unique idea. India is perhaps the only land where the female is looked upon as Devi and given that status in the household. There is a Sanskrit saying that Devas do not enter places where women are not respected and loved. The woman of the house is even addressed as Devi by her husband and community. Are women venerated and raised to the status of divinity in this manner in any other part of the world? No, India is the only land that can be called the home of the Devi!

In *Samaya Tantra*, the sixty-four parts of Devi are superimposed upon oneself. This tradition of tantra believes that the body is a temple in which the divine resides, and awakening the divinity in oneself through mantras and worship is most important. This tantra proclaims that one does not have to go anywhere or seek anything; everything is within. That potential can awaken through worship, prayer and the attitude of devotion, and the divine will reveal itself within. Right now that divinity is hidden behind a veil.

Vision of tantra

This is one of the most important revelations that tantra offers to humanity, because the entire perspective of life changes through this concept. Man is not an impure sinner, who has to rise from the mire and ask for forgiveness so that he may be redeemed and attain salvation. This whole world is the abode of God. One can behold that divinity everywhere, as well as within oneself. All one has to do is awaken the inner eye to see the light within.

Due to this grand vision of tantra which led to the emergence of many hitherto unknown techniques, it emerged as a vast and unique science, encompassing the myriad ideas developed by man in his spiritual quest right from the beginning of civilization. In fact, the birth of tantra took place with the birth of man. From the very beginning it was noticed that some people were born with supernatural powers. For instance, some were able to predict events which actually did happen, to heal, or to know the mind of another. These paranormal faculties, which certain people exhibited, aroused the curiosity of others and they started to investigate this phenomenon.

Thus the birth of tantra took place. So tantra is a science in which a systematic investigation into life and creation takes place. Side by side with this investigation and subsequent claims, tantra also provides practical methods to validate those claims. The uniqueness of tantra lies in the fact that the practitioner is the investigator and also the object of investigation. In order to validate the claims of this sacred science, one will have to commence an investigation into one's own self. In that sense tantra predates history.

Perhaps the texts of tantra can tell the true history of man down through the ages, if they are studied by research scholars. Was man originally a savage, as one is led to believe, or is the present humanity the outcome of an advanced civilization that has given sublime truths to man, which are extremely valuable for his further growth and evolution. The tantric scriptures, vedic hymns, upanishadic thoughts, and the pauranic lore are certainly not the works of primitive people. They show a maturity of thought that had reached a very high point of culmination, and which reflects the highly cultured and evolved mindset of the people at that time. Certainly no civilization up to the present day has been able to match the mine of knowledge and information available in the Tantras, Vedas and Upanishads. Thousands of years later, people are still trying to unravel their mysteries, and deriving solutions to many of their afflictions, whether physical, mental, emotional, spiritual, social or political.

Tantric symbology
Much later, when the systems of tantra were examined, grouped and arranged, five distinct traditions emerged, which prevail to the present day. Each tradition was named after the deity whom it venerated and they are: Shaiva or Shiva tantra, Vaishnava or Vishnu tantra, Saura or Surya tantra, Ganapatya or Ganesha tantra, and Shakti or Shakta tantra. This deification led to the misconception that tantra was a religion, because it alluded to gods and goddesses, rites and rituals, but this was not the case. Tantra was and always will be a science of the absolute.

However, unlike science, tantra does not use terms like infinite and absolute, which convey nothing concrete that a reader may conceptualize or imagine. Instead, tantra employs poetic imagery, which immediately becomes embedded in the mind, to convey the dry and abstract reality of the absolute. It is a hard task to explain the absolute and make it tangible. So tantra gave that reality names and forms, such as: Shiva, the three-eyed yogi with matted locks, a serpent coiled around his neck, smeared in ashes, and seated on a deer skin in rapt meditation; Shakti, with twelve hands, holding an assortment of weapons, lustrously beautiful, astride a tiger, granting boons to her devotees; or Ganesha, with the head of an elephant, seated upon a rat.

Tantra employs these concepts to convey the absolute, which in essence is formless and nameless. This rich imagery becomes a part of man's psyche, so he is able to relate to it at once and use it as a doorway to reach an otherwise closed room. Even a person who has never had any exposure to tantric images, such as: Chinnamasta, a naked woman, holding her severed head in one hand, with a stream of blood gushing from her neck, or of Kali, with protruding tongue, dripping blood, wearing a garland of skulls, standing naked with one foot on Shiva, cannot deny the strong impact they have on the mind. The immediate reaction may be one of repulsion rather than attraction, but the forces of attraction and repulsion are equal and opposite. Therefore, repulsion can also be a cause for awakening. These are images that one cannot forget in a hurry. They compel one to ponder over them and wonder exactly what they signify.

Matriarchal system
Out of all these traditions, Shakta tantra is regarded as most ancient, where Shakti or Devi is responsible for *srishti*, creation, *sthiti*, maintenance, and *pralaya*, destruction. She is the supreme and sole refuge of all! The *Srimad Devi Bhagavatam*, one of the classical texts of Shakta tantra, claims that God is not male, but female! Throughout creation it is the female species that creates life. Has anyone ever seen a father give birth to a child? No, never!

Similarly, it is irrational to believe that the creatrix of the universes, galaxies and solar systems would be male; it has to be female. Shakti is the name given to that root matrix of creation. Shakti is raw, potential energy, which has the power to manifest or create. The virgin power of Mother Nature manifests into the seas, mountains, skies and planets, and the 6,400,000 yonis, or species of life through which evolution has taken place.

The earliest traditions of humanity were matriarchal, not patriarchal. Gradually as man became a social animal, this concept changed to suit his convenience and to clarify the genealogy. After all, to whom will the wealth, progeny and status ultimately belong? In a matriarchal society it would belong to the mother. This must have posed certain problems and led to a clash of interests, where the male members felt disempowered and threatened. Gradually, the women were subjugated and relegated to lesser roles, and the men became the head of the family. Despite this, the matriarchal system is still alive today in some parts of India, and worshippers of Shakti abound throughout the world.

Three paths of Shakti worship

According to Shakta tantra, *shaktopasana*, or the worship of Shakti, is performed in three ways: Kaula marga, Mishrit marga, and Samaya marga. These are the three main paths of Shakta tantra. The practices of vama marga and dakshina marga, commonly known as the left hand and right hand path, are a part of Kaula marga. *Vama marga* deals with the practices for awakening and balancing the energy in ida nadi. *Dakshina marga* deals with the practices for awakening and balancing the energy in pingala nadi. Proficiency in vama and dakshina marga leads to the awakening of sushumna nadi, which houses the pathway for the ascent of kundalini.

In *Kaula marga*, this experience is generated through external means. In *Mishrit marga*, both external and internal methods are employed to attain the experience of Shakti. *Samaya marga* is the highest path, which is the basis of *Saundarya Lahari*. It deals with the awakening of Shakti within the framework of one's own body and mind, enabling one to enter into the realm of pure experience that transcends even knowledge. *Samaya* means 'You are in me', and thus external japa, pooja and ritual have no place in Samaya tantra.

According to this tradition of Shakta tantra, the worshipper and worshipped are one and the same, so who will worship whom? All rituals are visual experiences through an awakened mind. Here sahasrara chakra is the space in which the union with the divine consciousness is experienced. This is the epitome of yogic and tantric experience that one can have within the framework of the human body. Although there are higher chakras than sahasrara, they belong to the divine realms, which open up when the awareness goes beyond sahasrara.

The system of *shaktopasana*, or worship of Shakti, can be found in these three paths, which evolve from one to the other. The growth of awareness, which is the subject and goal of these traditions, is an evolutionary process and can never be static. As the awareness evolves, so does the perception. As the perception changes, there is a gradual change in the system of practice designed for the sadhaka. So, tantra contains practices for aspirants at every level of awareness, from the gross sensualist to the evolved yogi and sadhaka. For each individual, there is a path, a way. Tantra does not deny anyone the right to tread the path to self-knowledge, which is the birthright of everyone. No matter who or what one may be, no matter where life has stationed him, tantra has a way.

Shaktopasana is the worship of Shakti or energy, and all are shakti upasakas. Even without knowing it, one worships her in one form or other throughout life. But this worship is done in *avidya*, or ignorance. Due to the absence of reverence, it lacks the required energy, power or momentum to transform one's life. No one can live without shakti, whether it is the external energy that heats up the home and cooks the food, carries one up and down on the elevators from floor to floor in high rise buildings, runs the computers; the internal energy that digests and assimilates the food, allows one to think and act, sleep and rest, sneeze and blink, talk and look; or the subtle explosion of energy that generates an inner experience; or surpassing that, the energy that transcends the mind and is experienced as transcendental. In some way or other, we are all under the spell of Shakti, energy, and all our efforts go into keeping Shakti alive and vibrant within and without us.

Modes of Shakti worship

After the Shakta margas, the next classification which tantra gives is the mode of worship. Tantra outlines two modes of worship: *bahir yaag*, external worship, and *antar yaag*, inner worship. The word *bahir* means 'outer' and *antar* means 'inner'. The word *yaag* is the same as *yajna*, and implies 'worship' or something sacred that is consecrated. According to Shakta tantra, antar yaag should always precede bahir yaag, as first one has to perfect the inner awareness and cultivate the correct inner attitude towards external objects and persons. When this is done, the expression of thought, feeling and action, head, heart and hand, will be in perfect equipoise.

Antar yaag has five divisions, known as:
1. *Patal* – to establish Shakti in all the seven chakras, including sahasrara, through the medium of mantras
2. *Padhati* – to worship Shakti in the heart centre and also through the medium of mantras
3. *Kavacha* – to establish a protective armour around the physical body through the medium of *bija*, or seed, mantras and the numerous names of Devi
4. *Stotra* – to chant the secret hymns of Devi
5. *Sahasranam* – to worship Devi within the framework of the body.

Bahir yaag also has five divisions, known as:

1. *Japa* – to repeat any of the mantras of Mahashakti
2. *Homa* – to offer oblations into the fire
3. *Tarpana* – to offer oblations
4. *Marjan* – to destroy the samskaras
5. *Bhoj* – to feed the invoked divinity.

The greatness of Samaya tantra lies in the idea that the macrocosm is inherent in the microcosm. *Brahmanda*, the macrocosmic universe, which is incomprehensible to the human mind, is also present in its original form in *pindanda*, the microcosmic universe, which is the human body. The sublime idea of the cosmic experience being enshrined in the physical body in the form of kundalini, which has found its way to other systems and traditions, has its origin in Samaya tantra.

Today when one says that the aim of tantra and yoga is to awaken the sleeping kundalini entrapped in the body, or pindanda, he should also reflect on the origin of this mysterious and esoteric knowledge. This idea has filtered down from Samaya tantra. In fact, the first forty-one mantras of *Saundarya Lahari*, known as *Ananda Lahari*, or surge of bliss, deal with the ascent and descent of kundalini, and contain the very essence of Samayachara tantra.

The opening lines of *Purusha Sukta*, an early vedic hymn in praise of Purusha, starts with the words: *Sahasrashirshah-purushah Sahasraksha Sahasrapaat*, Purusha resplendent with thousands of eyes, hands and feet. This awakened purusha of the Vedas is symbolic of the descent of kundalini after it has united with Shiva in sahasrara. This event is the highlight of *Saundarya Lahari*, a text of Samaya tantra. Today, science has also discovered that in each cell of an individual exists the potential for an exact replica of that individual. Thus a thousand people can be born exactly alike.

Each atom, molecule and particle of one's being is designed according to the universal laws of mathematics. This is reflected in the fact that the nucleus of each atom has its own galaxy of protons and neutrons that are in constant motion. The space they maintain is dictated by interstellar space that exists between planets and by the intermolecular space in the human body. So, everything seen outside is an exact replica of what already exists within in geometrical form. The tree, cow, boy, field and house, all exist within, but one sees them outside; that is bahir yaag.

When one is able to see the object clearly inside, that is antar yaag. The mind perceives, experiences and enjoys, not the senses. The senses are mere tools of the mind. In fact, the mind can perceive experience and enjoy, even if the senses are absent. Beethoven wrote his Ninth symphony after he had gone deaf, but despite that he could still hear the music in his mind in a way that no one else could! So, bahir yaag utilizes the external senses to awaken and experience Shakti. In antar yaag the mind transcends the external senses and awakens to the inner experience, consisting of a more refined energy, which is not dependent on time, space and object.

Tantra calls this experience the expansion of mind, where the mind is able to break all the barriers that limit its flight into consciousness and dive deep into the unknown. The word tantra itself means expansion and liberation. The root *tan* is derived from the word *tanote*, meaning 'to expand' and *tra* is derived from the word *trayate*, meaning 'liberation'. So in tantra, something is supposed to expand and as a result something is liberated.

According to tantra, expansion takes place in the frequency of the mind, when it is not dissipated or distracted by the senses that deplete the energy of the mind. The expansion of mind causes an explosion that liberates energy from the field of gravity or matter to ascend upwards into the higher levels of the evolutionary process towards sahasrara and even beyond. At that time the spiritual energy, which is nothing but pure and absolute consciousness, begins to guide the aspirant to higher realms and experiences.

Tantric sadhana

Apart from the classification and modes of worship, tantra also outlines three categories of sadhakas or practitioners: *pashu*, instinctive nature governed by tamas, *vira*, heroic nature governed by rajas, and *divya*, divine nature governed by sattwa. Each tantric sadhana is designed for a particular type of individual, and the suitability of sadhana has to be decided by an authorized person known as a guru, not by oneself.

Without the direction and instruction of the guru, all tantric practices are fruitless and do not achieve the desired aim. One who practises without a guru is like a boat without a boatman, wandering aimlessly without any direction or sight of destination. The practitioner will never reach the shore unless a guru steers him onto the right path. This *chetavni*, or warning, is given profusely in all the tantric texts, and it should definitely not be ignored.

The aim of all tantric sadhana is refinement of awareness and *Saundarya Lahari* is no exception. This cannot be achieved just by knowledge gained from books. This is only possible under the skilled guidance of a guru, adept or master. A guru is not a yoga teacher, his skills supercede that of a teacher. A teacher can only convey knowledge to the student, but a guru can transmit both knowledge and experience to the deserving student.

Moreover, a teacher's method is verbal and linear, whereas a guru does not depend on speech alone and also employs methods which are non-verbal and non-linear. Knowledge can be passed from guru to disciple even in silence. Gurus are also known to transmit knowledge to a disciple who is physically thousands of miles away. This is what makes the guru more than a teacher. In fact, a guru can continue to transmit knowledge to a worthy disciple long after he has left this mortal plane.

Transmission of knowledge and experience is achieved only after a connection is established through the ritual of *diksha*, or initiation. The word diksha is derived from the root, *dik*, which literally means 'to assign a direction'. The guru assigns a direction for the movement of awareness in the disciple from gross to subtle realms. Tantric diksha is broadly categorized into three categories. The first is *aanvi*, when the guru whispers the mantra to the disciple and initiates him into the worship of yantra and mandala. The second and third categories of diksha are shakti and shambhavi. They are more subtle and are given in the form of *shaktipat* or direct transference of energy from guru to disciple. Shakti diksha accomplishes the piercing of chakras, *chakrabheda*, and opening of three granthis, *granthitraya*, by the ascent of kundalini. Shambhavi, which is the most intense, induces *tattwajnana*, the experience of the transcendental nature. The guru is one who has awakened Shakti within himself, and therefore is qualified to transmit that experience to the disciple.

Tantric sadhana takes the form of upasana, or worship, because from the Shakta point of view, the world is nothing but the manifest form of Shakti, which contains all the mountains, rivers, seas, skies, plants, vegetables, minerals, animals, aquatic and human life. Everything in life is regarded as an act of worship because Shakti is inherent in everything: the food one eats, the water one drinks, the clothes one wears, the bed one sleeps on, and the air one breathes. Since everything in creation is a medium of Shakti, whatever one beholds, all of one's actions, speech, thoughts and feelings are a means to experience or encounter the divine Shakti.

In tantra, the world is regarded as divine and worthy of reverence because it is the form of Shakti. The world is not an illusion; it is a giant temple, where one can pay obeisance to the divine, because everything in this world is teeming with divine energy, Shakti. Tantra in general and shaktas in particular view the whole of life as upasana or worship. Shaktas see the world as a beautiful shrine sculpted by Shakti, which enacts the play of Shakti in the manifest world. They believe that Shakti unites Shiva with creation. So, when one eats, one should feel that the divine is being nourished; when one speaks, it is the utterance of mantra; when one bathes, one is showering the divine with water; when one lies down, it is prostration to the divine; and when one sleeps, it is samadhi. Each and every act of life is designed to awaken the experience of Shakti, or divinity, abounding in the universe.

Kundalini shakti

Shakti, or energy, is transcendental as well as empirical. The main aim of the entire Shakti darshan and sadhana is to awaken the dormant, transcendental energy, known as kundalini, because there will be no liberation, or *mukti*, unless this occurs. *Kulashakti*, or kundalini, is entrapped in matter, lying in *Patala loka*, the lower chakras. She is the beloved of *akul*, or Shiva, who resides in sahasrara, and the entire effort of tantric sadhana is to bring these two lovers together.

Kulakundalini or kulashakti is the universal lineage of man. *Kula* means 'lineage'; it is the universal power or force which man has inherited from his cosmic mother, Mahashakti. Just as one has an individual lineage which relates to a particular family line, in the same way, one possesses a universal lineage by virtue of which he is related to all other human beings. Although the kundalini is present in all creatures, in man this latent energy has reached the point of evolution where it is ready for awakening.

Kundalini shakti has three states. The first is known as *kanya*, where she lies asleep at the base of the spine in mooladhara chakra. When awakened by the heightened level of prana, or energy, of the sadhaka, she emits a low hissing sound, like a snake that is stirred from its slumber. As a kanya, she is not yet aware of the power contained within her. The second state is *kumari*, where she raises her head and begins to ascend, gradually becoming aware of her power and sensuality. The third state is *shodashi*, or fully developed, when she is ready to unite with Shiva.

The word kundalini is derived from the root *kunda*, which means a 'deep pit' or 'hollow'. Kundalini shakti is the cosmic energy that lies asleep, like a snake, in three and a half coils within the *kunda* or pit. This description has given it the name 'serpent power'. The kundalini, or latent energy, exists not only in the human form, but in every atom of the universe. The kundalini shakti is *varna shariratmaka*, formed by light and sound. The entire universe is created by nada, cosmic sound, and from nada arises prana, or the life force, which holds the endless creation in existence. Nada exists within the serpent power that resides within each individual and is known as *para kundalini*. When the para kundalini erupts into sound, then it is known as *varna kundalini*.

Nada is in the form of *chitshakti*, energy of consciousness, and is at the root of each stage of its manifestation. Nada is also transformed into matter, and this entire manifest world is the result of transcendental sound. Everything that comes into being is a result of nada, or sound vibration, which transforms into the thirty-six elements of which all matter is composed. All the worlds are sound in different stages of manifestation, and sound is the result of the transformation of Shakti.

When nada enters into deep sleep, *sushupti*, it is known as *prana kundalini*. At the top of *brahmarandhra*, the spinal passage, is the *urdhva kundalini*, which is the basis of the *shakti tattwa* that later manifests as prana kundalini. This prana is known as *Hamsa*. The sound of *Ha*, or *Hakara*, is the inhalation, or *vimarshana roopa*, which symbolizes *tyaga*, renunciation, and the sound of *Sa*, or *Sakara*, is the exhalation, or *vimarsha roopa*, which symbolizes holding or receiving.

The kundalini is a symbol of receiving as well as renouncing. This is the way one should live life, so as to be in accord with the kundalini. That is the true worship through which she will surely awaken. Instead, however, one receives and clings onto what is received, and then craves and desires for more. So, one is living life in a manner which is anti-kundalini or opposed to the energy that one is trying to manifest in the body and mind.

In order to awaken kundalini, a few asanas and pranayama, or a little sadhana is not enough; the whole personality has to change. It is necessary to restructure and reorganize the entire pattern of association, reaction and response that one undergoes in life. In ancient India, the whole of life was structured in a manner that was conducive to kundalini awakening. The ways of modern life have stupefied the Indian mind for a time, but now more and more people are awakening to the knowledge of Kundalini Devi, which is man's highest potential. There is a trend to become more sensitive to this fine and sophisticated energy network that one is carrying without knowing.

Just as kundalini is varna shariratmaka, all the mantras or transcendental sounds, are *varnatmaka* and *shaktyatmaka*, sound and energy in motion. Shakti is indeed *matrika*, or indestructible as transcendental sound, as well as *shivatmika*, or indestructible as transcendental consciousness. Varna or matrika are embodied with immense *tejas*, or light, which has pervaded each and every speck of creation in all the *lokas*, or planes of existence.

Two energies or shaktis reside in all mantras: i) the *vakya shakti*, or energy generated by chanting the mantra, which is the atma of the mantra or the source of its illumination, and ii) the *vachaka shakti*, the corresponding energy generated within the sadhaka through the chanting of the mantra, which is *parabrahma*, or the highest consciousness. This is why mantra is one of the most important tools for kundalini awakening. In his book *Taming the Kundalini*, Swami Satyananda has said that by the repetition of the thirty-two names of Durga, and the chanting of *Saundarya Lahari* and *Tantroktam Devi Suktam*, in that order, one can awaken the mighty serpent power of kundalini enshrined within the physical body.

The existence of kundalini is not a myth or a product of imagination. Great thinkers, such as Sankara, have accepted that within the framework of man there is a supramental energy known as kundalini, which remains coiled and dormant at the base of the spine in mooladhara chakra. The awakening of this high voltage energy and its subsequent ascent to sahasrara is the experience of liberation, or moksha, from the bondage of gravity and matter into a dimension that transcends time, space and object. The awakening of kundalini is the transcendence of the body and mind, which culminates in the enriching experience of the Self.

In the language of modern science, the awakening of kundalini and its ascent mean the activation of the nine-tenths of the brain that are dormant in most people today. From birth, one comes into this world with the entire network of pranas, nadis and chakras for conducting this high voltage energy. All these systems are in place, but they are not connected to the power station. When the connection takes place, the entire body-mind structure, even the electrical impulses in the brain, are altered.

In the first part of *Saundarya Lahari*, Sankara worships the awakened kundalini as she ascends through the pranic field of the different chakras: mooladhara, swadhisthana, manipura, anahata, vishuddhi and ajna, on the *kulapath*, or direct path, which leads to union in sahasrara. This awakening in Sankara altered his consciousness, because after that he had the darshan of the highest Shakti.

Kundalini rises when the flow of energy in the body is balanced. This can be achieved through a number of ways, out of which the easiest and most effective is the worship of Shakti through mantra, yantra and mandala. This balanced energy charges the electrical current in the nerves, if maintained over a period of time, generating a tremendous pressure and force that arouses the kundalini.

Sri Vidya upasana

This awareness of the presence of Shakti in the manifold creation leads the practitioner of Shakta tantra to its main sadhana, which is *Sri Vidya* upasana. Any individual who becomes an upasaka of Sri Vidya is definitely most favoured and is nearing liberation. Sri Vidya creates a systematic esoteric discipline that combines elements of jnana, bhakti and upasana. The unrivalled Sri Vidya upasana, which confers the highest blessings upon the upasaka, is practised in the two ways previously described: bahir yaag and antar yaag.

In bahir yaag, the Sri Yantra, is worshipped with all the intricate rites and rituals of tantric worship, a ceremony that can last up to four hours. This is a most detailed and precise form of invocation of the divine Shakti, within the yantra, and the results are amazing. Antar yaag focuses on the inner experience of Sri Yantra, which is the subtle body of Tripura Sundari, superimposed on one's own body and mind through the medium of *bhakti*, devotion, and *bhavana*, inner attitude. This is the most powerful form of invocation, and the rule is that it should only be undertaken after preparing oneself through certain stages of purification, under the strict guidance of a guru. The guru will decide on the point where the yantra should be superimposed, according to the awareness of the disciple.

The outer upasana, or *bahyachar shaktyopasana*, derives its direction from the sixty-four tantras. The inner upasana, which is *antaronmukhi shaktyopasana*, has its basis in the *Shubagampanchaka* of Sankara, which is derived from the samhitas of Vasishtha, Sanak, Shauk, Sanandan and Sanat Kumar, who are amongst the original line of rishis and seers. As explained earlier, the outer upasana is derived from Kaula marga and Mishrit marga, whereas the inner upasana is derived from Samaya marga, which sees this body as a vehicle or abode of the divine. Sri Chakra or Sri Vidya upasana is the main sadhana in Samaya tantra. The outer upasana is necessary until kundalini awakens, and after that the inner worship begins. This form of tantra emerging from Shiva, which reveals the true, sublime and esoteric nature of Shakti, is independent of the sixty-four tantras and is the most revered of all.

Sankara was a promoter of Samayachara, which is not different from the vedic learning, disciplines and conduct. *Saundarya Lahari* is a work of Samaya in which Sankara highlights the awakening and ascent of kundalini that gives birth to the experience of Sri Chakra, the yantra form of Tripura Sundari, who forever resides in sahasrara chakra. Some of the original practitioners of Sri Vidya include such illustrious ancients as: Manu, Chandra, Kubera, Lopamudra, Manmatha, Agastya, Agni, Surya, Indra, Skanda, Shiva and Durvasa. Although there are several beautiful hymns composed by Sankara in worship of Shiva, Shakti, Vishnu, Ganesha and the nirguna Brahman, the attention given to this tantric poem, *Saundarya Lahari*, surpasses all his other work.

The two main meditations and branches of knowledge in Sri Vidya descend from the line of *Kamaraja vidya*, or *Kadi vidya*, and Lopamudra vidya, or *Haadi vidya*. Lopamudra, the wife of Rishi Agastya, is a rishi of the *Rig Veda*. She attained siddhi of Sri Vidya and her line is Haadi vidya. Although the goal of both Kaadi and Haadi vidyas is the experience of oneness with the supreme Shakti, Tripura Sundari, who is transcendental and beyond the three realms of awareness, their paths differ.

These differences lie in the mode of worship, the mantras that are used for invocation, and most importantly the point in the body where the supreme Shakti is meditated upon. These points relate to the higher centres, starting with anahata. Samaya tantra does not advocate meditation on any point below anahata, whereas Kaula and Mishrit tantra have practices involving the lower centres of mooladhara and swadhisthana.

Sri Vidya is Atma or Brahma vidya, which reveals itself through the mantra, yantra and *vigraha*, or mandala of Bhagavati Tripura Sundari, who is atma tattwa, shakti tattwa, vidya tattwa, prana tattwa, and this entire world of beings. In the *Nityashodshikarnava*, she is said to be the true yogini, who is none other than the *nakshatras*, or planets, the *rashis*, or astrological formations, *matrika*, or mantras, and peethas, or places where energy is enshrined. Moreover, it says that she is vidya, knowledge, and avidya, ignorance, too. She is both Shiva and Shakti, and the real form of Sri Vidya is revealed through her grace.

What lies beyond enlightenment? Through the practice of Sri Vidya, Samaya tantra reveals that it is Tripura Sundari. This vidya is known as Tripura Sundari due to its perfection of *saundarya*, or beauty. Tripura means three states, and Tripura Sundari signifies the sundara or beautiful experience that lies beyond the three states of *jagrat* or waking, *swapna* or dreaming, and *sushupti* or deep sleep, which correspond to the gross, subtle and causal dimensions of consciousness, or the conscious, subconscious and unconscious states. Tripura Sundari embodies the fourth state of *turiya*, which is transcendental, self-luminous and effulgent.

The three bija mantras, *Sa*, *Ka* and *La*, embedded in Sri Chakra are used for the sadhana of Sri Vidya. A combination of these three sounds creates the fifteen-lettered mantra of this sacred yantra. The *sampradaya*, or tradition, which practises this *panchakshari* mantra, beginning with the akshara *Ka*, is known as Kaadi vidya. Likewise, the sampradaya which practises the same fifteen-lettered mantra, beginning with the akshara *Ha*, is known as Haadi vidya. However, in both cases, this mantra becomes complete only when the sixteenth letter is added by the guru, making it *shodashi* or sixteen-lettered, which corresponds to the sixteen kalas or rays of transcendental nada.

Shodashi is the fully developed form of the mantra of Sri Yantra; it is born of sound in its primal form, without any modification or alteration. All the sixteen kalas emanating from this primal sound are contained in the Sri Yantra. This yantra is considered as the highest of all, because its structure is perfection to the utmost degree, making it the most suitable for attracting energy and projecting it back to the practitioner. This yantra leads to direct cognition, *aparokshanubhuti*, of the supreme, cosmic chitshakti, Tripura Sundari.

When the sadhaka's awareness transcends ajna chakra, he is guided through this formless and uncharted space of consciousness by the inner command of the guru, which is why ajna is known as the command centre. The sixteenth letter of the mantra is like a key that the guru hands over to the deserving disciple to enter higher states of awareness. Prior to that, the sadhaka practices the fifteen-lettered mantra. The shodashi mantra becomes complete or fully developed only when the sixteenth letter is added. Shodashi is *poornima*, the full moon, with all of its sixteen rays, or kalas. At that time it emanates a surreal hue, which is the reflection of Tripura Sundari, the shodashi of Sri Chakra.

The worship of Tripura Sundari is influenced by the lunar rays. The moon has sixteen rays, all of which are eternal. The first fifteen rays wax and wane, but the sixteenth does not. This sixteenth ray is Mahashakti Tripura Sundari or Lalita. She is the eternal jewel of *ananda* and *saundarya*, bliss and beauty. There is completeness and fullness only in shodashi, the sixteenth ray.

The body of Tripura Sundari is divided into three for the purpose of worship. The face of Bhagavati is *vagbhav kut*, the pinnacle of speech, ruled by *agneya* or fire, which has five kalas or rays. The *katipradesh* or middle portion of Bhagavati, from the neck to the waist, is *kamakala kut*, the pinnacle of desire, and is ruled by *Saura* or the sun, which has five kalas. The lower part of Bhagavati, from the waist down, is *shakti kut* or the pinnacle of energy, and is ruled by the moon, which has five kalas. The sixteenth kala is separate from these and is known as *madhukari*, the producer of nectar.

This concept of worship is peculiar to Shakta darshan, a system that is fully devoted to the worship of Devi. The part of Devi's body which is being worshipped assumes the main focus of the worship. For example, when the kamakala kut is being worshipped, then the other two portions recede into the background, and that portion alone becomes the pinnacle of worship. The awareness of the worshipper is totally absorbed only on that portion of Tripura Sundari, and he experiences the kala or rays emanating from there.

Worship of the fifteen kalas of the three parts of Tripura Sundari's divine body leads to the experience of the sixteenth kala, which is the nectar-producing ray. This is synonymous with kundalini's ascent to sahasrara and subsequent descent along with her consort down to the realm of the gross body, where she saturates every dimension of existence with her *madhu*, or nectar. Just as a bee produces nectar only at night, the yogi too awakens the kundalini at night, night being symbolic of the moment when the senses and lower awareness are asleep and the yogi ascends to greater heights. The upasakas of Sri Vidya worship her on the nights of *shukla paksha*, when the moon is waxing.

Rays of creation

According to Shakta darshan, the basic tattwas of creation are thirty-six in number, which corresponds to the concepts of Kashmir Shaiva Siddhanta and Shaiva darshan. This number differs slightly from the other philosophies, such as Nyaya which upholds sixteen; Samkhya, twenty-five; Vaishesika, six; Advaita Vedanta, one; Dvaita Vedanta, two; and Vishishta Advaita, three. The two principle tattwas of Shakta darshan are Shiva and Shakti, in their pristine purity. Here, Shiva is *prakasha*, the illuminating force, and Shakti is *vimarsha*, the vibratory force. Prakasha transmutes into vimarsha and assumes the form of bindu. Vimarsha, or Shakti, transmutes into prakasha, or Shiva, as a result of which bindu is split and nada is born. Prakasha is that energy inherent in Shiva, which exists independent of Shiva. Vimarsha is the nature of prakasha.

Moola bindu is the root of creation. When there is vibration in bindu, nada is born and the tattwas that arise out of nada are formed. Although in principle, nada and bindu are inseparable, like a mother and child, they separate at her behest for the supreme Shakti to manifest further. So there is evolution of sound into light, which gives rise to form. The break in their unity results in light. When they remain together, there is vibration or spandan in bindu, a kind of throb, like a heartbeat. This signifies that bindu is really the centre of existence in its highest potential, just before it bursts forth into the transcendental nada, *Aum*. When the awareness is in bindu, one thus experiences total peace, relaxation and unity with the cosmos.

The light emanating from the friction caused by the spandan in bindu and the subsequent emergence of sound is known as kala, or ray. This ray has a very high intensity and spreads out in all directions for further evolution into the gunas: sattwa, rajas and tamas, from which the entire creation springs forth. This ray, or kala, along with nada penetrates into all the tattwas that compose matter as it is being formed. Even in the human body, each and every organ, nerve and fibre is saturated with nada and kala, or sound and light. Of course, the intensity differs in each part of the body, as well as in the different *shariras*, or bodies: *sthoola*, gross, *sukshma*, subtle, and *karana*, causal.

In the sthoola sharira, sound and light have condensed to their grossest form and are thus hard to discern. The sthoola sharira is not really a producer of energy in the form of sound and light, but rather a consumer of it. The gross body is connected to the pranic field, and it is through the pranic body that the physical body is fed. Prana sustains the physical body, not the proteins and minerals that one ingests daily. If there were no prana in the body, the food that one eats would remain in the stomach undigested and putrefy. It is prana that causes digestion, respiration, circulation, excretion and reproduction. So, rather than focusing on different diet fads, it would be better to increase the quantum of prana in the body through tantric practices, so that it can be healthy and strong.

The sukshma sharira houses the pranic and mental bodies. Prana is nothing but sound and light energy, which is not perceived as solid matter, but in a purer form, as aura. This aura increases and decreases, according to the level of prana. The pranic channels are connected with the source of cosmic energy through the chakras and there is a constant influx of prana into the body. One of the main conduits for pranic intake from outside is the breath and this can be influenced by the practices of pranayama. The sukshma sharira also houses the six major chakras, from mooladhara to ajna, which are situated along the spinal column. The chakras are circular vortexes of energy which distribute prana through the nadis, or energy channels, to all parts of the body.

Sound and light are experienced in the karana sharira in their purest form. The chakras above ajna, such as *nirodhika*, bindu and sahasrara, which are energy points, rather than vortexes of energy, emanate sound and light that is very similar to the transcendental sound. As these points ascend, they become an identical replica of the transcendental nada and kala, which the saints have described as the cosmic reverberation of *Aum* and the effulgence of a thousand suns.

Shodashi – the sixteenth ray

The kala that emanates from the first nada is composed of sixteen rays. The sixteenth ray, which is known as *amritkala*, is present only when divinity manifests. Lord Krishna was born with sixteen kalas. The experience which Sankara was undergoing also comprised the sixteen kalas of divinity, because the form he was seeing was that of Adi Shakti, known in Samaya tantra as Tripura Sundari, who is responsible for the birth of the sixteenth kala.

These kalas are also present in the three shariras, or bodies, which comprise one's being. They exist in varying degrees of refinement in the gross, subtle and causal bodies. According to Samaya tantra, each and every organ of the gross body can be measured by the number of kalas it emits. In the same way, the subtle body that is composed of chakras can be measured by their number of rays, or kala. Similarly, the other evolutes of pure consciousness, such as *buddhi*, or intellect, *ahamkara*, or ego, *chitta*, or memory, and *manas*, or mind, can also be defined in this manner.

Although the mind, ego, intellect and memory cannot be seen by the naked eye, tantra has given unique definitions of these subtle, incomprehensible states by indicating the number of rays or kalas that each one is composed of. The mind is *ekadashi*, or eleven rays, and remains only until the awareness reaches ajna.

Once ajna is crossed, the mind does not remain in its present form, nor does it experience time, space and object, because of the direct relation between the transcendence of the mind and the cessation of time. Tantra states that as long as the mind is linked with the indriyas, or senses, it does not become *apaushya*, strong, pure and unlimited. The mind has to be purified by the fire of knowledge. Then there is transformation from the lower mind of eleven kalas to the higher mind. Buddhi is *dwadashi*, or twelve rays, chitta is *trayodashi*, or thirteen rays, and ahamkara is *chaturdashi*, or fourteen rays.

Amavasya, the no moon day, represents the state of *nirvikalpa*, transcendence, when all the rays recede back into their source. *Poornima*, the full moon day, represents bindu, but in fact it is not, because the sixteenth ray is still absent in bindu. When the kundalini shakti ascends to sahasrara, it pierces the *chandramandala* or *baindavasthana* and nectar streams down from the moon at bindu through the opening at brahmarandhra, making the ajna chakra *amrita maya*, full of nectar. Then all the sixteen rays of the moon begin to shine through the darshan, or inner experience, of the supreme vidya or knowledge, Tripura Sundari, who is the mistress of *baindavasthana*. This is the experience Sankara elucidates in *Saundarya Lahari*.

What is Shakti?

Shakti is composed of two syllables, 'sha' and 'kti'. *Sha* denotes 'auspicious prosperity' and *kti* denotes 'power', 'action', 'enactment'. So, Shakti is that power which is auspicious and brings prosperity to all. Thus Shakti is power, energy, life and creation in the true sense. The *Devi Bhagavatam* states that Shakti is the root as well as the source of creation. She is responsible for the evolution of all matter, animate or inanimate, which includes human beings. The universe is in a constant state of evolution, but until now people have been unaware of the great force behind this evolution.

Now the scientists call this force that cannot be seen, but exists everywhere, 'dark energy'. Apart from being responsible for the rapid evolution of the universe, this force also gives shape and form to the galaxies and maintains a suitable distance between them. This energy surrounds everything on all sides and holds the entire universe in its hands, but no one knows how it works or how it looks. Scientists are certain that dark energy exists and they consider it to be the most revolutionary discovery of this century. They also say that new equations of the material world can emerge once they gain knowledge of this dark energy. They have now started a long quest to ascertain what this dark energy is and where, if at all, it can be traced.

According to tantra, which seems to already have all the answers, this force of Mahashakti operates through kala, or waves. The first principle to emerge from the cosmic spandan, or vibration in bindu, at the time of creation was nada, the cosmic sound, and the second was kala. That supreme energy spreads out in waves, covering the entire world. Many of these waves have been discovered by scientists, and many more are yet to be discovered, some of which may totally revolutionize the concept of the world one lives in, as well as of oneself.

Shakti is the power that grants life and the power to think, desire, know and act. Through Shakti one conducts one's entire life; in the absence of Shakti one would cease to be. Shakti has three attributes through which it carries out all of these functions: *iccha shakti*, the power to will, *kriya shakti*, the power to do, and *jnana shakti*, the power to know. These three attributes which evolved out of the very first evolutes of Mahashakti, bindu, nada and kala, further evolve into the three gunas: *sattwa, rajas* and *tamas*, which pervade each and every dimension of existence, physical, mental and beyond as well. Everyone is greatly influenced by the effects of the three gunas, which are the manifest Shakti.

Although Shakti assumes attributes in order to manifest, there is also the unmanifest Shakti, which remains as *trigunatita*, without the three gunas or attributes. So, Shakti is both *nirguna*, without guna, and *saguna*, with guna. In her nirguna state, she is revered as Adi Shakti, and in her saguna state as Parvati, Durga, Kali, Lakshmi, Gauri, Ambe, Chandi, Bhavani and Saraswati. These are not merely names of goddesses; they are the forms that this magnificent Shakti assumes from time to time in the depths of individual consciousness as the awareness gains ascent. *Saundarya Lahari* is an ode to or worship of Parvati, who reveals her nirguna form as the highest Adi Shakti in union with Adi Shiva.

Just as a new born baby has the element of anger or a child of five has the element of passion, but they do not know it, in the same way, everyone has the supreme elements of Shiva and Shakti. They are hidden or concealed within and do not have to be brought from outside. They have only to be worshipped with love and devotion so that they manifest from within, just as passion manifests in the child when he grows up. This ultimate manifestation of one's highest potential is the sublime aim of tantra.

From the Shakta viewpoint, this creation is nothing but the *swaroopa*, or form, of Shakti. Unlike other darshanas, the Shakta agamas regard the world as a portrait or play of Shakti; it is the *parinama*, or result, of Shakti. The *Amritananda Deepika* says that just as butter is the result of milk, in the same way, this world is the result of that Parashakti. Shakti is *anadi*, eternal, and so is Shiva. But Shakti is not dependent on Shiva, both are eternal tattwas. Shakti is not the result or transformation of any tattwa, but exists independently and is the sole cause of the origin and transformation of all the tattwas. Mahamaya, Prakriti and Shakti are all the different stages of that one supreme Parashakti that is eternal.

Other darshanas insist that Shakti creates due to the desire of Shiva, but Shakta darshan holds Shakti as the sole cause of creation, nullifying the role of Shiva in the process of creation, and establishing him as the knower, or *sakshi*, of this process. Shiva and Shakti are inseparably united like the moon and its rays. The inward state of Shakti is Shiva, and the projection of Shiva is Shakti. This inward and outward projection continues endlessly. The feeling of Shakti is predominant in Shiva and vice versa. In the state of *tattwatita*, beyond the tattwas, neither Shiva nor Shakti is superior, both are equal. This is the blissful state of unity which Shaivas call Paramshiva and Shaktas call Parashakti.

Form of Shakti

Although all forms are the roopa of Shakti, the three main classifications are *nirguna roopa*, *purusha roopa* and *nari roopa*, which can be further classified as the sthoola, sukshma and pararoopa of Shakti. Mandalas are important because they comprise all three roopas, the gross, subtle and transcendental.

The *Tripurasiddhanta* is a tantric text that defines the concept of Tripura Sundari based on Adwaita principles. According to this philosophy, the Mahashakti Tripura Sundari is moola tattwa, one and single. Like a mirror, she reflects all forms in herself. Another important tantric text based on pure advaitic principles, the *Tripura Rahasya*, says that only the pure, untainted consciousness is real, and that is Tripura Sundari. This *Satyashakti* is known as Shiva, Vishnu and Mahesh. Although her creative power is independent in her undivided form, Devi Tripura Sundari is united with Shiva, who is none other than herself.

In the first sloka of the *Dakshinamurti Stotra*, it is said that from the enlightened point of view, this creation is seen as an extension of one's own self, like the reflection of a city or town in a mirror. In other words, the creation is held within itself. The extension of creation, which is experienced objectively, is only on account of *maya*, the power of illusion, which reverts back to its original state once maya is transcended. The governing principles of this creation are not *jada* or matter, but *chinmayi*, or pure awareness. In the second sloka, it is said that this creation remains established in the state of nirvikalpa, or transcendence, and is steady even in the state of *shoonya*, or void, which is beyond the differences created by the mind.

Pratyabhijna darshan as well as *Tripura* darshan give the same examples and are strongly linked to each other. The root of this creation is desire which springs from the combination of bindu and nada when it turns into mishra bindu. The *shveta*, white, and *rakta*, red, bindus are the result of this desire, out of which the sperm and ova are produced. When the shveta bindu, rakta bindu and mishra bindu unite, then the *kamakala tattwa* is born. This is known as *shakti chatushtaya*, the four parts of shakti: moola bindu, nada bindu, shveta bindu and rakta bindu, which give rise to kamakala, or the ray of desire. It is said that the Sri Yantra, too, came into being through the force of primordial desire.

Universality of Sri Yantra

Sankara was a worshipper of Sri Vidya. The Sri Chakra established by him in Sringeri Math is very sacred. Many tantric texts have explained the nature, construction, application and significance of Sri Yantra, the most powerful of all yantras. Sankara has described this sacred yantra in its most basic form in mantra 11. From that primordial sound full of the spandan or the vibration of desire, the Sri Yantra emerged as an interplay of triangles, circles, squares and lotus petals, each a manifestation of some aspect of creation.

The entire process of evolution of pure consciousness into matter and involution back to consciousness is enshrined in this yantra. This is why it is auspiciousness personified and can confer worldly as well as spiritual benefits. The diverse symbolism of Sri Yantra can be understood and its aesthetic appeal can be experienced immediately, but its potency cannot be grasped instantly. This requires regular sadhana, which in time unlocks its secret power so that the energy flows out of this yantra and illuminates the consciousness of the sadhaka.

The Sri Yantra is definitely the product of revelation, rather than the imagination of a human mind. The exact origin of this yantra is unknown, but it is most ancient. The universality of this yantra is evident when comparing it with the ancient monuments of the Maya civilizations in South America. These giant monuments were built in worship of Kukulklai, which has a striking similarity to the word kundalini, and depicted seven ladders with a serpent descending from heaven. The monuments were built with such precision that the reflection of the Sun throughout the day creates triangles, which become visible as the shadows change.

Adjacent to the main temple of worship are several smaller monuments placed in such a way that they guide the rays of the sun. It is astonishing to see that when the sun's rays are at a certain angle, these triangles all interlock with one another and light up to reveal a maze that is exactly like the Sri Yantra. The moon also exerts an influence on these monuments. On the sixteenth day of the lunar cycle, when the moon is in its full splendour, emitting the sixteen kalas, the serpent or kundalini is seen descending from the highest ladder down to the lowest, mooladhara or the earth. The serpent is only visible on that day when the moon is full. Similarly, Sri Yantra has the power to awaken kundalini, but the sixteenth ray for unlocking its power lies in the hands of the guru who can convert the yantra into Shodashi.

Saundarya Lahari sadhana

From the viewpoint of Shakti, there is no sadhaka, as there is no bondage or liberation. There is no place for sadhana or sadhaka, because the all-pervading, eternal, and illumined form of Shakti is the only reality. She is knowledge and absence of knowledge, and to know her is the highest knowledge. Just as one makes the body agile through the practices of asana and pranayama so that it can assume any posture, in the same way, the mind must become agile and capable of assuming any attitude. Eventually, the mind has to transcend itself, and the process of transcending the mind has to be selected skilfully.

This process may often appear to be beyond logic or any kind of rationale. The experience is also beyond logic and, therefore, it is natural that the process, too, will appear illogical. But if it works, why bother about satisfying the intellect? Knowledge alone is not enough; it is experience that has to take place. *Saundarya Lahari* sadhana can be utilized to achieve the agility of mind necessary for the free flow of spiritual energy in all dimensions of one's being. The mind blocks that experience on account of its rigid habits; it assumes a particular attitude and is unable to break out of it. The mantras and yantras of *Saundarya Lahari* allow one to transcend these habits and patterns.

The sadhana of *Saundarya Lahari* can be commenced at any age or stage in life, but the earlier one starts the better, to allow the full grace of Devi to shine in one's life. The mantras can even be chanted by mothers while their child is in the womb, to encourage expansion of awareness in the foetus itself. This sadhana is complete in itself. With the chanting of the mantras, it will be observed that one becomes accomplished in yama and niyama as a natural outcome of this sadhana, without any great effort. Pratyahara and dharana then follow as a consequence because they develop side by side.

An important aspect to keep in mind is the *bhava*, or attitude with which one practises. The mind should be soft, tender and fluid, not rigid and tense. This is possible only when faith and devotion to Shakti are developed along with the practice. The chanting of *Saundarya Lahari* enables one to maintain the correct attitude of mind, as it develops the experience of divinity within. The bhava, or mental attitude, is what makes this sadhana truly beautiful. If the bhava is soft, loving and tender, one will become beautiful, or *sundaram*, an embodiment of Devi oneself.

Any number of hidden meanings may be revealed to the sadhaka, according to his perception and understanding, as the grace of Devi descends while chanting the mantras. As the sadhaka becomes immersed in the sacred mantras, many esoteric truths may emerge from this treasure trove, which is a mine of bhakti, jnana and upasana.

Shakti is endless and so, too, are her explanations and descriptions, but the time comes when the experience should begin. Although the meanings of the mantras of *Saundarya Lahari* are sublime, beautiful and most inspiring, it is not necessary to understand them at all in order to have the experience. The important thing is to begin the practice. One should place the mandala or yantra of Devi before one, then sit in vajrasana with the hands in *avahaneya mudra*, and begin to chant the mantras. When the mantras are known by heart, the gaze can remain on the mandala while chanting. At first, one will see the mandala with the eyes open, and later when the chanting is over, with the eyes closed, the mandala will appear within the depths of one's consciousness.

Become a worshipper of Shakti!

Sri Saundarya Lahari
Commentary

Sri Yantra

1. Meditation on Shiva and Shakti

शिवः शक्त्या युक्तो यदि भवति शक्तः प्रभवितुं
न चेदेवं देवो न खलु कुशलः स्पन्दितुमपि ।
अतस्त्वामाराध्यां हरिहरविरिञ्चादिभिरपि
प्रणन्तुं स्तोतुं वा कथमकृतपुण्यः प्रभवति ॥१॥

shivah shaktyaa yukto yadi bhavati shaktah prabhavitum
na chedevam devo na khalu kushalah spanditumapi;
atastvaam-aaraadhyaam harihara-virinchyaadibhirapi
pranantum stotum vaa katham-akritapunyah prabhavati. (1)

shivah: shiva; *shaktyaa*: with shakti: *yukta*: when united; *yadi*: when; *bhavati*: becomes; *shaktah*; capable; *prabhavitum*: when capable of creating, protecting or destroying the universe; *na chet*: if not; *evam*: that way; *deva*: illumined one (meaning shiva); *na khalu*: not at all; *kushalah*: capable; *spanditum api*: even to stir; *ata*: so; *tvaam*: thee; *aaraadhyaam*: worshipped; *hari hara virinchi*: vishnu, shiva and brahma; *adibhih api*: even by the vedas; *pranantum*: worship, bow before; *stotum va*: praising through stotras or hymns; *katham*: how; *akritapunyah*: one who has not acquired merit; *prabhavati*: will be capable.

Translation
Shiva, the divine one, when united with Shakti is endowed with the power to create, protect and destroy the universe; otherwise he is unable even to stir. How can one who has not acquired great merit be capable of worshipping Thee, who art praised and worshipped by Hari (Vishnu), Hara (Shiva) and Virinchi (Brahma), and even by the eternal Vedas?

Commentary
Shiva is consciousness, the eternal, ultimate, unbroken and steady stream of awareness. Shakti is energy, immense power and potential. Shiva is chetana, the conscious and totally alert awareness, which is termed *jnana*. Shakti is both *jada*

and *chetana*, the dormant and conscious potential. Shiva knows, but cannot act; Shakti knows as well as acts. Shiva is transcendental; Shakti is transcendental as well as empirical. Shiva remains the *sakshi*, or witness, to the entire creation; Shakti is sakshi as well as actively involved in the entire creation. They are both one and the same, not separate entities, omnipresent throughout the entire manifest and unmanifest existence, and having no distinction of colour, gender, size, name, form, address or destination. Just as heat cannot be separated from fire, cold from snow, or light from the sun, in the same way Shiva cannot be separated from Shakti, because they permeate each other on a profound level.

Tantra has personified these two primary principles as Shiva and Shakti, so that the finite mind can grasp the infinite. This concept of Shiva and Shakti is one of the greatest contributions of tantra, whereby it has explained the origin of each and every facet of existence. In tantra, everything has a potential sound, linear dimension and form. This is understandable for objects and images, but tantra extends this imagery to the realm of feelings and emotions too. Each emotion that man experiences: passion, anger, greed, jealousy, compassion, innocence and purity, has been codified by tantra as sound, linear dimension and form, which are called *mantra*, *yantra* and *mandala*.

When one says the word cow, for example, the form of a four-legged creature with beautiful eyes, stocky frame, long ears and tail immediately comes to mind. In the same way, as soon as any word is pronounced, be it bell, drum, chair, table or tree, the form of that sound instantly and effortlessly etches itself upon the canvas of the mind. So, when one says the word consciousness, what form appears on the mental canvas? What is the form of consciousness? Tantra says the form of consciousness is *shivalingam*. Etymologically, the word *lingam* means 'source', not male phallus, as it has been misinterpreted on account of the shape. Lingam is an apt expression, because consciousness is the source of everything one sees, hears, speaks, senses, feels and perceives. It is the source of the manifest as well as the unmanifest creation, waiting to manifest itself in the bosom of consciousness.

The form of Shakti is *yoni*, the womb or holy grail, where creation germinates, sprouts, is nurtured and becomes manifest, so that all can witness, wonder and marvel at it. All of creation goes through this process in the microcosmos as well as the macrocosmos, the world which cannot be seen, but still exists all around us. At the microcosmic level each life form has physical parents, and at the macrocosmic level, too, each life has cosmic parents, whom tantra has identified and classified as Shakti and Shiva. They are the eternal parents, immortalized in the Sanskrit sloka:

> *Tvameva maataa cha pitaa tvameva,*
> *tvameva bandhushcha sakhaa tvameva,*
> *tvameva vidyaa dravinam tvameva,*
> *tvameva sarvam mama deva deva.*

Thou art my mother and father too, my friend and beloved,
Thou art knowledge absolute as well as matter;
Thou art all, O shining one.

Shiva is saturated with Shakti, and Shakti with Shiva. They are not just united, because union presupposes two separate entities coming together, but that is not the case. Shakti is inherent in Shiva, just as butter is inherent in milk. When milk is churned, the butter is exposed. Even though butter existed in the milk prior to that, it could not be distinguished as a separate entity; that is the relationship of Shiva and Shakti. Just as a crystal takes on the reflection of anything that it rests upon, in the same way, Shakti takes on the reflection of Shiva and Shiva of Shakti. So, the first important point to note in this relationship is that Shiva and Shakti permeate each other in such a profound manner that they cannot be distinguished and appear as one at the macrocosmic level. At the microcosmic level they appear to separate in order to manifest the entire creation, although they never really separate and forever exist as one homogeneous stream of consciousness and energy.

The second point to note is the subject matter of this opening verse of *Saundarya Lahari*. If it were not for Shakti, the inherent power of Shiva, that homogeneous stream of consciousness would forever remain motionless and inert. There would never be any *spandan*, or vibration, which is the very basis of motion. Shiva, devoid of Shakti, does not have the power to vibrate or set itself into motion. Thus it is motionless, timeless and eternal, as opposed to Shakti, which is motion, time, and both eternal and transient.

Thus, although Shakti is not different to Shiva, she has an additional quality which Shiva does not have, and that is to set things into motion. Shakti is both passive and kinetic, as opposed to Shiva, who is passive only. Is it not a great mystery or riddle how an eternal principle can also contain within it the germ or seed of transience? Tantra solves this mystery by stating that Shakti is an eternal principle that bestows the power to create, sustain and destroy, and thus gives birth to creation.

Shakti is the great power that moves what does not move. She makes Shiva aware of his own existence and not just Shiva, even we are aware of our existence on account of her. Sankara pays tribute here to the great compassion of Shakti in allowing us to know our existence, and to transcend the limitations that obstruct our experience of the state of stillness that is Shiva. Tantra says that it is to witness this grand spectacle that one is born.

The *shrutis*, such as *Ishavasya Upanishad*, declare that the eternal principle is vibratory as well as motionless: *Tadejati tanejati tadure tadvantike*; it vibrates and it does not vibrate. This raises the question whether spandan or vibration is the nature of Shiva or Shakti or both? Shiva stands for homogeneous awareness, so it is natural to assume a lack of motion in that which has been defined as uniform and without disturbance. Therefore, the question of Shiva being vibratory as well as motionless does not occur.

Shakti possesses the power to vibrate and to remain motionless, according to the situation. When united with Shiva, Shakti is passive, assuming her motionless and homogeneous nature; thus the nature of Shiva remains unchanged. When separated from Shiva, her spandan or vibration commences. Tantra speaks of the Shiva principle of homogeneous awareness as a state where Shakti is not absent, but present in her passive role. The passive and the dynamic roles of Shakti are beautifully allegorized through the two wives of Shiva. Sati is the passive principle and Parvati, the dynamic principle of Shakti.

In Vedanta, the homogeneous stream of awareness is called *Brahman*, a word derived from the root *brihad*, which means 'ever-expanding consciousness'. How can a motionless principle expand until and unless there is a movement? The passive principle of Shakti causes this expansion in a uniform and homogeneous manner, so that the expansion in all directions is equal and total, appearing as a steady stream. When Shakti functions separately from Shiva, her vibration sets all events into motion. However, despite the vibration that she instigates, Shakti still carries the homogeneous principle of consciousness, which she integrates into the objects she creates. This mantra says that the first vibration of creation is caused by Shakti. After that, there is vibration after vibration, movement after movement, *dhvani* after dhvani, which culminates in the vibrations of our daily lives.

The nature of Shakti is spandan, vibration or motion. Shakti is *trigunatmika*, which means that she expresses herself in three distinct ways: *iccha*, the power to will, *jnana*, the power to know, and *kriya*, the power to act. Thus the expression of spandan, or vibration, can take place in the homogeneous stream of awareness only at the behest of Shakti. However, as Shakti is an expression of Shiva's capability, they are equal and balanced. Shiva is the notion of *Aham*, 'I am', and Shakti is the notion of *Idam*, 'I do'. The experience of Shiva consciousness is *moksha*, or liberation, while the experience of shakti consciousness is *bhoga*, or enjoyment, on the one hand, and moksha, or liberation, on the other. In this way the range of Shakti is far more extensive than Shiva. Both materialists and spiritualists pay homage to Shakti, for she can bestow happiness in this life and liberation as well.

This mantra goes on further to say that only those who have acquired great merit are fortunate to worship her, which is an extremely valid and relevant point. Only those who have acquired great merit are able to see the magnificence, power and potential of Shakti. Others are enamoured of her glamour and drown in the enjoyment of the appearances of her power. Thus they are caught in *moha*, or delusion, but Sankara was not. He revered Shakti and worshipped her form with devotion, rather than passion or enjoyment; therein lies the difference.

A bhogi views the world, which is nothing but a manifestation of Shakti, as a playground of enjoyment; a yogi views it as a playground of worship. One is bound by his perception and the other liberated. But, according to this mantra, the attitude of reverence for Shakti does not arise in everyone. Only the fortunate, who have great merit, can worship Shakti without falling into delusion. They are fortunate because they live life with awareness and abiding wisdom, which most never realize, although these qualities are present in everyone. Those who are fortunate maintain this balance of awareness in life by perseverance and undaunted efforts. Thus they acquire merit through continued efforts, just as a hard working and diligent student acquires merit in his studies.

The only difference is that a student may acquire merit through the hard work of a few days, months or years, whereas in the worship of Shakti, great merit is acquired through endless lifetimes, which bring the devotee to the point of reverence, as was the case of Sankara. The greatness of Shakti is further elaborated in this mantra, where one is reminded that *Virinchi*, an epithet of Brahma, *Hari* of Vishnu, and *Hara* of Shiva, the three *mahadevas*, or great illumined ones, through whom Shakti creates, preserves and dissolves the universe, are forever in reverent worship of her. These three gods represent her three evolutes: *rajas*, signifying creation or Brahma, *sattwa*, preservation or Vishnu, and *tamas*, dissolution or Shiva.

The word *adi* in *adibhirapi*, which means the 'first' or the 'source', indicates the Vedas or shrutis, which are regarded as the source of all knowledge. This lends further support to the idea of Shakti's eminence, as it suggests that even the Vedas, which are regarded as the source of eternal truth and knowledge, sing her praise in worship. Scholars of tantra have understood that this verse contains many mantras for awakening Shakti. Some have even said that in this first verse itself Sankara has given the *shodashi*, or sixteen-lettered mantra of Sri Vidya, which can confer the highest grace.

This mantra neatly sums up the basic premise of tantra on which rest all of its theories on the interplay of consciousness and energy, where the main player is energy in the process of creation. *Na chedevam devo na khalu kushalah spanditumapi*; Shakti opens Shiva's eyes for the first time and the knowledge of Aham, I am, and Idam, I do, dawns. This is a state described as *sadakhya* or *sadashiva tattwa* that desires to create due to which the iccha or *sankalpa* shakti is born. Sankalpa shakti or will power is seen even at the level of the mind; in fact, the mind is an outcome of sankalpa shakti. It is Aham, I am, that becomes purusha and Idam, I do, that becomes prakriti at a later stage, when Shiva's eyes are fully opened by Shakti, after which Shakti begins her final stage of manifestation at different levels.

Without Shakti or energy, one cannot even blink an eyelid, let alone perform the innumerable activities that are required in life. The role of energy can be seen everywhere in the process of creation, whether of a living being, an object or idea, a business venture, a piece of music, a literary work, a painting, a dance repertoire or a music recital. Even the highest spiritual experience requires a great influx of energy. In the three states of mind: *jagrat*, *swapna* and *sushupti*, which correspond to the conscious, subconscious and unconscious, it is energy that directs the range of perception and experience. Finally, the transformation of energy from gross to subtle to causal states culminates in *turiya*, the transcendental state of consciousness.

Shakti is that energy which has a tremendous range of expression. *Saundarya Lahari* is an ode to Shakti, revered as the divine Mother. She is the cause of Shiva's evolution into this universe of sentient and insentient beings. As she is the cause of evolution, she must also be the cause of involution back to the source, which is Shiva. But this is only possible when one acquires great merit and becomes capable of worshipping her. Then only does she become compassionate. This is what Sankara is teaching in this mantra, how to evoke the compassion of Shakti. This compassion can only be invoked through devotion and *shraddha*, faith that renders an inaccessible entity accessible.

In this opening mantra itself, Sankara has indicated the overall theme of *Saundarya Lahari*. The very first two words, *Shiva Shaktya*, Shiva and Shakti, represent the two eternal principles. They are the source of all *vidyas* and knowledge, and through them Sankara introduces the main *upasana*, or worship, enshrined in *Saundarya Lahari*, which is the worship of Sri Vidya. They are the eternal parents of the universe, as everything seen and unseen emanates and evolves from them. Although they appear as a paradox, assuming opposite positions, such as passive and dynamic, they are one and the same.

In fact, this paradox has infiltrated down into human life at the gross level. Thus, when Sankara depicts Shiva and his shakti, Parvati, who exhibit the traits of lover and beloved or husband and wife, the attention is at once drawn to the fact that nothing in life is mundane. The human experience has its roots in the most sublime experience of unity between Shiva and Shakti. That abstract, absolute experience, which is just a concept until it is explained in this manner, becomes real, visible and concrete by assuming a name and form. Thereby Sankara at once elevates man and woman, the two opposites, who are eternally enacting their divine roles on the human plane.

2. Meditation on Sri Devi's feet

तनीयांसं पांसुं तव चरणपङ्केरुहभवं
विरिञ्चिः संचिन्वन् विरचयति लोकानविकलम् ।
वहत्येनं शौरिः कथमपि सहस्रेण शिरसां
हरः संक्षुद्यैनं भजति भसितोद्धूलनविधिम् ॥२॥

*taneeyaamsam paamsum tava charana-pankeruha-bhavam
virinchih sanchinvan virachayati lokaan-avikalam;
vahatyenam shaurih kathamapi sahastrena shirasaam
harah samkshudyainam bhajati bhasitoddhoolanavidhim.* (2)

taneeyaamsam: minute; *paamsum*: dust; *tava charana pankeruha bhavam*: from thy lotus feet; *virinchih*: brahma; *sanchinvan*: collecting; *virachayati*; creates; *lokaan*: the universe; *avikalam*: entire; *vahati*: bears, holds up; *enam*: it (this universe); *shaurih*: vishnu; *kathamapi*: somehow, with great difficulty; *sahasrena shirasaam*: with thousand heads; *harah*: shiva; *samkshudy*: reducing to ashes; *ainam*: it (this universe); *bhajati*: does; *bhasit oddhoolana vidhim*: besmears his body with it

Translation
Collecting the minute particles of dust from Thy lotus feet, Virinchi (Brahma) creates this universe. Shauri (Vishnu) holds this entire universe on his thousand heads, thus sustaining it with great difficulty, and Hara (Shiva) reduces it to ashes and besmears his body with it.

Commentary
The feet hold a special place of reverence in the worship of divine energies, such as God or Guru. Often the *paduka*, or feet, are worshipped instead of the form of the actual deity. The feet of an illumined person are seen as a point of refuge for the aspirant through which he receives divine protection and grace. Poems and odes dedicated to divine beings, saints and sages are filled with such references. In

the famous epic *Ramayana*, Lord Rama refused to end his exile in the forest and Bharata was chosen to rule Ayodhya for fourteen years. So Bharata requested his brother, who was divinity incarnate, for his *charan padukas,* or sandals, which he placed on the throne as the symbol of Rama in his absence. The same sentiment of veneration is expressed in this verse for the feet of Shakti.

The feet are also that part where the energy leaves the body. All the organs and glands, brain, nerves and nadis in the human body have their termination point at the feet. Thus, when personifying that great energy or shakti in human form, the feet are venerated as that would be the point where the energy flows outwards and graces the creation. Therefore, Sankara commences and concludes his esoteric poem of Shakti worship with the adoration of Devi's lotus feet. At the beginning this veneration bestows approval or sanction for her worship and in conclusion it offers the fruit or result of the worship to her.

The idea conveyed in the first mantra that Shakti is worshipped by Shiva, Vishnu and Brahma is further elaborated in the second stanza. The *trimurti*, or three Lords, Brahma, Vishnu and Shiva, who carry out the important functions of creation, sustenance and dissolution, owe their capacities to the trickle of Devi's compassion. The word Virinchi is derived from *rachna*, which means 'to create'. This is another name for Brahma, who creates all the worlds out of the smallest speck of dust from Shakti's feet.

The word *pamsum* means 'dust' and by using the phrase *taniyamsum*, Sankara indicates that in the particles of dust emanating from Mahashakti, the great energy, there are tiny specks which are even smaller. This tiniest speck of dust is sufficient to create the fourteen worlds. The word *lokaan* implies not just the universe we behold, but all the different worlds, which in esoteric terms signify planes of consciousness that the awareness passes through, from *bhuh, bhuvah, suvah, maha, jana, tapah, satya*, as well as the nether worlds: *atala, vitala, sutala, rasatala, talatala, mahatala* and *patala*.

Moreover, science, too, claims that the minutest subatomic particles of energy correlate with each other and thus are responsible for the creation of matter. Tantra calls these particles *anu*, atomic and *paramanu*, subatomic. The *pancha mahabhutas*, or five great elements, which are *prithvi*, earth, *apas*, water, *agni*, fire, *vayu*, air, and *akasha*, ether, are subatomic particles of nuclear energy. Together these five *tattwas*, or elements, are the building blocks of matter, which nature permutes and combines in a magnificent way to give solidity and density to the great cosmic energy.

So this mantra indicates that the dust emanating from Sri Devi's feet is enshrined in each atom that constitutes matter. This is why each atom has endless potential. Imagine that great moment when shakti, or cosmic energy, initiates the process of creation, the great upheaval that must occur in the homogeneity of Shiva and Shakti for energy to separate itself and become nuclear. The phrase *taniyamsum pamsum* is indicative of nuclear dust that emerges from the lotus feet of shakti, which is gathered by Brahma to create the universe.

The claim of the first mantra that consciousness is inert and incapable of any spandan, or vibration, without energy is further substantiated in the second verse. Here it asserts that shakti releases these subatomic particles on account of which Brahma creates, Vishnu sustains and Hara destroys the creation at the appointed moment. The trimurti, or three Lords, may have a great role to play in creation, preservation and annihilation, but they are dependent upon Her energy in order to perform their functions. The mahabhutas by which Brahma creates emerge from the cosmic energy only when Shakti is ready for creation, and at her will they permute and combine. Again, the primordial nature acts as the preserving agent through which Vishnu maintains and nourishes creation. Then again, at the behest of Shakti in the role of *Kali*, the consumer of time, Shiva, becomes *Mahakaal* and absorbs the universe back into its source.

After creation, comes sustenance or preservation, which is the task of Vishnu. In relation to this task of preservation assigned to Vishnu, the word *avikalam* means that this protection is not only carried out with perfection, but also assured until the final dissolution at the behest of Shiva. The thousand heads of *Sesha*, the serpent on whom Vishnu reclines in the midst of the waters, is also significant, as it is the serpent that bears the load of the universe and assists Vishnu in his role. The serpent is a symbol of cosmic energy, and one can easily assume that it is Shakti who provides this support and thereby empowers Vishnu to preserve.

Out of the three processes of creation, preservation and destruction, it is preservation that requires the most energy. Try creating anything, even a simple thing like a dress. To make the garment is not difficult; to destroy it is even easier, just rip it apart. But you will have to work very hard to preserve and maintain it, to keep it clean, neat and tidy, and keep it from tearing. So for the function of preservation, Vishnu has the support of the thousand-headed serpent, Sesha, which is none other than Mahashakti in the form of a fully awakened and alert serpent, which is the symbol of *kundalini*. After creating the matter of the body, the endless energy that remains is kundalini, or *adhara shakti*, the shakti which supports. Just as a mountain holds or supports the trees, kundalini holds and supports the body.

At the time of *pralaya*, dissolution, Shakti withdraws herself from creation, thus causing everything to disintegrate, decay and die. Shakti in the form of prana creates and preserves the manifest beings and objects. Although Hara or Mahakaal plays the role of destroyer, Shakti in the form of Kali cuts the noose of time, space and object, initiating the end or destruction of matter. Although Shiva is known as the destroyer, in actual fact he is the saviour. When this physical body becomes old and infirm and further progress is denied, then Shiva exchanges it for a new and beautiful form so that we may evolve further. Thus, hidden in destruction is the secret of transformation.

3. Meditation on Devi in the mudra of granting what you desire

अविद्यानामन्तस्तिमिरमिहिरोद्दीपनक री
जडानां चैतन्यस्तबकमकरन्दस्नुतिझरी ।
दरिद्राणां चिन्तामणिगुणनिका जन्मजलधौ
निमग्नानां दंष्ट्रा मुररिपुवराहस्य भवति ॥ ३ ॥

*avidyaanaamantas-timira-mihirodveepa-nakaree
jadaanaam chaitanya stabaka-makaranda-sruti-jharee;
daridraanaam chintaa manigunanikaa janmajaladhau
nimagnaanaam damshtraa muraripu-varaahasya bhavati.* (3)

avidyaanaam: for the ignorant; *antah timira mihira dveepa nakaree*: becomes the island city, where the luminous sunrise (of spiritual illumination) takes place, driving away the overcast darkness (of ignorance); *jadaanaam*: for the dull-witted; *chaitanya tabaka makaranda sruti jharee*: becomes the nectar (of awareness), gushing forth from the cluster of flowers; *daridraanaam*: to the poverty-ridden; *chintaamani gunanikaa*: (becomes) a necklace made of chintamani gems; *janma jaladhau*: in the ocean of worldly affairs; *nimagnaanaam*: for those immersed; *damshtraa*: tusk; *muraripu varaahasya*: of vishnu in his incarnation of the boar; *bhavati*: becomes

Translation

For the ignorant (the dust of Thy feet) is the island of shelter where the luminous sunrise (of spiritual illumination) dawns, driving away the overcast darkness (of ignorance). For the dull-witted it becomes clusters of flowers from which the nectar of awareness gushes forth. For the destitute it is a necklace of wish-yielding gems. And for those immersed in the ocean of samsara, it becomes their uplifter, like the tusk of Vishnu (which raised the earth from submergence) when he incarnated as Varaha, the cosmic boar.

Commentary

After asserting the primary role of Shakti in all aspects of creation subject to time and space, this mantra goes a step further, explaining that the minute particles of dust emerging from the lotus feet of Shakti give empirical experience as well as spiritual illumination. Matter and spirit are two sides of the same coin. Shakti is both transcendental as well as empirical.

The experience of Shakti depends entirely on one's vision and frequency of mind. Shakti illumines the mind, dispelling ignorance, and also enlivens the mind by drenching it with the nectar of awareness. Mind and awareness are both aspects of Shakti. Mind represents the *jada*, or dormant aspect and awareness the *chetana*, or conscious aspect. Mind without awareness is *moodha*, dull and inert, but with awareness it becomes attentive and attains *ekagrata*, one-pointed concentration.

There are five states of the evolving mind: *moodha* or dull, *kshipta* or dissipated, *vikshipta* or oscillating, *ekagrata* or one-pointed, and *niruddha*, a mind in total control. Each of these states is directly related to the degree of awareness that has trickled into the matter of the mind. Mind is matter, subject to time and space, like any object. But awareness is not matter; it is free from the clutches of time and space. So, when the mind links with pure awareness, it is liberated and attains freedom to move wherever it likes, without the restrictions of time, space and object.

Shakti is different things to different people. The experience of Shakti depends entirely on one's perception, as long as one remains in the state of *avidya*, or ignorance. So, for the ignorant, Shakti gives glimpses of illumination that dispel their darkness, and for the dull she gives awareness that guarantees perfection in whatever they do. Shakti also provides material wealth to the destitute, and becomes the support for those who are sinking in the trammels of *samsara* or worldly matters. Here there is a reference to Vishnu, who incarnated as a boar in order to lift the universe from the ocean into which it had sunk during the great deluge.

The last line of the mantra draws a comparison between the particles of dust emerging from Devi's feet and the tusk of Muraripu. The Puranas tell of an event long ago, when the demon Hiranyaksha stole the earth and disappeared with her into the underworld. At that time Vishnu incarnated as Varaha, the boar, and dived deep down into the ocean. Upon reaching the nether world, he redeemed the earth from Hiranyaksha and came up from the sea with the earth on his tusk.

In the same way, the dust of Devi's feet redeems her offspring from the never-ending cycle of pain and pleasure, and leads them to eternal happiness. Just as the light of the sun removes darkness, Devi's *upasana* or worship removes the tamas of avidya or ignorance from the mind. Avidya is the knot that blocks the free flow of energy within and obstructs one's progress. Desire is born out of avidya and gives rise to *aviveka*, lack of discrimination, which ultimately leads to egotistic behaviour. Ego gives rise to *raga* and *dwesha*, attraction and repulsion, which lead to fear and anxiety. In this way avidya is the root of all misery. In order to eliminate avidya, one must release the knot of ignorance that blocks the heart through Shakti upasana.

The way to worship Shakti is through mantra. Every aspect of Shakti has a particular *bija mantra*, or seed sound, which invokes or awakens it. These mantras are highly concentrated forms of energy which remain dormant until awakened. Just as a missile is not potent until it is mounted and launched at the target, in the same way the bija mantras become powerful through continuous repetition. As the mantra is repeated, it raises the frequency of awareness to different degrees. In this way the dark mind is illumined, the dull mind is activated, the destitute acquire wealth and material assets and those who have sunk in the worldly ocean of trials and tribulations are uplifted and able to sail through life.

There is indeed a wide range of benefits that shakti offers! Just as a mother gives her child the best things in the world, in the same way, the cosmic Mother bestows the most precious gifts upon her devotees. Through Shakti upasana, one can attain all her *aishwarya*, wealth, status, beauty, name and fame in a short time. Thus, in this verse Sankara establishes that the worship of Shakti will help every grade of aspirant or seeker to succeed in life. If one seeks knowledge, Shakti enlivens the mind with the nectar of awareness. If one seeks luxury, comfort and the pleasures of life, she provides all of these. If one is in dire affliction, she comes to the rescue. If one wants to be freed from the trammels of samsara, she raises one out of the worldly mire in which one is entrenched.

According to some commentators, this verse indicates the kamaraja mantra. *Kama* means the 'root of desire' and the suffix *raja*, means 'king' and stresses the superiority of this mantra for attaining all of one's desires. *Upasakas* or worshippers of Sri Vidya meditate upon this mantra.

4. Meditation on Devi's full form in abhaya mudra (mudra of fearlessness) and vara mudra (mudra of granting boons)

त्वदन्यः पाणिभ्यामभयवरदो दैवतगण-
स्त्वमेका नैवासि प्रकटितवराभीत्यभिनया ।
भयात्त्रातुं दातुं फलमपि च वांछासमधिकं
शरण्ये लोकानां तव हि चरणावेव निपुणौ ॥४॥

*tvadanyah paanibhyaam abhayavarado daivatagana
tvamekaa naivaasi prakatita varaabheety-abhinayaa;
bhayaatraatum daatum phalamapi cha vaancchaa-samadhikam
sharanye lokaanaam tava hi charanaaveva nipunau.* (4)

tvat anyah: excepting thyself; *paanibhyaam*: by (gestures) of the hands; *abhayavarado*: vouchsafe protection and boon; *daivatagana*: all deities; *tvam ekaa*: thou alone; *naivaasi*: art not; *prakatita varaabheeti abhinayaa*: given to any demonstrations of giving boons and shelter; *bhayat*: from fear; *traatum*: protecting; *daatum*: giving; *phalam api cha*: results (boons); *vaancchaa samadhikam*: more than what is desired; *sharanye lokaanaam*: shelter (resort) of the universe; *tava*: thy; *charanaav*: two feet; *eva*: by themselves; *nipunau*: are capable of

Translation
Excepting Thou, all other deities grant protection and boons by hand gestures (mudras). Thou alone art not given to such demonstrations of bestowing boons and shelter. Instead, Thy two feet alone are capable of providing protection from fear, the shelter of the universe and granting more than could ever be desired.

Commentary
It is commonly believed that where there is *bhoga*, or enjoyment, there is no *moksha*, or liberation, and similarly where there is moksha, there is no bhoga. In order to attain

one, it is necessary to sacrifice the other, but Shakti promises otherwise. Worship of Shakti offers both enjoyment and liberation on the same platter. Shakti ensures her devotees of *abhaya*, freedom from fear, which is synonymous with moksha, as well as *vara*, boons, which are synonymous with enjoyment. In this context abhaya is that state of mind designated to those who have transcended even the most deep-rooted fear of death. Fear keeps one in a state of ignorance about one's real nature. Vara denotes total satisfaction in the fulfilment of desire.

Shakti can fulfil both these aspects of life at the same time. The word *tvamekasi* further indicates that no other deity except her can grant both enjoyment and liberation at the same time. According to notable scholars, this sloka contains the *kamakala mantra* by which happiness in this life and moksha in the life beyond is ensured. To give a very gross example, the male species can produce seed but cannot germinate it, whereas the female species can produce the seed as well as germinate it. Thus, although the father may be acknowledged as the creator of the offspring, in actual fact the mother is the real creator. She may not overtly demonstrate this capability, but, if needed, she can bring forth progeny on her own.

In his talks on *Devi Bhagavatam*, a most important text on Shakti, the supreme energy, Swami Satyananda has said: "Ordinarily a woman cannot conceive a child without the help of a man, but it is said that Devi has both qualities within her. She can create anything within herself. It is also true that a female can produce sperm in her own body. Of course, the production of sperm does not take place in every woman; this is considered to be a freak of nature. But if a woman can create sperm within herself, she can produce a child that will be immaculate. A man cannot produce ova within himself; that is the limitation of the male body and the highest function of the female body. From this point of view, Devi is said to be the primal creator, because she has both possibilities within herself."

In the same way, all the deities promise boons as well as freedom from fear, but these are only a demonstration, for they cannot grant both at the same time, only one by one. But Devi can grant both and steadfast devotion to her can give fast results. This is because Devi is *matrika shakti*, which means she is endowed with immense power and compassion. Naturally, such a Goddess has the ability to grant whatever one may wish for, whether enjoyment or liberation.

This mantra reiterates the main assertion of Shakta darshan that Shakti rules over all the worlds, or *sapta loka*. There is none other than Shakti, the creatrix, who can give the experience of liberation as well as bondage. If she withdraws from the world, consciousness bereft of energy becomes uncontrollable, just as Shiva demonstrated when Sati immolated herself in the fire of *yogagni*, which she created through her yogic powers.

Although the arguments put forth by Shakta darshan may shakeup the ingrained notions of society and religion about the superiority of the Shiva principle, their claim is not illogical. Human birth, the enactment of karmas, the entire journey through countless lifetimes is merely witnessed by Shiva. As a witness, he remains a passive observer and, therefore, does not influence one's evolution in any way. Shakti, on the other hand, remains a passive observer as well as an active participant and is able to influence one's evolution. Thus, for the sake of progressive evolution, one ought to seriously rethink about whether the basis of upasana or worship, should be Shiva or Shakti.

5. Meditation on Devi's full form radiating light

हरिस्त्वामाराध्य प्रणतजनसौभाग्यजननीं
पुरा नारी भूत्वा पुररिपुमपि क्षोभमनयत् ।
स्मरोऽपि त्वां नत्वा रतिनयनलेह्येन वपुषा
मुनीनामप्यन्तः प्रभवति हि मोहाय महताम् ॥५॥

*haris-tvaam-aaraadhya pranata-jana-saubhaagya-jananeem
puraa naaree bhootvaa pura-ripum-api kshobham-anayat;
smaropi tvaam natvaa ratinayana-lehyena vapushaa
muneenaam-apy-antah prabhavati hi mohaaya mahataam.* (5)

harih: vishnu; *tvaam*: thee; *aaraadhya*: adoring; *pranata jana saubhaagya jananeem*: who bestows prosperity on all thy votaries; *puraa*: long ago; *naaree bhootvaa*: became a female; *pura ripum api*: even in shiva; *kshobham*: passion; *anayat*: stirred; *smara api*: even kamadeva; *tvaam*: thee; *natvaa*: having bowed before thee; *ratinayana lehyena vapushaa*: personality attractive to the eye of rati; *muneenaam api*: even sages; *antah*: in the minds of; *prabhavati hi*: becomes capable of; *mohaaya*: generating passion; *mahataam*: great

Translation
Long ago, adoring Thee who bestows prosperity on all Thy devotees, Vishnu, could become an (enticing) female and stir passion even in Shiva. Even Kamadeva, the god of love, having bowed before Thee (in devotion) has become such an attractive personality to his consort Rati and is thus capable of inciting great passion, even in the minds of sages.

Commentary
This mantra continues to list the powers conferred by Shakti. In the last mantra, Shakti bestowed fearlessness and boons; here she grants her devotees the power to infatuate not just lustful men, but even sages who have attained the states of *vairagya*, dispassion, and *tyaga*, renunciation. This is known as *sammohana shakti*, the force of attraction. Shakti

in the form of sammohana transformed Vishnu into Mohini, the enticing female referred to in this verse. Shakti always accomplishes everything through her agents whom she has programmed and designed to accomplish different tasks. This trend of Shakti can be seen in all the processes that she instigates; she remains behind the scenes and does not display herself.

Perhaps this is the reason why Shakti worship was relegated to the background, because people began to believe that Shiva, Vishnu and Brahma were doing everything. Even today, scientists are having a hard time understanding the mysterious laws of nature, because the very source from which all the forces emanate does not reveal Herself. She can only be known by her attributes, such as the law of gravity or the laws of electromagnetic or nuclear energy. But even after understanding these laws, she still remains a riddle because they do not reveal Shakti in her entirety. Maybe the only way to understand Shakti is through the realm of experience and not through intellect. For this, the quantum of devotion and reverence will have to be increased.

There is an age old Pauranic tale which speaks of an extremely significant event in the history of man. It is the story of the *samudra manthan*, churning the ocean, by the *devas*, gods, and *daityas*, demons. At that time, in order to protect the *amrita*, or nectar of immortality, which had emerged from the churning of the ocean, Vishnu assumed the form of Mohini an enticing female. In this form he infatuated all the daityas with the power of sammohana shakti, so that they began to chase Mohini, instead of the amrita. Thus, he was able to prevent the nectar from falling into the hands of the daityas and giving them immortality. In the Puranas it is well established that Vishnu was a great upasaka of Devi and the seer of the Devi mantra known as *Vaishnavi*. Vishnu acquired the power to assume any form that he wished by prolonged meditation and worship of Devi in the form of Sri Chakra. This is how he acquired the form of Mohini, which was so elegant and seductive that even Shiva, the greatest of ascetics and renunciates, was smitten.

Kamadeva, the god of love, popularly known as Cupid, also attained his power to incite passion in all through the worship of Devi in the form of Sri Chakra. Because of his meditation on Devi and the chanting of her mantras, she granted him sammohana shakti. Today, no one can resist the invasion of Cupid in the mind, but this verse says that the cause of attraction is not Kamadeva or Cupid, but Shakti herself, who transmits this power to those who worship her with devotion and try to experience her within their minds.

The phrase *ratinayanalehyena vapusha*, refers to Rati, the beautiful wife of Kamadeva, who restored Kama to life, after he was burnt to ashes by the fire that emanated from Shiva's third eye when he attempted to kindle passion in Shiva. Rati was able to bring Kama back due to Shakti's grace. Since then Kamadeva, or Cupid, has remained invisible to all except his wife Rati. But even though invisible, the force of attraction that he emits is invincible on account of Devi.

Science also speaks of the forces of attraction and repulsion. Just as a magnet attracts iron filings, honey attracts bees or sugar attracts ants, the same principle is applied in scientific technology. The force of attraction, or sammohana shakti, can be compared to electromagnetic waves pervading the universe, which science has claimed are responsible for the field of gravity. Gravity draws objects downwards, using the force of attraction inherent in the electromagnetic energy. The opposite field of repulsion is used when satellites are sent into space. After they reach a certain altitude, the force of repulsion separates the satellite from its launching shell.

Devi bestows this very same force of electromagnetic energy in the form of prana shakti as a boon to her devotees. The prana shakti that pervades the entire body as well as the whole of creation is the gift with which Shakti has endowed each and everyone. This electromagnetic energy has also revolutionized scientific theory, giving it a totally new dimension, which led to the discovery of the smallest particles, known as protons, neutrons and electrons, existing within an atom that hold everything in place. This force of electromagnetism brings everything together in the universe as well as in our daily lives. These are examples of the same force elucidated here as a boon from Devi that she bestows upon her devotees.

When the electromagnetic energy, or prana shakti, is intensified through worship of Shakti, it becomes a compelling force, attracting and creating polarity with other energy fields that come into its range and vicinity. This is what happens when one is drawn to a person, event or even an idea that emits a powerful electromagnetic force which is spellbinding. The other side of this force of attraction is the force of repulsion. Just as a magnet attracts, it repels too. The same principle applies in the case of Shakti, which pervades this universe as duality. Shakti exists in heat as well as cold, in day as well as night. If there is Shakti in love, there is Shakti in hatred also. One is negative and the other positive. Thus, the energy that Devi bestows is a dual force which can attract as well as repel, as the situation demands.

As mentioned in the previous mantras, Shakti can grant both experiences according to one's desire, which is rooted in karma. But even while granting desires so that one may enact one's karmas, the power of Shakti transforms through the lessons of pain and pleasure which one is subjected to throughout life. Pleasure is the energy of attraction and pain is the energy of repulsion. Both are teachers, but of the two, pain is the greater teacher. As the saying goes, "Pain and suffering is the crucible into which nature throws a man whenever she wants to make him a sublime superman."

The experience of attraction, love, desire and eroticism are serious factors that rule the entire gambit of life. In a single moment a man or woman caught in the pangs of love and passion is totally altered, physically as well as mentally. Even the temperature of the body changes, not to speak of the other characteristics. Passion overrules all the behaviours that a person may exhibit; therefore, the subject of attraction has to be understood in its entirety. *Saundarya Lahari* deals with this theme and especially divine eroticism as a means to higher experience.

This mantra can be used as a mantra for protection and progress in life by generating a strong force within to achieve one's desires.

6. Meditation on the divine and irresistible form of Devi

धनुः पौष्पं मौर्वी मधुकरमयी पञ्च-विशिखाः
वसन्तः सामन्तो मलयमरुदायोधनरथः ।
तथाप्येकः सर्वं हिमगिरिसुते कामपि कृपाम्
अपाङ्गात्ते लब्ध्वा जगदिदमनङ्गो विजयते ॥ ६ ॥

dhanuh paushpam maurvee madhukaramayee pancha-vishikhah
vasantah saamanto malaya-marud-aayodhana-rathah;
tathaapy-ekah sarvam himagirisute kaamapi kripaam
apaangaat-te labdhvaa jagad-idam-anango-vijayate. (6)

dhanuh: bow; *paushpam*: of flowers; *maurvee*: string; *madhu karamayee*: made of honeybees; *pancha-vishikhah*: only five arrows; *vasantah*: spring; *saamanta*: as assistant; *malaya marut*: southern breeze; *aayodhana rathah*: war chariot; *tathaa api*: yet; *ekah*: alone; *sarvam*: entire; *himagirisute*: oh! daughter of the snow-clad mountain; *kaam api*: some little; *kripaam*: favour; *apaangaat*: by thy sideways glance; *te*: thy; *labdhvaa*: having obtained; *jagat idam*: world; *ananga*: (even though) bodiless (i.e. kamadeva); *vijayate*: conquers

Translation

O Daughter of the snow clad mountain, having obtained some little favour by Thy sideways glance, Kamadeva, even though bodiless, is able to conquer the world with a bow of flowers, a bowstring made of honey bees, only five arrows in his sheath, the southern breeze as his war chariot and the spring season as his assistant.

Commentary

The *sammohana shakti*, force of attraction, of Devi can grant her devotee the power to make each and every living being go insane with amour. This is most evident in her staunch devotee, Kamadeva, the god of love. Although bodiless, with a bow made of flowers and honey bees for a bow string, with only five arrows in his sheath, the southern breeze as his chariot, and spring as his only aide, Kamadeva can drive even sages mad with passion. Kamadeva never misses his target, even though he has only five arrows in his sheath, which can be exhausted in no time. Moreover, these arrows are made of fragrant flowers such as lotus and jasmine that cannot hurt anyone.

In fact, Kamadeva really has nothing substantial in his favour, because even the spring season which is conducive to inciting passion is not permanent as it lasts only two months. The breeze, too, is unreliable and does not blow all the time, nor does it blow everywhere or in all directions. Yet he can sway and subjugate the entire world through the force of attraction, which is only due to the omnipotent grace of Devi, whom he adores.

Manmatha, another name for Kamadeva, is one of the celebrated devotees of Devi. There are others too, but he is one of the original devotees who have realized her potential within them. The *Kama-bija* mantra, which is the source of the Sri Chakra mantra, originates from Manmatha. He obtained this mantra after prolonged meditation on Devi. In fact, he is the seer of the mantra for Sri Vidya, and all other traditions of Sri Vidya upasana have emerged out of the mantra he realized. For this reason Sankara gives ample reference to Kama or Manmatha in the verses of *Saundarya Lahari*. Chanting of this mantra is most effective for invoking and awakening the Shakti within oneself that makes one a strong centre of attraction.

Charismatic leaders, film and pop stars drive hoards of people insane just by their appearance, even if they do not speak a single word. They have a mass appeal and people are attracted to them wherever they go by their charm and personality. If worldly charm and charisma can sway the minds of the masses so powerfully, then what would be the effects of the sammohana shakti of Devi?

Sammohana shakti is an extremely powerful force that she grants her devotees to use at will. Just as ordinary people protect and guard themselves with arms and ammunition, the evolved saints and sages, although defenceless, are extremely powerful, for they attain the power of sammohana shakti to capture the mind and heart of whoever they come in contact with. That is the weapon granted to them by Shakti. Arms and ammunition have a limitation, but the magnetic force of sammohana shakti can cross all boundaries and penetrate into the deepest core of the heart, captivating it in such a way that one may never be able to escape from it.

Here, Sankara deftly builds on the concept of beauty without any direct reference to the Devi's form of beauty. By merely referring to the force of attraction, which is the inherent nature of Shakti, one is led to the idea of how compellingly attractive Devi must be if she can readily grant such powers of attraction as boons to her devotees. In fact, she could mesmerize anyone who had the good fortune to behold her or have her darshan.

7. Meditation on Devi as a kanya with four hands holding a bow, arrows, noose and goad

क्वणत्काञ्चीदामा करिकलभकुम्भस्तनभरा
परिक्षीणा मध्ये परिणतशरच्चन्द्रवदना ।
धनुर्बाणान् पाशं सृणिमपि दधाना करतलैः
पुरस्तादास्तां नः पुरमथितुराहोपुरुषिका ॥ ७ ॥

*kvanat-kaancheedaamaa kari-kalabha-kumbhastana-bharaa
pariksheenaa madhye parinata-sharach-chandravadanaa;
dhanur-baanaan-paasham srinim-api dadhaanaa-karatalaih
purastaad-aastaam nah puramathitur-aaho-purushikaa. (7)*

kvanat kaancheedaamaa: girdled with jingling bells; *kari kalabha kumbhastana bharaa*: bent by the weight of her breasts, resembling the frontal lobes of a baby elephant; *pariksheenaa madhye*: slender waist; *parinata sharach chandravadanaa*: face blooming like the full moon in autumn; *dhanuh*: bow; *baanaan*: arrows; *paasham*: noose; *srinim*: goad; *api*: all these; *dadhaanaa*: holding; *karatalaih*: in the hands; *purastaat*: before; *aastaam*: manifest her presence; *nah*: us; *puramathituh*: shiva's; *aaho purushikaa*: pride

Translation
Slender waist, girdled with jingling bells, frame slightly bent by the weight of full breasts, like the lobes of a baby elephant, face blooming like the autumnal full moon, Thou who art the pride of Shiva. Please manifest Thy presence before us, holding all these, bow, arrows, noose and goad, in your hands.

Commentary
Any description of the female anatomy awakens some feeling within everyone, maybe curiosity, admiration, passion, dislike, disgust or indifference. Some may also be shocked to read such frank descriptions of the female anatomy, feeling that it is sinful even to read or think about it. Some may be

hypocritical about their interest in the descriptions, pictures or sights of the female anatomy. They project the impression of non-indulgence in such things, but in private they have great interest.

Everyone is aware of such reactions and has observed them. But does the female anatomy ever evoke reverence in anyone? Has it ever turned anyone towards God? Has it ever given anyone a deep spiritual awakening and experience? One knows that the female anatomy arouses passion, lust and craving, but does one know that it can also arouse spiritual ecstasy. These are the questions that come to the surface through this tantric poem, *Saundarya Lahari*.

When one sees the beauty of the female form through the eyes, feels her touch through an embrace, inhales the fragrance of her body and tastes the sweetness of her lips, that is an overwhelming experience. The entire world, without exception, is forever in pursuit of that experience. People are mad about it; they yearn and crave for it. They dream about it and experience sadness and depression if they cannot have it. Human beings are so enamoured of and attached to the beauty of ordinary things that they are forever hungry for beauty and thirsty for bliss. Thus they can never hope to attain the beauty of Devi, for she keeps those filled with desire forever ensnared at this level.

However, if this sensory experience of the female medium is so powerful, what would the inner experience of that same medium be? The gross experience is made up of flesh and blood and bones, but the inner experience is not. Then what is the female form that one experiences through the inner eye composed of? She is comprised of consciousness. Her outer form is made of matter, but her inner form is spirit. The outer form is subject to time and space; the inner form is beyond time and space. The outer form lives, decays and dies; the inner form, once created, is eternal.

The eternal nature of this inner vision lends it a divinity and effulgence that cannot be matched by any outer experience. Shakti reserves that vision for those who have transcended desire. Sankara was fully qualified for the experience of Shakti because he had transcended desire. The different parts of her anatomy described by him are the energy centres represented by the sixty-four *yoginipeethas*. These were created when the different parts of Bhagvati Devi fell on earth after she immolated herself at the Daksha yajna, and her body was dismembered by Shiva. There is a *yonipeetha* at Kamakhya, where her yoni fell; this is the most sacred shrine of Shakti. The *hridayapeetha*, where her heart fell, is at Deoghar, which is the *tapobhumi* of Sri Swamiji. In the same way different parts of her anatomy are worshipped at different places where they fell.

Aho purushika is indicative of Shakti or *Prakriti* as an entity equal to Shiva or *Purusha*. Shiva is Purusha and Shakti is Prakriti; they are two equal and opposite forces. *Aho* is an expression of amazement at the wondrous form of Purushika or Shakti, when she stands on a par with Shiva. At the very outset of *Saundarya Lahari,* Sankara invokes that form which even Shiva is very proud of and wishes to have her inner vision. Purusha is a word used for the male gender and thus by calling Shakti, Purushika, Sankara at once establishes her equality with Shiva, a fact that he maintains throughout *Saundarya Lahari.*

The word *karikalabha*, which has been interpreted as the frontal lobes of a young elephant to depict Devi's breasts, gives rise to poetic imagery of a very high order. The term *sharat chandravadanaa* that describes Devi's blooming face like the full autumnal moon also induces a sense of unmatched beauty. Her heavy breasts full of milk, her face like the full moon, her slender waist girdled with jingling bells, all invoke an image of beauty and completeness.

On a gross level, her four hands holding a bow, arrows, noose and goad indicate her victory and power over the different limitations that an individual has to face within himself. The noose is *kama,* or desire, which leads to attachment by which the entire world is tied. The goad is *krodha,* anger and hatred, which compels one to act against one's true nature. The bow is the mind, which is forever swinging like a pendulum between *sankalpa* and *vikalpa,* thought and counter-thought. The five arrows stand for the five senses that forever ensnare the mind and keep it bound to gross, mundane awareness. On a subtle level these weapons are represented by mantras that rule over these aspects of the mind.

This mantra describes the features of Devi in a way which an upasaka can at once relate to, thus making it easier to meditate on or contemplate her divine form within. Samaya tantra advocates the vision of Devi's form superimposed on the higher psychic centres in the body. To worship her mentally in this way, the sadhaka has to develop a clear image of Devi, which is beautiful and compelling to visualize, so that the mind is naturally drawn towards it. In fact, in this verse Sankara is introducing the preliminary worship of Devi to the followers of Sri Vidya by describing the first mandala of her features.

This vision of the Supreme Reality in female form, where her first appearance is preceded by the jingling of bells in much the same way as a beautiful dancer before she appears on the stage in full vision of the audience, gives a meaningful understanding of the relation between the essence and its manifest existence. Sankara's adherence to pinpointing this close link between the mysterious and unknown source of existence and the reality of everyday life renders the sacred verses of *Saundarya Lahari* a masterpiece.

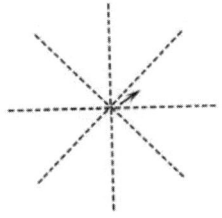

8. **Meditation on Devi at her abode made of gems, reclining on a bed made of Shiva, which is covered with a bed-spread made of Paramashiva**

सुधासिन्धोर्मध्ये सुरविटपिवाटीपरिवृते
मणिद्वीपे नीपोपवनवति चिन्तामणिगृहे ।
शिवाकारे मञ्चे परमशिवपर्यङ्कनिलयां
भजन्ति त्वां धन्याः कतिचन चिदानन्दलहरीम् ॥ ८ ॥

sudhaa-sindhor-madhye sura-vitapi-vaati-parivrite
manidveepe neep-opavanavati chintaamani grihe;
shivaakaare manche paramashiva-paryanka-nilayaam
bhajanti tvaam dhanyaah katichana chidaananda lahareem. (8)

sudhaa sindhoh madhye: in the midst of the ocean of nectar; *sura vitapi vaati parivrite*: surrounded by gardens of (kalpaka) trees; *manidveepe*: in the island of gems; *neepa upavanavati*: encircled by a small wood of nipa or kadamba trees; *chintaamani grihe*: in a mansion made of chintamani gems; *shivaakaare manche*: on a couch that is shiva; *paramashiva paryanka nilayaam*: reclining on the mattress that is supreme shiva; *bhajanti*: worship; *tvaam*: thee; *dhanyaah*: are fortunate; *katichana*: few; *chidaananda lahareem*: waves of blissful consciousness

Translation

In the midst of the ocean of nectar, surrounded by gardens of kalpaka trees, on an island of precious gems, encircled by groves of nipa or kadamba trees, in a mansion made of chintamani gems, reclining on a mattress that is the supreme Shiva placed on a couch that is Shiva, fortunate are the few who worship Thee (like this), for they experience ripples of bliss in their consciousness.

Commentary

Where does Shakti live? Does she have a home, and if so, what does it look like? The *peetha* or seat where Devi resides is now described. The entire concept of Shakti is personified here, yet there is a trace of the esoteric. She is described as reclining on Shiva and Paramshiva, both *shuddha tattwas* according to the evolution of the elements from shuddha to *ashuddha*, pure to impure.

In the *Devi Bhagavata Mahapurana*, the abode of Devi is described at length, enumerating the types of terrain that must be crossed to reach there: undulating mounds of earth, streams and rivulets, rivers that must be crossed, flora and fauna, as well as the birds and animals that inhabit the place. The minerals, gems and other precious and semi-precious gems found there are all described in the minutest detail.

The place where she resides is known as *Srinagara*, the island town of Sri. This island is set in a vast ocean of nectar or ambrosia. There are as many as twenty-five fortresses that lead to her innermost abode where she is enthroned in regal splendour. These fortresses are made of precious minerals, ranging from iron to silver and gold and also the nine precious gems. The inner, more subtle core of fortresses are made of mind, buddhi and ahamkara, followed by strong emissions of the sun, moon and *manmatha* or desire, which also create a type of fortress. Between these fortresses there are canals, lakes, streams, forests and parks. Between these and Tripura Sundari's palace, which is built of chintamani gems, is a canal of lotuses which serves as a protective moat.

Modern scientists have compared this topography with the human brain, stating that the abode of Shakti as described in the Puranas refers to the deepest recesses of the human brain. According to tantra, this region corresponds to sahasrara chakra. Moreover, Shiva and Paramshiva are also present in sahasrara in perfect union with Shakti, which is symbolized by Shakti reclining on a mattress, which is Paramshiva, laid on a couch that is Shiva. In other words the unmanifest form of Shiva is the bed laid out in the *shoonya* or space which is permeated by the waves of bliss and beauty that Shakti represents.

The bed is the bindu and stands on a *trikona* or triangular pedestal which is placed in a mansion of chintamani gems, surrounded by groves of Nipa trees in all four directions. These groves are set on an island studded with precious gems and surrounded on all sides by *kalpa vriksha*, or wish-fulfilling trees. The island itself rests on an ocean of *amrita*, or nectar of immortality. This is the resting place of Shakti, her home where she lives.

On that bed, Shakti as *chidananda lahari*, the first surge of supreme bliss, sports with the vibrationless Paramshiva, who is the fountain of bliss. The upasaka should imagine that and try to picture it in his meditation. By worshipping Devi, resting in her abode in this manner, in the inner space of the heart, which is the mid-point between the lower and higher psychic centres, one experiences *ananda*, unending bliss within oneself. This is a preparation for the experience of union in sahasrara, which takes place with the ascent of kundalini.

In fact, this mantra and the next accomplish the piercing of the six chakras through the tradition of *haadi vidya*. This sloka gives the description of *sahasrara padma*, the thousand-petalled lotus at the crown of the head where *Paramshiva*, who is ever-expanding consciousness, and *Chitshakti*, who is the first ripple of bliss that emanates from consciousness, both reside in permanent union. She is the first emanation of a movement in that motionless consciousness which spreads outwards.

As this ripple arises, *akshara* or indestructible sounds emanate, which are radiant with the energy of Devi; they are the gems that constitute her mansion home. From the radiant and luminescent akshara, or mantras of Shakti, divine rays radiate outwards, which are the trees surrounding her mansion. From these rays, or *kala*, the *kalpa vriksha* or *sankalpa shakti* dawns, and Shakti manifests into the tri-shaktis, jnana shakti, iccha shakti and kriya shakti, which later become sattwa, rajas and tamas. This stanza thus describes the entire process of *bindu, nada* and *kala,* the first evolutes of the supreme Shakti.

The phrase *manidveepe neepo* refers to the island abode of Shakti. *Manidvipa* is the abode of Parashakti. All the other lokas, such as: *Brahmaloka, Vishnuloka* and *Shivaloka,* are present in Manidvipa in the form of archetypes, and they come into existence at the behest of Parashakti. Although it has been argued by notable scholars that Manidvipa cannot be the stage of final liberation, because the seed of desire for the manifest world still exists there, Rishi Hayagriva proclaims that Manidvipa represents the state of *paramananda* or highest bliss.

According to Shakta darshana, the Manidvipa experience is *mukti*, liberation. By meditating on the endless form of Tripura Sundari, the fountain of beauty experienced in one's consciousness after transcendence, one realizes the sublime truths of Vedanta, such as: *Aham Brahmasmi*, 'I am Brahman', and *Tat Tvam Asi*, 'Thou art That'. By direct cognizance of this truth, or *aparokshanubhuti*, the sadhaka beholds the form of Shakti within his consciousness and becomes fully united with it. This was the experience attained by Sankaracharya through his invocation of Devi.

The upasaka then becomes free from the cycle of birth and death. His mind dissolves fully into that absolute power, or *nirbhasa shakti*, and he thus becomes drenched with the splendid power of Tripura Sundari, the most beautiful form of Shakti in all the three worlds. This is indicative of the ascent of kundalini shakti to the sahasrara padma. Only a select few have experienced the ripples of bliss in their consciousness through the worship and devotion of Devi Bhagavati. They are the truly fortunate ones whom Devi has chosen to shower her grace upon.

Puramathituraho purishika emphasizes that one must meditate on Shakti with Shiva, as has been elaborated in the previous verse as well. In fact, Devi's grace alone can give the inner experience of *Satchidananda,* truth, knowledge and bliss of the inner Self. This verse gives the second mandala of Devi in which her grandeur is established. It also describes the state of consciousness attained by the aspirant who transcends the lower sphere and reaches the transcendental level, which is revealed after the total dissolution of the mind, *buddhi*, *ahamkara* and *chitta*.

This mantra speaks of Shiva being the couch on which Devi reclines, and a more refined form of the same Shiva, whom Sankara calls Paramshiva, being the bedspread or mattress on which her beautiful form is in close contact. This is in keeping with mantra 24, where Sankara tells how all the other principles of existence disappear during the process of dissolution. Only Shiva remains on account of Shakti's infatuation with Him, but even so, it is Shakti who is the reigning deity.

This superiority of Shakti is justifiable, for she is the source of the lower prakriti that has dissolved into her. As a reward for the surrender of the aspirant, she gives a glimpse of the complete picture, herself with Shiva.

9. Meditation on the chakras forming a pathway for kundalini's ascent

महीं मूलाधारे कमपि मणिपूरे हुतवहं
स्थितं स्वाधिष्ठाने हृदि मरुतमाकाशमुपरि ।
मनोऽपि भ्रूमध्ये सकलमपि भित्वा कुलपथं
सहस्रारे पद्मे सह रहसि पत्या विहरसे ॥९॥

*maheem moolaadhaare kamapi manipoore hutavaham
sthitam svaadhishthaane hridee marutam-aakaasham-uparee;
manopi bhroomadhye sakalamapi bhitvaa kulapatham
sahasraare padme saharahasi patyaa viharase.* (9)

maheem: earth (element); *moolaadhaare*: in mooladhara; *kam api*: also water (element); *manipoore*: in manipura; *hutavaham*: fire (element); *sthitam*: stablized; *svaadhishthaane*: in swadhishthana; *hridee*: in the heart (anahata); *marutam*: the air (element); *aakaasham*: ether (element); *uparee;* above; *mana api*: also the mind (manasa element); *bhroomadhye*: between the eyebrows (ajna); *sakalam api kulapatham*: the whole path of kundalini; *bhitvaa*: piercing through; *sahasraare padme*: of the thousand-petalled lotus; *saha rahasi*: in the solitude; *patyaa*: (thou) with thy consort; *viharase*: sporteth

Translation
As earth and also water in mooladhara, (Thou art) established in swadhisthana, as fire in manipura, as air in the heart (anahata), and above as ether and also mind in bhrumadhya, between the eyebrows (ajna), also the entire path of kundalini, piercing which Thou sporteth with Thy consort in the solitude of sahasrara padma, the thousand-petalled lotus.

Commentary
The electromagnetic rays that emanate from the *spandan* or vibration of Shakti, manifest as the *pancha mahabhutas* or five elements. From a spandan in bindu, the primordial sounds emanate. These sounds are called *akshara*, which

means indestructible. The akshara are the *bija* or seed mantras of Shakti. They vibrate and resound at a very high frequency and emit rays, or *kala*, which travel outwards into the stratosphere. As they travel their frequency is altered and what emanated as a sound of high frequency condenses into the *tattwas* or elements. This is why the tattwas respond to *nada* or sound in the form of mantras.

The tattwas are cosmic evolutes of Shakti, and after coming into existence they permute and combine to form matter. Each and every form of matter has the tattwas as its building blocks. The tattwas exist within the body in their microcosmic form and throughout the universe in their macrocosmic form. This mantra describes their location and correlation to the chakras, according to Samaya tantra. The word chakra has not been used here; rather the chakras are described as the path of kundalini, or *kulapatha,* which is a direct reference to the Shakti cult.

Each tattwa has a corresponding bija mantra from which it has evolved, along with a related symbol and colour and a specific location in the physical body. The *prithvi tattwa*, or earth element, is the densest of the mahabhutas and has the form of a square. It vibrates at the frequency of golden light, emitting the bija mantra *Lam*, and is located at mooladhara. Subtler than prithvi is *apas*, the water element, which has the form of a crescent moon and vibrates as white light, emitting the bija mantra *Vam*.

According to this mantra, the water element is also located at mooladhara, as opposed to the other tantric texts, which unanimously state that apas is located in the region of swadhisthana. The phrase *kam api* establishes this claim. The word swadhisthana is composed of three roots: *swa* = one's + *adhi* = own + *sthana* = abode. Swadhishthana is kundalini's own abode, where she resides. Thus being the abode of the *Paramtattwa*, or Mahashakti, swadhisthana does not have any other tattwa nor does kundalini penetrate this energy centre. It simply circumambulates it three times and then moves upwards to penetrate manipura, the region of agni tattwa.

Subtler than apas is *agni*, the fire element, which has the form of an inverted triangle and vibrates at the frequency of red light, emitting the bija mantra *Ram*. More subtle than agni, is *vayu*, the air element, which is located in the region of anahata. It has the form of an octagon and vibrates as a bluish light, emitting the bija mantra *Vam*. Subtler still in frequency is *akasha*, the ether or sky element, which is located in the region of ajna and has the form of a circle. It is like the void, vibrating at the frequency of black light in which all colours are merged, and emits the bija mantra *Ham*. *Bhrumadhya* or ajna is also the place of the subtlest tattwa, known as the mind.

Again this text differs from other tantric texts that have fixed the place of akasha at vishuddhi chakra, whereas here there is no mention of vishuddhi. One must remember that *Saundarya Lahari* is a text of Samaya tantra, which sees the body as a receptacle of the divine, as opposed to other tantric texts which are according to the Kaula or Mishrit system of tantra.

According to Samaya tantra, the kundalini or mahashakti remains asleep in three and a half coils around the *swayambhu linga* at mooladhara. When she awakes, she begins to reside at swadhisthana with her mouth facing upwards, gazing at the fire, *huta vaham*, in manipura and emitting a hissing sound. Before rising up to manipura and piercing that centre, the kundalini circles around its abode in swadhisthana, which means that it does not penetrate this centre. This theory is also referred to in *Hamsa Upanishad*, an important text on kundalini yoga, where it is recommended to perform moola bandha and raise the prana shakti, or kundalini, from mooladhara. Performing three circles, or *parikrama*, of swadhisthana, the shakti then moves upward through the higher centres.

From manipura the kundalini ascends, piercing anahata. This is a significant step on her journey along the kulapatha or sushumna. Once the kundalini crosses manipura, it will not descend back to the lower centres, as the pull upwards becomes stronger than the gravitational pull downwards. As long as the kundalini has not crossed manipura, there is always the danger of it slipping back to slumber in mooladhara, but after manipura the kundalini will only move upwards.

Should the sadhaka leave his mortal body due to death after the kundalini has reached anahata, then the kundalini will continue from anahata in the next life. From anahata it pierces ajna, where akasha is located, and also is the seat of the mind. Here she is known as *Tripura*, as she gains victory over the three states of consciousness: *jagrat*, waking, *swapna*, dreaming, and *sushupti*, deep sleep. From there she moves on to sahasrara to attain oneness, or *sayujya*, with her beloved Shiva, where she is known as *Tripura Sundari*, the most beautiful in all the three worlds or states of mind.

Vishuddhi is the point where purification takes place, before the kundalini can meet with her beloved. The kulapatha through which kundalini ascends to sahasrara crosses mooladhara, swadhisthana, manipura, anahata, vishuddhi and ajna; however, at swadhisthana and vishuddhi the kundalini does not *bheda* or pierce through as in mooladhara, manipura, anahata and ajna, as there are no elements residing here. The first swadhisthana is the home of this mahatattwa and the second vishuddhi is the place where the poison is purified and made ready to move into the subtlest of tattwas.

This mode of worship, known as *chakrabheda*, is an essential part of Devi upasana, whereby the mahashakti kundalini is awakened from her slumber and the kulapatha is cleared for her ascent. Without this event the worship of Devi is fruitless. The final union takes place in sahasrara only after her full ascent, and then she descends to the gross plane to display the divinity that is enshrined within us. As a result of chakrabheda sadhana, a significant step in the ascent of kundalini is accomplished, the untying or loosening of the three *granthis*, or knots, which are located

Chakra	Location	Petals	Tattwa	Tanmatra	Deity	Region
Mooladhara	Anus	Four	Prithvi Apas	Smell Taste	Ganesh	Agni mandala
Swadhisthana	Genitals	Six	Abode of kundalini, emergence of agni	Abode of kundalini	Brahma	Brahma granthi
Manipura	Navel	Ten	Agni	Sight	Rudra	Surya mandala
Anahata	Heart	Twelve	Vayu	Touch	Vishnu	Vishnu granthi
Vishuddhi	Neck	Sixteen	Purifcation of tattwas, emergence of akasha	Emergence of sound	Jiva	Soma mandala
Ajna	Eyebrow centre	Two	Akasha Manas	Sound Mind	Guru	Rudra granthi

at three points in the chakra ladder as shown in the above chart.

The vision established by Sankara in the previous mantra of Devi's dignified and regal form as she reclines on Shiva is further explained here by describing how she reached there. The existence of kundalini is a discovery of tantra, which advocates the esoteric science of transcendence from matter to spirit. Initially kundalini shakti, which is none other than the supreme energy, lies asleep in the folds of matter at the base of the spine in mooladhara chakra, where it has fallen from its own abode at swadhisthana. Here she keeps the awareness rooted in the gross experiences of the senses and the material world of time, space and object.

By the efforts of the aspirant, the awareness is released from the clutches of matter as the kundalini awakens from her slumber and begins her ascent through the kulapatha. She pierces through the chakras and tattwas, which are her own evolutes, and finally reaches the highest point of human evolution the sahasrara chakra. Having left all her evolutes such as mind, intellect, chitta and ego far behind, she sports there in solitude with Shiva. The previous verse describes her reclining on Shiva, but now having rested after her journey and ensuring that she is on her own, she begins her amorous interlude with Shiva.

This amorous interlude, after she is fully satiated, will result in her most gracious and benevolent form, which will irrigate the entire creation with nectar. Once again Sankara has given a superb description of the essence of creation and existence through a rapt comparison with the nuances of an erotic experience between a man and a woman.

10. Meditation on the beautiful form of Devi seated on the lap of Shiva in close embrace

सुधाधारासारैश्चरणयुगलान्तर्विगलितैः
प्रपञ्चं सिञ्चन्ती पुनरपि रसाम्नायमहसः ।
अवाप्य स्वां भूमिं भुजगनिभमध्युष्टवलयं
स्वमात्मानं कृत्वा स्वपिषि कुलकुण्डे कुहरिणि ॥ १० ॥

*sudhaa-dhaaraa-saarai charana-yugala-antarvigalitaih
prapancham sinchantee punar-api rasa-amnaaya-mahasah;
avaapya-svaam-bhoomim bhujaganibham-adhyushta-valayam
svam-aatmaanam kritvaa svapishi-kulakunde-kuharini.* (10)

sudhaa dhaaraa asaarai: with the flood of nectar; *charana yugala antarvigalitaih*: gushing from thy feet; *prapancham*: manifested five (tattwas); *sinchantee*: irrigating, drenching; *punah api*: again; *ras aamnaaya mahasah*: six (chakras) from the region of illumination; *avaapya*: having reached; *svaam*: thy; *bhoomim*: home; *bhujaganibham*: like a serpent; *adhyushta valayam*: of three coils and a half; *svam aatmaanam*: the individual self; *kritvaa*: converting; *svapishi*: sleep; *kulakunde*: deep pit where kundalini resides; *kuharini*: hollow

Translation
With streams of nectar gushing from Thy feet, irrigating the five elements again from the region of illumination (sahasrara), Thou returnest to Thy home via the six chakras. Converting Thyself into the individual self, or jivatman, Thou sleepest in the deep pit of Thy own home, like a serpent of three and a half coils.

Commentary
On reaching sahasrara, the kundalini shakti sports with her consort Shiva for a while; she does not return at once. When talking about the kundalini experience, Swami Satyananda has said that the kundalini awakening and ascent lasts for a minimum of three days. During that period there is no

sleep, no hunger and no thirst, but there is ecstasy. The person having the kundalini awakening sees and experiences everything around him differently, although he remains in the same physical body. The perception, reactions and responses change, which is natural. This happens in a lower grade even in our daily lives without the awakening of kundalini, for as we grow our personality, behaviour, responses reactions and perceptions change and alter. But the change which occurs with awakening of kundalini is more dramatic and accentuated.

Moreover, the kundalini experience is not just a case of altered perception, but a complete takeover of this mind and body by higher voltage energy. There is a complete restructuring of the individual's body, mind and consciousness. The union with Shiva in sahasrara, the region of *prakasha*, or effulgent illumination, is total. Energy and consciousness become one homogeneous awareness. Shakti becomes Shiva and Shiva becomes Shakti; there is no difference between them. Then, they begin the descent together back to her own home, and the nectar of Shakti's union with Shiva gushes forth in streams from her feet. It rains amrita, irrigating the entire elemental structure of material existence.

Prapancha literally means 'the five' and is used as a substitute for the material world. In this case it would mean the five elements which constitute the material physical world, the five *jnanendriyas*, sensory organs, through which it is perceived or known, and the five *karmendriyas*, motor organs, through which one interacts with the material world. The kundalini irrigates all of them with the nectar gushing from her feet. Once again the significance of the feet is alluded to here.

Consciousness is present in each and every fibre of the body; the only difference is the degree of subtlety. The physical body has the grossest level of consciousness. The level of consciousness in the *indriyas*, or senses, is subtler than the physical body. The level of consciousness of the mind is more subtle than the indriyas. This process continues and at each level the consciousness becomes more and more subtle. The consciousness must also recharge itself. When it becomes depleted, the eyes become weak and cannot see, the ears cease to hear, the body becomes frail and cannot perform its functions. This happens as the consciousness begins to deplete, especially in disease and old age. Until this depletion takes place, one experiences youth and agility.

After the kundalini's ascendence to sahasrara and subsequent return, she irrigates all the *prapancha*, or senses, and once again the consciousness at these levels is restored and recharged, rejuvenating the entire elemental structure of the individual. This mantra says that after the highest experience in sahasrara, the kundalini once again returns to her abode and remains there as she did before the ascent. At this time, however, the connection with sahasrara is fully established and it becomes the controlling station, instead of mooladhara. The individual is then guided by the higher Self, as his awareness abides there and not in the senses.

Another important factor this mantra denotes is that the kundalini or Mahashakti is not alone when she descends; she is accompanied by Shiva. Just as two lovers in the throes of passion are inseparable, in the same way Shiva and Shakti are fully absorbed in one another. Thus the descent of Shiva-Shakti is as one homogeneous stream of energy and awareness, and not as two entities. That is the cosmic experience that the upasaka is endowed with through his worship. Moreover, this cosmic experience is firmly established in him, so that even his daily affairs are conducted with higher awareness, as opposed to others who operate from lower, mundane awareness.

The awakening of kundalini is always accompanied by dramatic changes in the mind and perception. The person whose kundalini has awakened becomes *abhaya*, or fearless, and experiences peace of mind and dispassion.

He has an intense desire to meditate, and meditation takes place spontaneously, without effort. He becomes selfless in all his actions and experiences *santosha* or deep contentment as his mind and nature begin to abide in the Self. This gives rise to the experience of bliss in spiritual pursuits and an inner spiritual strength. *Ekagrata*, or one-pointedness of mind, is also a sign of the awakened kundalini, as is intense faith and devotion to God. Stability of the body and mind, sweet speech, a radiant glow in the face and eyes and an attractive personality are further signs of a person whose kundalini has awakened and entered the sushumna passage.

As the kundalini ascends from one chakra to the next, the sadhaka's awareness transcends the mind and the influence of the lower chakras and tattwas one by one. The sadhaka is then guided by the mysterious force of Shakti, which continually illumines his path. During this time he must have abiding faith in the loving hand of Shakti, rest in her lap, and pray to her for help. Without the grace of Shakti one cannot traverse even an inch, let alone the entire journey to sahasrara.

11. Meditation on Sri Chakra

चतुर्भिः श्रीकण्ठैः शिवयुवतिभिः पञ्चभिरपि
प्रभिन्नाभिः शंभोर्नवभिरपि मूलप्रकृतिभिः ।
त्रयश्चत्वारिंशद्वसुदलकलाश्रत्रिवलय-
त्रिरेखाभिः सार्धं तव चरणकोणाः परिणताः ॥ ११ ॥

*chaturbhih-shreekanthaih shivayuvatibhih-panchabhir-api
prabhinnaabhih-shambho navabhir-api moola-prakritibhih;
trayash-chatvarinshad vasudala-kalaashra-trivalaya
trirekhaabhih-saardham tava charana-konaah-parinataah.* (11)

chaturbhih shreekanthai: four triangles that enclose the supreme energy; *shivayuvatibhih*: shakti triangles; *panchabhih api*: and also five; *prabhinnaabhih shambho*: severally distinct from shiva; *navabhih api moola prakritibhih*: (making up) the nine basic triangles of the root manifestations (of shakti); *trayah chatvarinshat*: as forty-three; *vasudala kalaashra trivalaya trirekhaabhih*: eight-petalled, sixteen-petalled, three circles and three lines; *saardham*: with; *tava*: thy; *charana konaa*: the angles which house thee (thy feet); *parinataah*: become

Translation

The four triangles that enclose the supreme energy and also the five shakti triangles form the nine basic triangles of the root manifestations (of Shakti). Then there are the eight-petalled and sixteen-petalled lotuses, three surrounding circles and three lines. Distinct from Shiva, these angles which house Thee become Thy mansion of forty-three triangles.

Commentary

This mantra describes the most sacred Sri Chakra, the mansion of Shakti. Sri Chakra is unique because it is a symbol of the *pindanda,* or microcosmos, as well as its relation with the *brahmanda,* or macrocosmos. The individual is the microcosmos and the universe the macrocosmos. One is limited, the other unlimited. Sri Chakra or Sri Yantra is a linear diagram that perfectly establishes the connection between these two different dimensions of existence. It symbolizes the evolution of consciousness into matter and the involution of matter back to consciousness. Therefore, this yantra bestows both material wealth and pleasure as well as liberation from the bondage of matter.

The entire kundalini experience described in the previous two mantras, where the kundalini ascends along the kulapatha to sahasrara to sport with Shiva and then returns to her abode, drenching the creation with her *amrita*, or nectar, is enshrined in the Sri Chakra. So, this yantra is the linear representation of the kundalini experience.

Moreover, the kundalini experience takes place in the human body or microcosmos as well as in the entire universe with all its infinite galaxies; it is happening all the time somewhere, some place.

This cosmic experience of the interplay of consciousness and energy at all levels is contained in Sri Yantra. This is the speciality of tantra that it offers a mandala, yantra and mantra for each and everything in the universe. These are utilized as tools for meditation, whereby one can attain higher states of consciousness by the awakening of kundalini. Sri Chakra is an intersection of four triangles facing upwards and five triangles facing downwards. These nine triangles, which represent the nine *moola prakritis*, or root manifestations, point in opposite directions. In the *Bhagavad Gita*, the nine moola prakritis are defined as one *paraprakriti*, supreme nature, and eight *aparaprakritis*: five tattwas, mind, buddhi and ahamkara.

The five triangles facing upwards, known as *shiva yuvati*, represent the paraprakriti or mahakundalini that is forever gazing upwards, poised for ascent. As paraprakriti, she is *yuvati*, the virgin goddess, who, interlaced with the four downward facing triangles known as *sri kanthe*, becomes entrapped in the sensorial world which is her own creation.

The word *kanthe* alludes to a sense of getting caught up in something, which is the exact condition of kundalini. Leaving aside the first triangle at the centre, which is the abode of Shakti, this intersection of the nine primary triangles creates a total of forty-three triangles. The four triangles of sri kanthe represent the *kalpa vriksha*, or wish-fulfilling trees, and the forty-three resulting triangles represent the Nipa trees, described in the eighth verse on the abode of Devi.

At the centre of Sri Chakra is the *bindu*, or nucleus, which is the seat of Shakti, who remains *asanga*, or separate, from the range of triangles that are created by the intersection of the nine triangles. The forty-three triangles are surrounded first by eight lotus petals, symbolic of aparaprakriti, and then by sixteen lotus petals, symbolic of the fifteen days of the waxing moon, culminating in shodashi, or *poornima*. Outermost is the *bhupura*, or square, which represents the earth element that contains all of this.

The thirty-six tattwas along with the *sapta dhatus*, which include *rakta* or blood, *mansa* or flesh, *meda* or fat, *snayu* or nerves, *asthi* or bone, *majja* or marrow, and *shukra* or semen, make forty-three, which is the number of triangles in Sri Yantra formed by the descent of energy. The intersection of the nine triangles, which creates an intricate mesh of forty-three triangles, is thus symbolic of the microcosmic experience of the manifestation of matter from pure unadulterated consciousness.

The macrocosmic experience is enshrined in the innermost forty-fourth triangle, which has a bindu at the centre. Thus some traditions advocate forty-four triangles instead of forty-three as the sum total of triangles that make up the Sri Yantra. This bindu is *Shambhu*, metaphorically described as the couch on which Shakti as Tripura Sundari majestically reclines in union with Paramshiva. At the cosmic level Sri Yantra represents the body of the supreme Shakti, who is *trigunatita*, beyond the gunas, as well as *tattwatita*, beyond the tattwas.

Evolution of the Thirty-Six Tattwas

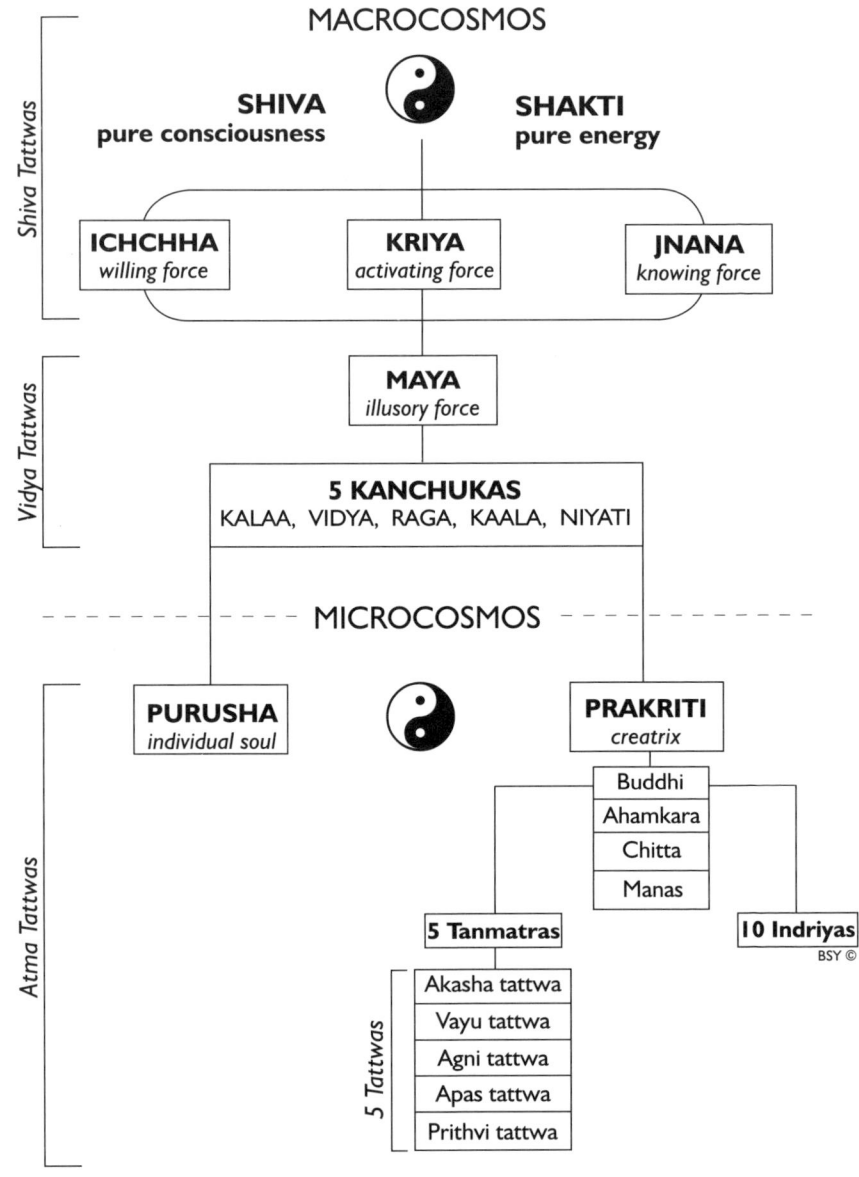

These forty-three triangles surrounding the bindu create five *avaranas*, or coverings. The bindu itself is also regarded as an avarana making it six avaranas. Apart from these six, there are three more avaranas made up of the two circles with lotus petals and the outer circle consisting of three walls. Avarana means to conceal or obscure, thus altogether Tripura Sundari has nine avaranas that keep her well concealed in the same way as the innermost core of a lotus is concealed by its closed petals.

In this cosmic experience Sri Chakra is meditated upon at three levels, which depict the three parts of Devi's body. The first corresponds to agni from the neck to the face and is known as *vaagbhav kut*; the second corresponds with surya from the neck to the waist and is known as *kamakala kut*, and the third corresponds with soma, the moon, from the waist down and is known as *shakti kut*. At the individual level Sri Chakra represents one's own body. Thus, it serves as a link between the individual and the cosmic Mother. When that link is established through mental worship of the yantra superimposed on one's body at a specific point designated by the guru according to the quality of the sadhaka's awareness, the supreme Shakti reveals her other half – Shiva, a homogeneous stream of pure, unadulterated awareness.

Thus, Sri Chakra provides a practical way to reach the goal of transcendence, and Sankara indicates the method is by meditation on this most sacred yantra. As sound migrates from causal to subtle to gross dimensions, the frequencies are altered to adjust to the dimension and space. Sri Yantra is a potent means to penetrate all the dimensions of sound, from the gross to the transcendental, because it is an exact replica of this experience in geometrical design.

Geometry is the measurement of the universe, utilizing lines, circles, triangles and squares, just as tantra does. However, the measurements of tantra enter those areas of calculation that are beyond the field of geometry.

For example, tantra has even attempted to define the calculation of energy contained in sound, as it alters from *para*, or transcendental, which is inaudible to the human ear, to a lower frequency which can be perceived through the subtle mind, or an even lower frequency that can be heard by the ear. Tantra has developed a very refined level of calculation in the geometrical designs, or yantras, the foremost being Sri Yantra.

12. Meditation on the beautiful form of Devi

त्वदीयं सौन्दर्यं तुहिनगिरिकन्ये तुलयितुं
कवीन्द्राः कल्पन्ते कथमपि विरिञ्चिप्रभृतयः ।
यदालोक्यौत्सुक्यादमरललना यान्ति मनसा
तपोभिर्दुष्प्रापामपि गिरिशसायुज्यपदवीम् ॥१२॥

tvadeeyam saundaryam tuhina-giri-kanye tulayitum
kaveendraah kalpante kathamapi virinchi-prabhritayah;
yad-aaloky-autsukyaad amaralalanaa yaanti manasaa
tapobhir-dushpraapaam api girisha-saayujya-padaveem. (12)

tvadeeyam saundaryam: thy beauty; *tuhina giri kanye*: oh! daughter of the snow clad mountain; *tulayitum*: to compare; *kaveendraah*: poets; *kalpante*: are not capable; *katham api*: even after taking great pains; *virinchi prabhritayah*: brahma and others; *yadaa*: which (beauty); *aalokya autsukyaat*: out of eagerness to glimpse that effulgent; *amaralalanaa*: undying youth and beauty; *yaanti*: attain; *manasaa*: mentally; *tapobhih*: through penance; *dushpraapaam api*: difficult to attain; *girisha saayujya padaveem*: condition of absorption into shiva

Translation
O Daughter of the snow clad mountain, Brahma and other greatest of poets, even after taking great pains, are not capable of comparing Thy beauty, which being eager to glimpse, they mentally try through penance to attain that most difficult state of absorption in Shiva with the hope that they will behold Thy effulgent and undying youth and beauty.

Commentary
Once again Shakti is considered superior to the chief deities, Brahma and Shiva. Even Brahma, the literary giant, who is forever singing the Vedas, the creator of the manifest worlds, whose daughter is the most eloquent Saraswati,

cannot compare the beauty of Devi. No words can express that experience. Her youthful splendour and effulgence are so enchanting that, in fact, Brahma and Saraswati pretend to do penance for Shiva so that by their absorption in him they will be granted a glimpse of Shakti. The beauty of Devi described in this mantra relates to her state after attaining Shiva *sayujya*, or total union with her beloved Lord. That can be compared to the state of a beautiful young girl of sixteen after union with her lover.

Worship of anything, whether a material object or pure consciousness such as Shiva, is actually the worship of Shakti. She is present as energy in the meditator as well as in the object of meditation. Her force of attraction joins them together in yoga or unity. This verse affirms the claims of Shakta darshan, which state that Shakti is the supreme tattwa. While other tantras speak of Shakti being the doorway to Shiva, Shakta darshan says that Shiva is the experience of Shakti in her most radiant form, that of Tripura Sundari, the most beautiful in all the three realms.

The experience of Sri Yantra superimposed on the body in sahasrara gives rise to absorption in Shiva, which is none other than the experience of the pristine Shakti, as they are forever absorbed in one another. As the awareness transcends ajna, it enters into open space. At that time Sri Yantra plays a significant role in directing the awareness towards absorption in the shuddha Shiva-Shakti tattwa. Thus, by absorption in Shiva, the divine Shakti is experienced in her purest form, which is the most rare and difficult to describe.

Ordinarily Shiva does not exhibit the Shakti tattwa, which is an integral part of him. But those who know the trick worship him in such a manner that he reveals Shakti in her purest form. In daily life people only experience her adulterated form and that has completely ensnared them. Imagine if they could see her pure form! The phrase *amarlalana* suggests that Devi has undying youth and beauty. She is not just beautiful, she is beauty personified.

Beauty and youth emanate from her because she is their source. She remains forever young and never ages. She does not get wrinkles and grey hairs as all the mortal beauties do. Human beauty is only skin deep, it withers and dies, but the beauty of Devi is perennial, because she upholds the principles of creation, preservation and thus of rejuvenation.

Even Brahma and Saraswati, who possess divine powers, are incapable of describing her youthful beauty, then what can be expected of us mortals. Her beauty cannot be described in words for the satisfaction of the intellect; it has to be known through experiential knowledge. Just as one has the personal experience of anger, passion, greed, worry and anxiety, in the same way and intensity, one can have an inner experience of the beautiful form of Devi. Her pure form can manifest as a reality for one to behold.

Once while Swami Satyananda was travelling in America, a famous artist came to meet him. He said that when he closed his eyes and looked within, he saw the most beautiful colours which could not be matched by anything he saw outside. His only problem was that he could not re-create these colours on his palette nor could he describe them to anyone. Whatever he tried would always fall short of the colours he saw in meditation. He had this experience in relation to colour, but the same idea applies to the experiences of smell, touch or sight.

One may smell fragrances that one has never smelt before and no words can convey what they are. One may feel the touch of something or someone that is completely overwhelming and takes him to another dimension, but upon returning he cannot convey this to others or recreate it. Or one may see something or someone which instantly elevates and touches him profoundly, but he cannot describe it. Such experiences just leave one yearning for more.

This is the exact same state that one has in relation to divinity; it is so beautiful that it is indescribable. All words are inadequate and so, too, are all descriptions.

The scriptures have said time and time again that divinity belongs only to the realm of experience. This is why tantra lays great emphasis on developing the experience rather than understanding the concepts intellectually. Sankara was undergoing such an experience, but the magic of it was that, unlike others, even the greatest of poets, he could convey it in a magnificent way on account of the grace of Devi.

13. Meditation on the compassionate form of Devi

नरं वर्षीयांसं नयनविरसं नर्मसु जडं
तवापाङ्गालोके पतितमनुधावन्ति शतशः ।
गलद्वेणीबन्धाः कुचकलशविस्रस्तसिचया
हठात् त्रुट्यत्कांच्यो विगलितदुकूला युवतयः ॥१३॥

naram varsheeyaamsam nayana-virasam narmasu jadam
tavaapaangaaloke patitam-anudhaavanti-shatashah;
galadveneebandhaah kucha-kalasha-visrasta-sichayaa
hathaat trutyatkaanchyo vigalitadukoolaa yuvatayah. (13)

naram: man; *varsheeyaamsam*: decrepit, old; *nayana virasam*: ugly or with ugly eyes; *narmasu jadam*: with dead (erotic) sensibilities; *tava aapaangaa loke patitam*: on whom thy gracious sideways glance has fallen; *anudhaavanti*: follow hastily; *shatashah*: hundreds of; *galat venee bandhaah*: with their hair unbound; *kucha kalasha visrasta sichayaa*: with their rounded breasts exposed by loosening of their upper cloths; *hathaat*: suddenly; *trutyat kaanchya*: their girdles broken; *vigalita dukoolaa*: letting their robes slip down; *yuvatayah*: young women

Translation
If Thy gracious sideways glance should fall on anyone, even a decrepit, ugly old man with dead (erotic) sensibilities, he will be hastily followed by hundreds of young women with their hair unbound, their robes slipping down, their girdles undone, and their rounded breasts exposed due to the loosening of their upper cloth.

Commentary
The *upasana* or worship of Devi leads to an awakening of energy and its subsequent liberation from the clutches of matter, which is the body. This liberated energy then ascends to a heightened state of consciousness that completely overrules mundane awareness, so that one can behold energy

in its pristine purity in all the myriad forms. In mantra 8, Devi is seen as the reigning queen who has subdued even her counterpart, the supreme consciousness, and is seen reclining upon him, which indicates her total control and presence in that state of awareness.

In mantra 9, she is seen present in the entire molecular (tattwa) and psychic (chakra) structure that everyone is made up of. Although fully present and in command at this level, she is also seen sporting with Shiva, the supreme consciousness, at the transcendental level. Thus she reveals herself at all levels of consciousness: *sthoola*, gross, *sukshma*, subtle, *karana*, causal, and having transcended these, *turiya*, superconscious, at the same time.

After that, in mantra 10, she is seen descending with the supreme consciousness as an integrated force to the level of *prapancha*, the senses, retaining the transcendental state of awareness without any alteration or drop in frequency. In mantra 11, she reveals her condensed form encapsulated in the Sri Yantra, which is her cosmic design. The worship of all these forms of Devi as mandala and yantra bestows her grace, which can totally transform and rejuvenate the practitioner. This verse says that even if her sideways glance falls on an old and decrepit man, his youth and beauty will be restored to such an extent that young and beautiful damsels will surround him, clamouring for his attention.

The vision of Mahashakti Tripura Sundari is not an ordinary affair; it is an elevating experience in every sense of the word. Here, Sankara speaks of *darshan*, or direct cognition, of Shakti's purest form that is not different from Shiva, which gives birth to *jnana*, or knowledge, as signified by the allegory of the old men. Jnana is always symbolized by a person who is old in years. Sankara speaks here of that state when jnana is flourishing in the individual due to the darshan of Shakti. The awakening of jnana is followed by the awakening of *siddhis*, perfections or powers that cluster around a person who has experienced inner knowledge. The females chasing after the old men represent the siddhis that surround a person with enlightenment.

Sankara is not describing an ordinary experience of young girls chasing a man, but a very high experience when one has transcended the lower mundane attractions. Yet the erotic imagery utilized to convey this elevated state is conveyed so vividly that one can easily identify it. Moreover, it shows that the higher experience is not separate from the mundane, but a transformed version of the same experience.

The electromagnetism of Devi transforms each and everything that comes into its range, because her intensity simply cannot be withstood by an impure substance. Purity is a prerequisite for the ultimate experience, and that is why greatest emphasis is given to *shuddhi* or purification in all sadhanas. This purification should not be understood in a moral, social or religious sense, but as the purification of the entire physical, pranic, mental, emotional and psychic structure of man.

Sadhana done in a lop-sided manner is not enough. The entire perspective has to be overhauled to become a vehicle of this powerful force. The emotions have to be refined, and one must have total control of the expressions of body and mind. Any mishap or misbehaviour, whether of the body or mind, can drive away forever the energy that is about to descend in the aspirant. Purity is also synonymous with beauty. The Devi is a reflection of one's own inner consciousness, or *atman*. The effulgence of the atman can only shine forth through a purified substance

Siddhis surround a person in whom the Mahashakti has begun to manifest or show herself. At first the person is endowed with jnana, inner and outer knowledge, which is both *para*, or transcendental, and *apara*, or empirical. Along with the blossoming of jnana, the siddhis arrive like a divine fragrance. They are wanton and free in expressing themselves through the jnanendriyas and karmendriyas in the form of speech, action and thoughts. Enormous powers are bestowed on one in whom the light of jnana has dawned through the grace of Tripura Sundari.

This mantra hints at the process of *kayakalpa*, rejuvenation of the body, whereby one's lost youth can be regained. Many yogis have been known to achieve this through sadhana and the awakening of kundalini. In fact, youth is synonymous with yogis, because a yogi can assume any body he wishes through the process of kayakalpa.

14. Meditation on the primeval form of Devi as Prakriti, the cosmic nature

क्षितौ षट्पंचाशत् द्विसमधिकपञ्चाशदुदके
हुताशे द्वाषष्टिश्चतुरधिकपंचाशदनिले ।
दिवि द्विःषट्त्रिंशन्मनसि च चतुःषष्टिरिति ये
मयूखास्तेषामप्युपरि तव पादाम्बुजयुगम् ॥ १४ ॥

kshitau shatpanchaashat dvisamadhika-panchaashad-udake
hutaashe dvaashashtish chatur-adhika-panchaashad-anile;
divi dvihshat-trimshan manasi cha chatuhshashtir-iti ye
mayookhaas-teshaamapi upari tava paadaambujayugam. (14)

kshitau: in earth; *shatpanchaashat*: fifty-six; *dvisamadhika panchaashat*: fifty-two; *udake*: in water; *hutaashe*: in fire; *dvaashashtih*: sixty-two; *chatuh adhika panchaashat*: fifty four; *anile*: in air; *divi*: in ether; *dvihshat trimshat*: seventy-two; *manasi*: in mind (ajna); *cha*: and; *chatuh shashtih*: sixty-four; *iti*: thus; *ye mayookhaah*: which rays (reach); *teshaam api*: those rays; *upari*: above; *tava*: thy; *paadaambujayugam*: two lotus feet (rest)

Translation
The rays: fifty-six in earth, fifty-two in water, sixty-two in fire, fifty four in air, seventy-two in ether and sixty-four in mind, emanate from Thy two lotus feet, which rest above.

Commentary
After worshipping Shakti in the tattwas, chakras and Sri Yantra, she reveals her presence as *kala*, or rays, that emanate directly from her two feet, which are beyond this manifestation of hers. The five elements from gross to subtle have to be realized and experienced as the kala of shakti. In this way the tattwas are transcended and the mind is transported to the vision of the two feet of the Supreme Beauty. The kalas, or rays of light, emanate from her feet in pairs to constitute the building blocks of matter, the

pancha mahabhutas. This further establishes the most basic philosophy of tantra that all are evolutes of that supreme Shakti, who has manifested in human form and every other form in creation by transmuting herself into nada, bindu and kala.

Nada, bindu and kala are the first evolutes of the supreme Shakti or energy. *Bindu* is a point or nucleus, which is the first manifestation of Shiva and Shakti. This stage of Shakti's manifestation is *shuddha vidya*, as it still retains the purity. *Nada* is sound, which arises on account of the *spandan* or vibration in bindu. Its range varies from inaudible to audible, transcendental to gross. *Kala* is a ray that emanates due to the spandan or vibration at bindu when the process of creation is set into motion.

The *agamas*, or tantric texts, say that bindu is *Shivatmaka*, of the nature of Shiva, and the seed or nucleus within it is *Shaktyatmaka*, of the nature of Shakti. The balance of both gives rise to nada tattwa. In tantra nada has been classified into four types: *vaikhari*, which emanates from the mouth; *madhyama*, which emanates from the navel; *pashyanti*, which emanates from the throat, and *para*, the transcendental sound beyond the range of hearing, which emanates from the heart.

Kala are rays of immense energy in the form of light, emanating from the unmanifest Shakti. They descend in a linear manner from the cosmic Shakti down to the lowest point of the pranic body, *sukshma sharira*, which houses the chakras, tattwas and organs that constitute the gross body. These rays which are full of nuclear potential, as they are reverberating with atoms, protons and electrons, belong to the realm of *avyakta* or unmanifest creation, as well as *vyakta*, or manifest creation. They are present even in the grossest matter which constitutes the physical body.

The body is composed of rays of light and waves of sound. However, the number of rays varies according to the density of the matter it occupies. In this mantra, Sankara gives the number of rays in each of the tattwas. The number of rays is indicative of the vibratory frequency of each element, and the elements are intimately related to the chakras. The position of Shakti's two feet from which the rays emanate is above ajna chakra, which indicates that Shakti is seated above the six chakras, sending out the rays.

Half of these rays are of the nature of Shakti, *Shaktyatmika*, and the other half of the nature of Shiva, *Shivatmika*, which really means that they emanate from her two feet in pairs of 28 in prithvi (earth), 26 in apas (water), 31 in agni (fire), 27 in vayu (air), 36 in akasha (space) and 32 in manas (mind). Together they add up to 360, which corresponds to the number of days in a lunar year.

From this, it can be seen that earth, water and air have fewer rays to exercise their influence than fire and space. Akasha has the greatest influence on the mind, which accounts for the creativity and brilliance that the human race has exhibited down the ages with all of its marvellous discoveries, such as aviation, electricity, telecommunication, computers, satellites and many more.

According to mantra 9, the tattwas are pierced by the ascending kundalini along with the chakras, because they reside in the chakras. On account of this the aspirant attains mastery over them. In yoga, this is known as *bhutajaya*, victory over the elements. Along with bhuta jaya, the aspirant also accomplishes *indriyajaya*, mastery over the senses, a natural consequence of which is *manojaya*, victory over the mind. The indriyas are governed by the flow of the tattwas as well as the breath. Thus it is natural that mastery over the tattwas divinizes the indriyas, enabling them to assume their sattwic vibrations.

This leads to the release of the *granthis*, or psychic knots: bhuta jaya releases brahma granthi; indriya jaya releases vishnu granthi and mano jaya releases rudra granthi. These granthis are psychic knots which obstruct the free flow of the supreme energy. Just as a person gets knotted with the problems of life, in the same way, consciousness, or *chetana*, becomes entangled with matter, or *jada*. By imagining the atman in the body, or the body as an extension of the atman, the knots are untied.

Although the notion is imaginary, it is so difficult to separate the atman from the body that it could take lifetimes of persevering endeavour to achieve this Herculean task. The release of the three granthis also signifies victory over *avidya*, the original, primordial ignorance, *kama*, or desire, and *karma*, or actions that bind one.

In raja yoga this state is attained by *sanyama*, simultaneous dharana, dhyana and samadhi on the gross, subtle, and causal dimensions of the tattwas. In tantra, the very same state is attained by *chakra bhedana*, piercing of the chakras when the kundalini ascends to sahasrara. In the same way the aspirant can attain victory over the indriyas and the mind, and thus over prakriti, by performing sanyama on the cognizable power of the indriyas, their form and individuality.

In this mantra the same process of overcoming the five tattwas, five indriyas and the mind takes place through the darshan of the rays that emanate from Shakti's feet. All these tattwas are doubly pierced by the two important nadis, ida and pingala, which emanate from the base of the spine, intersecting at each chakra. *Ida* is female or mental energy, and *pingala* is male or physical energy. Ida is related to *soma*, the moon, and pingala is related to *prana*, the sun. Both of these nadis unite in sushumna. In fact, all the rays of the tattwas travel upwards along the sushumna path to the two feet of Shakti.

All the rays converge in sushumna, and sushumna converges in the source of those rays, the feet of Devi, which are above ajna. The rays described here are of the gross, subtle and causal bodies, but Devi resides above these, as she is *kalatita* and *tattwatita*, beyond both the rays and the elements, which are her own products. The techniques for bhutajaya, victory over the influence of the elements, indriyajaya, victory over the influence of the senses, and manojaya, victory over the influence of the mind, are given here.

15. Meditation on Devi speaking

शरज्ज्योत्स्नाशुभ्रां शशियुतजटाजूटमुकुटां
वरत्रासत्राणस्फटिकघुटिकापुस्तककराम् ।
सकृन्न त्वां न त्वा कथमिव सतां संनिदधते
मधुक्षीरद्राक्षामधुरिमधुरीणा भणितयः ॥ १५ ॥

*sharaj-jyotsnaa-shubraam shashiyuta-jataajoota-mukutaam
vara-traasa-traana sphatika-ghutikaa-pustakakaraam;
sakrinna tvaam na tvaa kathamiva sataam samnidadhate
madhu-kshira-draakshaa madhurim-adhureenaa-bhanitayah.* (15)

sharat jyotsnaa shubraam: fair (lustrous) and spotless as the autumnal moon; *shashiyuta jataajoota mukutaam*: wearing the crescent moon in thy locks; *vara traasa traana*: thy two hands in the posture of granting shelter and boon; *sphatika ghutikaa pustaka karaam*: and the other two holding a rosary of crystals and a book; *sakrit na*: once; *tvaam*: thou; *natvaa*: having prostrated before; *katham iva*: how; *sataam*: good men; *samnidadhate*: cannot flow; *madhu kshira draakshaa madhurim dhureenaa*: excelling the sweetness of honey, milk and grapes; *bhanitayah*: words

Translation
How can words excelling the sweetness of honey, milk and grapes not flow from the good men who have prostrated before Thee, who are fair and spotless as the autumnal moon, who wears the crescent moon in her locks, whose two hands are in the gesture of granting shelter and boons, and the other two hands holding a crystal rosary and a book.

Commentary
In mantra 13, the worship of Devi granted youth and beauty, and in mantra 15, the good men who prostrate before her receive the gift of not just eloquence, but the *vashikarana* mantra of sweet speech. Here goodness is not equated with speaking truth or being kind and compassionate, but with

devotion and love for Devi. Those who exhibit this quality are considered good by Sankara. These good people receive that mantra of sweet speech that can hypnotize all living beings.

The comparison of sweet speech with honey, milk and grapes at once lends an erotic and attractive aura to the speech of a person who has been favoured by Devi, due to her being pleased by his worship. Sweet speech is a rare quality, which can bring even the strongest adversary under control if one possesses this quality. It is not easy to speak sweetly at all times, even in the face of adversity, calamity and disaster. But the devotee of Devi is granted her vision by which this art becomes natural.

In this vision of Devi, she is as fair as the autumnal moon, *sharajjyotsnashubraam*, with the crescent moon in her locks, *shashiyuta jataajootamukutaam*. Her two hands are in the mudras of granting boons and protection, while the other two are holding a mala and book. This view describes the sattwic form of Parvati, which is most beneficial to the devotee. When sattwa is increased, there is a generation of immense memory, which paves the way for the opening of the knots that conceal the Self.

The crescent moon lends a touch of intimacy which she shares with Shiva, on account of which she abandons her diadem. Her head is adorned with the crescent moon which is always seen on his crown, thus maintaining the underlying erotic imagery that runs through this entire work. Moreover, it hints at the philosophical truth of complete unity between Shiva and Shakti, even when they are separated.

This mantra elaborates the blossoming of *vak siddhi*, the power of speech, through the awakening of kundalini, which is the domain of Saraswati. Mantras and all forms of sound, whether repeated mentally, spoken or even written, as in the scriptures, have evolved from nada. When nada enters the dimension of deep sleep, or *sushupti*, it is known as *prana kundalini*. This is why one of the first outcomes of kundalini awakening is excellence in speech.

Vak, or speech, has four states and out of these, three are unmanifest or hidden, in the sense that they cannot be heard. These three are: whispered, mental and transcendental; they do not descend from their hidden stations. But the fourth kind of speech, which is known as *vaikhari*, is spoken, so it is not considered a siddhi as it is common in everyone.

Vak siddhi means several things. First, the words that one emits are most pleasing to everyone because they are sweet, like honey, milk and grapes. Second, whatever one speaks is enchanting to all. Third, whatever one speaks comes true. These three happen when the siddhi attained through perfection in the first three stages of sound begins to filter down to vaikhari and manifests in the spoken word.

An ordinary man like Kalidas became the greatest of poets on account of his devotion and worship of Kali, by which he got his name. *Kalidas* means 'servant of Kali'. Indian literature has acknowledged his greatness through the phrase *kavita kalidasasya*; one cannot speak of poetry without taking the name of Kalidas.

This mantra of Devi is meditation on *vaagbhav kut*, where the spotless face is the pinnacle of worship. The Devi offers Sankara protection, but more than that she is also ready to fulfil his prayer.

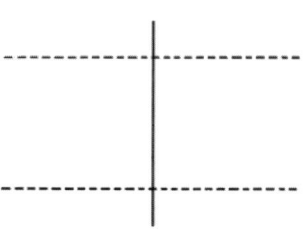

16. Meditation on the beautiful form of Devi bathed in the light of the sun, moon and fire

कवीन्द्राणां चेतः कमलवनबालातपरुचिं
भजन्ते ये सन्तः कतिचिदरुणामेव भवतीम् ।
विरिञ्चिप्रेयस्यास्तरलतरशृङ्गारलहरी-
गभीराभिर्वाग्भिर्विदधति सभाराञ्जनममी ॥ १६ ॥

kaveendraanaam chetah kamala-vana-baalaataparuchim
bhajante ye santah katichid-arunaameva bhavateem;
virinchipreyasyaas tarala-tara-shringaara-lahari
gabheeraabhir-vaagbhir vidadhati sabhaa-ranjanam-ami. (16)

kaveendraanaam: of gifted poets; *chetah kamala vana baalaataparuchim*: who art the rising sun's rays on the (lotus) mind; *bhajante*: who adore thee; *ye santah*: those devoted men; *katichid*: some; various; *arunaameva*: goddess of crimson colour; *bhavateem*: thou; *virinchipreyasyaah*: saraswati's; *tarala tara shringaara lahari gabheeraabhih*: majestic flow, surging like waves of erotic emotions, emanating from the youthful; *vaagbhih*: words; *vidadhati*: become capable; *sabhaa*: (minds) of good men; *ranjanam*: delighting; *ami*: those good men

Translation
O Aruna, Thou crimson-gold hued goddess, who art like the rays of the rising sun on the pure minds of gifted poets (helping their poesy to burst forth). Those who adore Thee become capable of delighting the minds of good people with the majestic flow of words that surge like waves of erotic emotions, emanating from the youthful Saraswati (the goddess of speech).

Commentary
The crimson-gold hue of Aruna, an aspect of Shakti, indicates her rajasic form, which is erotic in nature on account of the red colour. Here the aspect of Saraswati, which the supreme Shakti reveals in mantra 15, is replaced by

the aspect of Aruna in which rajas reigns supreme. After revealing herself as all the chakras up to ajna as well as their related tattwas, and then as the nada and kala inherent in them, Shakti now reveals herself as the *gunas* or inherent traits through which she pervades the entire creation.

Chetah kamalavanabaalaataparuchim or the rays of the rising sun in the mind signifies the blossoming of awareness that springs forth in her worshipper. Awareness and mind are two different things. Awareness is the seed of the mind. Just as the mango seed is different to the mango tree into which it has manifested, in the same way awareness is different to the mind. The tree cannot exist without the seed, but the seed can exist without the tree. In the same way, the mind cannot exist without awareness, but awareness can exist divested of mind.

When the awareness is linked with the mind, there is a marvellous surge of erotic emotions in the form of words, which delight each and everyone, as if Saraswati, the youthful consort of Brahma, were speaking through the person whom Devi has favoured. The phrase *kaveendraanaam chetah* defines a good poet as one who is able to link the awareness with the mind, for the words of such a poet are divine expressions, as in the case of Sankara.

Sringara is a word which describes the decorations a young girl in the throes of amour adorns herself with in order to attract her loved one. This word is profusely used in erotic imagery to convey a heightened emotional state, which is so necessary if one wants to meditate on Devi in all her bewitching forms. A heightened emotional state can generate the climate suitable for the higher experience or inner vision of Devi to unfold.

The rising sun in the forest of lotuses embedded in the consciousness is descriptive of the awakening of sahasrara, which is the main centre of Samaya tantra. When this happens the electromagnetic intensity of the awakened awareness, or *Purushika*, subdues the mind and gives birth to a completely new awareness. That awareness is full of eroticism, in the sense that it stimulates poesy in the sadhaka, which is what it did to Sankara, who burst forth into the verses of *Saundarya Lahari*.

The word *gabhiram* indicates a noble quality of eroticism as opposed to its vulgar form, for eroticism in art can never be vulgar. In this mantra there is a further elaboration of vak siddhi which is a sure and certain sign that Sankara has been blessed by Devi.

17. Meditation on Devi placing her hand on your head

सवित्रीभिर्वाचां शशिमणिशिलाभङ्गरुचिभिः
वशिन्याद्याभिस्त्वां सह जननि संचिन्तयति यः ।
स कर्ता काव्यानां भवति महतां भङ्गिसुभगैः
वचोभिर्वाग्देवीवदनकमलामोदमधुरैः ॥ १७ ॥

*savitreebhirvaachaam shashi-mani-shilaabhangaruchibhih
vashinyaadyaabhis-tvaam saha janani-sanchintayati yah;
sa kartaa kaavyaanaam bhavati mahataam bhangisubhagaih
vachobhir-vaagdevee vadana-kamal-aamoda-madhuraih.* (17)

savitreebhih vaachaam: (who are) sources of words or speech; *shashi mani shilaabhangaruchibhih*: (and) whose radiance resembles the lustre of freshly cut moonstone; *vashini aadyaabhi*: deities like vasini and others; *tvaam*: thee; *saha*: with; *janani*: oh mother; *sanchintayati*: meditates on; *yah*: whoever; *sa*: he; *kartaa*: author; *kaavyaanaam*: of poetical works; *bhavati*: can become; *mahataam*: of great ones; *bhangisubhagaih*: as delightful as; *vachobhih*: with words; *vaagdevee vadana kamala aamoda madhuraih*: sweet with the fragrance of saraswati's mouth

Translation
O Mother, whoever meditates on Thee as Vasini and other devis, who are the source of speech and whose radiance resembles the lustre of freshly cut moonstone, can become the writer of poetical works as delightful and interesting as those of the great authors, and emitting words sweet with the fragrance of Saraswati's mouth.

Commentary
Bursting into light is a function of the absolute principle of *sphota*, or sound that has attained clarity. The first glimpse of Shakti takes place when this occurs. Here Sankara describes that pristine form of Shakti when she first emerges into view

in all her sixteen kalas, by comparing her radiance to the lustre of a freshly cut moonstone.

A vision of Shakti in that form could turn anyone into a poet, even Valmiki and Kalidas. Until he had the darshan of Devi, Valmiki was a dacoit who looted innocent people on the highway. Kalidas was considered the most foolish man ever born, because he was seen cutting the branch of the tree on which he himself was sitting. But even he turned into a poet after his darshan of Kali. In this verse Sankara acknowledges the divine intervention in the lives of those who worship Devi, as they become immortalized through their poetry. The *Ramayana* of Valmiki and the works of Kalidas were not results of human effort but of the divine hand of Shakti, who wrote these words after overpowering their minds.

This mantra emphasizes vak siddhi, which occurs when the cosmic process unfolds. Was Sankara describing his own vision and inner experience when he beheld Shakti as the transcendental sound and light? Sweetness of speech is again highlighted here and this can easily be accepted as the *vashikarana*, or hypnotizing mantra of Devi, signifying an awakening of Shakti in the person who exhibits this quality. By sweet and pleasant speech one can win kingdoms and rule over the people, which is a sign of Devi's favour. Any good station that one enjoys in life is due to the influence of Shakti that has begun to manifest within, for Shakti and *Sri*, or auspiciousness, are synonymous.

This mantra is also a meditation on *vaagbhav kut*, symbolic of the tamasic nature of Shakti, in which the pinnacle of worship is the face. There is further highlighting of siddhis, which are a natural culmination of Devi worship.

18. Meditation on Devi in bhairavi mudra

तनुच्छायाभिस्ते तरुणतरणिश्रीसरणिभिः
दिवं सर्वामुर्वीमरुणिमनिमग्नां स्मरति यः ।
भवन्त्यस्य त्रस्यद्वनहरिणशालीननयनाः
सहोर्वश्याः वश्याः कति कति न गीर्वाणगणिकाः ॥ १८ ॥

*tanu-chhaayaabhiste taruna-tarani-shree-saranibhih
divam sarvaam-urveem arunimanimagnaam smarati yah;
bhavantyasya trasyad vanahari-na-shaaleena-nayanaah
sahorvashyaah vashyaah kati kati na geervaana-ganikaah.* (18)

tanu chhaayaabhih: thy form; *te*: thy; *taruna tarani shree saranibhih*: with young rays that resemble the rising sun; *divam sarvaam*: the sky (heavens); *urveem*: and the earth; *arunimani magnaam*: bathes in crimson radiance; *smarati*: meditates on; *yah*: whoever; *bhavanti*: exists; *asya*: he; *trasyat vana hari na shaaleena nayanaah*: with bashful eyes like those of frightened deer of the forest; *saha urvashyaah*: urvashi and other celestial courtesans; *vashyaah*: become fascinated; *kati kati*: how many; *na*: not *geervaana ganikaah*: heavenly damsels

Translation
How can the many heavenly damsels and celestial courtesans, like Urvashi, with bashful eyes like those of timid deer in the forest, not become fascinated by a person who meditates on the beauty of Thy form, like the early rays of the rising sun, which bathes the heaven and earth in a crimson radiance.

Commentary
Here the hue of the primordial Shakti in the form of light is compared to a crimson radiance. Perhaps the closest view one sees of that is the rising or setting sun. The sun is a source of prana shakti. It is a divine gift that Shakti has bestowed to nurture all living beings. In fact, the sun has

been compared to one of her breasts. Naturally the crimson glow of the sun is a reflection of her glory. *Arunima* is the crimson radiance which emanates from Devi and envelops the entire universe.

Today, even science proclaims that this universe is held together by a force which prevents it from falling apart. This force forms a type of grid which holds aloft all the planets and galaxies, including our earth, and bends with the weight of the object that rests in it. Thus the curve formed by the weight of the sun, around which all other planets revolve, determines the gravitational force of each planet. The nearer the planet is to the sun, as in the case of earth, the greater the gravitational force.

This radiance of Shakti is compared to the lustre of the rising sun. By comparing her to that, one can get some idea of how she would look when she makes her grand entry into the world. But her full glory surpasses even that. Her rays of crimson hue radiate into the whole of creation that is in the process of manifestation. The sky, the earth, everything is bathed with that pure light. Meditation on that light, which is none other than Devi's form, bestows immense power and siddhis. Even the most beautiful damsels become shy and subjugated in the presence of such a sadhaka.

Through the darshan of Devi, siddhis come to the sadhaka, but he is not a slave to them. Siddhis are a manifestation of the immense power of Devi. They are a realization of the *sthaniya devata*, the deity residing in that particular centre. It has already been pointed out that the human body has innumerable centres or points of illumination. As the sadhaka advances, he is bound to encounter them. They are a product of maya which is inherent in Shakti. So, without the grace of Devi, the awakening of siddhis can completely overwhelm even the most serious and alert aspirant.

Perhaps that is why Rishi Patanjali in his famous *Raja Yoga Sutras* has devoted the entire chapter entitled *Vibhooti Pada* to the dangers of falling prey to siddhis. If the sadhaka is not careful, siddhis can burn up his *tapas*, austerity, and *tejas*, effulgence, and reduce his spiritual accomplishment to ashes. Instead of gaining victory or ascent through his sadhana, he is defeated and descends to the lower planes, like a beggar with his begging bowl knocking on the door of the wide-eyed and credulous for something in return for the display of his siddhis.

In the course of sadhana, as the devatas of the different tattwa are awakened, various siddhis arise spontaneously. The devata of *ahamkara* or ego, which takes birth when the consciousness descends to the heart centre, is Rudra. The devata of *chitta*, equated with the collective memory of all the incarnations that the *jiva*, or embodied soul, has undergone, is Kshetrajna. The devata of *buddhi*, or intellect, is Brahma, the wise one, who also happens to be the deity of *maithuna*, or sexual interaction, being the creator. The devata of *manas*, or mind, is Soma, the moon, which waxes and wanes like the mind and is never steady.

The deity of *akasha*, space, the subtlest of the material tattwas, is hearing. The deity of *vayu*, air, is touch, which stays with the sadhaka right up to the point of asamprajnata samadhi. The deity of *agni*, fire, is sight. At this point ahamkara, which is born at the anahata centre, begins to assert itself, giving rise to self-identity by the vision of form. Form is also the basis of *Saundarya Lahari* in the sense that Sankara's experience was not of sound or touch, but of vision. He saw Devi's form, or the mandala of Devi. The deity of *apas*, water, is taste, and that of *prithvi*, earth, is smell.

There are several other deities, assuming various roles, but the essential feature of them all is that they link one with the cosmos when awakened through worship. Each of these deities is represented in tantra by a mantra, yantra and mandala to facilitate access into their domain. They lead the sadhaka into the realm of *siddhis* or accomplishment. The word *vibhooti* means 'accomplishment of yoga'. A vision of Devi in her pristine purity grants the devotee that accomplishment as well as the presence of mind to keep it under his sway, rather than being swayed by it. That is the greatest victory that a sadhaka can achieve, for this ensures his success in reaching the goal.

This mantra indicates that without subduing the fascination for siddhis, the aspirant can never hope to attain the highest experience. The manifestation of siddhi is a lower grade of experience. These days anyone who exhibits siddhi gains popularity in the mundane world. But in the spiritual world he is regarded as a fool who has fallen from great heights because he could not receive the blessings of Devi. Siddhis come under the control of a person who is devoted to Devi; he is not slave to them.

19. Meditation on the bewitching glance of Devi

मुखं बिन्दुं कृत्वा कुचयुगमधस्तस्य तदधो
हकारार्धं ध्यायेद्धरमहिषि ते मन्मथकलाम् ।
स सद्यः संक्षोभं नयति वनिता इत्यतिलघु
त्रिलोकीमप्याशु भ्रमयति रवीन्दुस्तनयुगाम् ॥ १९ ॥

*mukham bindum kritvaa kuchayugam-adhas-tasya tadadho
hakaaraardham dhyaayed-haramahishi te manmathakalaam;
sa sadyah samkshobham nayati vanita it-yatilaghu
trilokeemapy-aashu bhramayati ravindu-stanayugaam.* (19)

mukham: face; *bindum kritvaa*: (imagined) as bindu; *kuchayugam*: the twin breasts; *adha*: below; *tasya*: it; *tat adha*: below it; *hakaa ra ardham*: half akshara 'ha'; *dhyaayet*: meditates; *hara mahishi*: o, consort of hara; *te*: thy; *manmathakalaam*: cupid or kamadeva; *sa*: he; *sadyah*: instantly; *samkshobham*: of string the emotions; *nayati*: becomes capable; *vanita*: women; *iti*: this; *ya*: whoever; *ati laghu*: is a trifle; *trilokeem api*: even the ruler of the three worlds; *aashu*: instantly; *bhramayati*: can fascinate; *ravi indu stanayugaam*: with the sun and the moon as breasts

Translation

O Consort of Hara, whoever meditates on Thy face in the bindu, with Thy twin breasts below it, and the half akshara '*ha*' also below, Kamadeva evokes a string of emotions by which he becomes identified with Thee in meditation, and thus can quickly stir the mind of any woman. To instantly fascinate anyone is indeed a trifle for him who meditates on Thee as Triloki (the ruler of the three worlds) with the sun and moon as breasts.

Commentary

In meditation, the practitioner reaches a point where everything converges and then emerges again in the form of an experience. That point of focus is *bindu*, which is represented as the nucleus of the Sri Chakra. This mantra is a direct reference to that innermost point within the triangle of Sri Chakra, the abode of Shakti. By meditating on the bindu as the face of Shakti, with her twin breasts below, representing the sun and moon, or *ida* and *pingala*, and the akshara '*ha*' also below, one experiences union with the cosmic forces. Thereby the mind crosses its boundaries and limitations and new avenues open before it.

This verse is of special importance to Sri Vidya worshippers, as it highlights the innermost point or bindu. Ordinarily, one is only aware of the physical and mental experiences, not of the spiritual dimension. But with the union of the cosmic forces, this dimension opens. The gross experiences become a mere trifle for the person who can instantly travel through all the three levels of consciousness: waking, dreaming and deep sleep, and experience the cosmic or *turiya* state.

Manmathakalam is a name of Kamadeva, the god of love. When broken up, the word is composed of three roots: *man*, which is 'mind', *matha*, 'churning', and *kala* which means 'art' for example, the art of dancing, the art of speaking, the art of loving. Kala also means 'phase'; the phases of the moon are known as *chandrakala*, that of the sun are known as *suryakala*, the phases of beauty in a young woman are known as *roopakala*. Kala also means 'ray' or 'stream', as was its usage in previous mantras.

Kala is like the ebb and tide or waxing and waning that occurs in material substance. In the same way there are phases of emotion, such as anger, jealousy, hatred, passion, love and affection. The love one may feel for a particular person goes through different phases of intensity and indifference. Anger has many shades; sometimes it drives one to insanity, breakdown or even murder, and at other times it leaves one unruffled. The word manmathakalam should be understood in this context.

Here, however, instead of the physical or mental phases, Sankara is speaking of the spiritual phase, which comes as a surge and then a flood, through the churning of the mental wavelengths. Manmathakala is thus the art of churning the mind, which Kamadeva is adept at. Even in daily lives Cupid plays great mischief, churning out the emotions in abundance. The vedic and tantric traditions have always regarded kama as one of the *purusharthas*, or essential requisites of life. But they have also emphasized that its expression should not conflict with the other three, *artha*, material need, *dharma*, righteousness, and *moksha*, liberation.

The concept of triloki adds a new dimension to the meditation on Devi, as it lends a cosmic vision to her form. *Triloki*, the three lokas, are imagined as the *virat*, or universal, form of Devi in which the sun and moon are her two breasts. This awakens the *matri bhava*, or motherly feeling, in the aspirant. Just as a child is nourished by the milk of the mother's breast, in the same way, the sun, a symbol of prana, and the moon, a symbol of nectar, nourish the entire universe.

Philosophically, the word triloki is a significant epithet of Devi, because it lends credence to the fact that Shakti is present in the jagrat, swapna and sushupti states, and beyond them as well in the turiya state.

A passionate man may develop desire at the sight of a woman's body. But one who is able to transcend desire and awaken the thought of worship alone is able to realize the triloki, or cosmic form of Devi, and becomes a manmathari. Sankara had the ability to transcend desire; his vision was cosmic, not gross. He is not describing the body of a woman under the sway of passion and desire.

Manmatha is often regarded as synonymous with desire because the two always seem to go hand in hand. Rarely is one born who does not succumb to the element of desire. The roots of desire are so deeply entrenched that it is hard to say which came first, desire or vibration. The *Nasadiya Sukta* from the *Rig Veda* says that desire, or *iccha*, came first, out of which *sankalpa*, or resolve, was born, followed by vibration. This sequence is apparent even in daily life. First one desires, then one makes a resolve to accomplish that desire, and then one swings into action. However, all three are rooted in that infinite power, which Shaktas call Shakti and Shaivas call Shiva.

The emotional quality of a person largely determines his success in life. Today a lot of emphasis is placed on intellectual development and potential for achieving the goals of life, such as studies, career, or any other enterprise. However, if the emotional development is overlooked, one may become an intellectual giant, but an emotional pygmy. Unruly emotions, emotional immaturity and emotional imbalance can completely destroy what one has built up with his intellectual strengths.

Emotional outbursts can easily lead to a nervous breakdown and destroy the life of an intelligent person. These emotions can be channelled towards higher experience. Everyone has inherited an abundance of emotions which often remain locked within as there has never been a chance to express them fully. Even if one has a suitable environment for expressing the emotions, still there is always a surplus left over. These emotions should be developed for the inner experience to gain ascent.

Through constant reference to erotic emotions and ample involvement of Kamadeva, the master of emotions, this mantra offers a way to channel those erotic emotions and become easily identified with Shakti. In this way, one is elevated by those emotions, rather than being destroyed by them. It also reveals that erotic emotions, whether of love or passion, are highly coveted states of mind for inducing higher experience. At the height of erotic emotion, one can completely merge oneself with Absolute Beauty.

The organism of the body and mind evolves from the most subtle principle known as *kama*, or primordial desire. This same principle of kama, or *iccha shakti*, if understood properly can unveil the mystery of creation. It can open the door to enlightenment and lead one to the highest experience of absolute bliss and beauty. However, if not understood properly, kama propels the individual soul into the path of worldly transmigration.

This mantra depicts the body of Devi, and thus is *vaagbhav*, *kamakala* and *shakti kut* altogether.

20. Meditation on Devi's form emitting rays of light

किरन्तीमङ्गेभ्यः किरणनिकुरुम्बामृतरसं
हृदि त्वामाधत्ते हिमकरशिलामूर्तिमिव यः ।
स सर्पाणां दर्प शमयति शकुन्ताधिप इव
ज्वरप्लुष्टान् दृष्ट्या सुखयति सुधासारसिरया ॥२०॥

*kiranteem-angebhyah kirana-nikurumba-amritarasam
hridi tvaam-aadhatte himakara-shilaamoortim-iva yah;
sa sarpaanaam-darpam shamayati shakuntaadhipa iva
jvaraplushtaan drishtyaa sukhayati sudhaa-saarasirayaa.* (20)

kiranteem: sends forth; *angebhyah*: from thy body; *kirana nikurumba amritarasam*: nectar flowing from the rays; *hridi*: in the heart; *tvaam*: thee; *aadhatte*: meditates; *himakara shilaamoortim iva*: as an idol sculpted out of moonstone; *yah*: whoever; *sa*: he; *sarpaanaam*: of snakes; *darpam*: pride; *shamayati*: humbles; *shakunta aadhipa iva*: like garuda himself; *jvaraplushtaan*: those suffering from fever; *drishtyaa*: with looks; *sukhayati*: cures; *sudhaa saarasirayaa*: nectar-showering nadi

Translation
Whoever meditates in the heart on Thee as an idol sculpted of moonstone and on the nectar flowing from the rays sent forth from Thy body, like Garuda himself, humbles the pride of snakes and with mere looks cures the fever of the nectar-showering nadi.

Commentary
In this mantra Sankara firmly establishes the mandala of Devi and indicates that one should meditate in the heart centre, on her body, in the form of an idol sculpted of moonstone, from which rays of nectar flow and from which the nectar showering nadi emerges. The word *nadi* means flow. Just as blood flows in the veins and nerves that are

spread throughout the body, the nectar of awareness flows in the nadis, from the top of the head down to the toes.

The power of pure awareness assumes the form of nadi. The nadis flowing from the heart are especially important for carrying the experience of nectar, which induces a type of feverishness in one who has awakened this flow. Within the heart is the point from which a spark of energy is released that initiates the contractions of the heart and coordinates its activities. The ancient yogis and rishis located the higher mind in the heart.

The experience of Shakti triggers a mighty surge of energy in the sadhaka, just as a surge of electricity gives a jolt to all the equipment plugged into a line. After a surge the refrigerator may start vibrating and make a funny sound; the computer may go on the blink or give an alarm signal. In the same way, a surge can take place in the brain during meditation. This surge is not electrical or magnetic alone; it is electromagnetic, but it is also spiritual, which means a surge of awareness, the frequency of which is awesome.

This surge completely alters the circuits of the brain, which gives rise to an experience that differs from individual to individual. One may experience fear, nervousness, anxiety, or see himself lying dead, as was the case of Ramana Maharshi. One day during his meditation, he experienced a spiritual surge and in an instant saw his body lying dead before him. He had entered into the *sakshi* or observer state of awareness, where he began to see his body lying dead. At that moment the question arose: if I am laying dead, then who is sitting here and seeing that? In his case this event occurred spontaneously. He did not analyze how it had happened without any effort on his part. At that moment no logic works, nor is there any reasoning or understanding of the event. One just has to flow with the tide.

The same kind of surge is described by Sankara in this mantra. The nectar of supreme energy creates a surge as one meditates on the rays that flow from the form of Devi, which is seen as a sculpture of moonstone. Moreover, when one meditates on her in the heart, the surge is so powerful that all sorts of abnormalities can occur, such as the uncontrollable fever that arises due to the surge of nectar in the nadis. However, these are pacified by the meditator himself.

This mantra says that when a spiritual surge occurs through the spiritual vision of Devi, the abnormal experiences that arise at the physical and mental level can be cured by the great power the individual attains. The comparison Sankara gives is that of a snake, whose aggressive attitude is controlled by Garuda, who can pin him down at once. Similarly, the uncontrollable fever that arises due to an influx of spiritual energy into the body can be removed by a mere look.

Quite recently I was presented with a set of cds of a seminar on chakras given by Swami Satyananda in Vienna in the 1960s. Upon hearing them, I was simply astounded by the clarity and insight with which he had dealt with this extremely esoteric and secret subject. I showed them to Sri Swamiji, and while recalling the visit to Vienna and the course of the lectures, he told me that throughout that series of lectures he had high fever, which would only subside when he was at the place of the lecture. After that he would return to his hotel room and sleep, as if in a deep trance. When that seminar was over, he was again normal without any medicine or doctor. On another occasion when he was visiting Kamakhya, an important seat of tantric worship of Devi, throughout his stay of nine days he had a mysterious fever, which only left him on the last day when his worship was over with the kanya pooja. That fever is the surge of spiritual awareness in the nadis. He was experiencing the state of *sudhaa saarasirayaa* which Sankara describes in this mantra. However, this experience can be difficult to handle.

For this reason a guru is essential in the life of an aspirant who is keen on elevating his awareness and experiencing that which is beyond the confines of matter. When one treads on such unlimited boundaries, the dangers that befall him can only be rectified by a guru whose spiritual powers can cure him with a mere look and instil in him the faith that he is walking on the right path.

Except in very rare cases, meditation on the supreme reality in the form of absolute beauty and bliss is not possible without the direct guidance and company of an advanced spiritual personage. The strength to fight the most dreadful enemies, known as pride, lust and anger, comes only through this association.

Sarpaanaam darpam is a curious expression which has been understood to mean that snakes can be controlled through this mantra. Perhaps they can, but the term has a deeper meaning in this mantra. The word *sarpa* means 'snake' and *darpa* is the 'antidote' to the venom of the snake. A snake is always poised to poison an aggressor with its venom, but there is a darpa, or antidote to the snake's bite. *Shakuntaadhipa* is an epithet for Garuda, the king of eagles, who soars in the sky and preys on the poisonous snakes, hunting them out, one by one.

The impact of the nectar of Shakti on the meditator is compared to the bite of a snake, and the antidote is to allow that power to flow through one in the spirit of devotion and surrender to her, just as Sankara did. *Sudhaa saarasirayaa* describes the shower of nectar in the nadis or *sira* which Devi transmits to a worthy worshipper.

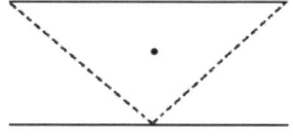

21. Meditation on Devi's glistening body in the form of lightning

तटिल्लेखातन्वीं तपनशशिवैश्वानरमयीं
निषण्णां षण्णामप्युपरि कमलानां तव कलाम् ।
महापद्माटव्यां मृदितमलमायेन मनसा
महान्तः पश्यन्तो दधति परमाह्लादलहरीम् ॥२१॥

*tatillekhaa-tanveem tapana-shashi-vaishvaanaramayeem
nishannaam shannamapi upari kamalaanaam tava kalaam;
mahaa-padmaatavyaam mridita-mala-maayena manasaa
mahaantah pashyanto dadhati param-aahlaada-lahareem. (21)*

tatillekhaa tanveem: (thy) lightning-like body; *tapana shashi vaishvaanaramayeem*: with manifestations of sun, moon and fire; *nishannaam*: located; *shannam api upari kamalaanaam*: above the six lotuses; *tava kalaam*: thy rays; *mahaa padma aatavyaam*: in the sahasrara lotus; *mridita mala maayena*: free from impurities of maya (like illusion and ignorance); *manasaa*: with a mind; *mahaantah*: noble aspirants; *pashyanta*: attain; *dadhati*: are filled with; *param aahlaada lahareem*: thrills of spiritual bliss

Translation
The noble aspirants with minds free from the impurities of maya (such as illusion and ignorance) are filled with thrills of spiritual bliss by (the vision of) Thy lightning-like body with its manifestations of sun, moon and fire, located above the six lotuses as Thy rays in the core of the sahasrara lotus.

Commentary
Maya is that state of mind which binds one to the manifest dimension of Shakti, which is the material world along with its objects: persons, events, feelings, mental associations, attachments, likes and dislikes. This power is inherent in Shiva and Shakti, and through it the *jivatman,* the individual

soul, experiences separation from its source, *paramatman*, the supreme soul, and enacts its karmas on the mortal plane. Maya, through her five *kanchukas* or veils obstructs the individual from perceiving the reality.

These five kanchukas are: i) *kala*, that which obstructs the power to do all; ii) *vidya/avidya*, that which limits the power to know all; iii) *raga*, that which gives rise to desire and attachment, and increasing discontent when they are not fulfilled or satiated; iv) *kaala*, that which limits perpetual existence by creating the notion of time, and v) *niyati*, that which limits free will by creating the notion of fate and destiny. Together these five cover the pure effulgent atman so completely that it begins to appear *apara*, or limited.

As the karmas are shed, the noose of maya subsequently loosens and the individual experiences shades of liberation or freedom from the clutches of attachment to the world. Such persons who are free of maya are noble indeed, for they have crossed one of the most difficult barriers that an individual has to encounter in life. Attachment is the biggest obstacle due to which one remains forever ensnared by *raga* and *dwesha*, like and dislike, and cannot rise above it.

Maya is the philosophical correlate to gravity. Just as gravity keeps one grounded and does not allow one to fly in the air, in the same way, maya binds one to worldly things that keep one tied to the endless cycle of pain and pleasure and birth and death. In the law of gravity cohesion operates on the physical plane as well as the mental plane through definite laws of association and relativity. In the same way, maya also operates on the physical and mental plane. Those who worship Devi and meditate on her should thoroughly understand these laws for better progress.

So, the first and greatest effort in spiritual life is to rise above maya, because by doing so one attains nobility and experiences the thrills of spiritual bliss. The physical substance is released from the pull of gravity and one is propelled towards the experience of Shakti as lightning.

Shakti, being pure energy, can be experienced as light, sound, form, colour, bliss or nectar, for they are all different frequencies of that one magnanimous power. As Shakti moves towards the core of sahasrara, it is experienced as lightning with its manifestations of *surya*, sun, *soma*, moon, and *agni*, fire.

Here, Sankara is not speaking of the manifest sun, moon and fire, but of their cosmic counterparts that compose the body of Shakti. Sahasrara represents the macrocosm and any experience related to it is macrocosmic, even if it is experienced within oneself. The sun, moon, stars, light, men and women that are seen in that high state of awareness are certainly not physical or individual. They are made up of pure awareness, which is the source of this manifest world. That is the kala of Shakti in its purest form. The one experienced in daily life is its grossest form, where it has lost much of its vibration and acquired density, thus appearing as solid matter.

This mantra refers to the vision of *jyoti* or light above ajna chakra. The phrase *mahapadmatavi* indicates this effulgence in the region of sahasrara. When the kundalini ascends, piercing through the six chakras up to sahasrara, the rays appear like lightning, which is a result of the combination of the luminosity of the sun, moon and fire. This vision gives rise to enlightenment, or jnana, and the siddhis are left behind as one rises above the influence of the chakras, which bestow the different siddhis.

Above the six lotuses refers to the state where the six chakras have been transcended to experience Shakti as kala; the specific term for this state of Shakti is *Sadakhyakala*, meaning her transcendental form. Again it is said that this kala of Shakti resides in the very core of sahasrara, where it can be experienced as lightning, and also manifests as thousands of suns and moons that illuminate the awareness to its fullest spiritual extent and potential. This glow of effulgence is then transmitted to all the lower realms of the body: the sthoola, sukshma and karana sharira.

While describing this experience, Swami Satyananda said that it can best be compared to a nuclear explosion within the individual, where time and space move towards each other with terrifying speed. The result of their collision with each other is a magnificent explosion at the very nucleus of sahasrara. This same experience is re-enacted at the mundane level when similar principles are applied to explode the atom bomb. While witnessing a nuclear explosion, the great scientist Oppenheimer exclaimed the following verse from the *Bhagavad Gita* (11:12):

> *Were a thousand suns to light up the sky,*
> *still they could not match the light*
> *of the absolute consciousness.*

22. Meditation on Devi sitting on a beautiful throne like an empress listening to the prayers of her worshippers

भवानि त्वं दासे मयि वितर दृष्टिं सकरुणाम्
इति स्तोतुं वांछन् कथयति भवानि त्वमिति यः ।
तदैव त्वं तस्मै दिशसि निजसायुज्यपदवीं
मुकुन्दब्रह्मेन्द्रस्फुटमुकुटनीराजितपदाम् ॥२२॥

*bhavaani tvam daase mayi vitara drishtim sakarunaam
iti stotum vaanchhan kathayati bhavaani tvam-iti yah;
tadaiva tvam tasmai dishasi nija saayujya padaveem
mukunda-brahmendra-sphuta-mukuta-neeraajita-padaam.* (22)

bhavaani: o bhavani; *tvam*: thou; *daase mayi*: me, thy servant; *vitara*: bestow; *drishtim*: glance; *sakarunaam*: with pity; *iti*: thus; *stotum*: praying; *vaanchhan*: desirous of; *kathayati*: starts uttering; *bhavaani*: bhavani; *tvam*: thou; *iti*: thus; *yah*: whoever; *tada iva*: instantly; *tvam*: thou; *tasmai*: for him; *dishasi*: bestow; *nija saayujya padaveem*: oneness with thyself; *mukunda brahma indra sphuta mukuta neeraajita padaam*: feet at which divinities like mukunda (vishnu), brahma, indra (and others) perform the ceremony with lighted lamp

Translation

O Bhavani, do Thou have pity and bestow Thy glance on me, Thy servant. Whoever is desirous of Thee, prays thus, even before he starts uttering your name. Thou instantly bestow on him oneness with Thyself, at whose feet divinities like Mukunda (Vishnu), Brahma, Indra (and others) perform the ceremony with lighted lamp.

Commentary

Bhavani tvam is indicative of a state when the aspirant says may I become yours. In this mantra, after awakening the Mahashakti kundalini, and raising it to sahasrara, where the kala of Devi is experienced by him, Sankara experiences a very high state, which is full of divine love and *sayujya*, or oneness with Devi. Sankara says that anyone who knowingly or unknowingly says *bhavani tvam*, which means, I want to become yours, is at once granted sayujya with the Devi. Fire burns even those who touch it unknowingly; in the same way, even if one speaks these words unknowingly, they bring him close to Devi.

Thus *Bhavani tvam daase* is a Mahavakya that can induce the state of sayujya, which literally means *moksha*, or absorption into the supreme Shakti. The other states of moksha, preceding sayujya, are *salokya*, coexistence with God, *samipya*, proximity to God, and *saroopya*, having the same form as God. Absorption leads to total dissolution of the individual self, which is the highest state. The lokas before that of Brahma, Vishnu and Indra are far below, and are seen as if their glittering diadems or headgear are waiving their lights in worship of that state of sayujya. This mantra also indicates that the path of devotion, or bhakti, confers quick results

There is a natural progression of experience in *Saundarya Lahari*, which becomes evident in this mantra. At first, Sankara beholds the vision of Devi as pure effulgence, which results in the awakening of an enlightened awareness that is hypnotic and magnetic. This awareness attracts all sorts of *siddhis* or accomplishments, which make him irresistible. When he is able to subdue these siddhis and make them subservient to him, he experiences sayujya, or oneness with Devi. In this mantra Sankara's sayujya with Devi is established. In the previous mantra he experienced total oneness with the experience of Shakti as the sadakhya kala in sahasrara, which here is expressed by declaring *Bhavani tvam daase*, I am totally surrendered to you; accept me as your servant.

Prayers are a medium through which one can directly interact with Devi. The efficacy of prayer depends entirely on how effectively one can establish contact with her. Often while praying the mind is not centred on Devi, instead it is centred on oneself. At other times the mind is so distracted that it runs here and there. This was not the case with Sankara; his mind was totally absorbed in Devi, and thus her response was also total.

Concentration or one-pointed awareness on the object of worship results in sayujya, oneness or union with the object. This oneness is attained when one is able to visualize the object of concentration very clearly, even in its absence. The practitioner should be able to recall the object of worship at a moment's notice. For this type of concentration one should have one-pointed awareness and tenacious faith. If these are lacking, one cannot attain concentration or total absorption on the form of devotion.

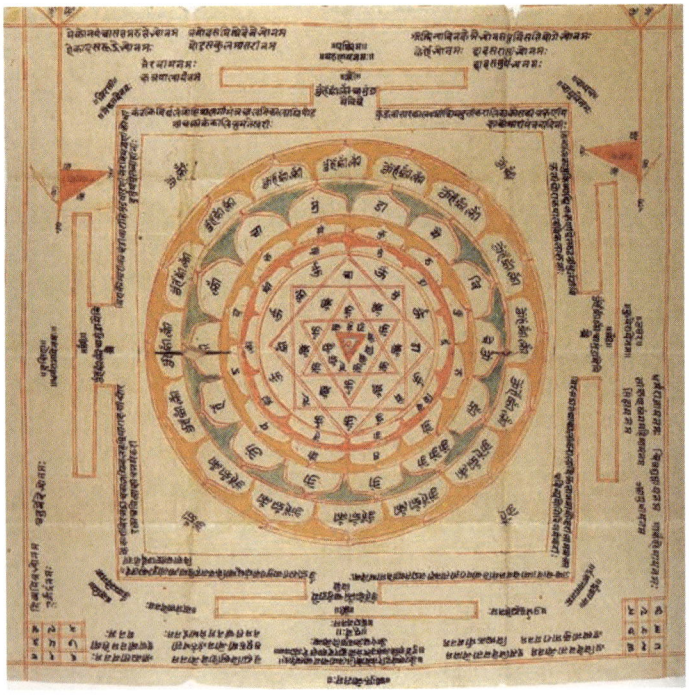

23. Meditation on the Ardhanarishwara (half woman and half man) form of Shakti

त्वया हृत्वा वामं वपुरपरितृप्तेन मनसा
शरीरार्धं शंभोरपरमति शङ्के हृतमभूत् ।
तथा हि त्वद्रूपं सकलमरुणाभं त्रिनयनं
कुचाभ्यामानम्रं कुटिलशशिचूडालमुकुटम् ॥ २३ ॥

*tvayaa hritvaa vaamam vapur-aparitriptena-manasaa
shareeraardham shambho aparamati shanke hritamabhoot;
tathaa hi tvadroopam sakalam-arunaabham-trinayanam
kuchaabhyaam-aanamram kutila-shashi-choodaala-mukutam.* (23)

tvayaa: thou; *hritvaa*: having appropriated; *vaamam vapuh*: left side of his body; *aparitriptena manasaa*: unsatisfied in mind; *shareer ardham shambho aparamati*: also shambhu's right half; *shanke*: I suspect that; *hritam abhoot*: hast invaded; *tathaa hi tvat roopam*: because of which thy form (that shines in my heart); *sakalam*: totally; *arunaabham*: crimson in complexion; *trinayanam*: having three eyes; *kuchaabhyaam*: by the weight of two breasts; *aanamram*: slightly bent; *kutila shashi choodaala mukutam*: and with the crescent moon in the diadem

Translation
Thou, having appropriated the left side of his body as Ardhanarishwara, Thy mind was not satisfied, I suspect, and hast invaded Shambhu's right half as well, because of which Thy form (that shines in my heart) is totally crimson in hue and slightly bent by the weight of Thy two breasts, having three eyes and the crescent moon adorning Thy crown.

Commentary
Shakti is all pervading, and there is no area of experience where she is not. From *bhu loka*, the worldly plane of gross objects, to *satya loka*, the highest plane of truth and bliss,

Shakti inhabits each and every speck of existence and experience. Shakti pervades the entire physical body, whether the left side, which is the flow of ida, or the right side, which is the flow of pingala.

Both ida and pingala are expressions of that one Shakti, even though they are opposite to each other, like day and night, heat and cold. Ida is the negative polarity of energy and pingala the positive. Ida governs the mental and creative tendencies and pingala the physical and dynamic tendencies. Ida corresponds to the parasympathetic nervous system and pingala to the sympathetic nervous system.

In electrical energy, there are three types of currents: positive, negative and neutral. Similarly, Shakti is present in the physical body as ida, pingala and sushumna, the neutral force, in the pranic field of energy that feeds the nervous system. The secret of spiritual awakening lies in bringing about a balance between the negative and positive energies, so that the third autonomous, neutral energy takes over and begins to flow. Sushumna is the spiritual energy which then overrides all the systems of the body.

Ardhanarishwara is a concept that is peculiar to tantric philosophy, which depicts Lord Shiva's body as half male and half female. In the famous Elephanta cave temple, off the shores of Mumbai, there is a gigantic statue of Ardhanarishwara. This image invokes the idea that the entire game of opposites is just a play of Shakti, who assumes different roles and different manifestations. In fact, the Shakti tattwa is so omnipresent and powerful that it has become difficult to recognize the Shiva tattwa.

In reality, they are not different from one another. This mantra indicates the state where the Shiva tattwa is subdued and Shakti tattwa is in predominance. According to Shakta darshan, this is a state where Shakti reigns supreme as the unified whole. That is the experience of Shakti as shodashi with all her sixteen kalas. At that stage Shiva is overpowered and absorbed by Shakti, and it may appear that Shiva has no role there.

Shiva is apparent as long as Shakti is not in her full intensity, which measures up to sixteen kalas, or rays. Once she attains that level of frequency, she simply overrides Shiva, and even takes over his half of the body, as depicted in the famous Ardhanarishwara (half man/half woman) form of Shiva and Shakti. From there, she reigns supreme as Tripura Sundari. This mantra depicts the total union of Shiva and Shakti, and describes a splendid meditation on sadakhya tattwa, or Ardhanarishwara.

Here there is no difference between Shakti and Shiva. The crescent moon and three eyes, which are character-

istic of Shiva, now adorn Shakti. This shows that they have amalgamated into one another in a wonderful way. Her full breasts indicate the full potential of this state, which nourishes and satiates the one who experiences it. The crimson colour of Devi's form indicates the richness of this experience, when the entire horizon of inner awareness is bathed with warm red light, emanating from the supreme Shakti.

What can be more comforting than this vision, as it is the light of Shakti that sustains the world and removes the darkness that keeps one bound in fear and ignorance.

24. Meditation on Kali

जगत्सूते धाता हरिरवति रुद्रः क्षपयते
तिरस्कुर्वन्नेतत्स्वमपि वपुरीशस्तिरयति ।
सदापूर्वः सर्वं तदिदमनुगृह्णाति च शिवः
तवाज्ञामालम्ब्य क्षणचलितयोर्भ्रूलतिकयोः ॥२४॥

*jagatsoote dhaataa harir-avati rudrah kshapayate
tiraskurvann-etat svamapi vapur-eeshas-tirayati;
sadaapoorvah sarvam tadidam-anugrihnaati cha shivah
tava-ajnaam-aalambya kshanachalitayor-bhroolatikayoh.* (24)

jagat: universe; *soote*: creates or brings forth; *dhaataa*: brahma; *hari*: vishnu; *avati*: protects it; *rudrah*: rudra; *kshapayate*: destroys it; *tiraskurvan*: absorbs (them) into himself; *etat*: these deities; *svam api vapuh*: his only body; *eeshah*: isha (maheshwara); *tirayati*: disappears into; *sadaapoorvah shivah*: shiva with the sound sada before, i.e. sadasiva; *sarvam tat idam*: all of them (brahma, visnu, rudra and isha); *anugrihnaati cha*: blesses them (into activity again); *tava*: thy; *ajnaam*: mandate; *aalambya*: depending on; *kshana chalitayoh*: by a single movement; *bhroo latikayoh*: of thy creeper like brows

Translation
Brahma creates the universe, Hari protects it, and Rudra destroys it. Then Isha absorbs these deities (which include the entire universe in involution) into himself, and all of them disappear into Sadashiva. Only a mandate from Thee through a single movement of Thy creeper-like brows confers Thy blessings (to spur them into activity again).

Commentary
Shakti is the benefactor of all, as *prabhava*, or creation, and *pralaya*, or dissolution, are both the activities of Shakti alone. Brahma, Vishnu and Rudra are her servants, who carry out their duties at her behest. This is why the next

mantra says that one need not worship them separately, for by the worship of Shakti they are all worshipped. Brahma presides over rajoguna, Vishnu over sattwa guna, and Rudra over tamoguna. These three gunas are the limbs of Shakti; therefore, their very existence depends on her. This theory shatters the traditional concepts in which the devas: Brahma, Vishnu and Mahesh, are regarded as *sarve sarva*, all in all.

The *nirguna* state of Brahma is *mayatita*, or equipoise of the three qualities or gunas, which can only be accomplished if Shakti allows it. Ishwara tattwa, too, is controlled by maya shakti. Although Sadashiva is supposedly the master of maya, the influence of Shakti is so strong that he, too, succumbs to the process of creation, for her shodashi form which is resplendent with all of her sixteen rays or kalas, is superior even to Sadashiva. In mantra 92, Sadashiva is referred to as the bedspread on which the Mahashakti Tripura Sundari reclines and commands her servants to do their respective tasks. Thus Sadashiva's role is also limited, because he operates at the behest of Shakti.

As the aspirant experiences oneness with Shakti, he becomes aware of the metaphysics of creation, maintenance and dissolution, which is Shakti's domain. She accomplishes these through her three main attendants: Brahma, Vishnu and Rudra, who become absorbed into Isha. All of them disappear into Sadashiva and await the next movement or *spandan* in the field of Shakti, who is reclining on Sadashiva. This verse describes Shakti's role and complete domination over the processes of the creation and dissolution of the universe.

This creation is not without a purpose, even though whatever is created by Shakti is destroyed by her whim. She is protective, concerned and mindful of the creation that she has instigated at all times, and acts efficiently at the appropriate time throughout its three processes of preservation, maintenance and destruction. It is her nod or consent that is required by the three devas for the work she has assigned to them, and although they appear to be independent, that is not the case.

Sadashiva appears to be a superior entity to Rudra, who destroys. Here it is seen that the essence of creation is absorbed by Isha (Maheshwara), who then disappears into Sadashiva, the only principle that remains. In fact, just like Shakti has many shades and roles, Shiva, too, enacts equal and opposite roles along with her.

In fact, when we relate this mantra to inner experience, which is the essence of *Saundarya Lahari*, the dissolution of the deities may also be related to the dissolution theories of the tattwas and chakras into supreme consciousness that are found in Samkhya and other schools of Tantra. For example, earth, water and fire (Brahma, Vishnu and Rudra) dissolve into air (Isha) and then air dissolves into space and mind (Sadashiva). Or it can be said that mooladhara, swadhisthana and manipura dissolve into anahata, and anahata into ajna. And all of them depend on the supreme mandate from sahasrara to descend again and continue their functions.

25. Meditation on Devi being worshipped

त्रयाणां देवानां त्रिगुणजनितानामपि शिवे
भवेत् पूजा पूजा तव चरणयोर्या विरचिता ।
तथा हि त्वत्पादोद्वहनमणिपीठस्य निकटे
स्थिता ह्येते शश्वन्मुकुलितकरोत्तंसमुकुटाः ॥ २५ ॥

trayaanaam devaanaam triguna-janitaanaam-api shive
bhavet pooja pooja tava charana yoryaa virachitaa;
tathaa hi tvatpaadod vahana-mani-peethasya nikate
sthitaa hyete shashvan mukulita-karottamsa-mukutaah. (25)

trayaanaam devaanaam: of the three deities (brahma, vishnu and shiva); *triguna janitaanaam api*: originated from your three gunas; *shive*: o! auspicious one; *bhavet pooja*: becomes the worship; *pooja virachitaa*: worship is done; *tava charana yo*: at thy feet; *yaa*: which; *tathaa hi*: because; *tvat paada ud vahana mani peethasya nikate*: near the diamond foot-stool that bear thy feet; *sthitaa hi*: are always waiting; *ete*: they; *shashvat*: always; *mukulita kara uttamsa mukutaah*: with their joined palms held above their crowned heads

Translation
O Auspicious One, the worship done at Thy feet becomes the worship of the three illumined ones (Brahma, Vishnu and Shiva), who have their origin in Thy three gunas (rajas, sattwa and tamas). (They require no special worship) because they are ever waiting by the side of the diamond foot-stool that bears Thy feet, with their joined palms held above their crowned heads (in salutation to Thee).

Commentary
The worship of Shakti is the worship of the entire creation, since the entire manifestation of beings, animate and inanimate, seen and unseen, are but forms of Shakti. The worship of other deities does not give the benefit of worshipping the totality. However, the worship of Shakti is

indeed a total experience, including even the three deities, Brahma, Vishnu, Shiva, who originate from the three gunas, sattwa, rajas and tamas, of Shakti.

In this mantra Sankara refers once again to the shodashi form of Shakti, which is the most superior of all. He is not describing the *amsha avataras*, or partial manifestations, but Shakti in her total splendour. Her feet rest on a diamond-studded stool beside which the three deities Brahma, Vishnu and Shiva stand with folded hands, forever raised in worship, awaiting her next order.

This mantra is a strong reaffirmation of the entire Shakta darshan in its purest form. According to the Shaktas, Devi is the supreme reality. The transcendental experience is a unified awareness in which Shakti's positive, negative and neutral energies become one current or flow, revealing Shakti as shodashi, the nature of effulgence. Moreover, the Samaya aspect of Shakta tantra is also emphasised here, as this experience takes place within Sankara in the confines of his body. According to tantra, Samaya is the highest experience, where the individual realizes the divinity within himself.

This mantra confers the highest eminence, and it is the samput given by Swami Satyananda for the chanting of *Saundarya Lahari*. *Samput* is the capsule which contains the heart and soul of the worship; all the other mantras complement and crystallize around the samput. This mantra is to be chanted at the beginning and end of all the anusthanas of *Saundarya Lahari* as per Swami Satyananda's tradition.

In this mantra the entire creation is worshipped through the worship of Shakti. This is an appealing idea, because one is often in confusion about which deity to worship in order to receive the ultimate benefit. Here Sankara reiterates once and for all that by the upasana of Shakti, worship is complete, total and unified. Shakti upasana is a superior worship, as she is the source of the three devas, Brahma, Vishnu and Mahesh, who are born of the three gunas, which are her innate qualities.

Pooja, or worship, falls under three categories: sattwic pooja, rajasic pooja and tamasic pooja. Each type results in some benefit to the worshipper; however, the perfect pooja is that which surpasses all these. Sankara clearly defines that as the pooja of Shakti, because she is the composite of all the three gunas, and as the supreme Shakti, she is *trigunatita,* or above the influence of the gunas.

In fact, Sri Vidya has been regarded by the rishis of yore as *atmavidya,* knowledge of the inner self. They clearly understood that the empirical experience, which has to be transcended in order to experience the beauty and bliss of the *antaratman* or inner self, cannot be withdrawn by anyone else except its creator. Shakti spreads herself out into the creation and she alone can withdraw it back to its source. Thus, this difficult task cannot be accomplished without the worship of Shakti, for she creates the notion of time, space and object, in which all jivas are ensnared.

26. Meditation on Shiva-Shakti in maithuna or union

विरिन्चिः पंचत्वं व्रजति हरिराप्नोति विरतिं
विनाशं कीनाशो भजति धनदो याति निधनम् ।
वितन्द्रा माहेन्द्री विततिरपि संमीलति दृशां
महासंहारेऽस्मिन् विहरति सति त्वत्पतिरसौ ॥२६॥

virinchih panchatvam vrajati harir-aapnoti viratim
vinaasham keenaasho bhajati dhanado yaati nidhanam;
vitandraa maahendree vitatirapi sammeelati drishaam
mahaasamhaaresmin viharati sati tvatpatir-asau. (26)

virinchih: brahma; *panchatvam*: elements; *vrajati*: is reduced into; *hari*: vishnu; *aapnoti*: attains; *viratim*: end; *vinaasham*: destruction; *keenaasha*: yama (god of death); *bhajati*: meets with; *dhanada* kubera; *yaati*: meets with; *nidhanam*: destruction, death; *vitandraa*: death; *maahendree vitati rapi*: indra, with his followers; *sammeelati drishaam*: closing his eyes; *mahaasamhaare asmin*: in such a state of dissolution; *viharati*: is sporting; *sati*: o! consort of shiva; *tvatpati*: thy consort, shiva alone; *asau*: this

Translation
Virinchi (Brahma) is reduced into the elements; Hari (Vishnu) meets his end; Kinasha (Yama, the god of death) himself dies; Kubera (the god of wealth) meets with destruction, and Indra with all his followers closes his eyes in the face of death. O Sati! Thy consort Shiva alone is sporting in such a state of dissolution as this.

Commentary
According to tantric philosophy, although Shakti and her consort Shiva are eternal concepts, the creation engineered by Shakti is not. It exists within a time frame known as *yuga*. There are four yugas: Satya yuga, Treta yuga, Dwapara yuga, and Kali yuga. Together these four form one cycle known as a *chatur yuga*, at the end of which there is total dissolution,

or *maha pralaya*. Even the devas such as Brahma, Vishnu, Yama, Indra and Kubera are not spared at the time of this final dissolution.

This mantra points out that at the time of dissolution, when the cause is absorbed back into the source, the only tattwa that remains apart from Shakti, who is both *jada*, inert, and *chetana*, conscious, is Shiva, who is pure chetana. The jada aspect of Shakti is absorbed back into her chetana aspect, and once again she is inseparably united with Shiva from whom she had separated to manifest the creation. Prakriti or Shakti absorbs everything into her womb, and assuming the state of a great slumber, remains united with Purusha or Shiva.

On account of this, the creation remains in *sadakhya tattwa*, seed form, because if that seed were also destroyed, then it would not be possible to initiate another creation after the resting period is over. Every seed has two parts, and so too this seed of the entire manifest as well as unmanifest creation. Even if the seed is eaten by worms, if the two parts from which it will sprout are intact, it shoots forth a stem. The seed of creation is desire or *iccha shakti*. This is the evolute of Devi; she can evolve the creation out of this seed at her own will, when the time is ripe. Until then she is able to contain the seed of desire, by merging the three shaktis: ichcha, jnana and kriya into herself.

Shakti's devotion to Shiva is what ensures his existence, even after the total dissolution, *mahapralaya*. At the time of mahapralaya, Shakti devours all except the pure Shiva tattwa. The entire creation of Brahma is reduced back into the primordial elements of earth, water, fire, air, and ether. Vishnu retires into seed form or an archetype. Kubera and Indra meet with death, but Shakti absorbs Sadashiva into herself and they become inseparable, sporting with each other until the great Tripura Sundari orders another creation. At that time Shakti and Shiva, energy and consciousness, once again separate, whilst still retaining their unity.

The idea presented by Sankara in the previous mantra that worship of Shakti is worship of all the devas is further developed in this mantra. Here he points out that the only eternal tattwa, apart from Shiva, is Shakti, who protects Shiva, as any pure and chaste wife would protect her beloved. Then why should one worship any other apart from her? By taking refuge in her, one will attain eternal protection, safety and security, which no other deva can grant, because they too are ultimately subject to death and destruction.

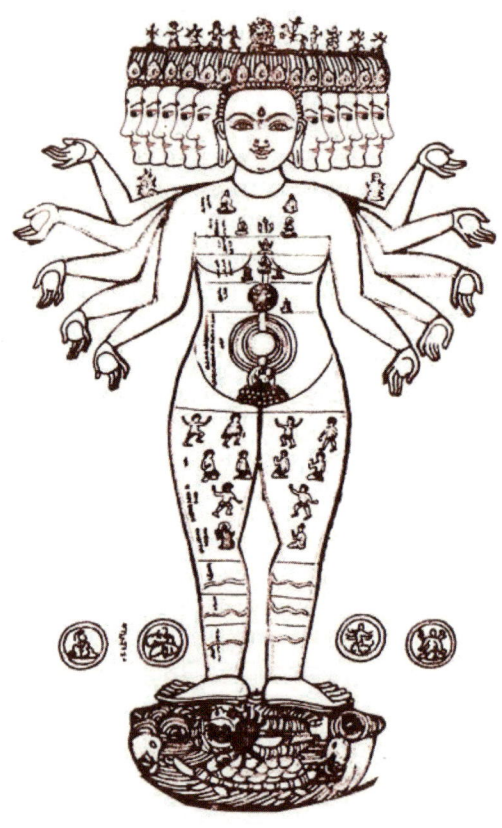

27. Meditation on worship of Devi being done by you

जपो जल्पः शिल्पं सकलमपि मुद्राविरचनं
गतिः प्रादक्षिण्यं भ्रमणमशनाद्याहुतिविधिः ।
प्रणामः संवेशः सुखमखिलमात्मार्पणदृशा
सपर्यापर्यायस्तव भवतु यन्मे विलसितम् ॥२७॥

japo jalpah shilpam sakalamapi mudraa-virachanam
gatih praadakshinyam bhramanam-ashanaady-aahutividhih;
pranaamah samveshah sukham-akhilam-aatmaarpana-drishaa
saparyaa-paryaaya tava bhavatu yanme vilasitam. (27)

japa: utterance of thy mantra; *jalpah*: my prattle; *shilpam sakalam api*: movements of my hands; *mudra virachanam*: hand gestures of thy worship; *gatih*: my walking; *praadakshinyam bhramanam*: circumambulation; *ashan aadi*: my eating and drinking; *aahuti vidhih*: fire sacrifice to thee; *pranaamah*: prostration to thee; *samveshah*: the stretching of my body (in sleep); *sukham*: various offerings made during thy worship; *akhilam*: all (my enjoyments); *aatmaarpana drishaa*: self dedication to thee; *saparyaa paryaaya*: as terms of thy worship; *tava*: thy; *bhavatu*: become; *yat me vilasitam*: all my actions

Translation
May my prattle be the utterance of Thy mantra; my hand movements, the gestures (mudras) of Thy worship; my walking, Thy circumambulation; my eating and drinking, oblations to Thee; the stretching of my limbs, prostration to Thee; all my enjoyments, the various offerings made during Thy worship. Thus may all my actions become acts of self-dedication performed in the worship of Thee.

Commentary
If Shakti is the only tattwa that does not end up in the melting pot at the time of total dissolution, then she should be considered the sole refuge of all beings, animate or

inanimate. At the moment when everything disintegrates and breaks up into the original tattwas, earth returns to earth, water to water, fire to fire, air to air and ether to ether, and then these elements involute further into the tattwas that precede them. Ultimately all that remains is Shakti, the root matrix of creation. Then it is her compassion and mercy alone that can redeem one. Shiva tattwa also remains, but that, too, is revealed only on account of Shakti.

Keeping this in mind, one should consider each and everything in life as a gift from her and feel forever indebted to her. Once this realization dawns, one is bound to remember her with every breath and feel that each and every act that one does, whether talking, eating or sleeping, is performed in worship of her. Samaya tantra offers the most unique concept that this body is a temple, and everything that it does is a worship of divinity. This same concept is highlighted here and it is a most wonderful idea, too. Whatever one speaks, does, thinks, consumes, even the most mundane gesture of stretching the body, can be divinized through this concept. This is pure tantra, because for a tantric each and every act of life is spiritual.

In tantra, the way in which one sits, bathes, combs the hair, decides what dress to wear, what food to eat, which direction to face while eating, sleeping or worshipping, all these are extremely significant. For a tantric no act is mundane or gross; each gesture is meaningful, as all are a part of that great divinity abounding in the universe, which resides within as the cosmic Shakti or kundalini. At the behest of that cosmic energy one moves, thinks, acts, dreams, laughs talks, sings and dances. The tantric practitioner understands that, accepts it and watches this idea unfold many mysteries before him.

Shakti is omnipresent, so naturally everything one does is in worship of her. While speaking, one is doing her japa; when one makes gestures with the hands, they are her mudras; while walking, one circumambulates her; while lying on the bed, one does *sashtanga pranam*, or prostrations, to her. Even while eating, one makes an offering to her, because *jatharagni*, the digestive fire, is also her form. (*Bhagavad Gita*, 15:14) So from this point of view, every act is an *ahuti* or oblation to her.

In reality the act of worship is related to one's feelings. When one begins to feel her presence everywhere, inside and outside, then one becomes connected to that mighty power, no matter what one is doing. To feel that every thought, word and deed is an act of worship of the divinity that is within and all around one is the epitome of life's experiences. This is total surrender to Devi, which results in *ananda*, supreme bliss, and the transformation of one's entire awareness from gross to transcendental.

Although the idea of total surrender may seem appealing and simple, on account of the maya of Shakti, the individual has a lapse of memory and forgets this divine truth which can sublimate his awareness to the greatest heights.

28. Meditation on the exquisite form of Devi oozing nectar

ददाने दीनेभ्यः श्रियमनिशमाशानुसदृशीम्
अमन्दं सौन्दर्यप्रकरमकरन्दं विकिरति ।
तवास्मिन् मन्दारस्तबकसुभगे यातु चरणे
निमज्जन् मज्जीवः करणचरणैः षट्चरणताम् ॥२८॥

*dadaane deenebhyah shriyam-anisham-aashaanusadrisheem
amandam saundarya prakara-makarandam vikirati;
tava-asmin mandaarah tabaka-subhage yaatu charane
nimajjan majjeevah karana-charanaih shat-charanataam.* (28)

dadaane: bestowing; *deenebhyah* to poor devotees; *shriyam*: wealth; *anisham*: always; *aashaanusadrisheem*: desired; *amandam*: abundant; *saundarya prakara makarandam*: honey of beauty; *vikirati*: dripping; *tava*: thy; *asmin*: these; *mandaarah tabaka subhage*: beautiful as a bunch of flowers; *yaatu*: may become; *charane*: on the feet; *nimajjan*: drowned; *majjeevah*: my life; *karana charanaih*: with six feet that are the six sensory organs; *shat charanataam*: six-footed honey bee

Translation
May my life become beautiful as a bunch of flowers on Thy feet, dripping with the honey of splendour, bestowing abundant wealth that is always desired upon Thy poor devotees, with its six sensory organs (including the mind) forever drowned at those feet, like a six-legged honey bee.

Commentary
The feet of Shakti are the point where pure, unadulterated energy leaves her body. They are dripping with the nectar of dazzling brilliance, which liberally blesses her devotee with wealth of all kinds, whether material, spiritual or both, if it should descend. The devotee's worship and desire for her will determine how Devi will bless him. The life one has received is a boon or gift granted by Devi. By her grace one is enjoying this wonderful time here,

indulging in all sorts of things through the medium of the senses and mind.

On account of the fleeting nature of the mind and senses, one chases the objects, events, people and experiences of life with the belief that they will give everything that one yearns for. The *avidya*, or ignorance, in which the mind is rooted blocks the knowledge that these transient things can never grant the wealth and happiness that one is seeking. The *jnani*, or wise person, has realized this and turns to Devi by fixing the senses and mind at her feet, from which he receives material and spiritual wealth in abundance.

In this mantra, the surrender of Sankara is complete. He offers Devi his mind and senses, his very life, and yearns with his heart and soul to forever worship her feet, because as one steeped in *jnana*, or wisdom, he has realized this truth. In fact, total surrender is the highest offering one can make to Shakti. She is not in need of wealth, luxury, comforts and nice things. She has given these in the first place. But she does respond instantaneously to the sincere love, devotion, remembrance and surrender of her devotee, which is pure, untainted and unconditional.

On account of his surrender, Sankara chooses to be a bunch of flowers placed at Devi's feet in worship, as those flowers receive in abundance the nectar dripping from her feet and thus remain always in full blossom. Just as bees swarm around flowers that are fragrant and full of nectar, in the same way, Sankara compares his senses and mind to the bees that swarm around the feet of Devi and remain immersed in her radiance, so that they can absorb the nectar which she is always emitting. That nectar can confer all that the heart desires.

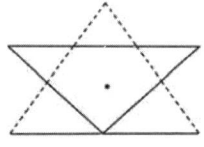

29. Meditation on the Devi bedecked like a bride

सुधामप्यास्वाद्य प्रतिभयजरामृत्युहरिणीं
विपद्यन्ते विश्वे विधिशतमखाद्या दिविषदः ।
करालं यत् क्ष्वेलं कबलितवतः कालकलना
न शंभोस्तन्मूलं जननि तव ताटङ्कमहिमा ॥२९॥

sudhaam-apy-aasvaadya pratibhaya-jaraa-mrityu-hareeneem
vipadyante vishve vidhi-shatamakh-aadyaa divishadah;
karaalam yat-kshvelam kabalitavatah kaalakalanaa
na shambhos-tanmoolam janani tava-taatanka-mahimaa. (29)

sudhaam: nectar; *api aasvaadya*: even after consuming; *pratibhaya jaraa mrityu hareeneem*: that confers immunity from frightful old age and death; *vipadyante*: perish at the time of the cosmic dissolution; *vishve*: all; *vidhi shatamakha aadyaa*: brahma, indra and others; *divishadah*: devas, divine beings; *karaalam*: dreadful; *yat*: if; *kshvelam*: poison; *kabalitavatah*: having consumed; *kaalakalanaa*: is (not) destroyed by time; *na*: not; *shambhoh*: shiva; *tat moolam*: give definition *janani*: mother; *tava*: thy; *taatanka mahimaa*: greatness of (thy) ear ornaments

Translation
Even after consuming the nectar that confers immunity from frightful old age and death, the divine beings like Brahma and Indra perish finally at the time of cosmic dissolution. O Mother, if (Thy consort) Shiva is not destroyed by time, despite having swallowed the dreadful poison, it is because of the greatness of Thy ear ornaments.

Commentary
In this mantra a reference is again made to the supreme consciousness, Shiva, being the only abiding principle apart from Shakti, as everything else undergoes death and dissolution, even those devas who have drunk the nectar of immortality emanating from Shakti. *Taataanka mahimaa*

indicates the abiding nature of Shakti's relationship with Shiva. *Tatanka* means 'ear ornaments', which are an important symbol of a bride.

Shiva does not perish due to his intimate association with Shakti, even though he had consumed the terrible poison that emerged during the *samudra manthan*, churning of the ocean, which could have easily killed him. Shakti's conjugal relationship with Shiva conveys the idea that Shiva and Shakti are essentially a homogeneous tattwa. Just as a husband and wife are considered one unit, in the same way, these two principles of the supreme reality are one and the same.

This mantra also makes an important reference to the healing and rejuvenating capacity of the great energy or Mahashakti. When invoked through worship, she can correct all the imbalances and diseases of the body, which is what Sankara had invoked her for. Practitioners of *Saundarya Lahari* can also attain benefit from this mantra, which removes all ailments, whether they be physical, intellectual or spiritual.

30. Meditation on Devi seated regally amidst her divine attendants

किरीटं वैरिञ्चं परिहर पुरः कैटभभिदः
कठोरे कोटीरे स्खलसि जहि जम्भारिमकुटम् ।
प्रणम्रेष्वेतेषु प्रसभमुपयातस्य भवनं
भवस्याभ्युत्थाने तव परिजनोक्तिर्विजयते ॥३०॥

*kireetam vairincham parihara purah kaitabhabhidah
kathore koteere skhalasi jahi jambhaari-makutam;
pranamreshveteshu prasabham-upayaatasya bhavanam
bhavasya-abhyutthaane tava parijanoktir-vijayate.* (30)

kireetam vairincham: brahma's crown; *parihara*: take care of; *purah*: body; *kaitabhabhidah*: vishnu's; *kathore koteere*: heavy diadem; *skhalasi*: tumbling over; *jahi*: beware of; *jambhaari makutam*: indra's crest; *pranamreshveteshu*: while they (brahma, vishnu and indra) are prostrated before thee; *prasabham*: the unannounced; *upayaatasya bhavanam*: arrival at thy abode; *bhavasya*: of shiva; *abhyutthaane*: springest up; *tava parijanoktih*: thy attendants; *vijayate*: cry out

Translation
Even while Brahma, Vishnu and Indra are prostrated before Thee, still at the unannounced arrival of Shiva at Thy abode, Thou springest up (in such a hurry to receive Him that) Thy attendants (have to caution Thee), crying out, "Take care of the crown of Brahma, avoid tumbling over the heavy diadem of Vishnu, and beware of the crest of Indra."

Commentary
In this mantra a word of caution is given to the aspirant. The goal is union with Shakti so that one may behold her in totality and experience her in union with Shiva. However, prior to that, the aspirant may have many experiences that are enough to shake him off the path. He may get distracted, swerve from the path and become entangled in

something that will create an obstacle in his reaching the goal.

Shakti is always in a hurry to receive Shiva, the supreme consciousness, and does not pay heed to Brahma, Vishnu and Indra, who here signify the siddhis and supernatural powers. Similarly, the aspirant should always be alert to and aware of that highest experience, because it could occur unannounced at any time. If an aspirant idles and plays with the powers that have manifested in him, he will not instantly recognize and pay heed to the arrival of Shiva.

As the kundalini awakens and moves towards union with Shiva in sahasrara, it leaves behind the deities of the lower chakras. Brahma resides in mooladhara, Indra is the lord of prithvi, Vishnu resides in swadhisthana. These lower centres represent darkness or lack of illumination, and there is always a danger of tumbling, falling or knocking down something when moving in the dark. This is precisely the state of kundalini shakti who wishes to reach sahasrara quickly. The attendants who caution her not to bump into the deities, represent the yoginis of all the chakras. In the physical body, Shakti in the form of kundalini is always in a hurry to experience final union with Shiva.

Imagine the scene of the beautiful, captivating enchantress, Shakti, seated regally in her mansion with her female friends at her service, attending to all her needs and forever mindful of her stature and regality. The devas have appeared in many of the preceding mantras as subservient to Devi, the great beauty. Once again they are prostrated before her, yearning for her attention, but she is impatient and forever looking toward the door, as if awaiting someone's arrival. As soon as she perceives the unannounced arrival of Shiva, she springs up from her seat in such a hurry that she is not even aware of the devas who are prostrated before her, awaiting her recognition and approval. In jumping up, she almost knocks off their crown, diadem and crest, and has to be cautioned by her attendants.

This mandala of Devi is very romantic and can easily be visualized by anyone. Shiva is once again singled out by Devi, who makes it absolutely clear to all whom she favours most. The ascent of kundalini also takes place in much the same manner. When kundalini first rouses from her slumber and is poised for ascent, the sadhaka has to create immense pressure in that region to counteract the downward pull due to the effects of gravity. In philosophical terms gravity is equated with *maya*, the illusory world, which accounts for the darkness that enshrouds the kundalini in that region.

As kundalini is in a hurry to move out of darkness and ascend towards the light, it tries to raise its head several times with a hissing sound, ignoring the protocol required for it to break free of its bondage. At that time the yoginis, or partial manifestations of Shakti, such as Dakini, Lakini, Hakini and others, assist the kundalini by assuring her swift and steady progress without creating too much upheaval in the lower chakras by her movement.

31. Meditation on sound emanating from the form of Devi

चतुःषष्ट्या तन्त्रैः सकलमभिसंधाय भुवनं
स्थितस्तत्तत्सिद्धिप्रसभपरतंत्रैः पशुपतिः ।
पुनस्त्वन्निर्बन्धादखिलपुरुषार्थैकघटना-
स्वतंत्रं ते तंत्रं क्षितितलमवातीतरदिदम् ॥३१॥

*chatushashtyaa tantraih sakalam-abhisandhaaya bhuvanam
sthitas-tat-tat-siddhi prasabha-para-tantraih pashupatih;
punas-tvannirbandhaad-akhila-purushaarthaika-ghatanaa
svatantram te tantram kshiti-talam-avaateetarad-idam.* (31)

chatuh shashtyaa tantraih: by sixty-four tantras; *sakalam bhuvanam*: all the worlds; *abhisandhaaya*: revealed to; *sthitah*: remained (satisfied); *tat tat siddhi prasabha para tantraih*: conferring only one or other of various psychic powers and worldly fulfilments; *pashupatih*: pashupati, a form of shiva; *punah*: later; *tvat nirbandhaat*: on thy insistence; *akhila purushaarthaika ghatanaa svatantram*: independent of all others and capable of conferring all the four aspirations of men (dharma, artha, kama and moksha.); *te*: thy; *tantram idam*: this tantra; *kshiti talam*: to the world; *avaateetarat*: revealed

Translation
Pashupati (Shiva) at first remained satisfied after giving to the world the sixty-four tantras (which expound practices), conferring only one or other of the various psychic powers and worldly fulfilments. Later, at Thy insistence, he revealed this, Thy own tantra, to the world, independent of all the others, and capable of conferring the four aspirations of men: artha, kama, dharma and moksha.

Commentary
Although Shakti is the supreme tattwa, Shiva is regarded as the father of tantra. He is the original yogi, who perfected all the states of consciousness and is forever established in the highest state of turiya. At Shakti's behest, Shiva,

the great authority, gives out this knowledge from time to time in the form of a dialogue with Parvati. The most knowledgeable and well-versed Parvati poses a question and Shiva in reply reveals the mysteries that abound in the universe. These dialogues form the *agamas*, which number sixty-four and are regarded as the recorded treatises on tantra.

The subject matter of these sixty-four tantras is varied and ranges from mundane to sublime. At one level they provide knowledge for gaining prowess in worldly affairs and at the other level they provide methods to attain liberation or *moksha*. A study of the agamas shows that there is absolutely no topic or subject which has been excluded in this vast and comprehensive literature.

In this mantra, Shakti gives Shiva the consent to reveal the sixty-fifth tantra. This tantra is hers exclusively and has never been revealed before. The sixty-four agamas reveal the highest transcendental knowledge, so what could possibly be left that Shakti is imploring Shiva to reveal in her most supreme tantra. In fact, the Samaya tantra is considered to be most supreme, even by Sankara.

If one examines the trend of human thought closely, a definite progression is seen in the line of thinking. At first, man wondered where divinity resides: in the skies, on land, in water, or in space. Is that divinity the sun, moon and planets? Is it the thunder, rain or lightning? Is divinity the awesome force of nature? He even worshipped these as God, so that he would not have to suffer on account of their anger or revenge because they had not been worshipped.

Later, when man's awareness became more refined, he personified God and confined him to a place which he believed was his home. Despite this, there were still unresolved issues in his mind, such as by confining God to one place, can it be inferred that God lives only there and nowhere else? Is God male or female or both? Thus many different paths, sects and beliefs arose. Some believed God to be male and others female. Some believed that God was formless and others that he could also assume form.

Each of these beliefs gave rise to certain practices that were peculiar to those beliefs. Gradually, however, man began to realize that divinity existed within him; he was, in fact, divine and his body was a shrine in which God lives. This is the highest realization that man can have, because everything changes once he realizes it. The entire view about himself and about life is transformed.

Thus, this revelation of tantra that Shiva only revealed after receiving the clearance from Shakti is most complete as it fulfils all the needs of man. Shakti could have disclosed this tantra herself as she is the supreme authority. Instead she asks Shiva to do it, thus demonstrating that Shakti fulfils all her tasks through others without revealing herself, except to the most deserving. Shiva explains this tantra to Devi, who needs no explanation as it has emanated from her, so that any deserving listeners nearby may overhear and convey it to others. Ganesha, their son, who also happens to be an expert stenographer, notes it all down and when he is finished conveys it to a rishi or siddha on the earthly plane to pass it on to others.

This traditional form of imparting knowledge has been going on since time immemorial and it will always continue. As the seer of these mantras, Sankara is an important personage in this line of luminaries, as he has handed this tantra down to mankind. This tantra is most supreme because it gives direct cognition or perception of energy and consciousness within the framework of one's own body, which is none other than consciousness.

The sixty-four tantras are related to the sixty-four *shaktipeethas*, where the different parts of Shakti fell. These sixty-four peethas are also associated with the sixty-four yoginis, but they represent the partial awakening of energy, as they are worshipped as a part of Shakti only. *Saundarya Lahari* is the worship of Shakti in the form of Tripura Sundari in her entirety, where each and every portion of her is venerated. Thus this tantra is independent of the sixty four tantras that can only bestow one or another of the *purusharthas*, or human aspirations. *Saundarya Lahari* fulfils all the purusharthas: *dharma, artha, kama* and *moksha*, righteousness, material need, emotional need and liberation, as well as something beyond that, which is absorption into the divine.

Tripura Sundari is the most beautiful form in all the three worlds; she is truly Miss Universe! She is the experience, which lies beyond enlightenment. The sixty-four tantras talk about expansion of mind and liberation of energy, which unites with consciousness. This is the enlightenment that the tantras speak of, but what lies beyond that? *Saundarya Lahari* is most important because it gives a glimpse of what lies ahead. This is the vision of Tripura Sundari in maithuna, or deep spiritual union with Shiva, where she is saturated from head to toe with nectar and ambrosia, radiating beauty and bliss, and appears as the reigning and most supreme tattwa.

Many texts elucidate not sixty-four but fifty-one and even 108 shaktipeethas. Here, in the following chart, we are concerned with the sixty-four siddhapeethas or awakened centres of Shakti worship.

Sixty-four Shaktipeethas

	Place	Body Part	Name of Shakti	Name of Shiva
1	Puri	Crown (kirita)	Vimala/Bhuvaneshi	Samvarta
2	Vrindavana	Hair	Uma	Bhutesha
3	Karveera	Third eye (trinetra)	Mahishmardini	Krodheesha
4	Sri Parvata	Right temple	Srisundari	Sundarananda
5	Varanasi	Ear ornament (karnamani)	Vishalakshi	Kaal Bhairava
6	Godavari Tata	Left cheek	Vishweshi/Rukmini/ Vishwa Matrika	Dandapani/ Vatspani
7	Shuchi	Upper teeth	Narayani	Sanhara/Sankura
8	Panchasagara	Lower teeth	Varahi	Maharudra
9	Jwalamukhi	Tongue	Siddhida Ambika	Unmatta
10	Bhairav Parvata	Upper lip	Avanti	Lambakarna
11	Attahaasa	Lower lip	Fullara Devi	Vishwesha
12	Jansthaana	Chin	Brahmari	Vikrutaksha
13	Kashmir	Throat	Mahamaya	Trisandhyeshwara
14	Nandipura	Necklace	Nandini	Nandikeshwara
15	Srishaila	Neck	Sri Bhramaramba Devi/Mahalakshmi	Mallikarjuna/ Sanvarananda/ Ishvarananda
16	Nalhati	Intestine	Kalika	Yogeesha
17	Mithila	Left shoulder	Uma/Mahadevi	Mahodara
18	Ratnavali	Right shoulder	Kumari	Shiva
19	Prabhaasa	Stomach	Chandrabhaaga	Vakratunda
20	Jalandhara	Left breast	Tripuramalini	Bhishana
21	Ramgiri	Right breast	Shivani	Chanda
22	Baidyanatha	Heart	Jayadurga	Baidyanatha
23	Vaktreshwara	Mind	Mahishmardini	Vaktranatha
24	Kanyakashrama	Back	Sharvani	Nimisha
25	Bahula	Left hand	Bahula	Bhiruka
26	Ujjaini	Elbow	Mangalya Chandrika	Kapilambara
27	Manivedika	Both wrists	Gayatri	Sarvananda
28	Prayaga	Fingers of hand	Lalita Devi	Bhava
29	Utkala	Navel	Vimla	Jagata
30	Kanchi	Skeleton	Devagarbha	Ruru
31	Kaal Madhava	Left buttock	Kali	Asitaanga
32	Shona	Right buttock	Narmada/Shonakshi	Bhadrasena
33	Kamgiri	Yoni	Kamakhya	Umananda

34	Hastinapura	Left thigh	Jayanti	Kramdeeshwari
35	Magadha	Right thigh	Sarvanandakari	Vyomkesha
36	Trisrota	Left foot	Bhramari	Ishwara
37	Tripura	Right foot	Tripura Sundari	Tripuresha
38	Vibhaasha	Left ankle	Kapalini/Bhimroopa	Sarvananda Kapali
39	Kurukshetra	Right ankle	Savitri	Sthanu
40	Yugandya	Right foot – big toe	Bhootadhatri	Ksheerkantaka
41	Viraata	Right foot – toes	Ambika	Amrita
42	Kalipeetha	Rest of the fingers	Kalika	Nakulesha
43	Manasa (Tibet)	Right palm	Dakshayani	Amara
44	Sri Lanka	Ankle	Indrakshi	Rakshaseshwara
45	Gandaki (Nepal)	Right cheek	Gandaki	Chakrapani
46	Nepal	Both knees	Mahamaya	Kapala
47	Hingula (Karachi)	Top of the head (brahmarandhra)	Bhairavi	Bheemlochana
48	Sugandha (Bangladesh)	Nose	Sunanda	Tryambaka
49	Kartoyatata	Left temple	Aparna	Vamana
50	Chattal (Bangladesh)	Right hand	Bhavani	Chandrashekhara
51	Yashora (Bangladesh)	Left palm	Yashoreshwari	Chandra
52	Karnataka	Both ears	Jaya Durga	Abheeru
53	Sarvashaila	Left temple	Shakini	Vatsanabha
54	Munger	Eyes	Chandi	Kaalabhairava
55	Himadri Hill	Not Available	Bhima	NA
56	Kishkinda Hills	NA	Tara	NA
57	Amarkantak	NA	Chandika	NA
58	Vindhyachal	NA	Vindhyavasini	NA
59	Chitrakut	NA	Sita	NA
60	Mathura	NA	Devaki	NA
61	Dwarika	NA	Rukhmini	NA
62	Gaya	NA	Mangala	NA
63	Pushkar	NA	Puruhuta	NA
64	Kanyakubja	NA	Gauri	NA

32. Meditation on Devi as mantra, in the form of Sri Yantra in the heart centre

शिवः शक्तिः कामः क्षितिरथ रविः शीतकिरण
स्मरो हंसः शक्रस्तदनु च परामारहरयः ।
अमी ह्ल्लेखाभिस्तिसृभिरवसानेषु घटिता
भजन्ते वर्णास्ते तव जननि नामावयवताम् ॥३२॥

shivah shaktih kaamah-kshitir-atha ravih sheeta-kirana
smaro hamsah shakras-tadanu cha paraa-maara-harayah;
amee hrillekhaabhis-tisribhir-avasaaneshu-ghatitaa
bhajante varnaas-te tava janani naamaa-vayavataam. (32)

shivah: 'ka'; *shaktih*: 'ee'; *kaamah*: 'ai'; *kshitih*: and earth – 'la'; *atha*: then; *ravih*: sun – 'ha'; *sheeta kirana*: moon – 'sa'; *smara*: kamadeva – 'ka'; *hamsah*: swan – 'la'; *shakrah tadanu cha*: and then; *paraa*: brahma – 'sa'; *maara*: kamadeva – 'ka'; *harayah*: vishnu – 'la'; *amee*: these (twelve syllables); *hrillekhaabhih tisribhih*: with there 'hrim' syllables; *avasaaneshu*: at the end; *ghatitaa*: added; *bhajante*: form; *varnaah*: mantra; *te*: thy; *tava*: thy; *janani*: oh! mother; *naama avayavataam*: name

Translation

O Mother! (the syllables) *Ka, Ee, Ai* and *La* indicated by Shiva, Shakti, Kama and Earth; *Ha, Sa, Ka* and *La* denoted by Ravi (sun), Sheetakirana (moon), Smara (Kamadeva) and Hamsa (swan); and then *Sa, Ka* and *La* denoted by Para (Brahma), Mara (Kamadeva) and Hari (Vishnu), form the mantra of Thy name when joined with the syllable *Hreem* at the end of each of the three groups.

Commentary

The linear dimension of that supreme Shakti in union with Shiva is Sri Yantra, which Sankara has already revealed in mantra 11. Here, the sound vibrations are given which induce that sublime experience, where energy is seen in union with consciousness. At the same time she is radiating her kalas towards creation, saturating it with her nectar. The beauty of creation is a testimony to this: the rivers, oceans, skies, mountains, trees, flora, fauna, animals and human life bear silent testimony to the fact that the creator of such beauty could be nothing less than beauty personified.

According to the tantric as well as vedic traditions, different deities are distinguished by particular syllables, such as *Ha, Sa, Ka, La Aim, Hreem, Kleem* and *Shreem*. These deities are none other than the energy residing in the sound syllables, known as *matrika* in tantra. The word Devi has often been translated as Goddess. This has caused a lot of confusion in the mind of the reader, because it alludes to a person sitting somewhere in the stratosphere, guiding our destiny. In fact, Devi means effulgence, a point of illumination, or *prakasha* that exists within all beings. This effulgence is also present in sound, as the energy residing in the mantra lends *tejas*, or brilliance, to the mantra.

This effulgent sound evokes an experience of illumination within, that is known as matrika and can best be described as the creative energy in sound. Matrika is transcendental sound and, therefore, it still has the quality of pure, unadulterated energy, containing *prakasha*, illumination and *vimarsha*, awareness. Thus matrika is regarded as the source of all *vidya*, or knowledge, and this is why it is given utmost importance in the field of mantra sadhana. Matrika assumes the form of *vedana*, or inward feeling that results in *ekagrata*, one-pointedness, through mantra. This vedana is full of the thrill of Shakti and provides a strong foundation for the experience of illumination or realization of the deity of the mantra.

In this mantra, Sankara gives the panchadasakshari mantra of Sri Vidya, which is made up of three sets of syllables: *Ka, Ee, Ai, La, Hreem*; *Ha, Sa, Ka, La, Hreem*; and *Sa, Ka, La, Hreem*. Each of these matrikas, or sound syllables represent a particular deity or luminary, such as: Shiva – *Ka*, Shakti – *Ee*, Kama – *Ai*, and Vishnu – *La*. The three sets of devatas each have to fix the mantra Hreem at the end.

The first four syllables of the panchadasakshari are related to Agni, or fire, which corresponds to the *kriya shakti* of Tripura Sundari, conferring the power to do all. In relation to the individual awareness, it correlates to *jagrat*, the waking state of consciousness, which has its cosmic counterpart, known as *Vishwa* or Vaishwanara. The guna prevailing at this level is tamas. In the worship of Sri Yantra, this first part of the panchadasakshari mantra with Hreem added at the end is known as *Vaagbhav kut*. It is the worship of Tripura Sundari's body from the neck up to the top of the head. This mantra confers immense power in learning, speech and wisdom.

The second five letters of the panchadasakshari are related to Surya, the sun, and correspond to the *iccha shakti* of Tripura Sundari, which confers the willpower to fulfil all that one desires. In relation to the individual awareness, it correlates to *swapna*, the dream state of consciousness, which has its cosmic counterpart, *Tejas*. The guna prevailing at this level is rajas. In the worship of Sri Yantra, this second part of the mantra with Hreem added at the end is known as *Kamakala kut*, which is the worship of Tripura Sundari's body from the neck down to the waist. This mantra confers immense power to fulfil all desires. In between these two locations of Vaagbhav kut and Kamakala kut is the rudra granthi, which is governed by the mantra Hreem.

The third three letters of the panchadasakshari are related to Soma, the moon, which corresponds to the *jnana shakti* of Tripura Sundari, which confers the power to know all. In relation to the individual awareness, it correlates to *sushupti*, the dreamless sleep state of consciousness, which has its cosmic counterpart in *Prajna*. The guna prevailing at this level is sattwa. In the worship of Sri Yantra, this third part of the mantra with Hreem added at the end is known as *Shakti kut*, which is the worship of Tripura Sundari's body below the waist. This confers immense power to fulfil all goals in life, whether they be material or spiritual. In-between these two locations of Kamakala kut and Shakti kut is the vishnu granthi, governed by the mantra Hreem.

This panchadasakshari mantra becomes efficacious and most potent when the sixteenth syllable, which is heard from the guru, is added, making it *shodashakshari*, the sixteen-syllabled mantra that invokes the Mahashakti Tripura Sundari beyond sahasrara, the energy residing in the Sri Chakra. The sixteenth letter corresponds to the fourth state of awareness, which is not individual, but universal in nature. It is also known as *chandrakala*, which corresponds to turiya and the experience beyond turiya, where the influence of the gunas does not prevail.

This confers the highest power and grants the four attainments of bhakti: sayujya, samipya, salokya and sarooupya. The devotee becomes the Devi Tripura Sundari. This shodashakshari mantra is meditated on in sahasrara, where the Sri Yantra is visualized to reveal the effulgent form of Tripura Sundari that reigns supreme beyond sahasrara. In between Shakti kut and this experience, the release of the third and final knot of rudra granthi takes place, enabling the awareness to ascend to the higher centres above sahasrara.

The sixteenth syllable conferred by the guru makes the mantra shodashi or complete, with all the sixteen rays emanating from Mahashakti Tripura Sundari. This shodashi mantra can grant the highest blessings of Devi and is only given to the qualified disciple. The qualification here is determined by where the awareness of the disciple abides. As sadhana is practised, the sadhaka's awareness may get stuck or stagnate at a certain point on account of his karmas.

At times he may be overwhelmed by passion, greed, fear, sorrow, disappointment, revenge, or even name and fame, and his awareness remains at that level if he is not cautious. So the sixteenth syllable is given or not given according to the level of awareness of the disciple. If his awareness is caught up in the lower spheres, then he has to refine it further. But if his awareness easily transcends all experiences, then he can be considered as a worthy recipient for the shodashi mantra.

The point used for meditation on the symbol, whether it be anahata, ajna or sahasrara, is most important. That is the point where one's actual journey will start. If the practitioner starts at the wrong point, the results will not be forthcoming. Thus the disciple's qualification is determined according to the point where his awareness is most drawn to. The worship of Sri Chakra, which involves superimposition of the mantra, yantra and mandala on one's body, mind and consciousness, is the keynote of Samaya tantra. In this mantra, Sankara experiences the mantra, yantra and mandala of Sri Chakra in the heart centre, or anahata chakra.

33. Meditation on Devi as mantra, in the form of Sri Yantra at the eyebrow centre

स्मरं योनिं लक्ष्मीं त्रितयमिदमाद्ये तव मनो-
निधायैके नित्ये निरवधिमहाभोगरसिकाः ।
जपन्ति त्वां चिन्तामणिगुणनिबद्धाक्षवलयाः
शिवाग्नौ जुह्वन्तः सुरभिघृतधाराहुतिशतैः ॥ ३३ ॥

*smaram yonim lakshmeem tritayam-idam-aadye tava mano
nidhaaya-ike nitye niravadhi-mahaa-bhoga-rasikaah;
japanti tvaam chintaamani-guna-nibaddha-akshavalayaah
shivaagnau juhvantah surabhi-ghrita-dhaara-ahuti-shataih.* (33)

smaram: syllable of kamaraja; *yonim*: syllable of bhuvaneshwari; *lakshmeem*: syllable of lakshmi; *tritayam idam*: these three syllables; *aadye*: in the beginning; *tava*: thy; *mano*: panchadasakshari mantra (mentioned in mantra 32); *nidhaaya*: adding; *eke*: some; *nitye*: oh! eternal being; *niravadhi mahaa bhoga rasikaah*: connoisseurs of the highest enjoyment; *japanti*: do japa; *tvaam*: thee; *chintaamani guna nibaddha akshavalayaah*: adorned with a rosary of chintamani gems; *shivaagnau*: in the fire of shiva; *juhvantah*: worship thee; *surabhi ghrita dhaaraa ahuti shataih*: with oblations of countless streams of ghee from the celestial cow

Translation

O Eternal One! Some connoisseurs of the highest enjoyment do japa of Thee adorned with the rosary of chintamani gems, adding the syllables of Kamaraja (*Kleem*), Bhuvaneshwari (*Hreem*) and Sri (*Shreem*) at the beginning of Thy mantra. (Thus do they) worship Thee with the oblations of countless streams of ghee from Surabhi (the celestial cow) in the purified fire of Shiva (i.e. Shakti established as the trikona in the anahata chakra).

Commentary

Worship of Shakti grants both sensorial pleasures and liberation from the senses. Mantras 32 and 33 transmit two distinct systems of Shakti vidya, namely *haadi* and *kaadi vidya*. Mantra 32 gives the mantras of haadi and mantra 33 the mantras of kaadi. *Tripuropanishad* also gives a description of the sequence of haadi and kaadi vidya, although it differs from that of *Saundarya Lahari*. Here, haadi vidya precedes kaadi vidya, whereas in *Tripuropanishad*, kaadi is the moola vidya from which the haadi mantra emerges.

The kulapatha is endowed with chakras, vortexes of pranic energy which is distributed to all parts of the body and brain. Each chakra is directly connected to the brain and, although all the centres are connected by the kulapatha, they operate independently until the kundalini ascends. At that time the flow of prana becomes unified and begins to flow in one upward direction. This unified flow of energy completely overrides the voluntary nervous system and the autonomic nervous system takes over these functions. Loss of hunger, sleeplessness, and lack of interest in daily activities may be experienced, but that depends entirely on the condition of the autonomic nervous system. Yogic asanas and pranayama help to strengthen the nervous system and keep it balanced.

In different traditions the centre for starting the awakening of energy differs. Some start from manipura and others from mooladhara, as in the case of Kaula marga. In fact, the entire world is following the Kaula path, as the majority of people are focused at mooladhara. Psychologically, mooladhara relates to survival and security. swadhisthana to desire and attachment, and manipura to accomplishment and self-assertion. These are the levels at which the whole world operates and is focused. However, those who have transcended these levels to some degree by dint of their past efforts, qualify for meditation on the higher centres of the heart and beyond. Sri Vidya or Sri

Chakra has many traditions, but the two main ones that have emerged are haadi vidya, which advocates the heart centre or hridayapeetha, and kaadi vidya, which advocates the eyebrow centre, in the region of the third eye, or ajnapeetha.

The fifteenth letter added to the mantra of haadi vidya is *Hreem*, the akshara of Lakshmi, and the fifteenth letter added to the mantra of kaadi vidya is *Kleem*, the akshara for Kali. The heart centre is the point where the kundalini energy, travelling up from mooladhara, first unites with consciousness. After this they travel upwards together to vishuddhi, where the final purification takes place before they enter the uncharted space beyond ajna. The mind transcends its boundary of time, space and object at the eyebrow centre and enters the unified field of quantum physics. From there the ascent to bindu and sahasrara becomes a close reality.

The sadhaka may perform Sri Vidya upasana according to haadi or kaadi vidya, but the final akshara known as shodashi, the sixteenth, is given by the guru directly to the disciple. Only then does the mantra become complete, allowing the awareness to enter the domain of sahasrara. Thus, the panchadasakshari mantra of haadi vidya with the mantra *Hreem* at the end is practised in anahata chakra. The panchadasakshari mantra of kaadi vidya with the mantra *Kleem* at the end is practised in ajna chakra, and the shodashi mantra of Sri Vidya added to either of these two traditions qualifies its practitioner to enter the meditation at sahasrara chakra.

The awakening of kundalini takes place through mantra japa, which results in the knowledge of the atma, or self. This is why mantra is considered as devata. The chanting of mantra develops the awareness and the aspirant attains accomplishment in mantra yoga, raja yoga, laya yoga and hatha yoga. But the awakening of kundalini is the greatest yoga. *Niravadhimahaabhogarasikaah*, which alludes to one who is a connoisseur of the highest enjoyment, is a person who is well established in the experience of kundalini awakening, which confers the highest bliss or enjoyment. *Chintaamanigunanibaddha* gives an indication of the highest experience of Shakti as pure nada, where the garland of letters *akshavalayaah*, from *Aa* to *Ksa*, are strung around her neck like a necklace of chintamani gems.

Smaram yonim lakshmeem at one level indicates the bija mantras of Shakti: *Kleem, Hreem* and *Shreem*, which are extremely efficient in generating the kundalini experience. These three words have a double meaning, as do many phrases in this highly esoteric tantric hymn. When these three words are associated with *shivaagnau juhvantah surabhighritadhaaraahutishataih*, they take on a deeper meaning. Sankara is speaking of the highest worship, or *yajna*, where countless streams of mantras are poured, like Surabhi's ghee into the fire of consciousness *(Shivalingam)* with full remembrance of the fire of energy *(Shaktiyoni)*. This is the *maithuna*, total union, of Shiva and Shakti, consciousness and energy, that confers the highest experience. Just as Surabhi, the celestial cow is the granter of all desires, so too this supreme worship grants all the desires of the practitioner.

This mantra gives the panchdashakshari, or fifteen syllable mantra for the worship of Tripura Sundari, according to kaadi vidya, for which the centre is ajna chakra. However, it also talks about oblations into the fire of consciousness, which give birth to the highest experience, the vision of Tripura Sundari, the supreme shakti. A similar concept is also found in *Lalita Sahasranam*, the 1,008 names of Devi, an important text of Shakti worship. *Chidagni kunda sambhootaa devakarya samudhyata* means born out of the fire of consciousness to fulfil the divine mandate. The following mantra elucidates the result of this worship.

srimaata shrimahaaraagni shrimatsimhaasaneeshwari
chidagni kunda sambhootaa devakarya samudhyata

(Lalita Sahasranam v.1)

34. Meditation on Shiva-Shakti in maithuna

शरीरं त्वं शंभो शशिमिहिरवक्षोरुहयुगं
तवात्मानं मन्ये भगवति नवात्मानमनघम् ।
अतः शेषः शेषीत्ययमुभयसाधारणतया
स्थितः संबंधो वां समरसपरानन्दपरयोः ॥ ३४ ॥

shareeram tvam shambho shashi-mihira-vakshoruha-yugam
tava-atmaanam manye bhagavati navaatmaanam-anagham;
atah sheshah shesheety-ayam-ubhaya-saadhaaranatayaa
sthitah sambandho vaam samarasa-paraanandaparayoh. (34)

shareeram: body; *tvam*: thy; *shambho*: shambhu's; *shashi mihira vakshoruha yugam*: with the sun and moon as breasts; *tava aatmaanam*: thy atma; *manye*: I realize; *bhagavati*: oh! bhagavati; *navaatmaanam*: nine manifestations; *anagham*: pure; *atah*: hence; *sheshah shesha iti*: of principal and accessory; *ayam sambandha*: this relationship; *ubhaya saadhaaranatayaa*: in common; *sthitah*: exists; *vaam*: among you; *samarasa paraanandaparayoh*: equipoised as transcendent bliss and consciousness

Translation
O Bhagavati! I realize Thy body as Shambhu's with the sun and the moon as Thy two breasts. This relationship exists in common between you. Thy pure atma, having nine principal and accessory manifestations (is thus the atma of the entire universe, which is none other than Shiva). Hence Thou art equipoised as transcendent bliss and consciousness.

Commentary
According to the agamas, Shakti in her purest form before mingling with matter has nine manifestations, which are the atma of the universe, as they percolate into each and every form of creation. These nine manifestations are: i) *matrika*, the energy residing in sound, ii) *kula*, lineage, iii) *nama*, form, iv) *jnana*, knowledge, v) *chitta*, individual

consciousness, vi) *nada*, the varying frequencies of sound, vii) *bindu*, nucleus, viii) *kaala*, time, and ix) *jiva* or *atman*, the self who enjoys.

Similarly, Devi is also characterized by the nine triangles of Sri Yantra. The four downward triangles represent her as: i) *Vami*, the one on the left side of the body, ii) *Jyestha*, the most supreme, iii) *Raudri*, the awakened one, and iv) *Ambika*, the mother of all. The five upward pointing triangles represent her as: i) *Iccha*, desire; ii) *Kriya*, action; iii) *Jnana*, knowledge; iv) *Shanta*, peaceful; and v) *Para*, supreme and transcendental.

The characteristics of Shambhu are identical. Thus, they are in equilibrium as transcendental bliss and consciousness. Since Shiva and Shakti are equal at all levels, they are respectively known as Samaya and Samayaa. *Samarasaparaanandaparayohoh* defines them as evenly balanced in power and bliss. Their equality is fivefold: i) they are equal in action, *anusthana samaya*; ii) they have equality in position, *adhisthana samaya*; iii) they are equal in station, *avasthana samaya*; iv) they are equal in name, *nama samaya*, and v) they have equality in form, *roopa samaya*.

The indications of this equal relationship between Bhagavati Tripura Sundari, the supreme cosmic energy, and Shambhu, the supreme cosmic consciousness, are that the *spandan*, or vibration, of both is at the same frequency and both emit the sixteen shodashi kalas. Just as Shakti has *navatman*, or nine expressions which manifest in the universe, Shiva also has nine expressions, and they are intertwined with one another, like the two sides of a coin. The entire creation inherits their nine expressions, as they are the source or original atman.

In the Vedas and Puranas, the cosmic Purusha is described as having the sun and moon as his two eyes; here the sun and moon are depicted as the two breasts of the cosmic Prakriti. As Purusha is the witness, the two eyes signify that he is the *drashta*. As Paraprakriti is the creator of the universe, the breasts are emphasized, signifying that the sun as prana and the moon as soma nourish the entire universe. Thus Purusha and Prakriti together are regarded as the mother and father of creation.

Although the meditation in this mantra is on Devi, the supreme Shakti, Shiva is included because Devi is conceived as the body of Shiva. Just as a cup becomes the support for milk, in the same way, Shakti is the support for Shiva. She is his body and the two cannot be separated. In the meditation on Devi, the sun and moon are treated as eyes and ears in the worship of vaagbhav kut, the portion from head to neck, and as breasts in the worship of kamakala kut, the portion from neck to waist.

The highest experience, according to Samaya tantra, is when Shakti is beheld in her purest form, which is none other than the radiant and effulgent consciousness, or Shiva. *Shariram tvam shambho* signifies that the experience Sankara is having supersedes sahasrara, where Shiva and Shakti amalgamate into one body and no longer appear separate. The phrase *samarasaparaanandaparayoh* further establishes that they are one and at par with each other. The path of Shakti is the experience of ananda through the awakening of kundalini, and the path of Shiva is the awakening of jnana through *dhyana* or meditation. Both are in fact one and the same.

The panchadasakshari mantra and the oblation of fire in the sacrificial pit of Shakti's yoni is followed by the *maithuna*, total union, of the supreme tattwas, Shiva and Shakti, or consciousness and energy, as depicted in the previous two mantras. Now Sankara experiences the fullness of shodashi, the sixteen kalas of Shiva and Shakti that shine from the region above sahasrara, and Shakti has made all this possible.

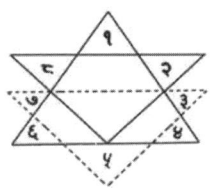

35. Meditation on the nirakara Shakti

मनस्त्वं व्योम त्वं मरुदसि मरुत्सारथिरसि
त्वमापस्त्वं भूमिस्त्वयि परिणतायां न हि परम् ।
त्वमेव स्वात्मानं परिणमयितुं विश्ववपुषा
चिदानन्दाकारं हरमहिषि भावेन बिभृषे ॥३५॥

manas-tvam vyoma tvam marudasi marutsaarathirasi
tvamaapas-tvam bhoomi tvayi parinataayaam na hi param;
tvameva svaatmaanam parinamayitum vishvavapushaa
chidaanandaakaaram haramahishi bhaavena bibhrishe. (35)

manah: mind; *tvam*: thou art; *vyoma*: ether; *tvam*: thou; *marut asi*: thou art air; *marutsaarathi asi*: thou art fire; *tvam aapah*: thou art also water; *tvam bhoomih*: thou art earth too; *tvayi parinataayaam na hi param*: there is nothing beyond what is not included in thee; *tvam eva*: thou; *svaatmaanam*: thy form; *parinamayitum*: transform thy self; *vishva vapushaa*: into the form of the universe; *chidaananda aakaaram*: this form of consciousness and bliss; *haramahishi bhaavena*: assumest the form of consort of shiva; *bibhrishe*: rules

Translation
O Consort of Shiva! Thou art mind; Thou art ether; Thou art air; Thou art fire, water and earth too. When Thou hast transformed Thyself into the form of the universe in this way, there is nothing beyond what is not included in Thee. This form of Consciousness and Bliss that Thou assumest rules in the form of Shiva's consort.

Commentary
All upasana is done for Shakti, for it is she who transforms herself into the universe. Here the term *parinamayitu* indicates that Shakti is the cause who continues to exist in the effect. The evolution of Shakti, or cosmic energy, into the universe is described here, starting with *manas tvam*, 'Thou art mind', right up to *tvam bhumi*, 'Thou art

the earth tattwa'. This transformation into the various elements is a process that she initiates herself, without the help of any outside agency. Within her are all the qualities required for the transformation of the subtlest energy into the densest matter, while still retaining the element of consciousness.

Consciousness is present in all the manifestations of Shakti. There is consciousness even in stone, and this accounts for the worship of stone images which has been prevalent from ancient times. Trees also have consciousness and have been worshipped down through the ages. Similarly, rivers and mountains, flora and fauna, sun and moon and stars also have consciousness.

This transformation of Shakti starts as a mere throb or pulsation, like a heartbeat, and ends up in the universe. During the course of evolution, Shakti manifests as the universal mind, or *hiranyagarbha*, which means 'golden womb'. She also manifests as the individual mind, which is a part of the universal mind in which it is stored. This golden womb contains the seed of all the individual minds of the universe. Whatever is stored in the mind of every individual is also there.

There are two aspects of mind, higher and lower. The lower mind operates through the senses, and the higher mind through the self or atman. Shakti is present in both, but the quantity and quality of her presence differs greatly. When one realizes that Shakti pervades the entire mind and body, which is composed of the elements: ether, air, fire, water and earth, one wonders at her all-pervasiveness. She is present in all forms and objects; wherever one looks her divine presence is there. She has assumed all these forms to help each being in the journey to self-realization.

The matter into which she has evolved is also in a process of its own individual evolution. The mind is evolving all the time, and so too are the emotions. Any further evolution in the physical structure does not seem likely, apart from the brain perhaps becoming subatomic as more and more people awaken the kundalini. In this process the dormant centres of the brain are illumined and awakened, so the structure of the brain is bound to alter. There may even be a complete change or reversal in the flow of energy.

The basic elements or *tattwas* are always in a state of evolution, because Shakti also transforms her *chetana*, conscious, aspect along with her energy, and injects it into the creation. The entire creation, which includes every sentient and insentient being, is in a constant state of evolution because of consciousness. If consciousness were removed, everything would decay and die. The form or mandala of Devi is meditated upon for the elevation of consciousness.

In order to worship, one needs a manifest form, and Shakti is manifestation. For the sake of evolution, she has assumed the role of consort of Shiva in the form of bliss and consciousness. She is the supreme Tripura Sundari, who is beyond maya and can grant *aparokshanubhuti*, or direct cognition of herself. She can create anything out of her own will, as the power of creation is inherent in her, just as the power to think is inherent in each individual. Did anyone teach man how to think? No, he started thinking on his own.

According to the classical interpretation of her transformation into the microcosm, Shakti assumes the roles of *vishwa*, *tejas* and *prajna*, and in the macrocosm of *virat*, *hiranyagarbha* and *ishwara*, the knower of all. The seven *lokas* or planes of existence: *bhuh, bhuvar, svah, mahah, janah, tapah* and *satya*, are her expressions. The five tattwas and tanmatras are her forms. Separated from Shiva, she transforms into these. In this mantra Shakti's evolution from *chidananda*, the blissful consciousness, right down to *annamaya kosha*, the material body, is defined. The tattwas exist in the annamaya kosha as well as in the *pranamaya kosha*, energy body, *manomaya kosha*, mental body and *vijnanamaya kosha*, psychic body.

Once again, Sankara acknowledges that Shakti in her purest form as Tripura Sundari is above the state of Shiva, but in order to create and rule creation, she becomes Shiva's consort and thus assumes the state of consciousness and bliss, or chidananda. After establishing Shakti's total union with Shiva, Sankara clarifies why she entered this state of union. Sankara experiences and acknowledges the totality of Shakti's presence, right down to the mahabhutas, or physical elements that constitute all matter.

36. Meditation on Shiva-Shakti at ajna

तवाज्ञाचक्रस्थं तपनशशिकोटिद्युतिधरं
परं शंभुं वन्दे परिमिलितपार्श्वं परचिता ।
यमाराध्यन् भक्त्या रविशशिशुचीनामविषये
निरालोके लोके निवसति हि भालोकभवने ॥ ६३ ॥

*tava-agyaa-chakrastham tapana-shashi-koti-dyutidharam
param shambhum vande parimilita-paarshvam-parachitaa;
yam-aaraadhyan bhaktyaa ravi-shashi-shucheenaam-avishaye
niraalokeloke nivasati hi bhaloka-bhavane.* (36)

tava: thy; *agyaa chakrastham*: residing in ajna chakra; *tapana shashi koti dyutidharam*: resplendent as millions of suns and moons together; *param shambhum*: the supreme shambhu; *vande*: I salute; *parimilita paarshvam*: whose left side is integrated; *parachitaa*: with the supreme consciousness; *yam*: whom; *aaraadhyan bhaktyaa*: adores with devotion (the devotee); *ravi shashi shucheenaam*: of sun, moon and fire; *avishaye*: out of reach; *niraaloke*: which is beyond the grasp; *aloke*: of the world; *nivasati*: lives; *hi*: that; *bhaloka bhavane*: effulgent plane

Translation
I salute the supreme Shambhu, residing in Thy ajna chakra, resplendent as millions of suns and moons together, whose left side is integrated with the supreme consciousness (Thyself), who adores Thee with devotion, and lives in that effulgent mansion (where Thou reside), which is outside the reach of sun, moon and fire, and beyond the grasp of the world.

Commentary
This mantra and also the next five comprise meditations on Shiva-Shakti in *maithuna*, or total union, at the different chakras. This is evident as now the invocations of Sankara pay obeisance to both Shiva and Shakti, who have

amalgamated into each other and become a unified field of the highest potential. So, everything that they come into contact with during this great descent of divine consciousness is totally transformed and rejuvenated. It is through this descent that the actual healing of the entire molecular structure takes place.

The kundalini has already ascended to sahasrara and the union between Shiva and Shakti has taken place; they have even enjoyed their honeymoon. Shakti has also revealed her highest form to Sankara, where she is seen radiating her purest energy in reverberation with Shiva. Now, just as a young bride returns to her home after her first conjugal bliss, accompanied by her bridegroom, Shakti too is returning home accompanied by Shiva.

Her return home is the descent through the same kulapatha, via the chakras, through which she ascended. But this time, on account of her maithuna with Shiva, she is drenched with *amrita*, or nectar, which is oozing out of her and irrigating the entire creation that in this case happens to be the physical body of Sankara. This is the great descent of divine consciousness to the human realm, a concept that is unique to Indian philosophy.

From this concept arose the belief in *avataras*, the descent of manifestations of God to the mortal plane, which no other philosophy advocates. Tantra is the mother of all philosophies and believes that the divine consciousness does manifest in human beings. At such times it completely overrides the mundane awareness, converting man into a divine being akin to God. Sri Aurobindo, the twentieth century yogi, advocated the descent of divine consciousness, leading to a supramental awareness in which man becomes unified with God. He said that the future evolution of man will lead to a supramental human race.

In this and the following mantras, the descent of Shiva-Shakti through the kulapatha must be understood in this light. The first point of their descent is ajna chakra, which is the seat of both akasha and manas tattwas. In addition, it is the hot link to bindu and sahasrara chakras. As such, the effulgence of sahasrara pervades this region. From ajna to sahasrara, the two nadis which emerge, *varna* and *asi*, denote the place where Shiva resides, *Varanasi*.

As explained earlier, nadi is a flow of awareness within the physical matter that constitutes the body. According to the *Guruvansh Purana* there are over 72 crores (720 million), 72 lakhs (72 million), 72 thousand and 682 such nadis throughout the body, spreading energy and awareness to each and every pore and cell. Imagine that! Some of these nadis are *drishya*, seen, and some *adrishya*, unseen. The nadis that emerge from ajna are adrishya. The flow of awareness cannot be seen at this point, but has to be experienced. At this point the practitioner hears the *taraka mantra* whispered by Shiva by which his awareness instantly pierces the darkness that surrounds him and crosses over to the blissful land of beauty and effulgence.

The point of ajna at the eyebrow centre, known as the command centre, is now inundated by the effulgent world, which is the mansion of Shiva-Shakti, and thus the influence of sahasrara on this region is experienced. The smells, sights and sounds all remind one of the unified state of Shiva-Shakti, consciousness and energy, and the divine experience comes within the grasp of the individual. Ajna is pervaded by the energy of both Mahadeva and Mahashakti, making it a very powerful centre for higher experience. *Tavaagyaachakrastham* indicates that Paramshambhu and Paramshakti are the presiding deities of ajna chakra.

Ajna is also the point where ida and pingala merge and become one stream. In this mantra Paramshambhu and Parachitta, presiding over the 64 eternal *kalas* or rays of the mind in ajna chakra, are described. The phrase *parimilita-paarshvam parachita* indicates that this steady stream of effulgence consists of both Shiva, in the form of supreme individual consciousness, and Shakti, supreme energy, integrated into one circuit.

The 350 rays of surya, chandra and agni in mooladhara, anahata and ajna do not extend beyond ajna, as they cannot penetrate the integrated circuit of Shambhu and Shakti in *maithuna*, or total union. The sun represents pingala or day, the moon, ida or night, and agni, sushumna, which is in-between day and night. The transcendental experience is beyond their range, so when this takes place, they are left behind, along with *samsara*, the world. This description of *paramadham* or the supreme abode is also given in the *Bhagavad Gita* (15:6): "Where the sun and moon do not shine, nor does fire light the space, reaching this place no one returns; that is my supreme abode."

Up to the point of ajna, the awareness is illumined by the light of the sun, moon and agni; or pingala, ida, and sushumna. But what happens when the awareness enters the zone where these three cannot penetrate? The consciousness enters total darkness for a time until it comes under the effulgence of Paramshambhu and Parashakti. This darkness has been described as the void, or *shoonya*. It is also known as the dark night of the soul which the consciousness has to pass through before it encounters the illumination of Shiva-Shakti in maithuna.

This passage from darkness to light is depicted in the ceremonies of *Shivaratri* and *Navaratri*. On Shivaratri the devotee keeps vigil the whole night, repeating Shiva mantras and conducting elaborate ceremonies of rudra abhisheka, so that the awareness is guided towards the experience of cosmic union. In Navaratri, which is an anusthana of nine nights, Devi mantras are chanted to guide the awareness to the abode where Shiva and Shakti reside in perfect maithuna. The nine nights symbolize the eight *aparaprakritis*, consisting of the five mahabhutas, mind, ego and buddhi, and the one *paraprakriti*, which is transcendental in nature. Paraprakriti guides the awareness with the help of the *dasamahavidyas* through the darkness of shoonya and leads it into the blissful union of Tripura Sundari, *paramchit*, and Shambhu, *paramchetana*.

Bhalokabhavane, the mansion of Shakti referred to here is not made of bricks and mortar, but of effulgence. The effulgence surrounds Mahashakti and Mahashambhu in union, just as bricks and mortar surround the space of one's home. Imagine the throb or pulsation of Shakti, which unilaterally sends out sixteen rays in equal measure from each direction. The rays at that point are so dense that they surround the pulsation, creating walls around them, just as bricks are joined to create the walls of one's home. The walls that surround one's being are the *koshas*, or sheaths, which have to be penetrated to experience the effulgent walls of pure light emanating from Shakti's feet.

Earlier the rays, or *mayukhas*, of Shiva-Shakti were described in the tattwas when kundalini was ascending. Here and in the following five mantras, they are described in the chakras, where Shiva and Shakti are descending in the state of maithuna, or total union. Now, their total potential is acting on the intuitive, mental, pranic and material levels of being. In this way the entire structure of man: the *saptalokas*, or seven states of consciousness, the *panchakoshas*, or five sheaths, the *manas chatushthaya*, or four tools of inner cognition, the *satchakras*, or six psychic centres, the *dasamindriyas*, or ten sensory perceptions, the *panchatattwas*, or five cosmic elements, the *shariras*, or three bodies, are all activated by the combination of Shakti-Shiva during their great descent.

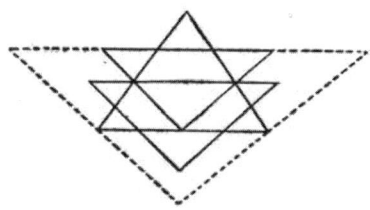

37. Meditation on Shiva-Shakti at vishuddhi

विशुद्धौ ते शुद्धस्फटिकविशदं व्योमजनकं
शिवं सेवे देवीमपि शिवसमानव्यसनिनीम् ।
ययोः कान्त्या यान्त्या शशिकिरणसारूप्यसरणिं
विधूतान्तर्ध्वान्ता विलसति चकोरीव जगती ॥३७॥

*vishuddhau te shuddha sphatika-vishadam-vyoma-janakam
shivam seve deveem api shiva-samaanavya-sanineem;
yayoh kaantyaa yaantyaa shashikirana-saaroopya-saranim
vidhoota-antardhwaantaa vilasati chakoreeva jagatee.* (37)

vishuddhau: in thy vishuddhi chakra; *te*: thy; *shuddha sphatika vishadam*: clear like pure crystal; *vyoma janakam*: and the creator of ether; *shivam*: shiva; *seve*: I meditate; *deveem api*: and devi; *shiva samaanavya sanineem*: who is equal to shiva in all respects; *yayoh*: which shiva-shakti's; *kaantyaa*: by the radiance; *yaantyaa*: emanating from; *shashikirana saaroopya saranim*: resembling moonlight; *vidhoota antardhwaantaa*: enveloped in the darkness of ignorance; *vilasati*: rejoices; *chakor iva*: like the chakori bird; *jagatee*: the universe

Translation

I meditate in Thy vishuddhi chakra, on Shiva and Devi, who is equal to Shiva in all respects, the creator of ether, shining like pure crystal. By the radiance emanating from Shiva-Shakti, resembling moonlight, the universe enveloped in the darkness of ignorance rejoices, like the chakori bird bathing in the rays of the moon.

Commentary

Shivasamaanavyasanineem indicates the perfect blending of Shakti with Shiva, just like milk and water when mixed cannot be distinguished from one another. Only the paramahamsa is adept at experiencing the two tattwas. In this mantra, Shakti in union with Shiva enters the plane of vishuddhi, which does not have any tattwa associated with it according to Samaya tantra, but instead is the place where the all pervading akasha emerges. While descending with Shiva, the akasha shines even more brightly like pure crystal, because it is rejuvenated by the effulgence of Devi's body which is oozing with nectar from her union with Shiva.

Akasha is undifferentiated matter. Although it contains all the ingredients for creation, it has yet to evolve into cohesive building blocks of matter. This undifferentiated matter of ether is pure like crystal, as it has emanated directly from Devi's body which is equal to Shiva's body in all respects. When they both grace the plane of vishuddhi, their effulgence lights up the inner consciousness and expels the darkness of the mind.

This mantra provides two clues about the quality of their radiance at this level. The first is *shuddha sphatika vishadam,* clear as pure crystal, and the second is *shashikirana saaroopya saranim,* which resembles moonlight. If one catches the rays of the full moon in a pure crystal, in a place devoid of light, the entire area will be filled with effulgence. The poetic imagery of the chakori bird highlights this state quite aptly, as it lives on moonbeams. This bird is forever looking at the moon with its beak open, waiting for any drops of nectar that may fall. The true devotee also waits for that divine nectar to fall on him and remove the dark clouds of ignorance. Meditating thus on Shiva-Shakti in vishuddhi, the devotee expels the darkness from the mind.

After experiencing Shakti as the mahabhutas, Sankara realizes Shakti with Shiva in each of the chakras in descending order. The descent after their union at sahasrara is the main feature of Sankara's worship, because as they descend the divine union of consciousness and energy fulfils his wish to rejuvenate himself. Their splendour flows through sushumna like moonbeams and floods the entire body. Finally reaching mooladhara, it removes all of Sankara's ills.

This worship of the supreme Shakti descending through the chakras in union with Shiva is highly efficacious and removes the ills of the practitioner.

38. Meditation on Shiva-Shakti at anahata

समुन्मीलत् संवित् कमलमकरन्दैकरसिकं
भजे हंसद्वन्द्वं किमपि महतां मानसचरम् ।
यदालापादष्टादशगुणितविद्यापरिणतिः
यदादत्ते दोषाद् गुणमखिलमद्भ्यः पय इव ॥ ३८ ॥

*samunmeelat samvit kamala-makarandaika-rasikam
bhaje hamsa-dvandvam kimapi mahataam maanasacharam;
yadaalaapaad-ashtaa dashagunita-vidyaa-parinatih
yadaadatte doshaad gunam-akhilam-adbhyah paya iva.* (38)

samunmeelat: full-blown; *samvit kamala*: lotus of knowledge; *makaranda eka rasikam*: who delight in the honey of; *bhaje*: I adore; *hamsa dvandvam*: pair of swans; *kim api*: which; *mahataam*: of the great; *maanasacharam*: who swim in the minds; *yat aalaapaat*: from their mutual conversation; *ashtaa dashagunita vidyaa parinatih*: have emerged the eighteen arts; *yat aadatte*: separate; *doshaat*: from the evil; *gunam akhilam*: all the good; *adbhyah*: from the water; *paya iva*: like milk

Translation

(O Mother!) I adore the pair of swans (Shiva-Shakti), who delight in the honey of the full-blown lotus of knowledge (anahata chakra), and who swim in the minds of the great. From their mutual conversation the eighteen arts have emerged. They separate good from evil, like (swans separate) milk from water.

Commentary

In this mantra there is a poetical reference to the descent of the divine couple, Shiva and Shakti, to anahata chakra, using the allegory of a pair of swans, *hamsadvandvam*. Swans symbolize purity and discriminating wisdom. Thus, as swans, the Shiva-Shakti tattwas would be swimming in the minds of great men who are full of discrimination and purity. Swans are also the symbol of adept yogis, or paramahamsas, as they can extract truth from untruth. *Kimapi mahataam maanasacharam* refers to the great paramahamsa yogis, who realize the existence of this couple swimming in their hearts and minds while they discourse on the supreme knowledge which they are able to grasp through their inner eyes and inner ears.

This pair of swans dwells in the hearts of all beings, but most have not awakened to this fact, as they are unaware of the inner phenomena. By awakening the inner ear, the practitioner can listen to their dialogues also. Here, surrounded by the fifty-four rays of vayu, Shiva-Shakti initiate the devotee into the *Hamso-Soham* mantra, the ajapa mantra that forever resounds in one's deeper being. The sound *Ha* represents Shiva or Purusha, and *Sa*, Shakti or Prakriti. The mantra *Hamso-Soham* denotes these two tattwas in maithuna, and the forms on which they are to be meditated are those of *Hamseshvara* and *Hamseshvari* in anahata.

This mantra indicates meditation on the heart centre, or anahata chakra, which is described as the lotus of knowledge in full bloom. Vibrant, pure and appealing, this knowledge engages even Shiva and Shakti, the supreme tattwas, who spend some time together at this plane during their descent, swimming in the pure blue lake of anahata.

In the confines of matter, Shakti meets her beloved Shiva for the first time at the heart centre during her ascent to sahasrara, and they are polarized at once. In that meeting Shiva is present as *jivatman*, the embodied soul. Jivatman is the individual soul separated from *paramatman*, the supreme soul, and entrapped in matter. Imagine its plight, separated from the one it loves, with hardly any chance of getting out of that condition. One feels a yearning for the supreme soul at times on account of this separation of jivatman from paramatman. If this feeling has an impact, one takes up the quest for paramatman.

However, the jivatman is an *ansha*, a part of paramatman, and even though separated has all the qualities of paramatman. This accounts for the first union of Shiva and Shakti at anahata, which is the abode of jivatman. From there they ascend together through vishuddhi, where their tattwas of energy and awareness are purified from the side-effects of the entanglement with samsara. Then they ascend to ajna, where they merge into one stream of awareness and ascend to sahasrara to engage in total maithuna, or total union, in the region of the thousand-petalled lotus.

Now, while descending the kulapatha, they drench each plane of awareness with the amrita or nectar that arises out of their union. At anahata they delight in the honey of the full bloomed lotus of knowledge that is known as *paravidya*, or transcendental knowledge. This knowledge is perceived without the medium of the senses; that is why it is called transcendental. In this state the external senses are left far behind, and the inner senses that operate give rise to extra-sensory perception. Although no music is playing, still one can hear the melodious sounds of the vina or flute, or rain clouds bursting into thunder.

As Shiva-Shakti swim in the blue lake of anahata, they are engaged in deep conversations about a wide range of topics, which are sometimes overheard by others. The great yogi Matsyendranath transformed himself into a fish in order to hear the discussions of Shiva-Shakti while they sat on the shores of the Anahata Lake and spoke on yoga. This knowledge, which the great souls imbibe directly through the realization of Shiva-Shakti in anahata, swims in their *mansarovara*, or mind lake, and is transmitted into thought, word and speech for the upliftment of mankind.

Ashtaadashagunitavidyaaparinatih refers to the eighteen kalas, or rays emanating from anahata, which are a result of the high level interaction of Shiva-Shakti at this centre. These eighteen kalaas relate to the shodashi, sixteen-lettered mantra, which is now complete with the supreme Shiva-Shakti tattwas and becomes the source of the totality of knowledge, both transcendental and empirical.

This supreme knowledge was originally heard as *shruti* in heightened states of meditation and later compiled into the four Vedas: *Rik, Sama, Yajur* and *Atharva*. These Vedas are a revelation which emerged from the source of the highest knowledge that is none other than Shiva and Shakti. The sound frequencies emanating from them in the form of mantras were picked up by the finely tuned consciousness of the rishis, who in their heightened states of receptivity retained the sounds and handed them down to the future generations in the form of the Vedas, which are regarded as the final authority on all matters, whether empirical or transcendental.

39. Meditation on Shiva-Shakti in swadhisthana

तव स्वाधिष्ठाने हुतवहमधिष्ठाय निरतं
तमीडे संवर्तं जननि महतीं तां च समयाम् ।
यदालोके लोकान् दहति महति क्रोधकलिले
दयार्द्रा या दृष्टिः शिशिरमुपचारं रचयति ॥३९॥

tava svaadhishthaane hutavaham-adhishthaaya-niratam
tameede samvartam janani mahateem taam cha samayaam;
yadaaloke lokaan dahati mahati krodhakalile
dayaardraa yaa drishtih shishiram-upachaaram rachayati. (39)

tava: thy; *svaadhishthaane*: in svadhishthana; *hutavaham*: the fire element; *adhishthaaya*: invoking; *niratam*: always; *tam eede*: I adore him; *samvartam*: the lord of the fire of dissolution; *janani*: oh! mother; *mahateem taam cha samayaam*: I adore thee, great samaya; *yat aaloke*: looks; *lokaan*: the universe; *dahati*: burn up; *mahati*: great; *krodhakalile*: with angry; *dayaardraa yaa drishtih*: thy glance drenched with kindness; *shishiram*: cool; *upachaaram*: treatment; *rachayati*: renders

Translation

O Mother! I worship him, who is always invoking the fire in Thy swadhisthana, as Samvarta, the lord of the fire of dissolution. I adore Thee, great Samaya (his potent power). When the angry looks of the great (Samvarta) burn up the universe, Thy glance drenched with compassion renders a cooling treatment.

Commentary

As the divine pair descends to swadhisthana, which according to Samaya tantra is the source of agni, or fire, they are worshipped amidst the sixty-two rays of *tejasa*, luminosity, as *Samvarteshwara* and *Samaya*, the deities of agni. Here the divine Shakti is addressed as Samaya, which is also the school of tantra that *Saundarya Lahari* advocates.

Samvarteshwara is the lord of transformation, who dissolves prithvi into apas, apas into agni, agni into vayu, vayu into akasha, which recedes into mind, mind into ego, and ego into mahat, at the time of dissolution. This process also takes place in meditation, as a result of which the body would be destroyed if it were not for the cooling and healing glance of Devi, *dayaardraa yaa drishtih*.

Shakti is the power and potency of Shiva. Just as a wife balances the aggressive nature of her husband, in the same way Shakti, as Samaya, at the level of swadhisthana, balances the destructive aspect of her Lord by offering compassion to her devotees at the time of destruction, when Samvarta, or Rudra, burns up everything with a mere look.

Rudra's anger is directed towards the devotee whose awareness is unable to break out of the mire of swadhisthana, the influence of which keeps one rooted in the world of *vasanas*, deep-rooted desires. Thus, his anger is compassion in disguise, as he is in a hurry to burn up the false notions of one's existence and reveal the grandeur of one's true nature. Rudra is free to conduct this traumatic surgery on the devotee, because Shakti will take care of any mishap that may occur. One is surely in good hands as both are expert and master surgeons!

At the time of kundalini awakening, Shakti has to be worshipped in order to balance the effects of the ascending energy, which can be quite awesome. In these mantras, which describe the descending path, Sankara worships both Shiva and Shakti as having an equal but opposite effect on the aspirant. If Rudra burns the universe, Samaya or kundalini cools it down by drenching it with compassion.

The feelings described in the mantra personify the abstract principles like energy and consciousness in such a beautiful manner that they become at once vivid and appealing to the mind. On the other hand, they also denote that energy and consciousness, although abstract, are not devoid of feelings. Energy too grieves and rejoices, and feels compassion and benevolence. Energy guides as well. So, the worship of Shakti is imperative for everyone; there is simply no other way to succeed in all aspects of life.

40. Meditation on Shiva-Shakti at manipura

तटित्वन्तं शक्त्या तिमिरपरिवृत्तिस्फुरणया
स्फुरन्नानारत्नाभरणपरिणद्धेन्द्रधनुषम् ।
तव श्यामं मेघं कमपि मणिपूरैकशरणं
निषेवे वर्षन्तं हरमिहिरतप्तं त्रिभुवनम् ॥४०॥

*tatitvantam shaktyaa timira-parivritti-sphuranayaa
sphuran-naanaa-ratnaa-bharana-parinaddh-endra-dhanusham;
tava shyaamam megham kamapi manipoor-aika-sharanam
nisheve varshantam hara-mihira-taptam tribhuvanam.* (40)

tatitvantam: with lightning; *shaktyaa*: of shakti; *timira parivritti sphuranayaa*: dispelling darkness; *sphurat naanaa ratnaa bharana parinaddha indra dhanusham*: with the rainbow formed by the dazzling gem-decked ornaments; *tava*: thy; *shyaamam*: dark-blue; *megham*: cloud; *kam api*: unique, indescribable; *manipoor eka sharanam*: which resides in the manipura chakra; *nisheve*: I worship; *varshantam*: sending showers; *hara mihira taptam*: burnt by the sun of rudra; *tribhuvanam*: the universe

Translation
I worship that unique and indescribable dark-blue rain cloud which abides ever in manipura with the lightning form of Shakti, dispelling darkness, and the rainbow formed by her dazzling gem-decked ornaments, sending showers upon the universe burnt by the sun of Rudra.

Commentary
This mantra speaks of Shiva as a dark rain cloud and Shakti as a ray of lightning in the cloud. According to Samaya, the rays of vayu in anahata mix with the rays of fire in swadhisthana and cool down into water upon entering manipura. Thus the entire universe scorched by *kamagni*, the fire of desire, which resides in swadhisthana, gets drenched and experiences relief in manipura. In

meditation, the aspirant experiences immense relief when the kundalini reaches manipura, where it breaks out of the clutches of vasanas and samskaras that are forever pulling it down.

In manipura, this divine pair is worshipped amidst the fifty-two rays of apas, water, as *Megheshwara* and *Saudamini*. In the last mantra Shakti drenched the universe with compassion; here, the dark blue rain cloud bursts into lightning and she sends showers to cool down the universe, which has been burnt by the sun of Rudra. In this text, during the descent, Sankara worships swadhisthana before manipura, but as explained earlier the kundalini path according to Samaya differs from other systems. Moreover, *Saundarya Lahari* describes the psychic passage when Sankara was in the throes of experience, which is always superior to knowledge.

There are two paths: *jnana*, knowledge, and *anubhava*, experience. The path of jnana is guided by *buddhi*, intellect, whose basis is *tarka*, logic. The path of anubhava is based on purity and innocence and guided by *shraddha*, faith, and *vishwas*, belief. Both paths lead to knowledge, but experiential knowledge is superior to intellectual knowledge. Sankara was in deep meditation and prayer; thus he was following the path of experience. Due to the purity and innocence of his prayer, sublime truths were revealed to him that one cannot find in books written by intellectual giants. Even though he worships the kulapatha in a different order to the other systems of tantra, we cannot discredit his experience.

As Shiva and Shakti descend, Sankara experiences their full grace through different forms and intensities which complement one another in a dazzling and unique manner. This mantra speaks of Shiva as a dark blue cloud pregnant with rain, and Shakti as a streak of lightning in that cloud. This is an apt symbol for manipura chakra, which has the nature of water according to Samaya tantra. Lightning is also a form in which Shakti frequently manifests; she is always electrifying, being the source of electromagnetic energy.

Perhaps this is why her experience is described as a surge, or *lahari*. The dark blue clouds pregnant with water aptly describe Shiva, whose skin is a bluish tint from swallowing the *halahala*, poison of the world, so that all may live and breathe in comfort. Moreover, manipura is also the centre where the ascending kundalini shakes off the last vestiges of impurities from the lower centres and becomes light, so that her ascent is fully ensured.

41. Meditation on Shiva-Shakti at mooladhara

तवाधारे मूले सह समयया लास्यपरया
नवात्मानं वन्दे नवरसमहाताण्डवनटम् ।
उभाभ्यामेताभ्यामुदयविधिमुद्दिश्य दयया
सनाथाभ्यां जज्ञे जनक-जननी-मज्जगदिदम् ॥४१॥

*tava-adhaare moole saha samayayaa laasya parayaa
navaatmaanam vande nava-rasa mahaa-taandavanatam;
ubhaabhyaam-etaabhyaam-udaya-vidhim-uddishya-dayayaa
sanaathaabhyaam jagye janaka-jananeemaj-jagad-idam.* (41)

tava: thy; *adhaare moole*: in the mooladhara chakra; *saha samayayaa*: in the company of samaya; *laasya parayaa*: who is dancing the lasya; *nava atmaanam*: form of Shiva, expressing the nine emotions; *vande*: I venerate; *nava rasa mahaa-taandava natam*: is engaged in the mahatandava dance; *ubhaabhyaam etaabhyaam*: in you both; *udaya vidhim uddishya*: for the regeneration of the universe; *dayayaa sanaathaabhyaam*: come together graciously; *jagye*: has come to have; *janaka jananeemat*: a father and a mother; *jagat idam*: this universe

Translation
I venerate Navatmana, who is engaged in the mahatandava dance, expressing the nine emotions, in the company of Samaya, who is dancing the lasya in Thy mooladhara chakra. In you both, this universe has come to have a father and a mother, who have come together graciously for its regeneration.

Commentary
Samaya is the Devi worshipped by the Samyacharins, and her name is referred to in the meditations on mooladhara, swadhisthana and manipura. There is no reference to Samaya Devi in the higher chakras, which is understandable, because Samaya represents the ability to divinize

the body. She is worshipped in the lower centres in order to divinize them, as they are the points where the aspirant can go astray.

Lasya is the dance of Devi and tandava the dance of Shiva. *Laasyaparayaa* signifies the dance of women, and *mahaatandava-natam* is the dance of men, known as the dance of creation. The tandava that is done with nine *rasas*, feelings or emotions, is known as the mahatandava. The nine rasas are: i) *sringara*, erotic, ii) *vibhatsa*, anger, iii) *raudra*, angry, iv) *adbhuta*, wondrous, v) *bhayanaka*, fearful, vi) *vira*, courageous, vii) *hasya*, joyful, viii) *karuna*, kind and compassionate, and ix) *shanta*, peaceful. They form the limbs of literature, poetry, dance and music. *Navatma* refers to Shiva expressing the nine sentiments or rasas. When all the pranas are directed to mooladhara in preparation for the awakening of kundalini, the yogi begins to tremble and dance with the explosion of energy.

Sankara calls the mahatandava and lasya nritya, the dance of the father and mother of the universe, Shiva and Shakti. After their union in sahasrara, Shiva accompanies Shakti all the way back down the kulapatha. Upon reaching mooladhara, where the kundalini shakti sleeps, Shiva begins to dance the mahatandava, and in response Shakti begins the lasya. Perhaps this could be called a homecoming party.

When kundalini awoke in mooladhara at the time of ascendence, she journeyed upwards alone. At anahata she met Shiva for the first time since her separation, and from there they travelled together through vishuddhi and ajna up to sahasrara. After honeymooning for some time at sahasrara, the effulgent mansion of Shakti, she begins her descent. This time, however, she entices Shiva to return with her and their return journey together is what these mantras of *Saundarya Lahari* describe.

Once the awakening of kundalini takes place, the individual becomes a divine entity, or God incarnate. Although remaining in the physical body, he operates through the

Self and not through the mind and senses. A total rewiring and restructuring of his energy circuits takes place. If the power station moves right into where one lives, the wiring and electrical circuits will have to be changed to adjust to the proximity.

The coming together of Shiva and Shakti at mooladhara, where Sankara has proclaimed them as the mother and father of the universe, is a cause for celebration because it is the secret of regeneration. This experience rejuvenates each and every cell along with the DNA structure of one's entire being, so it is like being born again, being given a new life in the same body. *Udayavidhim* indicates the regeneration process that these two forces trigger at the level of cause and effect, which filters into all the levels of matter, whether gross or subtle, animate or inanimate, static or dynamic.

For this reason Sankara had originally invoked Devi to remove an illness that afflicted his body. Instead of running to the doctor, he invoked the Mother of the universe. Naturally the father also came with her, and together they rejuvenated him. Simple story, but with divine implications! Sankara has shown the way to remove one's afflictions, whether physical, mental, emotional, psychic or spiritual. The worship of Devi can remove all of them.

The power of kundalini shakti enables energy and consciousness to move out of the fold of matter and carries the jivatman back to paramatman. The power of kundalini shakti also brings the fully awakened awareness down to the material realm and displays it in all its splendour. The claim of Shakti, the Mother of the universe, that she can give the devotee an introduction to the father, Shiva, is validated here by Sankara. *Sanaathabhyaam* indicates their equal prowess in every aspect.

42. Meditation on the crown of Devi

गतैर्माणिक्यत्वं गगनमणिभिः सान्द्रघटितं
किरीटं ते हैमं हिमगिरिसुते कीर्तयति यः ।
स नीडेयच्छायाच्छुरणशबलं चन्द्रशकलं
धनुःशौनासीरं किमिदमिति बध्नाति धिषणाम् ॥४२॥

*gatair-maanikyatvam gaganamanibhih saandraghatitam
kireetam te haimam himagirisute keertayati yah;
sa neede-yach-chhaayaa chhurana-shabalam chandra-shakalam
dhanuh-shaunaaseeram kimidamiti badhnaati dhishanaam. (42)*

gataih: attaining; *maanikyatvam*: ruby colour; *gagana manibhih*: gems that glitter like stars; *saandra ghatitam*: densely bedecked; *kireetam haimam*: golden crown; *te*: thy; *hima giri sute*: oh! daughter of the snow-clad mountain; *keertayati*: praises it; *yah*: (one) who; *sa*: he, the poet; *neede*: in the round crown; *yat chhaayaat chhurana shabalam*: multi-colour sheen of the inlaid gems; *chandra shakalam*: that the crescent moon; *dhanuh shaunaaseeram*: (rain)bow of indra; *kim idam iti badhnaati*: is likely to think; *dhishanaam*: understanding, impression

Translation
O Daughter of the snow-clad mountain! The golden crown on Thy head is densely bedecked with precious gems that glitter like the stars attaining a ruby colour. The poet who praises it is likely to have the impression that the crescent moon on Thy crown is a rainbow, because of the multicolour sheen of the inlaid gems.

Commentary
The amber coloured akasha is the crown on Devi's head. During the dark fortnight, just before amavasya, the sky at the time of dawn takes on a ruby-coloured hue that covers the akasha like a carpet. This can be imagined as the crown bedecking Devi's head. Hence, the fourteenth day of the

dark fortnight of the lunar cycle, which occurs just before the dark moon, is considered to be the most appropriate day for Devi worship, especially in the month of *Kartik*, which is known as *roopa chaturdashi*. On this day, meditation on the akasha as Devi's crown, inlaid with gems of many hues that glitter like stars, appearing as an *indra dhanush*, or rainbow, is most auspicious.

The first part of this text until mantra 41 is known as *Ananda Lahari*; the following mantras from 42 to 103 are the actual *Saundarya Lahari*, although the complete text is also known by the same name. The purpose of *Ananda Lahari* is to give the experience of *ananda*, or bliss, which is achieved by the awakening of kundalini. From this mantra onward the vision of Devi starts, resulting in the hymns that praise Devi's beauty in her many different forms, colours and expressions.

This mantra is the actual point where *Saundarya Lahari* starts. From here on, Sankara experiences the waves of *sundaram* or beauty, which is an epithet of the supreme consciousness. It should be remembered that this is an inner experience. Everything is happening within the enlightened consciousness of Sankara. He worships the many shades of beauty which Devi assumes to bless and shower grace upon those who come to her. In *Saundarya Lahari*, worship does not imply the performance of rituals, but a mental attitude through which total surrender and union with Devi are experienced.

By Sri Vidya pooja, or the worship of Sri Yantra within oneself at the appropriate centre, the Mahashakti is awakened from its slumber and ascends to higher centres, even beyond sahasrara. When the awareness awakens to its full potential in sahasrara, it then expands and experiences states beyond sahasrara, which belong to the realm of the divine. The chakras below mooladhara belong to the instinctive forms of life. In the animal kingdom mooladhara is the highest centre, just as sahasrara is the highest centre for human beings. From mooladhara human evolution begins, which culminates with sahasrara. The ascent after that has its own rules and conditions.

The experience beyond sahasrara is what Sankara is now describing. In the divine realms Devi is realized as sundaram. Just as she pervades the entire manifest universe, she also pervades the unmanifest. There she reigns over the three worlds as the queen of beauty; sundaram is her divine epithet. What Sankara perceives within himself as Devi is divinity. Along with sundaram, she is also *satyam*, truth, and *shivam*, auspiciousness. Devi in any form is auspicious. As *Ardhanarishwari*, she is the creator of the three worlds, and as Tripura Sundari, she permeates the entire creation with beauty, truth and auspiciousness.

After Shiva and Shakti descend to mooladhara, the entire structure of man's awareness is metamorphozed and a new awareness dawns, even while inhabiting the physical body. As if a new person were born in the same body, one lives, eats, sleeps, walks and talks in a state of divine union. Such an adept is able to experience the godhead, even while conducting everyday life like an ordinary person. However, one who has not mastered yoga, which gives control over this dual state of awareness, may lose control over the voluntary actions and require someone to clothe, feed and look after him while in this state.

In that state of union, the awareness abides in a divine, inner vision of God, *paramatman* or supreme consciousness. Sankara had the vision of Devi as the supreme consciousness in her many nuances, which are depicted in the profuse allegories of Sanskrit literature, such as the Puranas that recount instances from the life of the great goddess Parvati and her consort Shiva. These descriptions are highly esoteric; they are not just allegorical, nor do they just reveal an event which took place at a certain time in history.

Hidden within the folds of these stories are supercharged mantras, which are like missiles that can materialize matter, cure deadly diseases, overcome a vengeful enemy, restore lost status, earn enormous wealth, and much more than one could ever dream of. In fact, they can bestow whatever one may desire. The intelligent reader should see these mantras in this light, rather than wondering why Sankara has described Devi in this manner. The true and discerning sadhaka has to know in his heart that the power of Devi can achieve what no other power on earth can.

43. Meditation on the locks of Devi's hair

धुनोतु ध्वान्तं नस्तुलितदलितेन्दीवरवनं
घनं स्निग्धं श्लक्ष्णं चिकुरनिकुरुम्बं तव शिवे ।
यदीयं सौरभ्यं सहजमुपलब्धुं सुमनसो
वसन्त्यस्मिन्मन्ये बलमथनवाटीविटपिनाम् ॥४३॥

dhunotu dhvaantam nas-tulita-dalit-endeevara-vanam
ghanam snigdham shlakshnam chikura-nikurumbam tava shive;
yadeeyam saurabhyam sahajam-upalabdhum sumanaso
vasanty-asmin-manye balamathana-vaatee-vitapinaam. (43)

dhunotu: destroy; *dhvaantam*: the darkness of ignorance; *nah*: our; *tulita dalit indeevara vanam*: a forest of full-blown, blue lotus flowers; *ghanam snigdham*: dense, soft and shining; *shlakshnam*: soft; *chikura nikurumbam*: braid of locks; *tava*: thy; *shive*: oh! consort of siva; *yat eeyam*: of that hair; *saurabhyam*: fragrance; *sahajam*: natural *upalabdhum*: to absorb; *sumanasa balamathana vaatee vitapinaam*: the heavenly flowers of indra's garden; *vasanti*: reside; *asmin*: in these locks; *manye*: I presume

Translation

O Consort of Shiva! May Thy dense, soft and shining braid of locks, resembling a forest of full-blown, blue lotus flowers, remove the darkness of ignorance (in our hearts). I presume that the heavenly flowers of Indra's garden have taken a place in these locks to absorb a little of their natural fragrance.

Commentary

Just as dawn removes the darkness pervading everywhere, in the same way the vision of Devi can remove the darkness of ignorance in our hearts. One of the main features of Samaya tantra is that everything is superimposed on oneself in its practices. The mantra, yantra and mandala are seen as a part of oneself, visualized at a particular point in the body and not as an outside object. Through this focused visualization, the energy awakens and is directed upwards. After the full awakening, when the energy returns to the material dimension, there is an integrated awakening of all the energy points of the body due to the connection established between them.

Then the vision of Devi in her totality takes over. The divine and lustrous Devi blesses each and every part of one's being. Through the worship of her *angas*, or parts, one is totally rejuvenated. From this point onwards the healing propensities of Shakti are awakened and directed to each and every part of one's own body. So, by the worship of Devi, one directs her rarefied energy to all the different parts of one's body. This is not a mechanical or clinical process, but one that requires imagination, sensitivity and reverence, all at the same time. The result of this worship is miraculous, for the energy mends one's entire being and infuses energy into each and every cell of the molecular structure.

The mandala of Devi in this mantra is her beautiful face, adorned with a soft and shining braid of hair that is so dense it appears like blue lotuses. The divine beauty of Devi's locks, resembling the flowers of Indra's garden, are in fact the source of beauty that we see in all gardens The source of beauty is always enshrined in Devi, whether it be on earth or in heaven. However, the emphasis here is on the beauty of Devi's locks, banishing the darkness from within. Even the most educated person is in darkness, for this darkness is rooted in *avidya*, or ignorance of one's real nature. Therefore, no matter how intelligent, beautiful, wealthy or eminent one may be, one still needs the vision of Devi to banish this deep-rooted darkness from within.

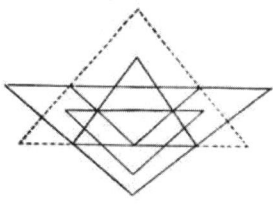

44. Meditation on the parting line of Devi's hair

वहन्ती सिन्दूरं प्रबलकबरीभारतिमिर-
द्विषां बृन्दैर्बन्दीकृतमिव नवीनार्ककिरणम् ।
तनोतु क्षेमं नस्तव वदनसौन्दर्यलहरी
परीवाहस्रोतः सरणिरिव सीमन्तसरणिः ॥४४॥

*vahantee sindooram prabala-kabaree-bhaara-timira
dvishaam brindair-bandee kritam-iva naveena-arka-kiranam;
tanotu kshemam nastava vadana-saundarya-laharee
paree-vaaha-srotah saranir-iva seemanta-saranih.* (44)

vahantee sindooram: by the streak of vermilion (on the parting line); *prabala kabaree bhaara timira dvishaam brindaih*: by the darkness of the thick locks of hair; *bandee kritam*: imprisoned; *iva*: appears to be; *naveena arka kiranam*: like the rays of the rising sun; *tanotu kshemam*: may we be blessed; *nah*: a thin band; *tava*: thy; *vadana saundarya laharee paree vaaha srotah saranih iva*: appears as a canal for carrying the overflowing flood of beauty of thy face; *seemanta saranih*: pathway formed by the middle parting line (of thy hair)

Translation
May we be blessed by the streak of vermilion (adorning Thy parting line) that appears like the rays of the rising sun, imprisoned as it were by the darkness of the thick locks of Thy hair. The thin band formed by the middle parting line of Thy hair appears to be a canal for carrying the overflowing flood of beauty of Thy face.

Commentary
In this mantra the poetic imagery of Devi's beauty with the streak of vermilion adorning the parting line of her hair, like the rays of the rising sun, conveys a striking image of Devi in her full form, radiant from head to toe. Her face is overflowing with beauty that spreads to the parting line in her dark tresses and carries the nectar to both

parts of her crown. This is the divine mandala of the fully awakened Shakti beyond sahasrara, which Sankara sees and conveys through poetic imagery. With the awakening in sahasrara the entire structure of the brain is illumined. This illumination spreads out to the deepest recesses in a homogeneous stream, awakening the full potential of Shakti. The effulgence of sahasrara then reveals Shakti in her most striking form, looking down on creation.

The vermilion mark adorning the parting line of a woman's hair is a sign of *saubhagya*, the happily married state that is Devi's condition after her union with Shiva. Sankara's description of this experience of transcendence is a rare feat that he accomplished through the grace of Devi. In this state the experiencer and the object of experience merge and one does not experience separateness. So, who is going to describe whom? The words which spring from Sankara, describing Devi, are the words of that highest Shakti, and not of Sankara. Devi speaks through him and thus these mantras are extremely important, because they can generate the same experience within anyone who chants them.

The vision of Devi's sublime beauty, attractive gait, lustrous hair, enchanting eyes, nose, lips and smile, breasts, waist, hips, arms, legs, thighs and ankles are described in vivid detail. In addition her jewels and decorations are also given in detail. These descriptions are the mandalas of Devi that can confer all sorts of boons on the practitioner. Each mantra conveys a different mandala of Devi that can be visualized while reciting the mantra. This offers the scope of generating an awakening within oneself, so that the grace of Devi can descend. One has to become qualified in order to invoke the grace of Devi within. In *Saundarya Lahari*, Sankara shows the way to do this by chanting the mantras and visualizing the mandalas of Devi within oneself in the regions of sahasrara, ajna or anahata.

45. Meditation on Devi's smile

अरालैः स्वाभाव्यादलिकुलहसश्रीभिरलकैः
परीतं ते वक्त्रं परिहसति पंकेरुहरुचिम् ।
दरस्मेरे यस्मिन् दशनरुचिकिञ्जल्करुचिरे
सुगन्धौ माद्यन्ति स्मरमथनचक्षुर्मधुलिहः ॥ ४५ ॥

araalaih svaabhaavyaad alikulahasashree-bhir-alakaih
pareetam te vaktram parihasati pankeruha-ruchim;
darasmere yasmin dashana-ruchi-kinjalka-ruchire
sugandhau maadyanti smara-mathana-chakshur-madhulihah. (45)

araalaih: curly; *svaabhaavyaat*: naturally; *ali kulaha sashreebhih*: beautiful like a swarm of bees; *alakaih*: forelocks; *pareetam*: surrounded by; *te*: thy; *vaktram*: face; *parihasati*: ridicules; *pankeruha ruchim*: beauty of lotus flowers; *dara smere*: little smile; *yasmin*: in thy face; *dashana ruchi kinjalka ruchire*: rendered charming by the brilliance of bud-like teeth; *sugandhau*: fragrant; *maadyanti*: gives great enjoyment; *smara mathana chakshuh madhulihah*: bees that are the eyes of shiva, the destroyer of kamadeva

Translation

Naturally, Thy face surrounded by curly forelocks, beautiful like a swarm of honey bees, ridicules the beauty of lotus flowers. The slight smile on Thy face, rendered charming by the brilliance of bud-like teeth, emits a fragrance that gives great pleasure to the bees that are the eyes of Shiva, the destroyer of Kamadeva (the God of love).

Commentary

Shakti's beauty surpasses even the pure lotus flowers that captivate all who see them. The lotus is a symbol of purity that is born in mud. Yet one never sees a trace of mud on its petals, which are forever glistening with beauty. The loveliness of Shakti naturally ridicules this concept of beauty. Her pure radiance, locks of hair like a swarm of bees, and half smile, revealing teeth that are brilliant and sparkling like crystal, far surpass even the beauty of the lotus which is held so dear. Even Shiva, who was not ruffled by the arrows of Kamadeva, is enchanted by the beautiful fragrance of Devi. In that sense the *nirguna* Shiva, who is without qualities, is also the enjoyer of Shakti.

The description of Shakti's exquisiteness ridiculing the beauty of lotus flowers conveys a sense of superiority which is not rooted in arrogance, but is just natural. She is totally confident and assured of her beauty, and thus of herself, which is not a minus point, but simply an assertion of the Truth. In this mantra Sankara also reveals Devi's smile and her beautiful bud-like teeth, which inflict the desire to go on gazing upon her without ever taking one's eyes away. This is precisely the state of Shiva, who becomes enchanted with her smile, even though he is an expert in mind control. The vision of her smile is also an indication of Devi being pleased with Sankara's worship.

The references to Shiva and Kamadeva abound in these mantras, because Shiva's encounter with Kamadeva is one of his most impressive achievements. No one has been able to thwart the attack of Kamadeva as Shiva did. Moreover, both Shiva and Manmatha are the devotees of Shakti, having perfected the shakti mantra to attain her grace. In fact, *Manmatha* is the original seer of the Sri Vidya mantra, which was later practised by the great rishis and munis, according to their own tradition, in order to obtain the grace and compassionate glance of Shakti.

Kamadeva was an upasaka of the kaadi moola mantra of Shakti. He represents her power to produce love and passion; her iccha shakti gave birth to him. At some time in life, everyone sees Kamadeva's prowess in producing the sentiment of amour. Rati is his wife and together they are the epitome of beauty. Although invisible, he is able to create something out of nothing and change the very course of one's life. This is the might of Kamadeva; he is so invincible that even the strongest rishis were unable to resist his invasion. This is all due to his worship of Devi. However, as Kamadeva's rasa is a product of rajas, he becomes an obstruction on the path of sattwa unless Devi's grace intervenes.

Thus, while describing the beauty of Devi, Sankara says that even the ascetic Shiva, who did not succumb to the arrows of Kamadeva, is stirred with pleasure and amour upon seeing Devi's smile, which reflects in an immediate change in his countenance. This is not due to passion, because Shiva is the destroyer of cupid, but to the supreme beauty of Shakti. Just as Shakti arouses the jivatman at anahata, she also arouses Shiva or the paramatman at sahasrara for the devotee to behold and experience. Until then Shiva remains inert and motionless. Both Shiva and Shakti are present in this vision of Devi, beyond the region of sahasrara.

46. Meditation on Devi's forehead

ललाटं लावण्यद्युतिविमलमाभाति तव यत्
द्वितीयं तन्मन्ये मुकुटघटितं चन्द्रशकलम् ।
विपर्यासन्यासादुभयकृ तसंधानमयितः
सुधालेपस्फू र्तिः परिणमति राकाहिमकरः ॥ ४६ ॥

lalaatam laavanya dyuti-vimalam-aabhaati tava yat
dviteeyam tanmanye mukuta-ghatitam chandra-shakalam;
viparyaa-sanyaasaad ubhaya-krita-sandhaanamayitah
sudhaalepasphurtih parinamati raakaa-himakarah. (46)

lalaatam: forehead; *laavanya dyuti vimalam*: with the pure brilliance of its youthful beauty; *aabhaati*: shining; *tava*: thy; *yat*: that; *dviteeyam*: another, second; *tat*: it; *manye*: I think; *mukuta ghatitam*: attached to the crown; *chandra shakalam*: crescent moon; *viparyaa sanyaasaat*: inverted; *ubhaya krita sandhaanamayitah*: came together and became joined with; *sudhaalepasphurtih*: with nectar dripping from it; *parinamati*: would form; *raakaa himakarah*: autumnal full moon

Translation
I think Thy forehead, shining with the pure brilliance of its youthful beauty, is the second (crescent moon in addition to) the crescent moon already attached to Thy crown. (As the upper is) inverted (both crescent moons) appear to be joined together by the nectar dripping from them and form the autumnal full moon.

Commentary
The moon represents *soma*, life-giving nectar. Here the nectar or *amrita* from the moon is beautifully allegorized to depict how the waxing and waning moon are joined together to form the full moon, symbolizing spiritual awakening. Earlier there was a reference to the rays of the rising sun adorning Devi's crown. This mantra describes the moon

dripping nectar or amrita on Devi's crown, which itself is like the autumnal moon.

The moon also symbolizes the most exquisite beauty. In any shade, form, colour, or time, the beauty of the moon is enrapturing. The different shades of the full moon are a sight to behold, as it waxes to the state of shodashi, vibrant with all of its sixteen rays. However, the beauty of the experience which Sankara describes in this mantra is magnified a thousandfold. Here the shodashi form of Devi, known as Tripura Sundari, who is full of youthful beauty and radiance, appears before him, raining nectar. This is called *amrita varsha*, the drenching of one's entire being with nectar, which is a sign of spiritual awakening.

Different traditions have pointed out that there is an *amrita bela*, or actual time of day, when the cosmic Shakti sends nectar in the form of prana into the universe to each and every creature. That time is known as *brahmamuhurta*, which occurs between four and six am, and that is the time prescribed for sadhana. At the exact moment before the sun rises over the horizon, there is a splendid burst of energy throughout the environment. The prana at that time is highest and everyone can avail of it by getting up early and doing sadhana. Conversely, at dusk or twilight time the prana shakti is less and one is not advised to do sadhana at that time, as it may lead to depression.

This mantra is a meditation on the shodashi form of Devi beyond the region of sahasrara, in which the forehead is highlighted. The meditations on Devi's body are in three categories. Those from the crown to the neck come under the category of *vaagbhav kut* and confer wisdom, learning, poesy, and skill in literature and fine arts. Those from the neck to the waist come under the category of *kamakala kut* and confer fulfilment of all that one may desire. Those from the waist down come under the category of *shakti kut* and confer the ability to fulfil one's goals.

Sanskrit poetry uses the allegory of the moon frequently to depict divine beauty. Here, however, the two crescent moons join together to form the autumnal full moon, *raakaa himakarah*, dripping nectar, *sudhaalepasphurtih*, which represents the esoteric experience of Devi as shodashi. In this form Devi emits all of her sixteen kalas, which signify her complete splendour and radiance that is unmatched with anything ever seen, imagined, dreamed, heard or thought about. This complete form of Devi drenches the creation with nectar as the rays descend upon the *srishti*, creation.

This shodashi form is Tripura Sundari, the unmatched beauty in all the three worlds of jagrat, swapna and sushupti. She is what lies behind the closed doors of the turiya experience, which the awareness perceives after it has made a quantum leap across the darkness of the void, or *shoonya*. She is the *para*, or transcendental, who comes within the grasp of all those who seek her with heart mind and soul.

47. Meditation on the captivating eyes of Devi

भ्रुवौ भुग्ने किंचिद्भुवनभयभङ्गव्यसनिनि
त्वदीये नेत्राभ्यां मधुकररुचिभ्यां धृतगुणे ।
धनुर्मन्ये सव्येतरकरगृहीतं रतिपतेः
प्रकोष्ठे मुष्टौ च स्थगयति निगूढान्तरमुमे ॥४७॥

bhruvo bhugne kinchid bhuvana-bhaya-bhanga-vyasanini
tvadeeye netraabhyaam madhukara-ruchibhyaam dhritagune;
dhanur-manye savye-tara-kara-griheetam ratipateh
prakoshthe mushtau cha sthagayati nigoodhaantaram-ume. (47)

bhruvo: eyebrows; *bhugne*: arched; *kinchit*: slightly; *bhuvana bhaya bhanga vyasanini*: who is bent on dispelling the fears of the world; *tvadeeye*: thy; *netraabhyaam*: eyes; *madhukara ruchibhyaam*: shining like bees; *dhritagune*: as the bow string; *dhanuh*: bow; *manye*: I consider; *savya itara kara griheetam*: held in the forearm; *ratipateh*: kamadeva's; *prakoshthe mushtau cha*: and clenched fist; *sthagayati*: is hidden; *nigoodhaantaram*: middle portion; *ume*: oh! uma

Translation
O Uma, who art bent on dispelling the fears of the world! I consider Thy slightly raised eyebrows to be the bow of Kamadeva, Thy eyes shining like bees as the bowstring held in the forearm of Kamadeva, whose clenched fist hides Thy middle portion.

Commentary
This mantra refers to the eyes of Devi that Sankara compares to the bow of Kamadeva, the fatal glance that makes one captive! If a beautiful young girl even looks at a young lad, he is captivated. He will dream about her day and night, even forgetting to eat, drink and sleep! But Devi's captivating glance gives freedom from fear by instilling faith, trust and belief in that one belongs to her. Her glance

is reassuring and soothing for the devotees whom she saves from the inherent fear of the world.

Everyone is born with an unseen and unknown fear, which surfaces on its own and often for no reason. The future is always uncertain; no one knows what will happen next. Apprehension of death, disease, loss of wealth and loved ones are the common fears. But there are other fears, which belong to subtler dimensions that attack during dreams or even in meditation. Due to these subtle fears, one often feels uneasy without knowing why.

The *Raja Yoga Sutras* of Patanjali has termed these inherent fears as *kleshas*, which dominate the mind in a deep-rooted way that influences and determines the very quality and structure of one's life. Klesha is an internal agony and its expression filters down to the very behaviour one exhibits in daily life. For example, one is usually not aware of the fear of death on a day to day basis, but it is there in the subconscious and one's actions are subconsciously guided by this powerful klesha. All living beings have this fear, not only humans.

Patanjali has identified the kleshas as five in number: i) *avidya*, ignorance; ii) *asmita*, ego; iii) *raga*, attraction; iv) *dwesha*, repulsion; and v) *abhinivesha*, fear of death. Through careful analysis one will discover that avidya, ignorance, is the root of all the kleshas. From avidya, asmita or ego is born; from asmita comes raga or attraction; from raga, dwesha or repulsion; and from dwesha, abhinivesha, fear of death.

This is the fear that Devi's glance removes from her devotees, which can alter and restructure the very course of one's life. On account of fear one is severely limited; fear makes one weak and destroys *atma-vishwas* or self-confidence. One who overcomes fear through the grace of Devi is able to rise high in life. No difficulty can overpower one who believes that Devi is protecting him all the time and no harm can befall him.

In this mantra Devi captures Sankara's imagination in order to divert the inherent fear that could ruin his inner experience. Thus, her eyebrows appear to him like the bow of Kamadeva, and her glistening eyes appear as the bowstring, which is drawn taut and firm as if to pierce Sankara with the arrows of love, so that he may overcome his fear. Eroticism is an apt means to disperse the thoughts of illness, disease and death, which was why Sankara invoked Devi in the first place.

In times of sickness, and despair, if one is successful in diverting the mind from the morbid and anxious thoughts that assail it, then knowingly or unknowingly, one initiates a process of repair and restoration. The secret lies in separating the mind from the cause of its sorrow or pain, and thereby from its influence and experience. If one can disturb the link in the chain of obsessive thoughts that invade the mind, the destructive process will be reversed. The removal of fear requires much effort on one's own; however, as stated in this mantra a mere glance of Devi will suffice.

48. Meditation on the three eyes of Devi

अहः सूते सव्यं तव नयनमर्कात्मकतया
त्रियामा वामं ते सृजति रजनीनायकममुम् ।
तृतीया दृष्टिस्ते दरदलितहेमाम्बुजरुचिः
समाधत्ते संध्यां दिवसनिशयोरन्तरचरीम् ॥४८॥

*ahah-soote savyam tava nayanam-arkaatmakatayaa
triyaamaa vaamam te srijati rajanee-naayakamamum;
triteeyaa drishtiste dara-dalita-hema-ambuja-ruchih
samaadhatte sandhyaam divasa-nishayor-antarachareem.* (48)

ahah: to the day; *soote*: gives birth; *savyam tava nayanam*: thy right eye; *arkaatmakatayaa*: being of the nature of the sun; *triyaamaa*: night; *vaamam te*: thy left eye; *srijati*: causes; *rajanee naayakamamum*: being of the nature of the moon; *triteeyaa drishtih te*: thy third eye; *dara dalita hema ambuja ruchih*: like a golden lotus slightly blossoming; *samaadhatte*: causes; *sandhyaam*: twilight; *divas nishayoh antarachareem*: in between day and night

Translation
Thy right eye, being of the nature of the sun, gives birth to the day. Thy left eye, being of the nature of the moon, causes night, and Thy third eye, resembling a golden lotus slightly in bloom, causes the twilight in between day and night.

Commentary
The cosmic nature of Shakti is emphasized here. The left eye of an ordinary mortal cannot create day nor the right eye bring about night. Day and night are the products of nature, which is another name for Prakriti or Shakti. Shakti is primordial nature and all the functions of nature in this wondrous world take place at her behest. She is the ruler of all the animate and inanimate creation. Every breath is controlled by her. This includes the movement of sun,

moon, stars, planets and galaxies; all are determined by Shakti.

Moreover, the three eyes of Shakti imagined by the seer of this splendid hymn indicate the three states of mind, jagrat, swapna and sushupti. Day naturally represents *jagrat*, waking consciousness; night represents *sushupti*, or deep sleep, and twilight represents *swapna*, dream state. All dreams occur when the consciousness is poised at the threshold of day and night. That is the twilight zone, which is neither day nor night, but a state in between.

The awakening of the third eye indicates the blossoming of transcendental experience, as the third eye is the seat of supreme knowledge, which lies beyond what the two outer eyes can see. For this reason the third eye is termed the inner eye, which induces the contemplative state. Just like Shakti, Shiva too has an awakened third eye. Awakening of the third eye is the aim of tantra, for without this significant milestone on the spiritual journey, the aspirant cannot cross over the twilight zone.

In philosophical terms the twilight zone is termed *madhya dasa*, the middle state, where the consciousness has a purview of what lies on both sides of the veil. By meditation on the three eyes of Devi, a crossover to the other side of the veil becomes imminent. The eyes are the mirror of the soul and are directly connected with the recesses of the brain, where all the images are stored. Thus sight is an important medium by which the mind can be influenced in its quest for transcendence.

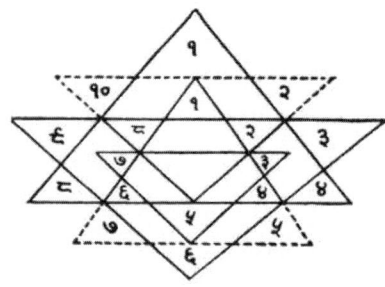

49. Meditation on the glories of Devi's eyes

विशाला कल्याणी स्फुटरुचिरयोध्या कुवलयैः
कृपाधारा धारा किमपि मधुरा भोगवतिका ।
अवन्ती दृष्टिस्ते बहुनगरविस्तारविजया
ध्रुवं तत्तन्नामव्यवहरणयोग्या विजयते ॥४९॥

*vishaalaa kalyaanee sphutaruchir-ayodhyaa kuvalayaih
kripa dhaaraa dhaaraa kimapi madhuraa bhoga vatikaa;
avantee drishtiste bahu-nagara-vistaara-vijayaa
dhruvam tattanaama vyavaharana-yogyaa-vijayate.* (49)

vishaalaa: wide; *kalyaanee*: auspicious; *sphutaruchih ayodhyaa kuvalayaih*: undefeated even by blue lilies; *kripaa dhaaraa dhaaraa*: shedding a continuous flow of grace; *kim api madhuraa*: subtly sweet; *bhoga vatikaa*: bestowing enjoyment; *avanti*: and offering protection of the world; *drishtih te*: thy eyes; *bahu nagara vistaara vijayaa*: surpassing all these great cities in their vastness; *dhruvam*: certainly; *tat tat naama vyavaharana yogyaa*: is fit to be referred to by the respective behaviour; *vijayate*: are glorious

Translation
Thine eyes are glorious, surpassing all the great cities in their uniqueness: wide, auspicious, undefeated even by the blue lotuses, shedding a continuous flow of grace, subtly sweet, bestowing enjoyment and offering protection to the world. Thy glance is fit to be referred to by their respective behaviour.

Commentary
The importance of a mere glance is familiar to everyone. The stern look of a teacher or elder, the loving look of a mother, the passionate look of a beloved, all invoke a corresponding response in the person who receives the look. No words need to be spoken between two lovers; just a look can convey passion and amour. One is so influenced

by a look that in a moment joy can turn into sadness or vice versa. One does not need any particular training to express the emotions through the eyes; it is a natural occurrence in everyone.

Just as the eyes are influenced by the emotions and appear frightening when one is angry or enticing when one is passionate, in the same way, the emotions can also be influenced by the eyes. An eye gesture can induce a state of mind, and in tantra this trick is utilized to induce higher states of awareness. With the flick of an eyelid one can enter into a trance or meditative state, if one knows how. The practice of *trataka*, one-pointed gazing on a candle flame or any chosen object, can induce an intuitive state of mind. The practice of *shambhavi mudra*, gazing upward at the eyebrow centre, can bring about transcendence of body awareness to the extent that the awareness begins to fly through space.

Devi has her own favourite eye *mudras*, or gestures, which she uses to induce states of mind in her devotees who approach her for a myriad number of reasons. These gestures instil the corresponding response in the devotee, generating the experience and the desired objective. The eight eye mudras described in this mantra cover the entire range of Devi's emotions: i) *vishala*, or wide, on account of her all encompassing nature, ii) *kalyani*, granting auspiciousness to all, iii) *ayodhya*, undefeated even by most beautiful blue lotuses, iv) *madhura*, sweetness, v) *kripadhara*, shedding a continuous stream of grace, vi) *bhogavati*, granting enjoyment, vii) *avantika*, offering protection to all, and viii) *vijaya*, unsurpassed in valour, courage and strength.

The eye mudras of Devi also depict *ucchatan*, disturbance, *akarshana*, attraction, *dravikarana*, awakening of sexual energy, *sammohana*, infatuation, *vashikarana*, control, *tadana*, striking, *vidravana*, defeating and *marana*, destruction. These are the eight powers of Shakti by which she accomplishes her tasks. They are also the qualities used to describe energy in a more gross sense. These eight bhavas are found in agni, or fire, and are therefore specially related to the awakening of the third eye.

50. Meditation on the allure of Devi's eyes

कवीनां संदर्भस्तबकमकरन्दैकभरितं
कटाक्षव्याक्षेपभ्रमरकलभौ कर्णयुगलम् ।
अमुञ्चन्तौ दृष्ट्वा तव नवरसास्वादतरलौ
असूयासंसर्गादलिकनयनं किंचिदरुणम् ॥ ५० ॥

*kaveenaam sandarbhas-tabaka-makarandaika-bharitam
kataaksha-vyaakshepa bhramara-kalabhau karnayugalam;
amunchantau drishtvaa tava navaras-aasvaada-taralau
asooyaa-samsargaad alika-nayanam kinchid-arunam.* (50)

kaveenaam: poet-devotees; *sandarbhah tabaka makaranda aika bharitam*: imbibing the honey dripping from the flower bunch of; *kataaksha vyaakshepa bhramara kalabhau*: the two honey bees of thy long eyes; *karnayugalam*: the two ears; *amun chantau*: inseparable (constantly hovering); *drishtvaa*: seeing; *tava*: your; *navarasa aasvaada taralau*: to enjoy the nine emotions; *asooyaa samsargaat*: out of jealousy; *alika nayanam*: the third eye on the forehead; *kinchit arunam*: looks slightly red

Translation
The two honey bees of Thy long eyes are constantly hovering about Thy ears, imbibing the honey dripping from the flower bunch of the nine poetic emotions poured into them by the poet-devotees (singing hymns of Thee). Seeing this good fortune of Thy two eyes, Thy third eye in the forehead looks slightly red out of jealousy.

Commentary
The eyes hold a special fascination because they are a reflection of one's deepest thoughts. Words can be manipulated, but the eyes can give one away. The eyes convey everything, even without a single word. One can know at once the state of mind of a person by looking into his eyes. The nine emotions, nine moods and nine spiritual

frequencies of Devi can be conveyed by her merely through a glance. Her glance can make the dumb speak, the lame walk, the blind see and the destitute acquire wealth beyond their dreams. The question is how to attract her gaze? What will make her aware of one's existence?

In this mantra Devi's eyes are seen hovering over her ears, because she does not want to miss the emotions offered by the poet-devotees in worship of her. Even her third eye, which cannot reach the region of her ears, is slightly red with jealousy due to missing this opportunity. So, her worship will draw her gaze towards the devotee. Her worship should be performed regularly and drenched with pure, untainted emotion; it should not be mechanical, terse and dry. One should feel immense attraction and love for Devi and an impatience to behold her form.

Worship can be ritualistic or devoid of ritual, depending on one's preference. Ritual plays an important role in creating the proper ambience to alter one's state of mind and draw out the appropriate emotions of immense love, surrender and devotion to the deity of one's worship. However, those who are supersensitive and have rich and abundant emotions do not require the support of rituals to dive deep into the experience of oneness with Devi, as in the case of Sankara. The alternative to ritual is closing the eyes and altering the frequencies of the mind, so that they are in tune with the richness of inner experience.

The seed or source of this mantra is *kama*, the root of desire; poetry, literature, music and art are granted when this kamabija mantra is perfected. Kalidas had perfected the kamabija mantra, and he became the greatest poet ever, *Kavita Kalidasasya*. The third eye of Devi, which is red with jealousy, indicates agni, which is the tattwa that governs this mantra.

51. Meditation on Devi's glance

शिवे शृङ्गारार्द्रा तदितरमुखे कुत्सनपरा
सरोषा गङ्गायां गिरिशनयने विस्मयवती ।
हराहिभ्यो भीता सरसिरुहसौभाग्यजननी
सखीषु स्मेरा ते मयि जयति दृष्टिः सकरुणा ॥ ५१ ॥

*shive shringaar-aardraa tad-itaramukhe kutsanaparaa
saroshaa gangaayaam girisha-nayane vismayavatee;
haraahibhyo bheetaa sarasiruhasaubhaagya-jananee
sakheeshu smeraa te mayi jayati drishtih sa karunaa. (51)*

shive: at shiva; *shringaara aardraa*: is softened by love; *tat itaramukhe*: at others; *kutsanaparaa*: with that of dislike; *saroshaa*: with that of anger; *gangaayaam*: at ganga; *girisha nayane*: on hearing of the heroic exploits of shiva; *vismayavatee*: with that of wonder; *hara ahibhya*: at the serpents forming shiva's ornaments; *bheetaa*: with that of dread; *sarasiruhasaubhaagya jananee*: red-tinged loveliness of the lotus flower; *sakheeshu smeraa*: at thy comrades with that of a smile; *te*: thy; *mayi*: at me; *jayati*: victory: *drishtih*: glance; *sakarunaa*: is compassionate

Translation
(O Mother!) Thy glance at Shiva is softened by love; at others (it is characterized) with that (feeling) of dislike; at Ganga with that of anger; on hearing of the heroic exploits of Shiva, with that of wonder; at the great serpents forming the ornaments of Shiva, with that of dread; at the sight of Thy comrades, with that of a smile; and at me, Thy devotee, with that of compassion. Moreover, Thy glance has the red-tinged loveliness of a lotus flower, indicating courage and heroism.

Commentary
In this mantra, Devi's glance falls on different kinds of people, generating nine different emotions, which are described through beautiful allegories. The first is *Shive shringaaraardraa*,

when her gaze falls on Shiva and transforms into the *sringaaradrishti*, which is a look that incites love and attraction. If her gaze falls on anyone other than Shiva, her drishti turns into *vibhatsa* or dislike. When she looks on Ganga, she is full of *raudra* or anger, as Ganga is a co-wife of Shiva, whom she considers her own.

When she hears of the adventurous exploits of Shiva, she is *adbhuta*, or wonderstruck. When she sees poisonous and dangerous snakes coiled around Shiva's body, she is *bhayanaka*, or fearful. When she sees her friends around her, she is *hasya*, or smiling and cheerful.

When she sees someone like Sankara, who worships her with love and is in need of her grace, she becomes *karuna*, or compassionate. This indicates that Devi responds to the bhava of the devotee. So, if the devotee wants her compassionate gaze to fall on him, then he must make his heart and feelings soft, tender and full of surrender, just as a small child before his mother. The serious practitioner should worship Devi with a mind that is intensely immersed in her, so that her compassionate gaze will fall on him, as it did in the case of Sankara.

The ninth bhava is *shanta*, or peace, which she confers on those who are ready for *moksha* or liberation. The specific mention of shringara and karuna in this mantra indicate that these two sentiments are the everlasting and most prominent characteristics of Devi. The others are transient emotions. Moreover, the mantra states that Devi's glance has the red-tinged loveliness of a lotus flower, which indicates that her nature is *vira*, or courageous.

In this mantra, Sankara beholds the most intimate and expressive side of Shakti where she expresses herself through emotions and feelings. Until now, Sankara perceived her physical form as clouds, lightning and the crimson radiance of the sun. This experience of Shakti has metamorphozed into a stream of emotions, which are easily identifiable because everyone undergoes them all the time.

Emotion is energy in motion. The nine emotions which Sankara describes here are also the form of Devi which he is experiencing. The intensity of her form is depicted through her emotions. The entire classical dance system of India has evolved from these nine emotions of Devi. They form the basis of all the postures, mudras and eye movements which the dances of *Bharat Natyam*, *Odissi* and *Kuchipudi*, to name only a few, are composed of. These traditions of dance form the rich culture and heritage of this diverse land.

In this mantra the silken rays of emotion emitted by Devi's glance are discussed in detail. This has become an important topic in science too. In the science of *drishti*, or vision, the shape, colour and movement of the pupils convey a myriad variety of sentiments and feelings. With just a single glance, one can convey an entire gamut of emotions. One can know a person just by looking at his eyes. One can know whether that person is benevolent towards him or not. This means that the rays of the mind or mental energy link up with the rays of the eyes to convey a feeling or an idea.

This is true of animals and other living beings too. Some animals attract and some frighten with their look; some repulse and some are playful. The effect that drishti, sight, exerts also applies to the planets when they look down in different conjunctions. Some have straight and others retrograde vision. The effects of their changing vision have an impact on everyone's life.

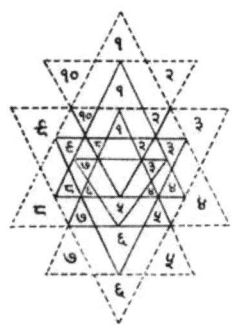

52. Meditation on Devi's seductive look

गते कर्णाभ्यर्णं गरुत इव पक्ष्माणि दधती
पुरां भेत्तुश्चित्तप्रशमरसविद्रावणफले ।
इमे नेत्रे गोत्राधरपतिकुलोत्तंसकलिके
तवाकर्णाकृष्टस्मरशरविलासं कलयतः ॥ ५२ ॥

gate karnaabhyarnam garuta iva pakshmaani dadhatee
puraam bhettush-chitta prashama-rasa-vidraavana-phale;
ime netre gotraa dharapati-kulottamsa-kalike
tavaa-karnaa-krishta smara-shara-vilaasam kalayatah. (52)

gate: extend; *karnaabhyarnam*: up to the ears; *garuta iva*: resembling the feathery wings; *pakshmaani*: with eyelashes; *dadhatee*: wearing; *puraam bhettuh*: of shiva; *chitta prashama rasa vidraavana phale*: engaged in disturbing the tranquillity of the mind; *ime netre*: these two eyes; *gotraa dharapati kulottamsa kalike*: oh devi, who art the bud on the crest of the mountain king's dynasty; *tava*: thy; *akarnaakrishta smara shara vilaasam*: aimed and drawn up to the ear like kamadeva's arrows; *kalayatah*: looks

Translation

O Devi, who art the bud on the crest of the mountain king's dynasty! Thy two eyes which extend up to the ears, with eyelashes resembling the feathery wings (attached to arrows), engaged in disturbing the tranquillity of the mind of Shiva, look like the arrows of Kamadeva, aimed and drawn up to the ear.

Commentary

In the previous mantra the nine emotions expressed through the eyes of Devi were described. Here and in the next mantra the *shringara drishti*, or vision of love expressed by decorating oneself in order to look beautiful, is highlighted. The word shringara is synonymous with love and contributes highly to eroticism. It literally means 'to decorate oneself beautifully'.

One dresses beautifully in order to impress, attract or win someone over. Devi adorns herself through the expression in her eyes, which is full of the essence of *shringara rasa*, the nectar of love for Shiva.

Here Sankara refers to the dynamic aspect of energy, which is symbolized in Parvati. Himavat, the king of the Himalayas, was Parvati's father. She was the fragrant flower born in the line of his dynasty. When she turned her shringara drishti, or amorous glance, upon Shiva his tranquillity was disturbed. *Saundarya Lahari* is an ode to Parvati, the daughter of the mountain king, Himalaya. Parvati is the beloved of the ascetic yogi, Shiva, and together they symbolize the mother and father of creation.

In the last mantra her eyes and eyebrows were compared with Kamadeva's bow poised to strike Shiva. Here in this mantra her eyelashes are described as the feathery wings of Kamadeva's arrows. With the inclusion of arrows, it is certain that Shiva will be struck by her. Shringara drishti strikes the heart, and devotees who wish to invoke Devi may worship by decorating her with beautiful clothes, flowers, gems and jewellery. When worshipped in this way, she removes all the obstacles in one's life.

The tantric view of worship highlights shringara or decoration. There is no spice in life without shringara. No one wants to see a person, place or event that is plain, dull and washed out. Everyone is subconsciously attracted to beauty, elegance and style. Tantra uses this innate tendency of man in all tantric rituals, as it works on the deities too. Man is a reflection of the gods. One's feelings are the same as the feelings of Devi, even though she is the Paramatman. She can generate feelings of eroticism, compassion, grace, kindness and even anger. Everyone has received these feelings from her, because all are part and parcel of her.

53. Meditation on Tri Devi, Kali, Lakshmi and Durga

विभक्त त्रैवर्ण्यं व्यतिकरितनीलाम्बुजतया
विभाति त्वन्नेत्रत्रितयमिदमीशानदयिते ।
पुनः स्रष्टुं देवान् द्रुहिणहरिरुद्रानुपरतान्
रजः सत्त्वं विभ्रत्तम इति गुणानां त्रयमिव ॥५३॥

vibhakta-traivarnyam vyatikarita-neelaambujatayaa
vibhaati tvannetra tritayamidam-eeshaanadayite;
punah srashtum devaan druhina-hari-rudraan-uparataan
rajah sattvam vibhrat-tama iti gunaanaam trayamiva. (53)

vibhakta traivarnyam: with three distinctive colours (red, white and black); *vyatikarita neelaambujatayaa*: beautified with collyrium; *vibhaati*: lustrous beauty; *tvat netra tritayam idam*: thy three eyes; *eeshaana dayite*: oh! consort of isha; *punah*: again; *srashtum*: to start them on their creative activity; *devaan*: devas; *druhina hari rudraan uparataan*: brahma, vishnu and rudra after their dissolution; *rajah*: rajas; *sattvam*: sattwa; *vibhrat*: shine; *tama*: tamas; *iti*: these; *gunaanaam trayam iva*: like (these) three gunas;

Translation

O Consort of Isha (Maheshwara)! The lustrous beauty of Thy three eyes shines with three distinct colours (red, white and black) when beautified with collyrium, like the three gunas: rajas, sattwa and tamas, which Thou assumest with a view to reviving Brahma, Vishnu and Rudra, after their dissolution (during the pralaya) and start them once again on creative activity.

Commentary

Here the three gunas of Devi, sattwa, rajas and tamas, are again alluded to. At the behest of Devi, they assume the forms of Brahma, Vishnu and Shiva. According to tantra, the three gunas arise from the three powers: jnana shakti, iccha shakti and kriya shakti.

Rajas is derived from *kriya shakti* or the power to do all, which goes to Brahma so that he can create the worlds. Sattwa is derived from *jnana shakti* or the power to know all, which goes to Vishnu so that he can sustain all that is created. Without sattwa, the entire creation would fall apart, as it is only on account of sattwa that it is being maintained. Tamas is derived from *iccha shakti* or willpower, which goes to Shiva so that he can destroy the creation through this extraordinary force.

In this mantra the three eyes of Devi are compared to the gunas, each having a distinct colour. Rajas has a reddish tinge, sattwa is translucent white, and tamas has a dark bluish tinge, like heavy rain clouds. Thus, the entire universe is born from Devi's divine vision. The expansion of the universe from her eyes is referred to here. At the time of *pralaya*, or dissolution, the three devatas, Brahma, Vishnu and Shiva, are absorbed into the gunas, where they remain in seed form. At the time of creation they emerge again out of her three eyes, which are white, red and blue, representing sattwa, rajas and tamas.

In order to understand Shakti it is most important to understand the three gunas, because she manifests the creation and conducts her myriad activities through these three qualities. Each and every speck of creation from the mightiest galaxy to the tiniest blade of grass is pervaded by these three gunas and acts according to them. It is these three gunas that restrain one's freedom of action by influencing one to act in a certain way.

Under the sway of tamas, one is dull, inert, procrastinating, destructive, negative, depressed, evil and vicious. Under the sway of rajas, one is dynamic, aggressive, ambitious, full of desire, full of ideas, persevering and accomplished. Under the sway of sattwa, one is knowledgeable, wise, balanced, equipoised, effulgent, highly creative and attractive.

By examining oneself, the situations and events in one's life and how one tackles them, one will be able to discern the influence of the predominant guna. This brings one closer to the realization that Shakti is acting at a very intimate and basic level within and no one can escape or avoid her influence on life. Would it not be wise then to propitiate her, so that she becomes compassionate towards one? These mandalas of Devi are intended for that purpose. This form of Devi is to be meditated upon in order to attain her compassionate *drishti*, or glance.

54. Meditation on the convergence of Devi's three eyes

पवित्रीकर्तुं नः पशुपतिपराधीनहृदये
दयामित्रैर्नेत्रैररुणधवलश्यामरुचिभिः ।
नदः शोणो गङ्गा तपनतनयेति ध्रुवममुं
त्रयाणां तीर्थानामुपनयसि संभेदमनघे ॥५४॥

*pavitreekartum nah pashupati-paraadheena-hridaye
dayaamitrai-netrai aruna-dhavala-shyaama-ruchibhih;
nadah shono gangaa tapanatanay-eti dhruvam-amum
trayaanaam teerthaanaam upanayasi sambhedam-anaghe.* (54)

pavitree kartum: to sanctify ourselves; *nah*: for us; *pashupati paraadheena hridaye*: oh goddess, who has surrendered her heart only to pashupati (shiva); *dayaamitrai*: thy compassionate; *netrai*: with eyes; *aruna dhavala shyaama ruchibhih*: having the three colours of red, white and black; *nadah shono*: shone river (with red water); *gangaa*: ganga river (with white water); *tapana tanayaa*: yamuna river, daughter of surya (with black water): *iti*: thus; *dhruvam*: definitely; *amum*: this; *trayaanaam teerthaanaam*: of the three sacred rivers; *upanayasi*: does; *sambhedam anaghe*: confluence that destroys sin

Translation
O Goddess, who has surrendered her heart only to Pashupati (Shiva)! (It seems certain that) with Thy compassionate eyes, having the three colours of red, white and black, Thou presentest to us the confluence of the holy rivers, Shone, Ganga and Yamuna, to sanctify ourselves by immersing in them.

Commentary
Only through surrender does union take place; surrender thus becomes the highest achievement of man. This form of surrender is different to that which is experienced in day to day relationships, where the son surrenders to the father's

orders, or the wife surrenders to the husband's dictates. Surrender in this way may be out of fear or helplessness because one has no other option. The basis of that surrender is through the mind and, therefore, union does not take place. Instead there is often strife and disharmony due to the surrender.

However, this does not undermine its importance, for this type of mental surrender is the training ground for the higher type of surrender, which is accomplished through the heart. Only by constant surrender in daily life does one become qualified and ready for that final surrender. The surrender to Devi takes place in anahata chakra, the heart centre, which is the resting place of Shiva. The consequence of this surrender is the experience of compassion or universal love, which is the quality of anahata. As the awakening stabilizes in anahata, the aspirant experiences universal love, compassion and mercy for all beings.

Usually it is imagined that surrender is for the weak and helpless, and that a strong, courageous person has no need to surrender. But here the mighty Devi, who commands the entire creation, in front of whom all the devas and ishwaras stand with their heads bowed in obeisance, also surrenders her heart to someone. Her surrender is not out of weakness, but pure, unconditional love. She does not need anything from anyone, yet she surrenders; that is the highest ideal of surrender. One should reassess the idea of surrender, because true surrender is not for the weak-minded, but for those who have a strong character and high standards and values. Devi surrenders to Shiva out of her immense, untainted and pure love and compassion. The aspirant should try to generate this type of surrender, for it will lead to higher experience.

This compassion further awakens the third eye of jnana in ajna chakra, which is the confluence of ida, pingala and sushumna, symbolized here as Ganga, Yamuna and Saraswati. Through the simple, but at the same time most difficult act of surrender, the aspirant is presented a higher experience of transcendental knowledge by the awakening of the guru tattwa or ajna chakra. This experience is most purifying and is compared to the sanctifying dip at the confluence of the three holy rivers at Prayag.

The convergence of the three holy rivers, Ganga, Yamuna and Saraswati at Prayag represents the merging of ida, pingala and sushumna at the eyebrow centre, or third eye. Ganga represents pingala or the right eye, Yamuna, ida or the right eye. Saraswati represents sushumna, the third eye at the eyebrow centre, which is the sacred tirtha of Prayag. This tirtha, situated on the Ganga near Allahabad, is the famous site for the *Kumbha Mela*, which is held every twelve years there at the confluence of the three sacred rivers.

This mela occurs during certain astrological constellations, which charge the water in that area with purifying and rejuvenating vibrations. A bath at Prayag during that period can absolve one of the karmas of many lifetimes, instantaneously removing the obstacles and difficulties one may have been facing on account of those unknown karmas. The Kumbha Mela is an ancient tradition which has continued over thousands of years. Millions of people throng there for a bath at the confluence, even in this twenty-first century. While visiting the Kumbha Mela with my guru, Swami Satyananda, I was awestruck at the scene there. As Sri Swamiji said, "The Kumbha is an experience of faith in motion." I went there as a disbeliever and I returned transformed.

The event of the Kumbha represents the experience of Sankara as he beholds the eyes of Devi. This mandala of Devi confers friendship and compassion in the heart of the devotee. Even the sternest person softens if Devi's glance falls on him with her three eyes emitting rays through the confluence at the third eye, just as when Ganga, Yamuna and Saraswati convene at Prayag.

A bath at Prayag removes all the dross of many lives. Similarly, a glance of Devi from her three eyes that are like a tirtha, *trayaanaam teerthaanaam*, emitting equal rays of white, red and blue frequencies, can remove all obstacles and purify one totally. A glance from her eyes can also rejuvenate one, as the frequencies of the rays that she emits are full of *amrita*, the nectar of immortality.

The elevated state of awareness, where the consciousness transcends the three gunas and enters the realm of the *shuddha vidya*, pure knowledge, composed of the *shuddha tattwas*, pure elements, is what Sankara is describing in this mantra. This state of awareness can be attained by a mere glance of Devi with her three eyes. Meditation on this mandala, focusing on the eyes of Devi Shambhavi, is most beneficial for rejuvenation.

55. Meditation on Devi Aparna's eyes

तवापर्णे कर्णेजपनयनपैशुन्यचकिता
निलीयन्ते तोये नियतमनिमेषाः शफरिकाः ।
इयं च श्रीर्बद्धच्छदपुटकवाटं कुवलयं
जहाति प्रत्यूषे निशि च विघटय्य प्रविशति ॥५५॥

tava-aparne karne japa-nayana-paishunya-chakitaa
nileeyante toye niyatam-animeshaah shapharikaah;
iyam cha shreer-baddha chada-putakavaatam kuvalayam
jahaati pratyooshe nishi cha vighatayya pravishati. (55)

aparne: oh! parvati; *tava karne japa*: carried to thy ear; *nayana paishunya chakitaa*: being afraid of the telltale activities of thy eyes; *nileeyante*: hide themselves; *toye*: in water; *niyatam*: surely; *animeshah*: without blinking; *shapharikaah*: female fish; *iyam cha shreeh*: sri, the goddess of wealth also; *baddha chada putakavaatam*: that have closed petals for doors; *kuvalayam*: blue lily; *jahaati*: abandons; *pratyooshe*: at dawn; *nishi cha*: at night; *vighatayya pravishati*: forcing open returns to it

Translation
O Aparna! The female fish hide themselves in water surely without blinking, being afraid of the telltale activities of Thy eyes. Sri, the goddess of beauty, also abandons the closed petals of the blue lily during the day (in order to reside in Thy lotus-like eyes) and returns again at night to the open blue lily.

Commentary
In this mantra the beauty of Devi's eyes is compared to the glittering eyes of the female fish and the blue lily; one keeps her eyes forever open and the other closed. The ability to keep the eyes open without blinking is a feature of divine beings; no human can do that. Devi always keeps her eyes open, so that she may shower special rays of compassion, love and friendship on her devotees without

interruption. A devotee who creates an environment of devotion and surrender through the worship of Devi draws these rays towards himself and is able to avail of them at all times.

Aparna is the name given to Parvati when she performed the *panchagni tapasya*, austerity of sitting amidst five fires, to obtain her beloved Shiva. At that time, she repeated the mantras to invoke Shiva while enduring the heat of the five fires, and lived for many years on air without eating even a leaf, thus obtaining the name Aparna. The great poet Kalidas has eulogized Parvati as Aparna in his famous work *Kumarasambhavam*, which holds an important place in Indian classical literature.

When my guru, Swami Satyananda, performed the Panchagni tapasya at Rikhiapeeth for nine long years, from 1989 to 1998, his eyes developed such immense *tejasa* and brilliance that it was often difficult to look him straight in the eyes. One had to lower one's eyes in respect and surrender to the beauty and brilliance that his eyes would emit. The female fish too must have faced the same situation when Parvati was doing panchagni tapasya. The brilliance of her eyes in which the goddess Sri, who is a symbol of the highest beauty and auspiciousness, had also begun to reside must have been to strong for them to bear.

Sri, the goddess of beauty, was so impressed by Aparna's selfless and unbroken devotion and surrender to her Lord that she abandoned the beautiful blue lily to reside in the eyes of Devi. Parvati faced hunger, heat, strong winds and heavy rains. The burning embers of the five fires burnt her skin, yet she remained undaunted. Surrender never goes unrewarded; it is the way to higher experience and the master key to all that one aspires for. All the gods and goddesses surrender before the one who lives in the spirit of true surrender to Guru and Devi. Meditation on this mandala of Devi Aparna, focusing on the immense beauty and brilliance of her eyes, confers the ability to achieve success in the most difficult tasks.

56. Meditation on Devi's unblinking eyes

निमेषोन्मेषाभ्यां प्रलयमुदयं याति जगती
तवेत्याहुःसन्तो धरणिधरराजन्यतनये ।
त्वदुन्मेषाज्जातं जगदिदमशेषं प्रलयतः
परित्रातुं शङ्के परिहृतनिमेषास्तव दृशः ॥ ५६ ॥

*nimesh-onmeshaabhyaam pralayam-udayam yaati jagatee
tavetyaahuh santo dharanidhara-raajanya-tanaye;
tvad-unmeshaaj-jaatam jagad-idam-ashesham-pralayatah
paritraatum shanke parihrita-nimeshaas-tava drishah.* (56)

nimesha unmeshaabhyaam: because of the closing and opening of eyes; *pralayam udayam yaati*: is dissolved and created (respectively); *jagatee*: universe; *tav*: thy: *iti*: thus; *aahuh*: say; *santa*: sages; *dharanidhara raajanya tanaye*: oh! daughter of the king of mountains; *tvat unmeshaat jaatam*: that has sprung at the opening of thy eyes; *jagat idam*: this universe *ashesham*: without any exclusion; *pralayatah*: from dissolution; *paritraatum*: to prevent; *shanke*: I suspect; *parihrita nimeshaah*: do not blink; *tava drishah*: thy eyes

Translation
O Daughter of the mountain king! The sages have said that the world is dissolved and created with the closing and opening of Thine eyes. I suspect that Thou dost not blink, but keepest Thine eyes always open to prevent this universe that has sprung up at the opening of Thine eyes from going into dissolution.

Commentary
Parvati is the daughter of Himalaya, the king of the mountains. She is Sati reborn. Both Sati and Parvati were wedded to Shiva, and together they represent the passive and dynamic aspects of Shakti. Parvati, who is the most exquisite beauty incarnate, is the dynamic and kinetic aspect of Shakti. Sati, who transformed herself into the Dasa Mahavidyas, is the passive aspect.

In this mantra, Parvati is recognized as the chief agent for creation and dissolution, being the dynamic aspect of Shakti. When she opens her eyes, creation takes place, and it is sustained as long as she keeps her eyes open. Whenever she decides to close her eyes, or even to blink, the entire world disappears. The jagrat state of mind keeps the universe or material world going. As soon as the mind slips into swapna, sushupti or turiya the whole world vanishes and fades away. Just as the individual experiences the jagrat state of mind, similarly the universal consciousness also has a corresponding state, which is known as *vaishvanara*.

Vaishvanara is the first dimension of universal consciousness, whose sphere is the waking state where the consciousness is associated with physical matter. Vaishvanara has awareness of the external objects and receives knowledge by means of its seven limbs, which are the seven lokas, and nineteen mouths, which are the five tattwas, five indriyas, five pranas, and four tools of antahkarana. Through these it enjoys and feeds on the gross objects and thus they form the avenues of knowledge and experience.

Devi, as cosmic consciousness, maintains this universe by keeping her eyes open all the time, so that the vaishvanara state is maintained. Shakti is the realm of manifestation. If Shakti disappears, the whole world will cease to exist. This is why Shakti is venerated. This was also the cause of Shiva's uncontrollable rage when Sati immolated herself in the fire of yoga at the grand yajna held by her father, Daksha. He had invited all the important dignitaries to this yajna, but had adamantly refused to invite his son-in-law, Shiva. Sati could not bear this insult to her dearest husband and jumped into the fire altar in front of all the guests.

When Shiva heard this news, he at once reached the yajna sthala with all his men and destroyed the entire ceremony. Then he picked up the body of Sati and wandered throughout the three lokas with it, violent with fury. With Sati dead and gone, the entire world went into disarray; there were earthquakes and floods, and the earth began to disintegrate. Out of concern for the creation, Vishnu, the preserver, sent forth his *sudarshan chakra,* or discus, to dismember the body of Sati so that the destruction would end and balance would be restored. As the sudarshan chakra struck Sati's body, it was severed into sixty-four parts, which fell in sixty-four places. These became the venerated shrines of Shakti, or *shaktipeethas*, which have existed until today.

Shakti is essential for creation, preservation, destruction and rejuvenation. This mantra describes the importance of her role in poetic language. Meditation on this mandala of Devi with her eyes open, looking at her creation, is beneficial for material success, wealth and status. The devotee should worship this mandala of Devi to attract her compassion and grace.

57. Meditation on Devi's compassionate eyes

दृषा द्राधीयस्या दरदलितनीलोत्पलरुचा
दवीयांसं दीनं स्नपय कृपया मामपि शिवे ।
अनेनायं धन्यो भवति न च ते हानिरियता
वने वा हर्म्ये वा समकरनिपातो हिमकरः ॥ ५७ ॥

*drishaa draadheeyasyaa daradalita-neelotpalaruchaa
daveeyaamsam deenam snapaya kripayaa maamapi shive;
anena-ayam dhanyo bhavati na cha te haanir-iyataa
vane vaa harmye vaa samakaranipaato himakarah. (57)*

drishaa: look; *draadheeyasyaa*: (with the) long, far reaching; *daradalita neelotpalaruchaa*: beautiful like the slightly blooming blue lotus; *daveeyaamsam*: being far removed from thee; *deenam*: and miserable; *snapaya*: bathe; *kripayaa*: with compassion; *maam api*: me also; *shive*: oh! auspicious one; *anena*: by this; *ayam*: I; *dhanya bhavati*: shall feel blessed; *na cha te haani*: to thee it involves no loss; *iyataa*: this; *vane vaa*: on the forest; *harmye vaa*: or on the palace; *samakaranipaata*: fall alike; *himakarah*: the rays of the moon

Translation
O Shive, Auspicious One! Grace me also, being far removed from Thee and miserable, with Thy far-reaching and compassionate look, beautiful like the slightly blooming blue lotus. By this I shall feel blessed, while to Thee it involves no loss. The rays of the moon do fall on the palace and on the wilderness alike.

Commentary
This mantra is a direct and most touching prayer of Sankara, asking Devi to bless him with her healing and compassionate look. Although Sankara expresses that he feels far removed from Devi, yet his intimacy with her is eloquently conveyed through the idea of being bereft of her grace and more so by addressing her in the first person.

Just as the rays of the moon fall equally on a palace as well as on the wilderness, Devi's grace also descends on the entire creation, thus her look would be no loss to Devi, but of great benefit to Sankara, who seeks restoration of his health and a cure of his disease. Sankara knows he will be cured if he can invoke her grace and direct her look towards him. He has utmost faith in the fact that Devi can eradicate his ailment. Thus he prays for her healing sight to fall on him.

One may argue that Sankara was a siddha who had performed many miracles, then why did he pray to Devi to bless him? This was not without reason. Paramahamsa Ramakrishna, a great saint and siddha who had contracted cancer, did not cure himself of this disease, although he healed many people who came to him. He must have had good reason to suffer in silence, or as in the case of Sankara to turn to a higher power for help. Ramakrishna lived with his ailment because it was the result of taking on other's karmas. Sankara's disease on the other hand was contracted due to black magic and sorcery. He was under a spell and thus the appropriate remedy had to be sought to nullify its effects.

He could have removed the effect of the magic by his own powers, but no enlightened person will use his own siddhis on himself. This goes against the laws and ethics of spiritual evolution. Those who act against these laws suffer greatly and their evolution is hampered. Thus Sankara prayed to Devi, leaving the ultimate decision to her. If his plea was legitimate and earned Devi's compassionate glance, she would surely bless him.

There is also an element of helplessness, innocence and humility in this mantra that is most touching. Saints and siddhas dedicate their whole life to others. They live selflessly, not caring at all for their own needs and comforts. They have no wants, desires, or needs. Even in times of great difficulty, they will not use their powers on themselves, but leave it to the higher powers to intervene in their lives. This is the sign of complete surrender, and their plight cannot be unnoticed or ignored by Devi, who is compassion incarnate, especially for those who are devoted to her body, mind and soul.

58. Meditation on the sideways glance of Devi

अरालं ते पालीयुगलमगराजन्यतनये
न केषामाधत्ते कुसुमशरकोदण्डकुतुकम् ।
तिरश्चीनो यत्र श्रवणपथमुल्लङ्घ्य विलसत्
अपाङ्गव्यासङ्गो दिशति शरसं धानधिषणाम् ॥ ५८ ॥

araalam te paalee-yugalam-agaraaja-nyatanaye
na keshaam-aadhatte kusuma-shara-kodanda-kutukam;
tirashcheeno yatra shravanapatham-ullanghya vilasat
apaanga-vyaasango dishati shara-sandhaana-dhishanaam. (58)

araalam: curved; *te*: thy; *paalee yugalam*: space between the eyes and ears; *agaraaja nyatanaye*: oh! daughter of the mountain king; *na keshaam aadhatte*: create the feeling of; *kusuma shara kodanda kutukam*: the beauty of kamadeva's bow; *tirashcheena yatra*: through them; *shravanapatham ullanghya*: beyond the ears; *vilasat*: cast; *apaanga vyaasanga*: length of the side glances; *dishati*: creates; *shara sandhaana dhishanaam*: impression of an arrow mounted on a bent string

Translation
O Daughter of the mountain king! The curved space between Thy eyes and ears creates the feeling of Kamadeva's beautiful bow. The length of Thy side-glances cast through them, reaching beyond the ears, creates the impression of an arrow mounted on a bowstring.

Commentary
In this mantra Devi is still in the mood of *shringara*, or amour. Her slanting side glances are intended for Shiva, as he is the cause of her amorous mood, but a true devotee can also avail of her full grace by meditating on her amorous look. Shringara and love are intense emotions that completely override an individual's perception of the world. For a person in love the whole world is beautiful and joyous.

For one who is not in love, the world appears drab, dry and devoid of joy.

When one is joyous, one feels alive and vibrant with a different kind of energy. At that time one thinks that one can take on the entire world; that is the effect of love. Everything begins to glow and shine with a new kind of lustre. If this is the result of ordinary love, then what would be the effect of divine amour, or the enticing glance of Devi? One would become spellbound and the whole world would appear magical. Each and every cell and pore of one's being would resound and reverberate with the pulsating, electromagnetic energy of the supreme Shakti.

Here there is a reference to the space inbetween Devi's eyes and ears being like the beautiful bow of Kamadeva and her long side glances being like the flowery arrows mounted on the bowstring and ready to strike their target. The descent of the highest prana shakti is insinuated here through the allusion of her glance poised to strike her devotee, who seeks her blessings in the way that Sankara did.

The enigmatic beauty of Devi is meditated on here. It makes all the difference as to whether one succeeds in this meditation, and if successful, it kindles new life in the meditator. It may seem surprising that the Devi, who is the epitome of beauty, purity, divinity, auspiciousness and truth, can also be erotic. She can attract others with her looks, convey jealousy and possessiveness for her beloved Shiva, or even pride in her unmatched beauty.

This is where tantra stands apart from other philosophies, for it believes that one does not have to be good in the moral, social or religious sense to be enlightened. To be good and to be correct are two totally different things. Often, when acting correctly, one's actions may not appear humane and good. So, tantra does not lay much importance on appearance, as it is more concerned with the correct outcome of the actions that one enacts.

Eroticism, love and amour are life-giving and life-rejuvenating principles. They do not detract from life;

rather they reinforce it. If the principle of love, or *prema*, is taken away from life, one will be left with nothing and will at once feel that the life force is ebbing away. Sankara's prayer was for life; he implored Devi not to forsake him, although he was far removed from her. He wanted the life force to re-enter his body, and the Devi responded to his prayer by generating her amorous, enticing and seductive look. This began to work on his body and mind as soon as it fell on him by generating the desire and will to live. When his mind was influenced by Devi's look, his body too responded and he started to get better.

This mandala of Devi is most effective for those who have lost the will to live on account of sickness or difficulties of body and mind. Devi is a symbol of love; the creation that she instigates is a labour of love. But the love that is highlighted here is not compassionate, filial or affectionate love. Erotic love is the focus in this mantra, because this quality of love works most effectively in generating the will to live.

59. Meditation on the erotic face of Devi

स्फुरद्गण्डाभोगप्रतिफलितताट्ङ्कयुगलं
चतुश्चक्रं मन्ये तव मुखमिदं मन्मथरथम् ।
यमारुह्य द्रुह्यत्यवनिरथमर्केन्दुचरणं
महावीरो मारः प्रमथपतये सज्जितवते ॥ ५९ ॥

*sphurad-gandaabhoga pratiphalita-taatanka-yugalam
chatushchakram manye tava mukham-idam manmatha-ratham;
yamaaruhya druhyaty-avaniratham-arkendu-charanam
mahaaveero maarah pramathapataye sajjitavate.* (59)

tava mukham idam: this thy face; *sphurad gandaabhoga*: glistening cheeks; *pratiphalita*: reflection; *taatanka yugalam*: two ear ornaments; *chatush chakram*: of four wheels; *manye*: I fancy; *manmatha ratham*: kamadeva's chariot; *yam aaruhya*: seated in which; *mahaaveera maarah*: great hero kamadeva; *druhyati*: inflicts pangs; *avaniratham*: earth for chariot; *arkendu charanam* with sun and moon as wheels; *pramathapataye*: lord of the pramathas (shiva); *sajjitavate*: is fully ready

Translation
I fancy that Thy face, having two ear ornaments that reflect on Thy glistening cheeks, is verily the four-wheeled chariot of Manmatha, the god of love. Seated in this chariot of Thy face, he inflicts pangs on the Lord of Pramathas (Shiva), who is fully equipped and ready (to fight back) with the earth for a chariot, whose wheels are the sun and moon.

Commentary
The battle of equals is about to take place. On the one side is Devi, whose face is the chariot of Kamadeva, the god of love, with her two ear ornaments and their reflection on her glistening cheeks as the four wheels of his chariot. On the other side is Shiva, who is fully equipped to fight back in his chariot that is the earth with the sun and moon as its

wheels. Inbetween is Kamadeva, who by taking refuge in the countenance of Devi builds up the courage to enter into combat with Shiva.

Devi alone can withstand the wrath of Shiva by sending him amorous glances, because Shiva responds favourably to her. She alone has this privilege. Kamadeva was previously unsuccessful in his efforts to stir Shiva's mind and was burnt to ashes by his third eye. Therefore, he hides in the amorous looks of Devi, so that he may take on Shiva. *Kama*, the root of desire, is one of the most deep-rooted influences that assail man. Victory over Kama is next to impossible for one who does not worship the great goddess. Even Kama is subject to her because he takes her help to inflict his arrows on Shiva.

Shakti is Shiva's equal in every respect. Thus, he at once succumbs as soon as he realizes that the person who is shooting the arrows of love is none other than Parvati. This is not mentioned in the mantra, but it is known, whereas Kamadeva's efforts on his own to instil love in Shiva for Parvati went in vain. This would be similar to the servant of the girl one loves trying to incite feelings of love for his mistress. Although his motives may be good, one is bound to react negatively, because the servant is not one's equal in any respect and has no business meddling in one's personal affairs. The girl should approach her beloved directly, rather than through her servant.

Actually, as the story goes, the devas had conspired to send Kamadeva to incite love for Parvati in Shiva. Parvati did not need the help of anyone; she alone was capable of winning over Shiva, which she eventually did by severe austerities and strict sadhana. The eroticism in this mantra is built up further by bringing Shiva into the picture, so that Devi's erotic emotions and glances become more enhanced. This bhava would work strongly in the rejuvenation process of Sankara. The doctor alone knows what will cure the patient. Meditation on this mandala of Devi's face will defuse the mightiest of enemies and any affliction they may impose.

60. Meditation on Devi's sweet speech

सरस्वत्याः सूक्तीरमृतलहरीकौषलहरीः
पिबन्त्याः शर्वाणि श्रवणचुलुकाभ्यामविरलम् ।
चमत्कारश्लाघाचलितशिरसः कुण्डलगणो
झणत्कारैस्तारैः प्रतिवचनमाचष्ट इव ते ॥ ६० ॥

*sarasvatyaah sooktee amritalaharee-kaushala-hareeh
pibantyaah sharvaani shravan-chulukaabhyaam-aviralam;
chamatkaarashlaaghaah chalita-shirasah kundalagano
jhanatkaarais-taaraih prativachanam-aachashta iva te.* (60)

sarasvatyaah: sarasvati, goddess of learning; *sooktee*: sweet speech; *amritalaharee kaushala hareeh*: that humbles the sweetness of nectar; *pibantyaah*: drinking, imbibing; *sharvaani*: oh! consort of shiva; *shravan chulukaabhyaam*: through the cups that are thy ears; *aviralam*: continuously; *chamatkaarashlaaghaah chalita shirasah*: shaking the head congratulating thy; *kundalagano*: (of) ear ornaments; *jhanatkaaraih taaraih*: by the loud clanging omkara; *prativachanam aachashta iva*: seen to reply (to thee) in the affirmative; *te*: thy

Translation
O Consort of Shiva! Saraswati continuously imbibing Thy sweet speech that humbles the sweetness of nectar, through the cups of Thine ears, is seen to reply in the affirmative by shaking her head, congratulating Thee by the loud clanging Omkara of her ear ornaments.

Commentary
Saraswati is the goddess of speech, wisdom and learning. She confers *vak siddhi*, the power of speech. Saraswati is said to reside on the tongue of one who shows genius in writing, speaking, dancing, singing or any of the fine arts. Other traditions have also symbolized wisdom as a female goddess; for example, the ancient Greeks worshipped the beautiful and wise Athena, after whom the city of Athens is named.

Saraswati is dressed in pure white, holding a vina and *pustaka*, book, in her hands, and seated on a white lotus.

This supreme goddess is also subservient to Shakti, who is the source of all sound and akshara. The first *dhvani*, sound vibration, emerged from her *spandan* or vibration in the form of *Aum*. All the alphabets are derived from this first dhvani. Saraswati imbibes that sound of *Aum* and responds in the affirmative, congratulating Shakti for this divine gift to the world.

From this transcendental nada the entire creation emerged as a ray or *kala*, which then diversified into the gross world of sight, sound, smell, form, and touch. Whatever is seen in this universe is nothing but vibrating energy in constant motion, which produces the most subtle sound inaudible to the human ear. But Saraswati is divine and she can hear the subtle sound of *Aum*, which is Devi's speech.

The sound of *Aum* is Shakti's conversation with creation and it offers peace, tranquillity, knowledge and enlightenment. This is the greatest wealth that one can aspire for. No amount of money can compare with these assets. Even if one has all the money in the world, but is devoid of the qualities that Shakti's speech endows, one is a pauper in the real sense of the word.

Sound vibration from which all are created is a powerful tool for restoring any imbalance that has occurred in life on the physical, mental emotional, intellectual, psychic or spiritual levels. In this mantra, Sankara's worship is rewarded for he hears the sweet speech of Devi, which is the transcendental sound of *Aum*. She speaks to him and he is restored. The mantra *Aum* is the *pranava*, which can elevate the awareness to the realm of *turiya*, the fourth stage of consciousness, in which the universe fades away and ceases to exist in its present form.

Aum is made up of three syllables: A+U+M. To pronounce the first syllable 'A' the mouth is opened wide and that represents the *jagrat*, or waking state of awareness.

To pronounce the second syllable 'U' the lips meet and the mouth is partially open and partially closed, representing the *swapna*, or dream state of awareness. To pronounce the third syllable 'M' the lips are joined together and the mouth is closed, which represents the *sushupti*, or dreamless sleep state, where the awareness comes very close to the Self. *Aum* is a mantra for transcending mundane awareness. Imagine the effect if Devi herself whispers it into one's ear, as she did in the case of Sankara!

Today, even medical science has recognized the curative powers of the mantra *Aum*. The chanting of *Aum* reduces anxiety and lowers the blood pressure. Sound therapy works its way to the body through the mind, heart and soul. Today there are scientists who have faith in this theory and risk their reputations by linking spirituality with health. They advocate that the human spirit has a healing force which guides the body. This healing force is awakened, activated and made powerful through mantra or sounds of high frequency. This belief challenges all the rules for treating illness and it also challenges one's own understanding of how the universe works. However, it is time to recognize that due to the infatuation with technology, people have not paid enough attention to the healing power of mantra. A daily dose of mantra can work wonders for one's wellbeing.

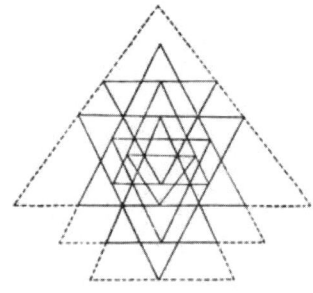

61. Meditation on Devi's nose

असौ नासावंशस्तुहिनगिरिवंशध्वजपटि
त्वदीयो नेदीयः फलतु फलमस्माकमुचितम् ।
वहत्यन्तर्मुक्ताः शिशिरतरनिःश्वासघटिताः
समृद्ध्या यस्तासां बहिरपि च मुक्तामणिधरः ॥ ६१ ॥

*asau naasaa-vamshas-tuhina-giri-vamsha-dhvaja-pati
tvadeeyo nedeeyah phalatu phalam-asmaakam-uchitam;
vahaty-antarmuktaah shishira-tara-nihshvaasa-ghatitaah
samriddhyaa yastaasaam bahirapi cha muktaa manidharah.* (61)

asau: this; *naasaa vamshah*: bamboo-like nose ridge; *tuhina giri vamsha dhvaja pati*: oh flag of the race of the snowy mountain; *tvadeeya*: thy; *nedeeyah phalam*: quickly the fruit; *phalatu*: bestow; *asmaakam*: on us; *uchitam*: suitable; *vahati antarmuktaah*: (that bamboo) which has pearls inside; *shishira tara nihshvaasa ghatitaah*: pushes out by the moon-cooled breath of the left nostril; *samriddhyaa yat taasaam*: out of their abundance; *bahi api cha*: outside also; *muktaa manidharah*: is worn (outside) as a nasal pendant

Translation
O Flag Bearer of the race of the snowy mountain! May Thy bamboo-like nose ridge quickly bestow the appropriate fruits on us. The moon cooled breath of Thy left nostril pushes out pearls from inside in such abundance that one pearl can be seen outside as Thy nasal pendant.

Commentary
The word *vansha* used in this mantra has a double meaning; it means *kula*, or race, as well as 'bamboo'. If the *dhwaja*, or emblem, of the race of Himachal to which Parvati belongs is held aloft on a bamboo pole from which it flies high, this brings glory to Shakti, as Parvati is none other than Shakti. In the other meaning Parvati is the pride of the race of Himachal, as she brought name and fame by her noble

and courageous deeds. The word *mukta* also has a double meaning: *moti*, or pearl, is known as mukta, and a liberated being is also known as *jivanmukta*. A bamboo does not bear fruit, but it produces moti, or beads, inside, and a kula, or race, produces jivanmuktas in its line.

When Sankara prayed for suitable fruits to arise out of Shakti's bamboo-shaped nostrils, what does he really mean? Being a sannyasin, he was free from the four earthly desires of: *dareshna*, the desire for a woman; *putreshna*, the desire for progeny; *viteshna*, the desire for wealth; and *lokeshna*, the desire for name, fame and status. As such, his prayer for suitable fruits could not be related to those. Just as a bamboo does not bear fruit, but instead produces pearls, in the same way, the upasakas of Shakti should produce jivanmuktas, or liberated beings, in her sampradaya.

The breath of the daughter of Himalaya should be cool as the mountain breeze, the touch of which freezes the sweat on the body into crystals that are like pearls. The left nostril, or ida nadi, on which all Indian ladies wear a nose ring or pendant made of precious gems, like pearls and diamonds, emits cool breath that make the droplets of pearl appear like the nose pendant of Devi. These beautiful descriptions and allegories tell that the Shakta worshippers, who belong to the kula or line of Shakti, are liberated souls, because this worship is the supreme path to enlightenment.

Although Sankara had a purpose for invoking the divine Shakti, his surrender to her was total, and thus he leaves it to her to bestow upon him whatever fruits she wishes. Sankara is confident that Shakti will fulfil his deepest wish, and he implores her to act without any delay. Perhaps he was in dire distress and his condition required immediate attention. One can surmise that a deadly assault was made on him by his enemies, because of the courage and valour he had displayed during his *digvijaya*, or spiritual conquest, of Bharatvarsha. During this period he had to face many difficulties and much resistance, so wherever he moved he had an army that followed him, which was granted by the kings and royal families who were his well-wishers and knew that his work was divinely ordained.

Meditation on this mandala of Devi's nose bestows the experience of *paranada*, or transcendental sound, within the aspirant.

62. Meditation on the redness of Devi's lips

प्रकृत्या रक्तायास्तव सुदति दन्तच्छदरुचेः
प्रवक्ष्ये सादृश्यं जनयतु फलं विद्रुमलता ।
क्व बिम्बं दृग्बिम्बप्रतिफलनरागादरुणितं
तुलामध्यारोढुं क थमिव न लज्जेत कलया ॥६२॥

prakrityaa raktaayaas-tava sudati dantachchhadarucheh
pravakshye saadrishyam janayatu phalam vidrumalataa;
kva bimbam drigbimba pratiphalana-raagaad-arunitam
tulaam-adhyaarodhum kathamiva na lajjeta kalayaa. (62)

prakrityaa: naturally; *raktaayaah*: red; *tava sudati*: oh goddess with beautiful teeth; *dantachchhadarucheh*: splendour of (thy red) parted lips; *pravakshye*: I shall mention; *saadrishyam*: likeness; *janayatu*: produce; *phalam*: fruit; *vidrumalataa*: let the coral creeper; *kva*: where; *bimbam*: the bimba fruit, which is like a bright red gourd; *drigbimba pratiphalana raagaat arunitam*: has turned red due to the reflection of thy (red) lips; *tulaam*: equal; *adhyaarodhum*: become; *katham iva*: how; *na lajjeta*: will it not feel ashamed; *kalayaa*: by even a little

Translation
O Goddess with beautiful teeth! I shall say the names of that which have a likeness to the splendour of Thy naturally red parted lips. (I am afraid I shall have to wait until) the coral creeper produces a fruit (which is redder than the bimba fruit). Will not even the bimba fruit feel a little ashamed to be compared with the redness of Thy lips, since it is the mere reflection of Thy lips that has made the bimba fruit so red.

Commentary
After dwelling on the eyes and then the speech of Shakti, Sankara now praises her lips, which part to reveal beautiful teeth that are pearly white. The whiteness of her teeth is in sharp contrast to the redness of her lips, which he

compares to the bimba fruit. Apart from the red colour, the sharpness of the contrast also extends to the fact that the lips are soft like fruit as opposed to the teeth that are hard like coral.

The mouth has a special significance in the art of eroticism as the lips and tongue are directly connected with the centres of passion in the brain. By dwelling on the parting of the lips to reveal the teeth, Sankara is using the most superior form of allegory to unconsciously develop a highly awakened and exalted state in the mind of the seeker. The imaginative, sensitive, psychic and esoteric mind will immediately respond to the ideas he is conveying.

Moreover, this mantra is a carryover from the previous mantras, for the erotic expression of the eyes always reflects on the lips. The *jnanendriyas*, sensory organs, are all linked and convey information to each other. It is Shakti that gives them the power to do so. From mantra 42 onwards, Sankara worships each jnanendriya in its subtle form through the mandala of Devi. By worshipping these parts of Devi, he divinizes himself.

The jnanendriyas, which are the eyes, ears, nose, tongue and skin, through which one sees, hears, smells, tastes and touches, exist on the gross as well as subtle levels. As the awareness transcends the gross level, it is the subtle jnanendriyas that transmit knowledge or jnana to the individual through the medium of the higher mind. In that dimension, however, they are not dependent on external objects for their knowledge. Then their source of knowledge is Shakti herself in the form of atman.

Meditation on the beauty of Devi's teeth and redness of her lips is an effective method to regenerate this jnanendriya.

Drigbimba pratiphalana raagaat arunitam refers to the crimson red colour of Devi's lips which here symbolizes prana shakti, the life force which is essential for existence. Sooner or later one must wake up to the idea that the life force is what sustains one, not the blood which runs through the veins, the bones that give the body a structure, the marrow or semen that carry vital fluids, nor the organs that conduct a myriad of tasks.

Tantra has defined the life force as prana shakti, which is electromagnetic in nature, but also much more than that. When this life force begins to deplete, one's life slowly ebbs away. No matter how many vitamins or how much nourishing food one takes, they will not have any effect. This is true for all living beings, such as people, plants, animals, aquatic life, and also for mountains, seas, sky and earth. Earthquakes, tsunamis, floods, famines and droughts all occur on account of a depletion of the life force in the earth and environment.

Although the earthquake occurs today, the process which led up to it started much before. In the same way one may have a stomach disorder today, but the signs of that began to develop earlier. Often one feels a lack of energy, dull, slow and tired, and not one's usual self, but one does not really know why. If one is alert to the signs and signals, one can know of impending illnesses and follow the method of prevention by altering the diet, fasting or practising yoga. There are several options for averting illness, but one does not heed what the body is trying to tell one.

This life force is Shakti, they are not different, but little attention has been given to this phenomenon. People talk a lot about the body and also about the atman, or spirit. However, prana shakti is the very important link between the two, which is actually the key to both the gross as well as the transcendental dimensions. One may not be at all interested in transcendental matters, but one cannot deny the need for good health, a strong mind, balanced emotions, strong willpower, clarity of thought, focus and concentration, a harmonious personality, positive attitude, contentment, relaxation and creativity. One's success in career and relationships depends on these.

The life force is responsible for each of these conditions, and this is the importance of *Saundarya Lahari*. Sankara brings home this vital truth in relation to one's functioning on this earth. Today there is a lot of conjecture about whether *Saundarya Lahari* is a text of Advaita or Tantra, of Samaya or Kaula. However, one needs to rise above these differences and just focus on the universality of his thought, which applies to each and every human being, no matter what his beliefs are. Then one can say that Sankara has succeeded in proving his point.

After all, there is an existence beyond dogma and belief, which are imposed on us by society. A Muslim suffering from an illness will go to a Hindu doctor if he knows that he is the only person who can cure him, because life is above all these limitations. It has got to be that way or else the human race will become extinct. All other creatures will survive, but humans will not because they have created this limitation for themselves in their ignorance and avidya.

Prana shakti, the life force, which is the domain of the supreme Shakti that Sankara is invoking, is a universal phenomenon. Shakti is essential for everyone, no matter to which country, race, nationality, religion, gender or status of life one belongs. If one can accept this, then Sankara will have made his point.

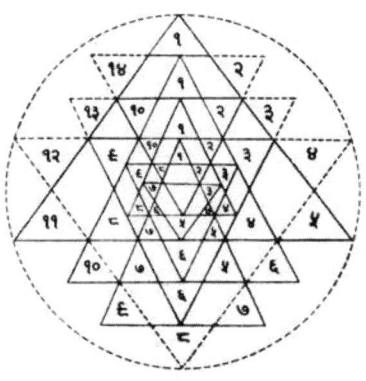

63. Meditation on Devi's sweet smile

स्मितज्योत्स्नाजालं तव वदनचन्द्रस्य पिबतां
चकोराणामासीदतिरसतया चञ्चुजडिमा ।
अतस्ते शीतांशोरमृतलहरीमम्लरुचयः
पिबन्ति स्वच्छन्दं निशि निशि भृशं काञ्जिकधिया ॥ ६३ ॥

*smita-jyotsnaa-jaalam tava vadana-chandrasya pibataam
chakoraanaam-aaseed-atirasatayaa chanchu-jadimaa;
ataste sheetaamshor-amritalahareem-amla-ruchayah
pibanti svachchhandam nishi nishi bhrisham kaanjikadhiya.* (63)

smita jyotsnaa jaalam: luminous light of thy smile; *tava*: thy; *vadana chandrasya*: on thy moon like face; *pibataam*: drinking; *chakoraanaam*: to the chakora birds; *aaseet*: got; *atirasatayaa*: because of extreme sweetness; *chanchu jadimaa*: insensitivity of tongue; *atah*: so; *te*: they; *sheetaanshoh*: from the moon; *amritalahareem*: waves of nectar; *amla ruchayah*: to obtain sour taste; *pibanti*: drinks; *svachchhandam*: as much as it wants; *nishi nishi*: every night; *bhrisham*: much; *kaanjikadhiyaa*: under the impression that it is gruel

Translation

The chakora birds have developed insensitivity of the tongue by drinking the extreme sweetness of the luminous light of Thy smile on Thy moon-like face. For this reason every night they drink as much as they want of the waves of nectar from the moon to obtain some sour taste under the impression that it is gruel (that will relieve the insensitivity of their tongues).

Commentary

The chakora bird is used extensively in Indian poetry when describing the longing for union. This bird is known to wait patiently for the nectar which drips only in a certain constellation, or *nakshatra*. It constantly pines for that nectar, sitting on a tree with its mouth open, waiting for those drops to fall by which it is satiated. These drops fall when nature, or *prakriti*, smiles; nature also feels happy or pleased and smiles. One of those periods when nature smiles is *Kartik*, the month when the chakora bird receives its drops of nectar.

This mantra describes the smile of Devi as so sweet that the chakora birds become satiated by drinking the rays emanating from it. The excessive sweetness of her smile makes the chakora bird's tongue insensitive to the rays of the moon. In contrast to Devi's smile, the moon's rays appear like sour gruel, which they drink to regain the sensitivity of their tongues so that they can once again enjoy the rays emanating from Devi's smile.

Once the smile of Devi falls on one, everything else appears tasteless. One simply wants more and more of that exquisite experience, developing indifference to any other form of enjoyment which may have appeared very inviting prior to the experience of her luminous smile. Each and every nuance of Devi is unmatched with any experience one may have had before. The experience of Devi, the epitome of beauty, is not dull or puritanical, but extremely enjoyable and exciting. It does not kill the senses; rather it magnifies them a thousand-fold, with the result that mundane experience is no longer inviting or inspiring.

A smile immediately connects one with the people around. It is a most effective way to reach out to people and draw them closer. Everyone responds to a smile and reciprocates immediately, especially if it arises from the heart. This is the case with Devi, whose smile is totally bewitching, not just to humans but to birds as well. When Devi smiles, the entire creation smiles, for Devi is the creation.

Meditation on the smile of Devi stimulates the energy centres in the region of the mouth, above and below the tongue. When this connection between the brain and the mouth is established, extreme sensitivity is generated within an individual, enabling him to become a great writer, poet, artist or musician.

64. Meditation on the redness of Devi's tongue

अविश्रान्तं पत्युर्गुणगणकथाम्रेडनजडा
जवापुष्पच्छाया तव जननि जिह्वा जयति सा ।
यदग्रासीनायाः स्फटिकदृषदच्छच्छविमयी
सरस्वत्या मूर्तिः परिणमति माणिक्यवपुषा ॥ ६४ ॥

avishraantam patyur-gunagana-katha-amredanajadaa
javaa-pushpa-chhaayaa tava janani jihvaa jayati saa
yad-agr-aaseenaayaah sphatika-drishad-achha-chhavimayee
sarasvatyaa moortih parinamati maanikya-vapushaa. (64)

avishraantam: constantly; *patyuh*: of thy consort; *gunagana katha-amredanajadaa*: forever articulating the glories; *javaa-pushpa-chhaayaa*: and of the colour of hibiscus; *tava*: thy; *janani*: oh mother; *jihvaa saa*: that tongue; *jayati*: glory to; *yat agra aaseenaayaah*: who dwells on the tip of it; *sphatika drishad-achha chhavimayee*: her crystal like white complexion; *sarasvatyaa*: sarasvati; *moortih*: body; *parinamati*: changes; *maanikya vapushaa*: colour of ruby

Translation
O Mother! Glory to Thy tongue that defies the lustrous redness of the hibiscus flower and is constantly engaged in articulating the glories of Thy consort. (The redness of Thy tongue is so intense that) the white crystal-like complexion of Saraswati, the goddess of speech who dwells on the tip, changes into the colour of a ruby.

Commentary
Shakti upasana does not alienate the aspirant from Shiva. On account of the sectarian nature of one's upbringing and mind, one ordinarily assumes that if Shakti is worshipped, then Shiva is absent and has no role to play in one's practices and evolution. However, when Shakti herself is constantly engaged in singing the glories of Shiva, then the Shakti worshippers also find themselves in awe of

Shiva. Shakti is always engaged in repeating the mantra of Shiva. Parvati repeated the panchakshari mantra of Shiva for thousands of years to regain him as her husband and consort. It is through Shakti that one finds Shiva. This does not mean that Shakti is merely the cab driver who takes one to the destination. Shakti is chetana or Shiva; they are one and the same.

The tongue is an important centre which houses many points of energy or Shakti. This is exactly what is meant by the saying that Saraswati resides on the tongue of an individual who is gifted in music, speech, and all the eighteen arts that distinguish the superiority of man from animal life. Art, music and culture have evolved with the growth of man's awareness. Without them man is no better than the animals. The awakening of the heart centre, anahata, and the higher mind, ajna, bring man closer to the subtle vibrations emitted by higher ideas and thoughts depicted in all forms of art.

On the gross level the energy points on the tongue are activated through speech and repetition of the akshara or bija mantras with correct pronunciation and intonation. But on a subtle level, according to Samaya tantra, these points are activated by meditation on those parts of Devi. The quality of crystal is reflection. Saraswati is pure and translucent as crystal, but when she sits on the tongue of Shakti which is red like the java or hibiscus flower, she also appears ruby red. So, even Saraswati is overshadowed by the supreme Shakti.

In tantra, each deity has its own favourite offerings in terms of flowers, fruits, colours, ornaments, clothes, incense, trees and so on. The hibiscus flower is most dear to Devi and is included in the traditional offerings made to her. When the Sat Chandi Mahayajna commenced at Rikhiapeeth in the year 1996, my guru, Swami Satyananda, had over a thousand hibiscus bushes of different varieties and shades planted at his *tapobhumi* to offer to Mahashakti during the yajna.

Devi's tongue is compared to the java or hibiscus flower because it is very attractive. They say that java and Devi are synonymous. The tongue of Devi is most venerated, especially in the case of Kali, who is depicted with her red tongue protruding for devotees to see. Many Devas reside in the tongue and by worshipping this centre, one gets instant and immediate gratification.

65. Meditation on Devi's worship by the devas

रणे जित्वा दैत्यानपहृतशिरस्त्रैः कवचिभिः
निवृत्तैश्चण्डांशत्रिपुरहरनिर्माल्यविमुखैः ।
विरिञ्चीन्द्रोपेन्द्रैः शशिशिशिरकर्पूरधवला
विलिप्यन्ते मातस्तव वदनताम्बूलशकलाः ॥ ६५ ॥

*rane jitvaa daityaan apahrita-shirastraih kavachibhih
nivrittaish-chandaamsha-tripura-hara-nirmaalya-vimukhaih;
virincheendropendraih shashi-shishira-karpoora-dhavalaa
vilipyante maatas-tava vadana-taamboolashakalaah. (65)*

rane: in war; *jitvaa*: victory over; *daityaan*: asuras; *apahrita shirastraih*: with their head gear removed; *kavachibhih*: clad only in armour; *nivrittaih*: returned; *chandaamsha tripura hara nirmaalya vimukhaih*: rejecting the remains of the offerings to shiva, which are the share of chanda; *virinchi indra upendraih*: brahma, indra and vishnu; *shashi shishira karpoora dhavalaa*: with camphor pure as the moon; *vilipyante*: chew them until they melt away; *maatah*: oh! mother; *tava*: thy; *vadana taamboola shakalaah*: betel leaf rolls from thy mouth

Translation

O Mother! Rejecting the remains of the offerings made to Shiva, as those are the share of Chanda, celestials like Brahma, Indra and Vishnu, after their victory over the asuras, (come to Thee) clad in armour with their head dress removed (to receive as Thy gracious gift) the betel leaf rolls from Thy mouth with white camphor pure as the moon and chew them until they melt away.

Commentary

Shakti is both *para*, transcendental, and *apara*, empirical. In the scheme of evolution, Aparashakti is known as Prakriti and Parashakti is equivalent to Shiva. Aparashakti or Prakriti operates through the ten indriyas, which have two vrittis each, one auspicious and the other inauspicious.

Thus, the ten indriyas have twenty vrittis of which ten are auspicious and ten inauspicious. When an individual sets out in life, he is free to choose which vrittis he wants to develop for himself. The auspicious vrittis initiate a cycle of progress towards knowledge, light and truth, and the inauspicious vrittis lead to ignorance, darkness and despair.

The celestials also underwent this process and gained victory over the demons, who are none other than the inauspicious vrittis, such as anger, pride, jealousy, lust, avarice, selfishness and infatuation. That is how they became divine and celestial. However, after they attained victory over the demons, instead of going to Shiva, they approached the feet of Shakti to receive her gracious gift.

Shakti is a dual force; she thrives on opposites. This is apparent in every aspect of nature, which is her expression. Night is followed by day, cold is balanced by heat, love by hatred, youth by old age, passion by vairagya. For each and everything there is an equal and opposite reaction. Shakti is able to achieve this through her *trigunatmika* nature of sattwa, rajas and tamas.

Thus, when the demonic, inauspicious tamasic vrittis subside, the rajasic vrittis emerge, which are also an aspect of Shakti. Although rajas is not her transcendental nature, it represents Prakriti in a state of motion, where there is growth, progress and development. Her rajasic vrittis are the devas, Indra, Brahma and Vishnu. Shakti's sattwic and transcendental nature is none other than Shiva, which she reveals only to the chosen few.

Tripurahara is a name for Shiva, and this mantra again establishes the power and sway that Devi holds over creation. The devas reject the remnants of Shiva, but vie with each other for the betel leaf rolls that Devi has been chewing. The Puranas are full of stories about the devas, who always fought against evil and inauspiciousness, but still they had pride, jealousy, greed and all the demonic qualities. The difference was that these were subdued and within their control.

The three devas depicted here are not the usual trinity of Brahma, Vishnu and Mahesh; instead they are Brahma, Vishnu and Indra, the lord of the devas. Brahma had been a protagonist in many of the battles against the demons. Indra, too, led many battles against the demons by virtue of which he became the Lord of the devas and the ruler of Swarga, or heaven. Vishnu had taken many *avataras*, divine manifestations, to destroy the rakshasas and demons and to restore dharma.

However, each time these devas return from their battle to Devi, to whom they pay obeisance, removing their head gear as a mark of respect, as is done before entering a sacred place or appearing before a very important person. They turn away from the offerings of Shiva, leaving them for Chanda, to receive the betel leaves from Devi's mouth and chew them until the white pieces of refined camphor contained in them dissolve.

Whenever the devas went to battle against the *daityas*, or demons, they first propitiated Devi, who granted them the power to emerge victorious, for she is the actual ruler of the devas. She energizes them and makes them a potent and viable fighting force. As prana shakti, she offers them the vitality, skill and expertise to conquer the daityas in all respects. She gives them the presence of mind to work out strategies to counteract their every move. After these lengthy battles, they return to Shakti to renew their prana shakti which becomes depleted in combat.

The betel leaves chewed by Devi are traditionally known as *paan*. They are rolled up with different herbs, nuts and flavours and taken by ladies while relaxing after meals. Although these leaves are commonly taken, it is a sign of aristocracy to indulge in this luxury. Devi's regality is suggested by this scene, where she is relaxing in her chamber, chewing betel leaves that are specially prepared with fragrant camphor. At that moment, the three devas enter still wearing their armour. They remove their head gear and bow before her, and she gifts them the betel leaves that she has been chewing, which they are eager to accept.

This scene can be understood as an analogy to the constant inner battles that are raging within between the demons and devas. The amount of prana that is depleted by fighting one's inner demons and the anxiety and stress one faces as a consequence has to be renewed. In this light one should understand the importance of worshipping Devi and eating her prasad in order to renew one's vigour and also develop the strength to keep the demons under siege. Without Devi's help it is simply impossible to continue this enormous task throughout life.

Meditation on this mandala of Devi being worshipped by the devas confers all four purusharthas: artha, kama, dharma and moksha, according to the qualification of the aspirant.

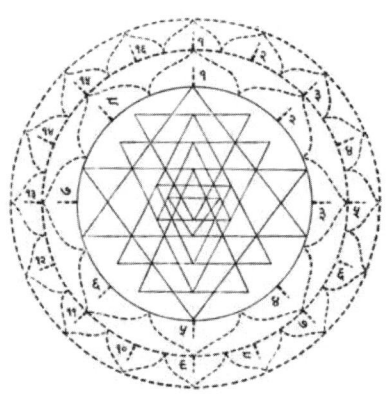

66. Meditation on the sweetness of Devi's voice

विपंज्या गायन्ती विविधमपदानं पशुपतेः
त्वयारब्धे वक्तुं स्खलितवचसा साधुवचने ।
तदीयैर्माधुर्यैरपलपिततन्त्रीकलरवां
निजां वीणां वाणी निचुलयति चोलेन निभृतम् ॥ ६६ ॥

*vipanchyaa gaayantee vividham-apadaanam pashupateh
tvaya-arabdhe vaktum skhalita-vachasaa saadhu vachane;
tadeeyair-maadhuryair-apalapita-tantree-kalaravaam
nijaam veenaam vaanee nichulayati cholena nibhritam. (66)*

vipanchyaa: with her vina; *gaayantee*: sings; *vividham*: various; *apadaanam*: glorious deeds; *pashupateh*: shiva's; *tvaya*: thou; *arabdhe*: begins; *vaktum*: to express; *skhalita vachasaa*: nodding thy head; *saadhu vachane*: words of appreciation; *tadeeyaih*: of those words; *maadhuryaih*: due to the sweetness; *apalapita tantree kalaravaam*: soft melody feeling ridiculed; *nijaam veenaam*: her instrument (vina); *vaanee*: saraswati; *nichulayati*: covers; *cholena*: with its cover; *nibhritam*: silently

Translation
While Saraswati sings with her vina, extolling the glorious deeds of Pashupati (Shiva), Thou beginnest to express words of appreciation, nodding Thy head. The sweetness of Thy voice (however seems to ridicule) the soft melody of her musical instrument, and hence Saraswati silently covers the vina with its cloth.

Commentary
Saraswati is the goddess of fine arts, music and dance. She is propitiated for excellence in this field, as she is the epicentre of this potential. Clothed in pristine white and seated on a white lotus, she is forever the symbol of higher expression. In one hand she holds the vina and in the other a book. Music, dance, art, sculpture, poetry and prose are the hallmark of an awakened mind that can express sublime

emotions. They do not belong to the ordinary plane of mind.

Saraswati marks that point of illumination and expression within an individual, which enables him to break out into poetic ecstasy, as Sankara did when he sang the *Saundarya Lahari* in praise of Devi. However, Shakti represents the full potential of the higher mind, which surpasses even the excellence bestowed by Saraswati. When that mind awakens within an individual, Saraswati is overshadowed and takes a back seat. She secretly covers her favourite musical instrument, the vina, because she understands that some greater power is present.

The manifestations of Shakti fall into different grades. Although each of these is capable of conferring the epitome of excellence on an individual, they pale next to the magnitude of Shakti's full power. Lakshmi bestows *riddhi*, immense wealth and glamour, Saraswati bestows *buddhi*, heightened intellect, and Kali bestows *siddhi*, perfection and power. If the aspirant is not swayed by any of these accomplishments, he can experience the awakening of the highest Shakti. Music or nada yoga is very beneficial for the awakening of Shakti and is one of the most powerful means to transcend time and space.

In this mantra Saraswati is singing about the glories of Shiva, which is what Devi likes to hear. However, Devi sings his praises in such a sweet and melodious voice that she surpasses Saraswati, who has to recede into the background. Once the supreme Shakti starts to sing, the transcendental quality of her voice supersedes all other sounds in terms of frequency and range. Once that sound is heard, all other sounds are obliterated and only the *dhvani* or *paranada*, transcendental sound vibration, of Aum is heard. Shakti forever emits this dhvani on the transcendental or *paravak* level in worship of Shiva, whom she has separated from for the purpose of creation.

However, this truth does not negate the importance of the different frequencies of sound that exist at the lower levels of awareness. Through *abhyasa*, or constant, uninterrupted practice of mantra at the gross level, one can attain the experience of paravak. Saraswati, the goddess of music and speech, helps the aspirant at this stage. She is a manifestation of Shakti, who exists within a particular range of awareness. But as soon as the Devi begins to speak directly to the devotee or to whisper the praises of Shiva into his ear, Saraswati recedes into the background, knowing that her role is over.

67. Meditation on Devi's matchless chin

कराग्रेण स्पृष्टम् तुहिनगिरिणा वत्सलतया
गिरीशेनोदस्तं मुहुरधरपानाकुलतया ।
करग्राह्यं शंभोर्मुखमुकुरवृन्तं गिरिसुते
कथंकारं ब्रूमस्तव चिबुकमौपम्यरहितम् ॥ ६७ ॥

*karaagrena sprishtam tuhinagirinaa vatsalatayaa
gireeshen-odastam muhur-adhara-paanaakulatayaa;
karagraahyam shambhor-mukha-mukura-vrintam girisute
kathamkaaram broomas-tava chibukam-aupamyarahitam.* (67)

karaagrena: with tips of his fingers; *sprishtam*: touched; *tuhinagirinaa*: by (thy father) himavan, the mountain king; *vatsalatayaa*: with affection; *gireeshen*: and by shiva; *udastam*: lifted; *muhuh*: again and again; *adhara paanaakulatayaa*: in the intensity of his desire to kiss thy lips; *kara graahyam*: to hold and view; *shambhoh*: shambhu's; *mukha mukura vrintam*: forms the handle of the mirror of thy face; *girisute*: oh! daughter of the mountain; *kathamkaaram*: how; *broomah*: can I describe; *tava*: thy; *chibukam*: (thy) chin; *aupamyarahitam*: and matchless

Translation

O Daughter of the mountain! How can I describe the matchless beauty of Thy chin, which is touched with affection by Thy father Himavan, the mountain king, and lifted again and again by Thy consort Shiva with the intensity of his desire to kiss Thy lips, and which forms the handle of the mirror of Thy face for Shambhu to hold and view.

Commentary

Prakriti's face is the mirror in which the face of Shiva is reflected. The poetic excellence of this mantra is indeed worth commending. The idea it conveys is sublime, yet the expression is of ordinary amour between a man and woman. The scriptures unanimously proclaim that Shiva and Shakti are inseparable; they never exist apart, they remain united, although they may appear to separate for the purpose of creation. The upanishadic mantra: *Poornamadah poornamidam poornaat poornamudachyate, poornasya poornamaadaaya poornamevaa vaashishyate* means exactly this.

How is it possible that Shiva and Shakti separate for the purpose of creation, yet still remain united? This claim seems to defy all logic. But Shakti has that power to separate from Shiva and show him his own reflection in her embrace. When he sees his reflection in her face, he imagines that he is separated from her, and on account of the notion of separation, desires to kiss her again and again, and drink from her lips.

In this mantra Devi's beautiful chin is described by Sankara as caressed both by her father Himavan when she was a child and her husband Shiva when she grew up into a young lady. The mantra thus effectively conveys two sentiments, one of affection and the other of intense attraction. Meditation on this mandala, describing the beauty of Devi's chin restores peace, love and harmony in relationships.

68. Meditation on Devi's graceful neck

भुजाश्लेषान्नित्यं पुरदमयितुः कण्टकवती
तव ग्रीवा धत्ते मुखकमलनालश्रियमियम् ।
स्वतःश्वेता कालागरुबहुलजम्बालमलिना
मृणालीलालित्यं वहति यदहो हारलतिका ॥६८॥

*bhujaa-shleshaannityam puradamayituh kantakavati
tava greeva dhatte mukha-kamala-naala-shriyam-iyam;
svatah-shvetaa kaalaagaru-bahula-jambaala-malinaa
mrinaalee-laalityam vahati yadaho haaralatikaa.* (68)

bhuja ashleshaat: by the embrace; *nityam*: always; *puradamayituh*: of the destroyer of cities (shiva); *kantakavati*: thrilled (with tiny hairs standing on end); *tava*: thy; *greeva iyam*: this neck; *dhatte*: displays; *mukha kamala naala shriyam*: the gracefulness of the stalk of the lotus; *svatah shvetaa*: naturally white; *kaalaagaru bahula jambaala malinaa*: darkened by the application of agaru, a scented paste; *mrinaalee laalityam*: charm of the fibrous root of the lotus stalk; *vahati*: presents; *yat adhya*: below this neck; *haaralatikaa*: garland

Translation
Thy neck, always thrilled by the embrace of the destroyer of cities (Shiva), displays the gracefulness of the lotus-stalk. Below this neck with the naturally white garland (of pearls), darkened by the application of agaru paste, presents the charm of the fibrous root of the lotus.

Commentary
In this mantra Sankara proceeds to describe the beauty of Devi's neck. This systematic glorification of Devi's parts suggests that he is directing the divine energy of Devi, awakened through his worship, to the different parts of his body in order to cure the ailment that he was afflicted with. The graceful neck of Devi, forever in the thrilling embrace

of Shiva, is adorned with a garland of white pearls that sets off the colour of her neck darkened with the application of the muddy agaru paste, making her look even more beautiful. Ordinarily, dark paste would detract from the beauty of a lady; here, however, it is shown to enhance Devi's beauty.

The concepts of beauty are set by the society and one never ventures beyond that, but this is a limited view. One always imagines that fairness is akin to beauty, but in reality darkness is equally attractive. One attributes long and shining tresses to beauty, but the shaved head of an ascetic is even more beautiful, as the source of this beauty is not external but internal. True beauty is not the result of artificial creams, lotions and shampoos, but of a limitless inner glow.

The most beautiful diamonds, gems, gold and silver are found in the mud of river beds. The delicate lotus is born in mud, but its beauty is incomparable. Sankara's description of Devi's neck highlights this contrast. Absolute beauty is complete in itself; it does not need any outside agent. Even if something unattractive and non-appealing is kept nearby, absolute beauty will make it look beautiful.

The term *puradamayituh* refers to Shiva, who is the destroyer of the three levels of individual awareness: jagrat, swapna and sushupti, and is forever established in *turiya*, the universal consciousness. Devi is always in his embrace, which means that she too is forever established in turiya. Shiva's relationship with Devi is eternal and everlasting. His embrace of her is not limited to a few seconds, minutes or hours, as it is with humans. The thrill and bliss that emanates from their embrace is total, complete, and unending. Meditation on Shiva and Shakti in this way can induce samadhi.

Meditation on this mandala of Devi's neck purifies the devotee and absolves deep-rooted samskaras, or impressions that obstruct his progress.

69. Meditation on the three strands at Devi's throat

गले रेखास्तिस्रो गतिगमकगीतैकनिपुणे
विवाहव्यानद्धत्रिगुणगुणसंख्याप्रतिभुवः ।
विराजन्ते नानाविधमधुररागाकरभुवां
त्रयाणां ग्रामाणां स्थितिनियमसीमान इव ते ॥६९॥

gale rekhaastisro gati-gamaka-geetaika-nipune
vivaaha-vyaanaddha triguna-guna-sankhyaa-pratibhuvah;
viraajante naanaa-vidha-madhura-raagaakara-bhuvaam
trayaanaam graamaanaam sthiti-niyama-seemaana iva te. (69)

gale: on (thy) throat; *rekhaah*: lines; *tisro*: three; *gati gamaka geetaika nipune*: oh! mistress of the musical modes, modulations and songs; *vivaaha vyaanaddha triguna guna sankhyaa pratibhuvah*: indicating the number of strings in the auspicious chord fastened at the time of thy wedding; *viraajante*: shine; *naanaa vidha madhura raagaakara bhuvaam*: which form the source of the various melodies of musical notes; *trayaanaam graamaanaam*: three musical scales; *sthiti niyama seemaana*: boundaries demarcating; *iva*: like; *te*: thy

Translation
O Mistress of the musical modes, modulations and songs! The three lines on Thy throat, indicating the number of strings in the auspicious cord fastened at the time of Thy wedding, shine like boundaries demarcating the three musical scales which form the source of the various melodies of musical notes.

Commentary
From *Omkara,* the first vibration, sprang forth all other sounds, including the seven notes of the musical scale out of which all music is composed. The seven notes of the musical scale: *sa, re, ga, ma, pa, dha, ni, sa*; or *do, re, mi, fa, so, la, ti, do* that form all music originate from Omkara. As Shakti herself is Omkara, when she vibrates to emit the first nada, she is

declared as the mistress of all sound, its varied modulations, musical modes and songs.

The beautiful allegory of the three strings on her throat fastened at the time of her wedding signify the *mangala sutra,* auspicious thread, worn by brides as a sign that they are married. This further indicates that it is none other than Shiva, her husband, who gently caresses these lines on her throat to produce the first dhwani. Just as music is born when the strings of an instrument are gently and skilfully caressed by a musician, in the same way, the different sounds are born of the original dhwani through Shiva's caress.

Gati gamaka geetaika nipune indicates one who has prowess in *gati,* movement or rhythm of the voice, *gamaka,* modulation of the voice and *gita,* singing a song. Timing is an important factor in music and Devi is mistress of time. The three factors that govern one's entire existence from birth to death are time, space and object, which are the three categories of the finite mind. The minute these are transcended, the entire world fades away, just as in deep sleep. At the time of sleep, one has no knowledge of the time or space in which one is sleeping or the objects around one.

Devi rules over time as *Kali,* the destroyer of time. Shiva as *Mahakaal,* timelessness or eternity, is the master of time. Time, as past present and future, governs one's entire life and the quality of one's experience. One is born, becomes young, turns into an adult, grows old and dies. This experience of life takes place within a time-frame, and one has no control over it. Time rules one's life, but it is a mere puppet in the hands of Shiva and Shakti, for together they are the source of time, which governs creation.

This factor is highlighted here in a subtle way. The three essential factors that relate to all forms of music: gati, movement of the voice; gamaka, modulation of the voice, and gita, the resulting song, are dependent on time. Without correct timing, music does not stir the soul.

These three aspects of music are beautifully connected with the intimate relationship of Shiva and Shakti. Just as the intimacy between husband and wife is defined by the three strands of the mangala sutra, which adorns the neck of a married woman, in the same way the intimacy between Shiva and Shakti is defined by the emergence of nada, which is achieved by a pulsation in Shakti that occurs when Shiva gently caresses the three strands at her throat.

The three strands referred to here cover a wide range of connotations and levels of experience from gross to transcendental. At a finite level they refer to time, space and object; at a cosmic level to sattwa, rajas and tamas. In terms of awareness they refer to jagrat, swapna and sushupti; in terms of nada to vaikhari, madhyama and pashyanti. At a transcendental level they represent Tripura Sundari, the beauty that abounds when the three levels of gross, subtle and causal experience are transcended, as well as Maha Tripura, the experience that lies beyond the range of the three.

The wide range of Shakti's influence is described here, as she is mistress of the modulations of music as it is heard in everyday life from pop, rap and disco to classical ragas, as well as mistress of the first vibration that emanated as Omkara, the sound of creation.

70. Meditation on Devi's protective arms

मृणालीमृद्वीनां तव भुजलतानां चतसृणां
चतुर्भिः सौंदर्यं सरसिजभवः स्तौति वदनैः ।
नखेभ्यः संत्रस्यन् प्रथमदमनादन्धकरिपोः
चतुर्णां वक्त्राणां सममभयहस्तार्पणधिया ॥ ७० ॥

*mrinaalee-mridveenaam tava bhuja-lataanaam chatasrinaam
chaturbhih saundaryam sarasija-bhavah stauti vadanaih;
nakhebhyah samtrasyan prathama-damanaad-andhaka-ripoh
chaturnaam vaktraanaam samam-abhaya-hastaarpanadhiyaa.* (70)

mrinaalee mridveenaam: smooth like the lotus stalk; *tava*: thy; *bhuja lataanaam chatasrinaam*: of (thy) creeper-like four arms; *chaturbhih vadanaih*: with his four heads; *saundaryam*: beauty; *sarasija bhavah*: brahma; *stauti*: is praising; *nakhebhyah*: fingernails; *samtrasyan*: afraid of; *prathama damanaad*: due to the earlier mishap (in which shiva nipped off one of brahma's five heads); *andhaka ripoh*: shiva's; *chaturnaam vaktraanaam*: to his surviving four heads; *samam*: simultaneously; *abhaya hastaarpanadhiyaa*: hoping that thou might give protection

Translation
Brahma, being afraid of the fingernails of Shiva due to the earlier mishap (when he nipped off his fifth head), is now praising the loveliness of Thy creeper-like four arms, smooth like the lotus stalk, with his remaining four heads simultaneously hoping that Thou might give him protection.

Commentary
This mantra refers to the age old story about Shiva's offensive behaviour towards Brahma. References are made to this event in many of the songs, stotras, and chants to Shiva and Shakti. The reason for this offensive behaviour was none other than Saraswati. Brahma is the creator, acting at the behest of Shakti, the energy principle. He created the

universe and its many galaxies. He also created the fine arts, music, song and dance, and Saraswati, the goddess of fine arts, is his daughter.

After creating Saraswati, however, Brahma became infatuated with her and started chasing her, as an amorous man would chase his lover. Shiva was offended by this lack of control or discrimination on the part of Brahma and resorted to violence in order to correct him. In fact, he tore off one of Brahma's five heads with his fingernails, and would have done more damage, but for the protection of Shakti.

Everyone is destroyed by his own wrong actions. Outside agencies, such as job, boss, husband/wife, children and so on, are only the catalysts that propel one towards right or wrong actions. According to the choice one makes, one derives pain or pleasure, happiness or sadness. If one has the good sense to make a right choice, there is no problem, but supposing one makes a wrong choice, as in the case of Brahma who chased his own daughter out of uncontrollable passion. Is there no redemption?

Yes, there is! The worship of Devi can save one from the evil effects of one's karma. She absorbs one's wrong actions and one is thereby freed from that adversity, just as Brahma lost only one head at the hands of Shiva and was able to retain his other four. He could have lost all five, but due to his adoration of Devi, she redeemed him. Everyone can be redeemed and absolved of their wrong actions through worship of Devi.

This mantra again sheds new light on the intimacy and equality of Shiva and Shakti that was established in the last mantra. Sankara develops this theme right through *Saundarya Lahari*. There are many levels of Shiva that he exposes in these mantras. For example, he introduces Sadashiva as the cot on which Devi reclines, and Shiva as the bedspread that covers the cot, thus implying that this level of Shiva is a degree closer to Shakti than Sadashiva, as the bedspread lies between the cot and Devi. Then there is Shiva with whom she is in eternal embrace. He seems to be an integral part of her and the one she keeps with her even after the dissolution of all the other tattwas, or elements. This Shiva is highlighted in the last mantras as he is incessantly embracing her.

However, this mantra highlights the fact that Shakti also has a life of her own, which exists apart from her intimacy with Shiva. She offers protection to her devotees, even from the wrath of Shiva, as she did to Brahma when Shiva became angry with him. As the mother of creation, she is forever kind and compassionate to her offspring. Just as a mother protects her children from the wrath of a stern father, in the same way, Shakti protects her devotees from all kinds of mishaps throughout life. Even in the jaws of death, when one is about to be devoured by Mahakaal, the great time, she comes to one's rescue.

In order to gain Shakti's protection, however, the aspirant must develop an intimate connection through worshipping and praising her, just as Brahma did. One develops connections and relationships with different people throughout life by offering them love, dedication, appreciation and praise. This becomes the basis of a strong bond, which one uses as and when needed. In the same way, the devotee develops a strong bond with Devi.

71. Meditation on the splendour of Devi's hands

नखानामुद्योतैर्नवनलिनरागं विहसतां
कराणां ते कांतिं कथय कथयामः कथमुमे ।
कयाचिद्वा साम्यं भजतु विधयाा हन्त कमलं
यदि क्रीडल्लक्ष्मीचरणतललाक्षारुणदलम् ॥७१॥

*nakhaanaam-udyotair-nava-nalina-raagam vihasataam
karaanaam te kaantim kathaya kathayaamah katham-ume;
kayaachidvaa saamyam bhajatu vidhayaa hanta kamalam
yadi kreedallakshmee charana-tala-laakshaaruna-dalam.* (71)

nakhaanaam: of the nails; *udyotaih*: lit up with the radiance; *nava nalina raagam*: the brightness of the newly bloomed lotus; *vihasataam*: surpasses; *karaanaam*: of (thy) hands; *te*: thy; *kaantim*: splendour; *kathaya*: tell us; *kathayaamah*: can we describe; *katham*: how; *ume*: oh! uma; *kayaa chit vaa*: somehow; *saamyam*: similarity; *bhajatu*: can attain; *vidhayaa*: perhaps; *hanta*: alas; *kamalam*: lotus; *yadi kreedat lakshmee charana tala laakshaaruna dalam*: if it comes in to contact with the red dye on the feet of the sporting goddess, lakshmi

Translation
O Uma! How can we describe the splendour of Thy hands, lit up with the radiance of Thy nails, which surpasses the brightness of the morning's lotus blooms? Alas, the lotus can perhaps attain some similarity (with Thy hands), if its redness is enhanced by contact with the red dye on the feet of goddess Lakshmi, who sports in it.

Commentary
Lakshmi is the consort of Vishnu, and Uma the consort of Shiva. Lakshmi is considered one of the *poorna avataras*, or total manifestations of Shakti's powers. She arose from the *samudra manthana*, churning of the ocean, when the devas and *daityas*, demons, were in pursuit of *amrita*, the nectar of immortality. At that time different divine objects arose from

the ocean, such as *kamadhenu*, the celestial cow, *airavata*, the celestial elephant, and *parijata*, the celestial tree. When Lakshmi emerged from the ocean, both the devas and daityas were astounded by her beauty and wanted to take her, but she went to Vishnu because he alone was fit to receive her.

Lakshmi is seated on a red lotus and is the symbol of progress, growth, fertility, auspiciousness and wealth. This mantra, however, says that despite her divine attributes, Lakshmi is also a manifestation of that supreme Shakti at whose behest even Brahma, Vishnu and Mahesh carry out their respective duties. The lotus can be compared with the hands of Devi only because it is the seat of Lakshmi and is tinged by the red colour of her feet. Lakshmi is the manifest reflection of Shakti. She is the accomplishment of *riddhi*, pomp and show. No wonder the lotus is elevated by the presence of Shakti as she sports in it.

From the neck Sankara proceeds to describe the hands and nails of Devi. Once again, as in earlier mantras, the reflection of Shakti is seen in Saraswati. Previously, the redness of Devi's tongue gave Saraswati a red hue. In this mantra there is a reflection of the redness of Shakti's hands and nails in the feet of Lakshmi, which are dyed red, as is the custom with young brides who do this as a type of *shringara*, or ritual to appear more beautiful. Again Sankara emphasizes that beauty and higher experience go hand in hand. Beauty elevates the soul and transports the awareness to another realm altogether. Spiritual experience is not devoid of youth, beauty, eroticism and passion, although the quality differs from that of the mundane experience.

In this mantra Shakti is addressed as Uma, which is a name for Parvati. So, Parvati is referred to as the supreme Shakti, apart from Lakshmi and Saraswati. Parvati was named Uma by her mother as a plea not to perform the severe austerities that she did to attain Shiva. Parvati was a poorna avatara, complete manifestation in herself, and so did not need any outside agency to achieve wholeness. Although she did not need to perform penance for Shiva, she did it out of love for him, which is the highest type of bhakti.

Uma is an example of unconditional love. She did not want anything from Shiva as she was complete in herself, yet she did the severe panchagni tapasya out of her intense love and devotion for Shiva.

This is how the devotee should develop bhakti towards Devi. One should love her for the sake of love, and not for the sake of fulfilling one's desires, needs and wants.

72. Meditation on Devi's overflowing breasts

समं देवि स्कन्दद्विपवदनपीतं स्तनयुगं
तवेदं नः खेदं हरतु सततं प्रस्नुतमुखम् ।
यदालोक्याशङ्काकुलितहृदयो हासजनकः
स्वकुम्भौ हेरम्बः परिमृशति हस्तेन झटिति ॥७२॥

samam devi skanda-dvipavadana-peetam stanayugam
tav-edam nah khedam haratu satatam prasnuta-mukham;
yad-aalokyaa-shankaa-kulitahridayo haasajanakah
svakumbhau herambah parimrishati hastena jhatiti. (72)

samam: simultaneously; *devi*: oh! devi; *skanda dvipavadana peetam*: suckled by both skanda and ganesha; *stanayugam edam*: these pair of breasts; *tava*: thy; *nah*: our; *khedam*: sorrows; *haratu satatam*: may always expel; *prasnuta mukham*: from which milk is overflowing; *yat*: which; *aalokya*: seeing; *ashankaa akulita hridayo*: with suspicion in his heart ganesha; *haasajanakah*: causing great amusement; *sva kumbhau*: his frontal lobes; *herambah*: ganesha; *parimrishati*: feels; *hastena*: with his hands; *jhat iti*: suddenly

Translation
O Devi! May Thy pair of breasts from which milk is overflowing, suckled simultaneously by both Skanda and Ganesha, always expel our sorrows. Suddenly, with suspicion in his heart, Ganesha feels with his hands to see whether the pair of frontal globes of his elephant face are there (or whether they have become Thy breasts before his eyes), thus causing great amusement (to his parents).

Commentary
Siddhis arise from a metamorphosis in the original tattwa, or element. As Shakti is transformed, different attributes arise from her, such as beauty, intelligence, intellect and ego. However, Skanda and Ganesha are her sons. They were not born out of a metamorphosis in Shakti, but emerged

from her being. Ganesha was born from her hands when she etched him into the mud and blew life into him. So Ganesha is her offspring and Shiva was not involved in his birth.

Shiva did not even recognize Ganesha when he returned home one day and found him standing guard in front of his mother's innermost chamber. Ganesha, too, did not recognize Shiva and denied him entry, at which Shiva was outraged and cut off his head. When Uma came running out and saw what had happened, she cried loud that Shiva had cut off her son's head. This proves Shakti's independence in the process of creation, as even Shiva, who is her most intimate companion, does not know of her creations until she acquaints him with them.

In the human skull also, Ganesha stands entry at the gate to the cranium. The exact replica of Ganesha has been found in the dissection of the human skull by a Lebanese scientist, who has even released pictures of the same, and the resemblance is amazing.

Thus, in all rituals obeisance is first paid to Ganesha; otherwise one will not gain entry to the secret chamber where Devi resides. Not even Shiva can enter without the consent of Ganesha because he will not violate the wish of Shakti. Once again, the idea of reflection arises here as Devi's breasts are mistaken by Ganesha for the frontal lobes on his elephant face, and the whiteness of the steady stream of milk that overflows from them is mistaken for the whiteness of his own tusks. So he begins to feel with his hands to see if his frontal lobes and tusks are still in place or not.

According to tantra this idea of reflection is one of the chief attributes of Devi, who is a master of the art of creating illusion. She accomplishes this through her power of *maya*, which is the seed of illusion. Everything in creation is her maya. The tantric and vedic philosophies stipulate that the world is a reflection of that supreme Shakti who is the absolute beauty. What one beholds in this beautiful world is only an illusion or reflection of her.

The experiences of the world are illusory and fade away, but the experience of Shakti is timeless and eternal. The gratification one gets from the world is incomplete and leaves one craving for more, but the gratification one gets from the experience of Shakti, who is the source of all beauty, is fully rewarding and satisfying. The phrase *prasnuta mukham* gives an image of wholeness and fullness, a never-ending supply of sustenance and nourishment, which Devi bestows.

This experience of total gratification is different to the reflection she creates that one mistakes for the real stuff, just as Ganesha did. His plight was the same as that of everyone. The only difference is that Ganesha at once came out of his illusion due to the succour of Devi's milk. The aspirant, too, can expel the darkness and come out of his misery by meditating on this image of Devi's breasts.

Matter is purified through the medium of energy. When the potency of energy is high as in the case of Shakti, the purification is total and one becomes pure, refined and divine. Ganesha and Skanda are regarded as divine, because they are direct recipients of Devi's milk from her two breasts, the left and the right. The aspirant can also avail himself of this if, like Ganesha, he becomes like her child and meditates on her in this way.

In this mantra the erotic image of the young girl enticing her lover in so many ways and then succumbing to the erotic passion of embrace and union develops into the eroticism of a young mother with two offspring, who are feeding simultaneously on her full breasts which incessantly emit a steady stream of milk.

Quantum physics speaks of the revolution of electrons, which spin from the right and the left as they journey from the great source of energy to form the building blocks of matter. The breasts of Devi which are suckled by Ganesha and Skanda represent this absolute phenomena that occurs in the realm of the cosmos, unseen and unknown, at the behest of Shakti.

In the process of meditation too, the aspirant has to overcome the reflection which he sees outside by first developing an image within himself, just as Ganesha did, and then transcending it altogether to become one with the great energy of Shakti.

73. Meditation on the nectar of Devi's breasts

अमू ते वक्षोजावमृतरसमाणिक्यकुतुपौ
न संदेहस्पन्दो नगपतिपताके मनसि नः ।
पिबन्तौ तौ यस्मादविदितवधूसङ्गमरसौ
कुमारावद्यापि द्विरदवदनक्रौञ्चदमनौ ॥७३॥

*amoo te vakshojaav amritarasa maanikyakutupau
na sandehaspando nagapatipataake manasi nah;
pibantau tau yasmaad-avidita-vadhu-sangamarasau
kumaaraav-adyaapi dvirada-vadana-krauncha-damanau.* (73)

amoo te vakshojaau: these two breasts of thine; *amritarasa maanikyakutupau*: are jars made of ruby, filled with nectar; *na sandehah spando*: have no doubt at all; *nagapati pataake*: oh! mountain king's flag of victory; *manasi*: in the mind; *nah*: we; *pibantau tau*: by drinking their contents; *yasmaat*: because; *avidita vadhu sangamarasau*: not having known the pleasure of the company of women; *kumaaraau*: (have remained) young boys; *adyaapi*: to this day; *dvirada vadana krauncha damanau*: kumara and vinayaka

Translation

O Mountain King's flag of victory! We have no doubt at all in our mind that these two breasts of Thine are jars of ruby filled with nectar, because by drinking their contents, Thy two sons, Kumara and Vinayaka, (have remained) young boys to this day, not having known the pleasure of the company of women.

Commentary

Shakti is pregnant with potential, or *vibhooti*, which manifests as *pratibha*, the genius in an individual. Genius in any form relates to the awakening of Shakti within the individual. Genius in an individual can easily be spotted, but what form would genius assume in that supreme Shakti? The immense power of Shakti, if aroused, can confer anything on an individual. This has happened in the lives of many people who have been geniuses in their fields.

However, what would be the outcome if Shakti were aroused to create something from herself? That form would be the ultimate symbol of *riddhi*, prosperity, *buddhi*, innate intelligence, and *siddhi*, ultimate accomplishment. That is the form of Ganesha, whose co-wives are riddhi, siddhi and buddhi. Ganesha stands for skill and Kumara, or Kartikeya, stands for valour. One needs strength, courage, dexterity and skill in order to accomplish any task, whether it is running a business, building mansions, solving intricate problems, or even achieving spiritual goals. To overcome the demons and monsters within also needs skilful manoeuvring of one's innate tendencies.

The potency of these two symbols, Kartikeya and Ganesha, nurtured by Shakti is made more convincing by the allusion to them being fed on the milk from Shakti's breasts. Mother's milk is nectar for the child, which nourishes and sustains him throughout life. The entire molecular structure is influenced by the milk the infant drinks immediately after birth. In India, great emphasis is placed on the exclusive diet of mother's milk for the newborn child for this reason.

If an infant is fed on powdered milk that is full of preservatives and chemicals, its body, mind and intellect will undoubtedly be influenced. Kumara and Vinayaka are most fortunate because they have been suckled on the breasts of Shakti. Thus they will never be subject to the decay and destruction of the elements that an ordinary person who is fed on the breast of a human mother would have to undergo.

The pure Shakti element is present within human beings too, but it has not been awakened. Rather, its influence is very limited due to negligence, poor lifestyle, and erratic thinking patterns. How can one generate the high potency minerals of *amrita*, or nectar, which can confer the boons which Shakti granted to Ganesha and Kumara through her breast milk.

Milk is a substance that is born out of the mother's body. If the mother has maintained her purity, there is nothing that can compare with it. Here, however, mother's milk alludes not just to a diet of minerals and vitamins, but to the very stuff that can arouse one's dormant potential and make one aware of his greatness. Shakti offers *stan paan*, or breast milk, not just to her sons, but even to her husband, Shiva. In Tarapeetha, one of the sixty-four *shaktipeethas* or awakened shrines of Shakti where the parts of her dismembered body fell, the ritual of Shiva feeding on Shakti's breast is carried out daily as a form of worship in front of thousands of devotees.

Shiva, or consciousness, feeds on the breast of Shakti. This image shatters all the concepts of Shiva supremacy, because here he can be considered subservient to Shakti. However, in the interplay of Shakti and Shiva, many roles are assumed by them. In these roles subservience and superiority are frequently interchanged. They also have roles of balance and equal strength, for they are not different from each other.

Shakti is that power which stops degeneration. If something is devoid of Shakti, it begins to decay and die. This is true in a physical as well as a spiritual sense, but more importantly, it is relevant for spiritual awakening, experience and ecstasy. One wastes energy in useless and trivial matters, so there is not enough left for inner experience. Inner experience requires a great deal of prana or energy. This is why prana has to be built up, conserved and channelled to the higher centres.

However, prana is usually depleted by the hundred and one tasks that one is compelled to perform. Thinking uses a lot of prana, especially if the thought patterns centre around worry and agitation. The sexual act consumes a lot of prana. That is why most people fall asleep after sexual intimacy, because sleeping allows them to recoup from the depletion of prana.

Ganesha and Kumara have no cause to worry on this point, because they have received pure, unadulterated prana from Shakti, so they have a head start. This prana does not drop to the lower centres and create nervous titillation in them, so they are never swayed by the company of women. Thus they have also become objects of worship with the power to confer blessings on the devotees.

74. Meditation on the pearl necklace adorning Devi's breasts

वहत्यम्ब स्तम्बेरमदनुजकुम्भप्रकृतिभिः
समारब्धां मुक्तामणिभिरमलां हारलतिकाम् ।
कुचाभोगो बिम्बाधररुचिभिरन्तः शबलितां
प्रतापव्यामिश्रां पुरविजयिनः कीर्तिमिव ते ॥७४॥

vahaty-amba stamber-ama-danuja-kumbha-prakritibhih
samaarabdhaam muktaa manibhir-amalaam haaralatikaam;
kuchaabhogo bimbaa-dhararuchibhir-antah shabalitaam
prataapa-vyaamishraam puravijayinah keertimiva te. (74)

vahati: bears; *amba*: oh! mother; *stambeh ama danuja kumbha prakritibhih*: got from the frontal globe of gajasura; *samaarabdhaam*: made; *muktaa manibhih*: of pearls; *amalaam*: pure; *haaralatikaam*: creeper-like necklace; *kuchaabhoga*: the expanse of (thy) breasts; *bimbaa dhara ruchibhih*: by the brilliance of thy bimba-like lips; *antah shabalitaam*: variegated from within; *prataapa vyaamishraam*: confluence of the valour; *pura vijayinah*: of thy consort, shiva; *keertim iva*: and fame; *te*: thy

Translation
O Ambe! The expanse of Thy breasts bears a creeper-like necklace made of pure pearls obtained from the frontal globe of Gajasura, variegated from within by the brilliance of Thy bimba-like lips, as if it were the confluence of the fame (white) and the valour (red) of Thy consort Shiva, the destroyer of the cities.

Commentary
Gaja, or elephant, is the largest and mightiest of animals, most difficult to subdue or eradicate. Dinosaurs, mammoths and many creatures from the wild have become extinct, but the elephant has survived down through the ages. This quality of the elephant likens it to the strongest emotion in

man, which is *kama*, passion. If there is any one emotion that rules over man's life, it is kama; everything else pales beside it. A man afflicted by kama is like a monkey drunk on champagne and stung by a scorpion. He just cannot sit still until kama is satisfied.

A man under the sway of kama has no shame or fear, *'na bhayam na lajja'*. So, it is quite natural to venerate a person who has controlled kama, as this is no ordinary feat. An ordinary person cannot even conceive of this idea, let alone achieve it. Even in old age, when the body is infirm and weak and the grave is nearby, still the passions run high. They consume and torment a man, even though he is no longer fit to express and fulfil them.

Mahatma Gandhi was venerated because he attempted to subdue kama. The view held by millions of people is that one who can subdue this mighty giant is no less than a mahatma. By destroying Kamadeva, Shiva instantly elevated himself to this status. The story about the encounter of Kamadeva with Shiva when he was deep in meditation verifies this. Kamadeva did not spare any guiles to tempt Shiva with passion and lust. By generating the befitting fragrances, scenery, sounds of music, laughter and the tinkling of bells, Kamadeva tried to create the season of romance, which could have swayed even the strongest of yogis. But Shiva was so maddened with rage at Kamadeva's attempt to disturb his meditation that he reduced him to ashes in an instant. Since that time Kamadeva has been invisible. His arrows strike painlessly without leaving any marks or bleeding, but the wounds are so deep that they last a whole lifetime!

The act of Shiva destroying Kama is compared with the difficult feat of destroying an elephant, the mightiest of animals. Kama, passion, starts in the mind and from there it travels to the body. In the same way, Shiva won the pearls that were hidden in the head of the elephant, Gajasura, and thus subdued him. These pearls were the sign of his great victory, which he then offered to Shakti to adorn her neck and breasts. A valiant man likes to offer the objects of conquest to his lady love waiting for him back at home. By doing so, he is assured of her love in greater measure! Who will not love a strong and powerful man?

So the necklace of pearls which adorns Shakti has been given to her by Shiva, who is forever enamoured by her and wants her to look more beautiful. Shakti adorns herself with this necklace of pearls, which hangs between her breasts and become tinged with red.

Victory over kama is victory over the *vasanas*, seed desires, because if the strongest vasana can be rooted out, the weaker ones will definitely be eradicated. Although the vasanas are active and volatile in mooladhara and swadhisthana, they reside as dead matter in anahata. The vasanas remain as traces there, so anahata is the seat of the vasanas in limbo. They no longer torment the individual; rather victory is in sight and ensured, as long as the sadhaka remains vigilant.

The vasana do not have to be exterminated, but transformed into a more dynamic and creative force. The universal nature of vasana has to manifest. This is possible at the level of anahata, which is the seat of universal love, as opposed to the lower centres where the individualistic desire to own or possess is expressed. Love for the sake of loving is an expression of anahata; this is unconditional love. The same lower vasanas are churned and transformed into divine love, compassion, higher intelligence, and memory of higher planes. The *Tantroktam Devi Suktam*, an ode to the transformed vasanas that manifest as the influence of Devi begins to catch hold of an individual, explains this in a beautiful, poetic way.

It would not be correct to say that Shiva and Shakti are devoid of vasana. If that were so, then what is the relevance of creation? Creation is born out of desire. The desire that mortals experience is a mere tiny reflection of the desire of the creator. The same vasana, or nervous titillation, that one experiences in daily life, if transformed, can create this mighty universe. That is *iccha shakti*, the power of desire, which can manifest anything.

The desire to create arose in the universal creator out of unconditional love and compassion, as opposed to the ordinary desire of creating, owning, or dominating over something. The relationships that one creates around oneself are just an expression of craving for power, status, success, fame and money. One does not really love others unless they fulfil one's wishes and demands.

Atmanastu kamaye sarva priyam bhavati: the Upanishads declare that it is for one's own sake that one loves another. The son's love for the father, the miser's love for money, the lover's love for his beloved are all just forms of an inner desire that is being expressed. If the beloved betrays the lover, he soon turns into an enemy ready to kill the one for whom he had expressed undying love. Is that real love or just a temporary arrangement?

The pearl necklace adorning the neck and breasts of Shakti is Shiva's tribute to her, for she too has annihilated the hold of the vasanas. So this mantra expresses an excellent blend of poetry and mysticism.

75. Meditation on Devi's breast milk

तवः स्तन्यं मन्ये तुहिनगिरिकन्ये हृदयतः
पयः पारावारः परिवहति सारस्वत इव ।
दयावत्या दत्तं द्रविडशिशुरास्वाद्य तव यत्
कवीनां प्रौढानामजनि कमनीयः कवयिता ॥७५॥

*tavah stanyam manye tuhinagiri-kanye hridayatah
payah paaravaarah parivahati saarasvata iva;
dayaavatya dattam dravidashishur-aasvaadya tava yat
kaveenaam praudhaanaam-ajani kamaneeyah kavayitaa.* (75)

tavah stanyam manye: I remember thy breast; *tuhinagiri kanye*: oh! daughter of the mountain king; *hridayatah*: from thy heart; *payah paaravaarah*: the milk ocean; *parivahati*: emerges; *saarasvata iva*: as poetic inspiration; *dayaavatya*: graciously kindly; *dattam*: given; *dravida shishuh*: dravida child; *aasvaadya*: by drinking it; *tava*: thine; *yat*: due to which; *kaveenaam praudhaanaam*: among great composers; *ajani*: became; *kamaneeyah kavayitaa*: noted poet

Translation
O Daughter of the mountain king! I remember Thy breast, the milk ocean emerging as poetic inspiration from Thy heart, graciously given to the Dravidian child (Sankara) by which, due to drinking it, among great composers, he became a noted poet.

Commentary
We all know that the heart is the seat of poesy and the breasts the source of sustenance. Today the breasts are associated with erotic imagery, but traditionally they were the symbol of sustenance, nourishment and preservation. All the different parts of Devi, the cosmic mother, symbolize important facets of life. Out of these, four stand out in the tantric tradition: *yoni*, reproductive organ; *stan*, breasts; *vakshasthal*, heart, and *trikuti*, eyebrow centre.

The breasts of Devi offer spiritual succour to those who are hungry for it. To those who wish for other things, Devi's breasts offer the accomplishments of their choice. So potent is the milk from Devi's breasts that even Shiva does *stan paan*, drinking milk from her breasts. As was previously discussed in mantra 73, every day devotees gather in the temple of Tarapeetha, a few hours east of Deoghar, to worship Devi feeding Shiva with her breast milk.

This is a unique concept found in tantra. Each and every facet of life has a deeper esoteric meaning, thus making it sacred. Even a mundane act like a mother breast feeding her child has great significance when viewed in this manner. Breast feeding is also symbolic of *shaktipat*, the transference of energy from shakti to the devotee. In the Puranas, there are many incidents where Devi offered her breast milk to abandoned children who were crying out in distress and hunger because there was no one to feed them.

Children who are favoured by Devi in this manner turn out to be prodigies in their field. One such reference occurs in this mantra: *dravidashishuh*, a Dravidian child became a notable poet because Devi fed him with her milk. Dravidas are the race which inhabits the southern part of India. In fact, they are classified as the *panchdravidas*, which includes: Maharashtra, Karnataka, Kerala, Tamil Nadu and Andhra Pradesh. The Dravidians have their own dialect, script, art, literature, poetry and culture, which are exclusively theirs. The Dravidians are a distinct civilization of India, traces of which have been found in the excavations of Harappa and Mohenjodaro.

Kerala, the region where Sankara was born, is included in the area of Dravidas. In reference to *dravidashishuh*, it is assumed that Sankara was speaking of himself. As a young child, Sankara had gone to the Devi temple in his father's absence with an offering of milk. When the idol did not consume the milk, Sankara began to cry. On seeing the innocence of the child, Devi manifested in the idol and drank the entire pot of milk. However, on seeing that there was none left for him, Sankara again started to cry. Out of compassion, Devi began to suckle him from her breasts, and as a result of that shaktipat or transference of Devi's energy, the child received the blessings of poesy.

The phrase *tavah stanyam manye*, which literally means, 'I remember your breasts', gives the impression that Sankara is talking about himself. Moreover, if he is talking about himself, it means that he saw her breasts and also suckled them as the story about his childhood seems to suggest. If that story is true, then when he grew up and meditated on Devi, he remembered each and every part of her as he had seen her when she gave him darshan in the temple. But he remembers her stan, or breasts, most clearly, for the Devi has fed him with her breast milk. There are several other stories which creep up in relation to this *dravidashishuh*. However, more important than trying to establish who this most favoured Dravida child was, it is important to understand that *stan paan*, or suckling of the breasts, is a tantric ritual which confers *shaktipat*, or transference of powerful divine energies.

This mantra relates to the child who became a poet by drinking Devi's breast milk. In tantra there are also references to Shiva as an adult suckling the breasts of Devi, which induces a very elevating experience. Shakti is the source of prana and meditation on her breast milk in this way confers creativity and genius. The devotee can remember Devi in this way to elevate his thoughts and emotions.

76. Meditation on the navel of Devi

हरक्रोधज्वलावलिभिरवलीढेन वपुषा
गभीरे ते नाभीसरसि कृतसङ्गो मनसिजः ।
समुत्तस्थौ तस्मादचलतनये धूमलतिका
जनस्तां जानीते तव जननि रोमावलिरिति ॥७६॥

hara-krodha-jwaalaavalibhir-avaleedhena vapushaa
gabheere te naabhee-sarasi kritasango manasijah;
samuttasthau tasmaad-achalatanaye dhoomalatika
janastaam jaaneete tava janani romaavaliriti. (76)

hara krodha jwaalaa: flames of shiva's wrath; *avalibhih avaleedhena*: consumed; *vapushaa*: (his) body; *gabheere te naabhee sarasi*: in the deep lake of thy navel; *kritasanga*: took refuge (or immersed himself); *manasijah*: manmatha, kamadeva; *samuttasthau*: rose up; *tasmaat*: from it; *achala tanaye*: oh! devi, daughter of the mountain; *dhoomalatika*: a creeper-like column of smoke; *janah* people; *taam*: it; *jaaneete*: describe; *tava*: thy; *janani*: mother; *romaavalih*: line of hair; *iti*: as

Translation

O Devi, daughter of the mountain! When the flames of Shiva's wrath consumed the body of Manmatha (Kamadeva), he took refuge in the deep lake of Thy navel from which arose a creeper-like column of smoke, which people describe, Mother, as the line of Thy hair below the navel.

Commentary

Manmatha as a name of Kamadeva is actually the process through which Kamadeva emerges. Kamadeva or Cupid, the god of amour, is actually a point of expression within one's own mind. The word *man* means 'mind' and *matha* means 'churning'. Many points of illumination spring up through the churning of the mind, which are converted into expression and action. The idea of sweetness is converted into the action of eating chocolate. In the same way, the idea of passion that arises through a process of mental churning gives rise to the desire and subsequent action of union.

The desires, or vasanas, have to be rooted out or consumed by the flames of knowledge. Only Shiva, the personification of knowledge, can eradicate these vasanas by burning them to ashes, as he did in the famous story of Kamadeva, when he dared to tempt Shiva with his prowess. But even when the vasanas are scorched, their residue remains and Sankara beautifully compares this to the line of hair below Devi's navel. The hair on the head and in the different parts of the body is nothing but residue. Although long tresses are regarded as a sign of beauty, in reality they are nothing but the residue that the body emits after absorbing the nutrients.

So, the line of hair beautifully illustrates the residue that remains even after the vasanas are extinguished. However, why does Sankara compare the residue of vasanas to the line of hair below the navel and not to the hair on her head or any other part of the body? This is because the navel is the location of manipura chakra, which is the seat of the gross residue of the vasanas. Although the vasanas lie dormant in mooladhara and swadhisthana, with their awakening the aspirant is tormented by the *panchagni*, or five fires, of their expression: i) *kama*, passion; ii) *krodha*, anger, iii) *lobha*, greed; iv) *moha*, attachment, and v) *mada*, intoxication of ego. These five fires can be extinguished through yogic sadhana, grace of guru, merits acquired in the past or potent herbs. When the aspirant transcends swadhisthana, the fire or heat of swadhisthana scorches them to ashes and leaves the residue in manipura.

Once again Sankara ascribes Shakti with a role or life apart from the one she shares with Shiva. By crediting her with saving the devotees from the wrath of Shiva, and reiterating this again and again, Sankara firmly establishes the tenets of tantra. Shakti exists in both the manifest and unmanifest realms simultaneously; she is the mistress of the empirical as well as the transcendental worlds. Even in her transcendental role, she is supreme and not subservient to Shiva. Thus, she is able to completely nullify the wrath, or *krodha jwaalaa*, of Shiva.

77. Meditation on Devi's slender waist

यदेतत्कालिन्दीतनुतरतरङ्गाकृति शिवे
कृशे मध्ये किंचिज्जननि तव तद्भाति सुधियाम् ।
विमर्दादन्योन्यं कुचकलशयोरन्तरगतं
तनूभूतं व्योम प्रविशदिव नाभिं कुहरिणीम् ॥ ७७ ॥

yadetatkaalindee tanutara-tarangaa-kriti shive
krishe madhye kinchij-janani tava tadbhaati sudhiyaam;
vimardaad-anyonyam kuchakalashayor-antaragatam
tanoobhootam vyoma pravishadiva naabhim kuharineem. (77)

yat etat: which; *kaalindee tanutara tarangaa kriti*: in the shape of subtle ripples in the kalindi; *shive janani*: oh! auspicious mother; *krishe madhye*: slender middle region; *kinchit*: thing; *tava*: yours; *tat bhaati sudhiyaam*: appears to devotees; *vimardaat anyonyam*: compressed by their pressure; *kuchakalashayoh antaragatam*: in between thy bulging breasts; *tanoobhootam vyoma*: as the ether; *pravishat iva*: forced into; *naabhim kuharineem*: into the cavity of the navel

Translation
O Shive, auspicious mother! Thy slender middle region, which appears to devotees like the subtle ripples of the river Kalindi, being compressed as the ether in between Thy bulging breasts, is forced into the cavity of Thy navel.

Commentary
In this mantra Sankara has given beautiful expression to the metaphysical process of the elements, *akasha*, ether, and *vayu*, air, being compressed into the navel centre, where they are transformed into *agni*, fire. Sankara describes Devi's bulging breasts compressing the flow of akasha and thus forcing it down to the navel, suggesting that Shakti is causing this to happen, which is a fact.

In the scheme of creation ether, which is undifferentiated matter comprised of infinite potential energy begins to vibrate, creating movement so that akasha is transmuted into vayu. Then the excessive and unhindered movement of vayu creates friction which generates heat for the emergence of agni. Devi herself causes this transformation of the elements by creating a pulsation, which starts off a vibratory process. When the breasts of Devi collide, they send out ripples of vibrations.

Devi has the potential within herself to create vibration after vibration and ripple after ripple, so that the unending process of creation is unhindered. She is fully endowed with the capacity to complete the process of creation that she has started without the help of any outside agency. Sankara intuitively clarifies many metaphysical mysteries that are hard to grasp, even by the most contemplative of thinkers.

The dark blue hue of the Kalindi, the river Yamuna, is also the colour of akasha and vayu intermingling, whereby vayu reduces the darkness of akasha and gives it a bluish tinge. Yamuna is also a symbol for ida nadi, and as the tattwas also flow in the *swara* or breath, it would indicate that the negative polarity of Shakti is working here to create that pressure.

Akasha is the subtlest tattwa and the flow of mental energy in ida nadi is also subtle. The Yamuna river flows downward from Yamunotri, and as it descends onto the planes at Mathura and Vrindavan, its ripples flow more like a subtle undercurrent. On the surface it appears smooth, but as one steps into the water the ripples below the surface are felt. Thus the comparison given in this mantra is most apt.

Tanoobhootam vyoma refers to that great moment when the supreme energy transforms itself and emerges as ether, the first element. The creation takes place on the unmanifest level up to this point, but with the emergence of ether the manifest creation begins. At the level of agni matter is realized, because with the emergence of fire the ego is born and the awareness becomes individual. This individual awareness then begins to perceive something outside of itself.

The birth of creation takes place at this moment, and thus Sankara refers to Devi as *shive janani*, auspicious mother, who has finally expelled the creation from the region of her navel for the individual awareness to experience and behold.

78. Meditation on the glory of Devi's yoni

स्थिरो गंगावर्तः स्तनमुकुलरोमावलिलता
निजावालं कुण्डं कुसुमशरतेजोहुतभुजः ।
रतेर्लीलागारं किमपि तव नाभिं गिरिसुते
बिलद्वारं सिद्धेर्गिरिशनयनानां विजयते ॥७८॥

sthiro gangaa-vartah stana-mukula-romaavali-lataa
nijaavaalam kundam kusuma-shara-tejohuta-bhujah;
rateerleelaagaaram kimapi tava naabhim girisute
biladvaaram siddher-girishanayanaanaam vijayate. (78)

sthira gangaa aavartah: steady whirlpool on the surface of the river ganga; *stana mukula romaavali lataa*: wet soil-bed for the creeper of thy navel hair, bearing two flower buds, which are thy breasts; *nijaa aavaalam*: your gentle depression; *kundam kusuma shara tejohuta bhujah*: sacrificial pit wherein resides the fire of the prowess of kamadeva; *rateh leelaagaaram*: pleasure house of rati; *kim api*: which also; *tava naabhim*: thy navel; *girisute*: oh! daughter of the mountain; *biladvaaram siddheh*: opening of the cave for yogic success; *girishanayanaanaam*: to the eyes of shiva; *vijayate*: is the glory

Translation

O Daughter of the mountain! Glory to Thy navel, (which is like) a steady whirlpool on the surface of the river Ganga. The wet soil-bed for the creeper of Thy navel hair bears the two flower buds of Thy breasts. The gentle depression (of Thy yoni) is the sacrificial pit, wherein resides the fire of the prowess of Kamadeva, which is also the pleasure house of his wife, Rati, opening the cave for yogic success to the eyes of Shiva.

Commentary

In this mantra Sankara describes the most intimate parts of Devi's anatomy with such skill that he converts them into a sacred image. The beautiful and apt reference to her navel being like a whirlpool on the surface of the Ganga lends a mystic touch. Tantra is an occult science, which explains the abstract concepts of space, time, consciousness, awareness, energy and all of its evolutes in a secret manner so that only the discerning can extract the meaning.

For this reason most of the tantric texts have a double meaning. The wet soil-bed of the Ganga is indicative of a most passionate state of awareness. But this passion is different to the physical passion, in the sense that everything is taking place on the subtle dimensions of inner awareness, which transcends the mind and its supports of time, space and object. The description of Devi's *yoni*, womb, is also most classical and mystical. By describing the yoni as a sacrificial pit, Sankara has at once made it into an altar, not for pleasure or progeny, but for samadhi and worship.

That sacrificial pit burns with the fire of Kamadeva and is the source of intense pleasure as well as yogic success. As long as one is after pleasure, Rati and Kamadeva, Cupid and his amorous wife, will be pulling one's strings. But if one is intent upon yogic attainment like Shiva, then through the worship of Devi one will have to discover the opening of the cave that leads to kundalini awakening, which is a symbol of yogic success.

The *Lalita Sahasranam* begins with the lines *chidagni kund sambhuta deva karya samudhyata*: born out of the fire of consciousness to fulfil the task of illumination. Here, too, there is a reference to a sacrificial pit out of which Shakti in the form of kundalini emerges to fulfil a great task, that of illuminating the world. Shakti illuminates the mind, enabling it to understand, perceive and grasp, along with a myriad other tasks. If Shakti were not present, one would be like a corpse, lying there like Shiva, knowing but unable to act.

The creation of something requires tremendous passion. Without a passionate desire, it is impossible to achieve what one sets out for. Most achievers are passionate about what they do. If the passion dwindles, they drop out, diversify and dissipate. Devi's passion is very high, for she is one-pointedly devoted to creating the entire universe. This is passion aroused in the sacrificial pit, which is the region where Kamadeva and Rati meditate to acquire their skill of infatuating the world. This pit also leads those who have prowess in yoga, like her consort Shiva, to the secret cavern where the oblations are poured for the opening of the third eye of Shiva, *girishanayanaanaam*, on account of which he has been glorified.

Passion is the source of pleasure and progeny. But in this mantra Sankara says that passion can also be the source of samadhi, enlightenment, and opening the third eye of knowledge. Hence, passion can be the source of the highest glory and achievement when it is dealt with by yogic prowess. Then even Kamadeva and Rati can be the doorway to the secret cavern *biladvaaram siddheh*.

79. Meditation on Devi before giving birth to creation

निसर्गक्षीणस्य स्तनतटभरेण क्लमजुषो
नमन्मूर्तेर्नाभौ वलिषु शनकैस्त्रुट्यत इव ।
चिरं ते मध्यस्य त्रुटिततटिनीतीरतरुणा
समावस्थास्थेम्नो भवतु कुशलं शैलतनये ॥७९॥

nisarga-ksheenasya stana-tata-bharena klama-jusho
naman-moorter-naabhau valishu shanakais-trutyata iva;
chiram te madhyasya truti-tatatinee-teera-tarunaa
sama-avasthaa-sthemno bhavatu kushalam shailatanaye. (79)

nisarga ksheenasya: naturally slender; *stana tata bharena*: under the weight of thy breasts; *klama jusha*: labouring; *naman moorteh*: and so slightly bent body; *naabhau valishu*: oh! ornament of womankind; *shanakaih*: gradually; *trutyata iva*: threatening to break; *chiram*: always; *te*: thy; *madhyasya*: waist or middle region; *truti tatatinee teera tarunaa sama avasthaa sthemna*: is like the precarious stability of a tree on a cracking river bank; *bhavatu kushalam*: be safe; *shailatanaye*: oh! daughter of the mountain

Translation
O Ornament of womankind! May Thy naturally slender waist, labouring under the weight of Thy breasts and therefore slightly bent and threatening to break under that weight, whose precarious stability is like that of a tree on a cracking river bank, be safe, O Daughter of the mountain!

Commentary
The full and bulging breasts of Devi, which were described in the previous mantras, are now so full that their weight threatens to break the slender waist of Devi. In this mantra Sankara deftly builds up the concept of motherhood, or *prasuti*, by presenting the form or image of Devi in the throes and pangs of giving birth to creation. Just as one's own mother in the blossom of her youth would have undergone

the pangs of childbirth or prasuti, in the same way, Devi too prepares for the birth of creation.

The breasts of the cosmic mother, bulging with fullness, are so heavy that her slender waist can hardly carry that extra weight which comes with the presence of new life ready to be pushed out of her body. Just as human mothers undergo a precarious moment when they are about to give birth, in the same way, the cosmic mother also undergoes a critical situation. Sankara compares this to the precarious stability of a tree on a cracking river bank: *truti tatatinee teera tarunaa sama avasthaa sthemna*.

The birth of a child from the mother's body is a wondrous moment full of speculation, tension and uncertainty, because one never knows what turn the event will take until the baby emits the first cry, giving assurance that its entry into the world was successful. In the same way the creation that ensues from Mahashakti, the supreme energy, also generates a precarious uncertainty. For this reason Sankara refers to Devi as *naabhau valishu*, the ornament of womankind. She goes through a difficult and dangerous time, during which her slender frame has to labour very hard to produce the creation out of her own self, and then present it to her Lord to behold.

This entire section seems to be a form of *anga nyasa*, tantric practice placing mantras at different parts of the body, which Sankara is performing while visualizing Devi. As he sees her beautiful awakened form within himself in the region of sahasrara and beyond, he becomes aware of each and every part of her body, starting from the parting middle line of her hair to her forehead, eyes, lips, chin, and then onto her most intimate parts, the breasts, navel and yoni. Each of these can be used as a mandala for meditation, first externally with the eyes open and then internally superimposed on oneself.

By using these mandalas, one can direct the healing energy of Devi to the different parts of one's own body for relief of ailments as well as rejuvenation. The great difference in the minds of people regarding *sakara*, with form, and *nirakara*, formless, worship has to be seen in this light. The purpose of mandala worship, or sakara pooja of Devi, is to intensify the quantum of energy within oneself. Whether God has form or is formless has no relevance here.

The mandala is merely a tool, albeit an extremely effective one, to achieve the very difficult task of developing inner awareness. Unless the aspirant can increase the quantum of energy within, he may as well forget about spiritual experience. For higher experience and meditation, a great quantity of energy is required. Mandalas are effective in helping one to make that quantum leap.

80. Meditation on Devi giving birth to creation

कुचौ सद्यः स्विद्यत्तटघटितकूर्पासभिदुरौ
कषन्तौ दोर्मूले कनककलशाभौ कलयता ।
तव त्रातुं भङ्गादुदरमवलग्नं तनुभुवा
त्रिधा नद्धं देवि त्रिवलिलवलीवल्लिभिरिव ॥ ८० ॥

*kuchau sadyah svidyatata-ghatita-koorpaasa-bhidurau
kashantau dormoole kanaka-kalash-aabhau kalayataa;
tava traatum bhangaad-udarama-valagnam tanubhuvaa
tridhaa naddham devi trivali-lavalee-vallibhiriva. (80)*

kuchau: breasts; *sadyah*: quickly; *svidyatata ghatita koorpaasa bhidurau*: perspiring and bursting from the brassiere covering them; *kashantau dormoole*: touching thy armpits; *kanaka kalasha aabhau*: bright as golden pots; *kalayataa*: made; *tava*: thy; *traatum*: and to support; *bhangaat udarama*: to prevent from breaking; *valagnam*: in (thy) middle region; *tanubhuvaa*: by kamadeva; *tridhaa naddham iva*: three folds look like; *devi*: oh! devi: *trivali lavalee vallibhih*: three-stranded lavali creeper wound; *iva*: like

Translation
O Devi! The three folds in Thy middle region look like three strands of lavali creeper wound by Kamadeva for support to prevent Thy middle region from breaking under the weight of Thy quickly perspiring breasts, bright as golden pots, touching Thy armpits and bursting the brassiere covering them.

Commentary
The predicament of Shakti, facing *prasuti*, the birth of creation in the previous mantra is further accentuated here by Sankara's description of Devi's middle region being supported by the three folds, which look like a creeper wound by Kamadeva. Unless the waist is supported, it would break under the weight of Devi's breasts, which have

swollen to the point of bursting the cloth that is covering them.

The reference to perspiration further emphasizes the labour that Shakti is undergoing, even though the situation is an outcome of passion. Moreover, intensity of passion is best described through the breasts, which swell during passion. Here the intensity of experience which Shakti undergoes is parallel to the intensity of experience that is taking place within Sankara. He is seeing the many forms of Devi, as he worships all her different *angas*, or parts.

The references to Kamadeva and Rati and the incident of Shiva burning Kamadeva to ashes are profuse in *Saundarya Lahari*. There is a beautiful balance between passion and dispassion. This is exactly the state that the sadhaka has to develop. Passion has to be developed and sublimated, only then does this balance occur. When this happens, there is a balance in the flow of energy, as Shakti is both passion and dispassion as well.

Moreover, Kama is the most elemental desire deep-rooted in man. It is most difficult to sublimate desire into worship, but those who succeed attain the highest yogic attainment of awakening the kundalini, which gives birth to a new experience within the individual. Prior to the birth of the kundalini experience, each sadhaka goes through similar pains of labour. However, the passion and intensity for higher experience is so great at this time that he proceeds nevertheless, even though the outcome of his situation is precarious and uncertain.

Whether it is the birth of a child by a human mother, the birth of creation through Shakti or the birth of a higher experience through the labour of a sadhaka or devotee, all three experiences are clearly described in this mantra.

81. Meditation on Devi's expansive hips

गुरुत्वं विस्तारं क्षितिधरपतिः पार्वति निजान्
नितम्बादाच्छिद्य त्वयि हरणरूपेण निदधे ।
अतस्ते विस्तीर्णो गुरुरयमशेषां वसुमतीं
नितम्बप्राग्भारः स्थगयति लघुत्वं नयति च ॥८१॥

*gurutvam vistaaram kshitidharapatih paarvati nijaan
nitambaad-aachchhidya tvayi haranaroopena nidadhe;
ataste visteerno gurur-ayam-asheshaam vasumateem
nitamba-praagbhaarah sthagayati laghutvam nayati cha.* (81)

gurutvam: heaviness; *vistaaram*: expansiveness; *kshitidharapatih*: mountain king (thy father); *paarvati*: oh! parvati; *nijaan nitambaat*: from his flanks; *aachchhidya*: cut off; *tvayi*: to thee; *harana roopena*: as dowry; *nidadhe*: has presented; *atah*: so; *te*: thy; *visteerna*: extensive; *guruh*: and heavy; *ayam*: this; *asheshaam vasumateem*: entire earth; *nitamba praagbhaarah*: (thy) stupendous hips; *sthagayati*: covers; *laghutvam nayati cha*: and thus lighten its weight

Translation

O Parvati! Thy father, the mountain king, has presented to Thee as dowry (at the time of Thy marriage), the heaviness and expansiveness cut from his flanks. For this reason Thy stupendous hips, extensive and heavy, cover this entire earth and thus lighten its weight.

Commentary

Shakti renders an object heavy by decreasing her *spandan*, vibration, thus increasing the density of the object. Then again, Shakti intensifies the vibrational frequency whereby the same object loses density and becomes light. This technical idea is beautifully conveyed through the idea of Paravati's anatomy.

In this mantra, Himalaya, her father, represents the *shveta bindu* which is responsible for creation. There are two shades of bindu, one rakta and the other shveta. *Rakta* means 'red'; the drop of nectar in the form of *retas* from rakta bindu becomes the ova in women. *Shveta* means 'white'; the drop of nectar in the form of *ojas* that becomes sperm in men. The downfall of this vital fluid is reversed through the practices of yoga. When the ojas and retas are balanced and reversed back up to bindu, the yogi attains higher experience, lightness and elevation. Gravity loses its hold and he becomes free.

Parvati has received the gift of heaviness, or *gurutvam*, from her father, Himalaya, who being the king of the mountains gives this gift to his daughter at the time of her wedding to Shiva. Parvati also has the ability to lighten the heaviness; being pure, unadulterated energy she can expand and liberate the heaviness of matter into the lightness of consciousness. This expansion of the guru tattwa, *gurutvam vistaaram*, gives birth to a higher experience.

Gurutvam refers to gravity or time, and *vistaram* to expansiveness or space. The interaction of time and space, which are always moving in opposite directions, when reversed and made to move towards each other causes an explosion when they meet at the centre or nucleus, which gives rise to anti-gravity, where lightness is experienced and the awareness is liberated from the clutches of matter to expand in all directions of space.

The hips are actively involved in the process of childbirth, because on account of their heaviness, they are able to push out the newborn baby through contraction and expansion. In the same way by meditation on this mandala of Devi, the devotee can generate new life and experience within himself.

82. Meditation on Devi's thighs and knees

करीन्द्राणां शुण्डान् कनककदलीकाण्डपटलीम्
उभाभ्यामूरुभ्यामुभयमपि निर्जित्य भवति ।
सुवृत्ताभ्यां पत्युः प्रणतिकठिनाभ्यां गिरिसुते
विजिग्ये जानुभ्यां विबुधकरिकुंभद्वयमति ॥८२॥

kareendraanaam shundaan kanaka-kadaleekaanda-pataleem
ubhabhyaam-oorubhyaam-ubhayamapi nirjitya bhavati;
suvrittaabhyaam patyuh pranati-kathinaabhyaam girisute
vijigye jaanubhyaam vibudha-kari-kumbha-dvayamati. (82)

kareendraanaam shundaan: trunks of majestic elephants; *kanaka kadaleekaanda pataleem*: and the stems of golden coloured banana trees; *ubhabhyaam oorubhyaam*: thy two thighs; *ubhayam api*: both (the trunk and the stem); *nirjitya*: surpass; *bhavati*: oh! devi; *suvrittaabhyaam*: thy perfectly rounded; *patyuh pranati kathinaabhyaam*: and hardened by prostration to thy consort; *girisute*: oh! daughter of the mountain; *vijigye*: oh! observer of all ordained duties; *jaanubhyaam*: (thy) two knees; *vibudha kari kumbha dvayam ati*: (surpass) the two frontal lobes of airavata

Translation
O Daughter of the mountain! The beauty of Thy thighs surpasses both the trunks of lordly elephants and also the stems of golden coloured banana trees. O Devi, observer of all ordained duties! Thy perfectly rounded knees, hardened by repeated prostrations to Thy consort, rival the frontal lobes of the heavenly elephant, Airavata.

Commentary
Sankara was in the realm of inner experience while composing these mantras of *Saundarya Lahari*. His worship of Devi gave birth to a higher experience, indicated in the last mantra, where he depicted Shakti as the creatrix of the universe, giving birth to animate and inanimate nature.

He was in the throes of bliss and ecstasy, while beholding absolute beauty in the form of Devi as the ruler and mistress of all the processes of creation. When physical and gross matter is transcended, there is only grace and beauty.

In this mantra, Sankara compares Devi's shapely thighs to the trunks of lordly elephants. In Indian literature, the elephant has always been a symbol of eroticism. Moreover, the elephant is also a symbol of earth, the element of mooladhara chakra, located in the region of the thighs, which Sankara is beholding. The knees also relate to mooladhara, and here Devi's knees are compared to the round frontal lobes of Airavata, the celestial elephant on which Indra, the Lord of the devas, is seated.

Everything that exists in this universe at the gross level is present in the higher dimension. The world does not disappear and die, it simply transforms into another dimension according to the level of one's awareness and perception. As the perception changes the world too changes. Here Airavata denotes the awakened state of the *prithvi tattwa*, earth element, when it is vibrating at a rarefied frequency to reveal its cosmic potential.

The inner experience of Sankara was not static. He did not just see Devi in one form, but in her entirety of a myriad forms. His inner experience had many shades and nuances. He saw her as the omnipresent ruler of all, but he also saw her in embrace with Shiva. Just as Shakti has many roles, Shiva also has. In mantra 8, as Sadashiva he is the cot on which Shakti reclines in her eternal abode. Again, in the same mantra, as Paramshiva he is the bedspread in between her and the cot, or Sadashiva, thus signifying that Paramshiva is a superior tattwa to Sadashiva. Shiva is further described as being in embrace with Shakti in sahasrara, and then accompanying her back to her home in mooladhara while they are in *maithuna*, total amalgamation or union.

In each of these roles Shakti assumes either a superior or equal position to Shiva. But this mantra says that Shakti worships Shiva, for her knees are hardened due to the repeated prostrations she makes to her consort. This shows a very tender aspect of Shakti in which her love and devotion for Shiva are total, even though she is complete, unified and powerful in herself and does not need anyone or anything for her existence or support.

Love has many shades but its purest form is bhakti, which is totally unconditional. Love for love's sake is bhakti, which does not arise on account of any need, want or fear. There is no compromise, adulteration or contamination in the love of a true bhakta. The love that Shakti has for Shiva is pure, unconditional love. That is the definition of divine love or *bhakti*.

Unfortunately this pure, divine love is compromised in human relations. One loves another due to insecurity, attachment or need, always wanting something in return. Under the guise of love, one wants to control, manipulate and own others. One barters love to get the things one wants. If these needs are not fulfilled, the love soon turns into hatred.

However, Shakti's love for Shiva is the epitome of love and devotion. The all powerful Shakti, before whom all prostrate, herself prostrates before her consort. She does not feel in the least bit humbled by this act of worship, nor does it demean her importance or make her inferior in any way in the eyes of those who worship her. Bhakti does not make one subservient; it elevates one in every way.

One who is devoid of bhakti, no matter how rich, important or eminent he may be, is a pauper in the real sense of the word. Many people, especially those who worship the intellect, are of the opinion that the expression of love and devotion for God is a sign of weakness. They think that devotion reduces one to a slave or servant who only looks to his master for guidance. This mantra is a hint for those people, because here the all mighty and powerful Shakti, who can reduce this entire creation to ashes, in front of whom even Brahma, Vishnu and Mahesh are subservient, has devotion for her Lord.

This mantra is a curious mix of elegant poetry and spiritual experience of the highest order. Here Sankara experiences Devi as omnipresence and also omnipotent, the ruler of all. She is the observer of all the duties ordained by her and forever mindful and aware of all the processes of creation, maintenance and dissolution which are being carried out by her. She is also aware of the enactment of karmas by each individual, and thus has a hand in the process of cause and effect that governs the lives of everyone.

Although one may feel the master of one's life, the philosophy of tantra says there is another supramental force that shapes and guides one to act in certain ways, according to one's karmas. The good thoughts as well as the bad are all influenced by one's karmas, and the karmas are governed by the three gunas, sattwa, rajas and tamas, which are the expressions of Devi. For example, if it is one's karma to be imprisoned, no force on earth can stop it.

However one's approach and attitude to this event can change everything. A jnani of sattwic temperament will react differently to someone who is rajasic or tamasic. Mahatma Gandhi went to jail many times in his life; in fact, he spent a major part of his life in Indian jails. However, this was not an agonizing experience for him; it did not make him bitter and vengeful. Instead, it reinforced his resolve to accomplish the independence of India. He saw it as a stepping stone to accomplishment, rather than as a defeat.

83. Meditation on Devi's thighs and toenails

पराजेतुं रुद्रं द्विगुणशरगर्भौ गिरिसुते
निषङ्गौ जङ्घे ते विषमविशिखो बाढमकृत ।
यदग्रे लक्ष्यन्ते दशशरफलाः पादयुगली-
नखाग्रच्छद्मानः सुरमकुटशाणौघनिशिताः ॥ ८३ ॥

*paraajetum rudram dviguna-shara-garbhau girisute
nishangau janghe te vishama-vishikho baadham-akrita;
yadagre lakshyante dasha-shara-phalaah paadayugalee
nakhaagra-chadmaanah sura-makuta-shaanaugha-nishitaah. (83)*

paraajetum rudram: to conquer rudra; *dviguna shara garbhau*: to store double the number of arrows; *girisute*: oh! parvati; *nishangau*: two quivers; *janghe te*: thy thighs; *vishama vishikha*: kamadeva; *baadham*: certainly; *akrita*: converted; *yat agre*: at the end; *lakshyante*: are seen; *dasha shara phalaah*: ten crescent-shaped arrow heads; *paada yugalee nakhaagra chadmaanah*: of thy feet, under the guise of thy toenails; *sura makuta shaanaugha nishitaah*: sharpened on the whetstone of the crowns of prostrating divinities

Translation
O Parvati, daughter of the mountain! Surely, in order to conquer Rudra, Kamadeva has converted Thy two thighs into quivers to store therein double the number of arrows. For at the end of Thy feet are seen ten crescent-shaped arrow heads under the guise of Thy toenails, sharpened on the whetstone of the crowns of prostrating divinities.

Commentary
The five arrows that Kamadeva normally carries are the five *agnis* or fires that one faces on account of desire: i) *kama*, passion, ii) *krodha*, anger, iii) *lobha*, greed, iv) *moha*, delusion, and v) *matsya*, attachment. These five fires forever surround one on all sides and accomplish this task through the ten *indriyas*, or sensory organs, which act as crescent-shaped

arrow heads. The indriyas act at the behest of the devatas residing in them. On their own they cannot accomplish anything. They are sharpened by the awakening of the devatas or residing energy. These devatas also act at the behest of Shakti and thus are forever prostrating before her.

In this mantra, passion and dispassion are once again eyeing each other, and it remains to be seen which one Devi will shower her grace upon, for he will surely be the winner. On the one hand there is Kamadeva, who hides between Devi's thighs so that he can conquer Rudra, who is a form of Shiva. Kamadeva is relying on Devi's sensuality to conquer the infallible Rudra, who reduced him to ashes when he tried to incite passion in him before.

What Kamadeva could not achieve, Devi's most secret part hidden between her thighs is sure to achieve. Kamadeva hides there, so that he too can take credit for the conquest of Rudra. The subtle and esoteric innuendoes of this mantra, which are authenticated by actual incidents and personalities, signify the enlightened and evolved level of awareness that Sankara had. Only a master craftsman can weave such a splendid blend of mysticism and poetry, and only the discerning reader can understand the depth of what he is saying.

After acknowledging that Devi prostrates before Shiva, in this mantra Sankara again reiterates that the devatas forever remain at her feet, prostrating before her and awaiting her orders. Thus the nails of her toes are sharpened on their crowns, which are here compared to whetstones. Devi's victory over and subjugation of Shiva is also ensured by her erotic appeal to which he will surely succumb. Even Kamadeva of unlimited prowess could not achieve this feat.

These mantras may appear absurd to the ordinary mundane awareness, seeming to convey nothing in terms of spirituality. However, upon deep reflection one sees Shakti as the supreme source of truth, auspiciousness and beauty, which are the principles of creation. With this heightened perception, all of Shakti's nuances fall into place and convey a divinely woven structure, wherein not a single idea, thought or reference is out of place.

Moreover, everything that is said in these mantras is in total conformity with the profound principles of Tantra and Vedanta; there is no contradiction in any way. Shakti, as the root matrix of creation, is the mistress, queen and ruler of all one beholds; one's very existence depends on her. All existence from bhu loka to satya loka is at her command. To worship her is to worship the supreme tattwa; to behold her form is to behold the formless reality, to feel oneness with her is to merge with the supreme tattwa. That supreme tattwa is known as Shakti to the Shaktas, Shiva to the Shaivites, and by other names to different groups of people.

84. Meditation on the feet of Devi

श्रुतीनां मूर्धानो दधति तव यौ शेखरतया
ममाप्येतौ मातः शिरसि दयया धेहि चरणौ ।
ययोः पाद्यं पाथः पशुपतिजटाजूटतटिनी
ययोर्लाक्षालक्ष्मीररुणहरिचूडामणिरुचिः ॥ ८४ ॥

*shruteenam moordhaano dadhati tava yau shekharatayaa
mamaapyetau maatah shirasi dayayaa dhehi charanau;
yayoh paadhyam paathah pashupati-jataa-joota-tatinee
yayor-laakshaa-lakshmeer-aruna-hari-choodaamani-ruchih.* (84)

shruteenam moordhaana: upanishads, the crown of vedas; *dadhati*: wear; *tava*: thy; *yau charanau*: (which) feet; *shekharatayaa*: as a crest ornament; *mama shirasi api*: on my head too; *etau*: those (feet); *maatah*: oh! mother; *dayayaa dhehi yayoh*: for which (feet); *paadhyam paathah*: is the offering of water in worship; *pashupati jataa joota tatinee*: river ganga, residing in the matted locks of pashupati (shiva); *yayoh*: for which (feet); *laakshaa lakshmeeh*: the bright red dye on them; *aruna hari choodaamani ruchih*: gives a crimson brilliance to the jewels on the diadem of vishnu

Translation
O Mother! Be pleased to place Thy two feet, which the Upanishads, the crown of the Vedas, wear as the crest jewel, on my head too. River Ganga, who resides in the matted locks of Shiva, offers them water in worship, and their bright red dye gives a crimson brilliance to the jewels on the diadem of Vishnu.

Commentary
From Devi's feet emanate the rays of creation, which shine and glitter like a myriad gems. As they spread outwards, they resonate and create sounds, which are the source of the *shrutis* that were heard by enlightened beings in deep states of meditation. As these rays are the very source of the shrutis,

Sankara designates Devi's two feet as the crest jewel, which sits upon their crown.

Here Sankara addresses Shakti as the Mother of the most sacred knowledge which has descended upon this earth. Knowledge is of two kinds, para and apara. *Para* is transcendental knowledge, and *apara* is empirical knowledge. All the knowledge that one learns throughout life, such as geography, history, science, art and music, comes in the category of apara and is grasped through the lower mind and intellect.

On the other hand, knowledge that is grasped through the higher mind or intuition is para, being the same as *atma jnana*, knowledge of the Self. Apara knowledge is limited to matter and energy because it does not include knowledge of the atman. Para knowledge is unlimited because it gives knowledge of matter, energy and consciousness, and brings one into contact with the source of knowledge, which is the Self.

The sources of knowledge are instinct, intelligence, intellect and intuition. The aim of tantra is to develop each one of these faculties to its fullest potential. When one perceives only through instinct, intelligence or intellect, one is limited and deprived of the knowledge which can liberate. Intuitive knowledge grants one access to unlimited knowledge. The Vedas are the source of the sublime philosophy of *Vedanta*, which literally means the 'culmination of knowledge'. They end with the words: *Neti, neti*: not this, not this.

Intuition does not kill the instinct, intelligence and intellect; rather it enhances them. An intuitive person is astute, shrewd, smart, perceptive, judicious, decisive, wise, intelligent, sharp, clever and insightful, for intuition provides knowledge that is not limited to the senses. Intuition does not rely on the eyes, nose, ears, touch or taste for knowledge, nor does it rely on the thinking mind, but on the higher mind and consciousness.

The shrutis were perceived by enlightened and liberated beings in deep states of meditation, where they had transcended the finite mind and senses. Later they conveyed this knowledge to deserving disciples and students through word of mouth. Shruti means 'heard' and then conveyed by the spoken word. What they spoke was heard and remembered by their enlightened disciples. Later, these shrutis were recorded and classified by the rishis and munis, the chief being Maharishi Vedavyasa, to whom the credit goes for compiling the Vedas, Upanishads, Puranas and Itihasas, which contain both para and apara knowledge.

What these enlightened beings heard in deep states of meditation were the sounds and mantras abounding in the universe, which emanated from the vibration caused by Shakti. These mantras are capsules of potent energy which can be exploded within the deep recesses of the mind through *japa*, or continuous repetition of the sound. These sounds are not names of God, but forms of energy which can catapult one into a different level of awareness.

Thus the shrutis should not to be mistaken for religious doctrines which aim to promote a certain sect or idea of godhead. They contain the vast potential energy in the form of sound which has emanated directly from Shakti in the process of creation. This is why Shakti's feet rest on the shrutis. Her feet are the sacred source from which the first sound emerged and resounded in the universe.

The reference to Ganga offering water in worship of Shakti's feet also has a deep significance. Mother Ganga is not just a river; she is a goddess who descended from the heavens. During her descent, she first rested on the matted locks of Shiva who broke her fall, and from there she came down to earth. This association with Shiva, the supreme consciousness, gives her the credit for being the source of salvation. Ganga liberates every soul from the bondage of samsara. Her waters are purifying, and to behold her is to bathe in knowledge, because Ganga stands for perennial knowledge.

The red dye adorning Devi's feet, which is applied to the feet of a young bride, also bestows grace on Vishnu, who sustains the creation and all the knowledge that Shiva and Shakti send into creation. If Vishnu did not preserve this knowledge, the creation would be devoid of all the wisdom, intelligence and learning that were showered upon it through the grace of Shakti. Here, Sankara asks for this grace to descend upon him also so that he too may wear that crest jewel on his head, which is offered water by Ganga and lends glitter and colour to Vishnu's crown. The shrutis, Ganga and Vishnu represent the manifest creation in this sense, and so too does Sankara.

85. Meditation on Devi in the mudra of granting happiness

नमोवाकं ब्रूमो नयनरमणीयाय पदयोः
तवास्मै द्वन्द्वाय स्फुटरुचिरसालक्तकवते ।
असूयत्यत्यन्तं यदभिहननाय स्पृहयते
पशूनामीशानः प्रमदवनकङ्केलितरवे ॥ ८५ ॥

*namovaakam broomo nayana-ramaneeyaaya padayoh
tavaasmai dvandvaaya sphuta-ruchi-rasaalakta-kavate;
asooyaty-atyantam yadabhihananaaya sprihayate
pashoonaam-eeshaanah pramadavana-kankelitarave.* (85)

nama vaakam brooma: our salutations; *nayana ramaneeyaaya*: a delight to the eyes; *padayoh dvandvaaya*: to (thy) two feet; *tava*: thy; *asmai*: this; *sphuta ruchi rasaalakta kavate*: because of the brilliance of the liquid lac dye applied to them; *asooyati*: is jealous; *atyantam*: very; *yat abhihananaaya*: to be kicked by those feet; *sprihayate*: desires; *pashoonaam eeshaanah*: thy consort, pashupati; *pramadavana kankeli tarave*: of the kankeli (ashoka) tree in thy pleasure garden

Translation
Salutations to Thy feet, a delight to the eyes, because of the brilliance of the lac dye applied to them! Thy consort, Pashupati, desiring to be kicked by those feet, is jealous of the kankeli (ashoka) tree in Thy pleasure garden.

Commentary
Once again Sankara establishes the superiority of Shakti despite her relation with all levels of creation. She is intimately connected with everything, yet remains aloof and superior. Sankara conveys this idea by the use of skilful imagery, establishing her familiarity with Shiva and the objects that surround the innermost region of her mansion. Shiva is so intimate with Shakti that he is jealous of anything or anyone receiving her touch. Shakti has her *amsa roopinis*, or partial manifestations, and *poorna roopinis*, or total

manifestations, but as Mahashakti and Mahamaya she is beyond everything and everyone, including her consort Shiva, who as Pashupati is the lord of the animal nature.

This mantra gives a vision of Shakti in a joyful mood, walking in her pleasure garden. Her feet hold prominence here and in the next few mantras, which arouse respect because of the dazzling brilliance of the rays emitted by them. These rays can confer anything the devotee desires. Sankara pays obeisance to Shakti's feet at the very beginning when he commences his worship. Now, having received her grace, once again he mentally pays obeisance to her feet. In traditional and ritualistic worship, the feet of gods, saints and gurus are profusely venerated. They are bathed and washed lovingly by devotees and later the water is drunk as *charana amrita*, life giving nectar of the feet. It is firmly believed that this act can confer the highest grace and blessings.

Thus Shiva is always anxious to receive Shakti's gentle kicks and is jealous of the ashoka tree, because Shakti playfully kicks at the roots of this tree while walking around in her garden. Most people believe that only sweet words and acts bestow grace, but this is not true. Even a kick, insult or abuse can confer grace of a very high order. Milarepa, the great yogi, was abused, insulted, beaten, humiliated and tortured by his guru. Any ordinary disciple would have cracked, but Milarepa did not react. Finally, when his guru kicked him off the mountain, he became light as a feather and began to rise, and entered the state of nirvana by the grace of his guru.

Shiva, who himself can confer the highest grace, also stands in line for Devi's kicks for he does not want to miss this sublime experience. The reference to the kankeli trees in Shakti's pleasure garden indicates that the experience described here is of sahasrara, where both the tattwas of Shiva and Shakti are forever abiding in the pure, effulgent state.

86. Meditation on the kick of Devi's lotus foot

मृषा कृत्वा गोत्रस्खलनमथ वैलक्ष्यनमितं
ललाटे भर्तारं चरणकमले ताडयति ते ।
चिरादन्तः शल्यं दहनकृतमुन्मीलितवता
तुलाकोटिक्वाणैः किलिकिलितमीशानरिपुणा ॥ ८६ ॥

*mrishaa kritvaa gotra-skhalanam-atha vailakshya-namitam
lalaate bhartaaram charana kamale taadayati te;
chiraad-antah shalyam dahanakritam-unmeelitavataa
tulaakotikvaanaih kilikilitam-eeshaana-ripunaa. (86)*

mrishaa: inadvertently; *kritvaa*: (for) calling (thee); *gotra skhalanam*: by the name of another woman; *atha*: suddenly; *vailakshya namitam*: hang his head in shame; *lalaate taadayati*: kicked at his forehead; *bhartaaram*: husband; *charana kamale te*: with thy lotus feet; *chiraat*: long standing; *antah shalyam dahanakritam*: rumour for consuming him in the fire of his anger; *unmeelitavataa*: to get rid of; *tulaakotikvaanaih*: of the bells in thy anklets; *kilikilitam*: in the form of the tinkling; *eeshaana ripunaa*: shiva's enemy, kamadeva

Translation
When Thou suddenly kicked at the forehead of Thy husband with Thy lotus foot, as He bent His head in shame for calling Thee inadvertently by the name of another woman, His enemy Kamadeva got an opportunity in the form of the tinkling of Thy anklets to get rid of the long-standing rumour about Shiva consuming him in the fire of his anger.

Commentary
Again, this mantra uses the feet to suggest extreme intimacy between Shakti and Shiva. It also alludes to worldly love, where lovers quarrel bitterly out of jealousy for one another. But more than that, it establishes the purity of the Shiva-Shakti experience that he is having. Just as naming another

woman would defile the relationship between husband and wife, in the same way, the presence of any *ashuddha* or impure tattwa would defile the pure experience of Shiva and Shakti in amorous union in the region beyond sahasrara, where no other tattwa can enter.

The kick that Shakti gives Shiva on the forehead is to chide him for allowing name and form to enter the domain of absolute purity. There is no place for them in this zone, where name and form are obliterated and pure effulgence reigns. The kick also denotes the entry into the most inner recesses of the brain, which transcend even sahasrara where the magnificent glory of Tripura Sundari is revealed. In tantra, Shakti is considered superior to Shiva; she conducts the rituals and decides the point to be meditated upon to open the closed doors of inner awareness.

The mention of Kamadeva is significant at this stage. The union that takes place here is between the highest cosmic forces in the universe, supreme consciousness and supreme energy. Just as the union between man and woman is erotic and sensual, this union is also full of the eroticism that is associated with Kamadeva. Eroticism is not just material pleasure, it is also spiritual bliss. Where there is bliss, whether born of matter or spirit, there has to be eroticism and sensuality. But the sensory experience of atman is different to that of daily life; here the awakened and refined senses have aligned themselves with their source, the spirit or atman.

The erotic union of Shiva and Shakti is a higher union, devoid of passion. This is only possible when name and form are obliterated and the ability to do that lies in the hands of Shakti because she has created name and form. Her reason for creating name and form is so that by beholding oneself, one can reflect on one's inner glory. The tantras claim that Shakti initiates the process of creation to allow Shiva to see himself reflected within it. Shakti is the main force behind all experiences, for on the one hand she is responsible for aligning Shiva with the creation, and on the other hand she is responsible for directing the individual towards liberation.

However, instead of basking in the absolute truth, auspiciousness and beauty that is one's innate nature, the individual is lost in the world of name and form and ensnared by it throughout life. This is why higher experience is denied. If one breaks out of this vicious cycle, eternal beauty and bliss await in the form of Tripura Sundari. The gentle kick on Shiva's forehead, when he hangs his head in shame, is a hint to those aspirants who aspire for oneness with the supreme reality, but are unable to transcend name and form or the duality in which they are steeped.

Duality is necessary in life, and at the beginning of the spiritual journey it is used as a support. Name and form help one to focus the vagrant tendencies of the mind. But this duality, or *dvaita*, has to remain at the level of *kriya*, or action, and should not enter into the *bhava*, or attitude. Thus the secret to success in sadhana is to maintain dvaita at the level of kriya and *advaita*, non-dual, at the level of bhava. When one's eyes are open, the object of worship and oneself are two entities. However, when the eyes are closed, the duality disappears; the object and oneself come very close and appear as one. The worshipper becomes the object of worship.

The guru-disciple relationship is based on this principle. They remain two entities on the physical plane as they inhabit two separate bodies, but they are united on the levels of emotion, understanding and atman. All beings are united in atman, but they have not realized this unity. A true disciple realizes this unity and thus becomes merged in the guru. Then he acts as a switch which the guru can turn on at any time. He becomes a medium for the thoughts of the guru to be enacted. The guru thinks and the disciple acts. This is only possible in a high quality disciple. Most disciples remain at the level of dvaita throughout their lives, but the disciple chosen by the guru is able to evolve to the level of advaita through the grace of guru. Then he transcends dvaita bhava.

Sankara had to transcend dvaita bhava to enter the highest experience of the Mahashakti. He was a qualified aspirant, but still Devi cautions him through her kick to Shiva's head.

87. Meditation on the lotus of Devi's feet

हिमानीहन्तव्यं हिमगिरितटाक्रान्तिचतुरौ
निशायां निद्राणं निशि च परभागे च विशदौ ।
परं लक्ष्मीपात्रं श्रियमतिसृजन्तौ समयिनां
सरोजं त्वत्पादौ जननि जयतश्चित्रमिह किम् ॥ ८७ ॥

*himaani hantavyam himagiri-tataakraanti-chaturau
nishaayaam nidraanam nishi cha parabhaage cha vishadau;
param lakshmeepaatram shriyam-atisrijantau samayinaam
sarojam tvatpaadau janani jayatash-chitramiha kim.* (87)

himaani hantavyam: which perishes in the snow; *himagiri tataakraanti chaturau*: which always remain on the snow mountains; *nishaayaam nidraanam*; closes at night; *nishi*: night; *cha parabhaage cha*: and day; *vishadau*: blooming; *param*: dependent; *lakshmeepaatram*: on lakshmi (as it is her seat); *shriyam*: prosperity (thy grace); *atisrijantau*: bestowing; *samayinaam*: on devotees; *sarojam*: lotus flower; *tvat paadau*: thy feet; *janani*: oh! mother; *jayatah*: are far superior; *chitram iha kim*: is undoubtedly

Translation

O Mother! The lotus flower of Thy feet, which always remain on the snow mountains (of the Himalayas), blooming day and night, and bestowing grace on devotees, is undoubtedly far superior to the common lotus flower, which perishes in snow, closes at night and is dependent for its prosperity upon Lakshmi, the goddess of wealth, whose blessings on devotees are quite temporary.

Commentary

In this mantra, Sankara clearly establishes the role of the different manifestations of Mahashakti, and her superiority to them. The grace of Mahashakti is always blossoming in the devotee, but the grace of her manifestations such as Lakshmi, comes and goes. Lakshmi is a *poorna amsha*, complete part of Shakti, who was born at the time of the *samudra manthana*, churning of the ocean, and became the consort of Vishnu. She is the goddess of *riddhi*, magnanimous wealth, but her blessings are temporary, like the common lotus flower that closes at night, perishes in the cold, and is dependent on Lakshmi, as her feet rest on the lotus flower.

Even Lakshmi is inferior to Mahashakti, who supersedes everything and can confer blessings that are not subject to time and space. They are eternal and stay with you life after life and guide your evolution. Sankara is preparing himself for the highest experience which Devi is about to grant him of her ultimate form of absolute beauty. This form is beyond every form of Devi that he has described until now. In order to behold that form one has to leave behind the glittering wealth bestowed by the enchanting Lakshmi, the gift of eloquence bestowed by the learned Saraswati, and the enormous power bestowed by glorious Durga.

This is only possible with the realization that all these siddhis are temporary, even though they are bestowed by the manifestations of Shakti. She keeps the aspirant in the realm of maya under the spell of their charms for as long as she wants. Only to her chosen devotee does she reveal what lies beyond Lakshmi, Saraswati, Durga and Kali, which is her true form. The three levels of mind, jagrat, swapna and sushupti, have to be transcended in order to reach the state of *turiya*, super consciousness. After being established in turiya for a period of time, which is the vision of Shiva and Shakti in maithuna at sahasrara, the awareness of the aspirant ascends to higher lokas above sahasrara, where Tripura Sundari reigns, sending forth her effulgence and radiance.

88. Meditation on the feet of Devi

पदं ते कान्तीनां प्रपदमपदं देवि विपदां
कथं नीतं सद्भिः कठिनकमठीखर्परतुलाम् ।
कथं वा हस्ताभ्यामुपयमनकाले पुरभिदा
यदादाय न्यस्तं दृषदि दयमानेन मनसा ॥ ८८ ॥

*padam te kaanteenaam prapadam-apadam devi vipadaam
katham neetam sadbhih kathina-kamathee-kharpara-tulaam;
katham vaa hastaabhyaam-upayamanakaale purabhidaa
yadaadaaya nyastam drishadi-dayamaanena manasaa.* (88)

padam kaanteenaam: (is) seat of fame; *te prapadam*: thy feet; *apadam*: beyond the reach; *devi*: oh! devi; *vipadaam*: of mishaps; *katham neetam*: how do; *sadbhih*: by great poets; *kathina kamathee kharpara tulaam*: equate it to the hardened shell of the tortoise; *katham vaa nyastam*: how (did he place it); *hastaabhyaam*: with his two hands; *upayamanakaale*: during the marriage ceremony; *purabhidaa*: by shiva; *yat aadaaya*: placed (them); *drishadi*: on a grinding stone; *dayamaanena manasaa*: with tender mind

Translation

O Devi! How can the great poets equate Thy feet, which are the seat of fame and beyond the reach of mishaps, to the hardened shell of the tortoise? And how did Thy consort Shiva, the destroyer of cities, in spite of all his tenderness towards Thee, place Thy foot on the grinding stone with his two hands during Thy marriage ceremony?

Commentary

The tortoise is a creature that can extend its head and limbs outside of shell, and then immediately withdraw them and close itself up inside the shell. Devi's forefeet have been compared with the tortoise shell because she too has this ability. The pulsation of Shakti emanating outwards and then withdrawing inwards happens all the time. The energy that one experienced a minute ago is not the same energy that is running through the body now. This movement of energy is going in and out continuously. But Sankara is not happy with this comparison of Devi's feet with the hardened shell of the tortoise that many poets make, for Devi's feet are most auspicious.

In the *Bhagavad Gita* (2:58) Lord Krishna compares the tortoise to the purusha of stable awareness. When the indriyas are withdrawn to their source, just as the tortoise withdraws its limbs back into the shell, *prajna*, or awareness, becomes a steady and homogeneous flow of consciousness. Only then does the consciousness gain ascent. But the question arises, how to withdraw the indriyas? This is the most difficult task of pratyahara. This task can be completed in a spontaneous and natural manner through the worship of Devi, because she is the creator of the indriyas and they are naturally attracted to her form. Thus, *pratyahara*, or sensory withdrawal, can be achieved without great effort.

The worship of Devi allows for highly intensified energy to be channelled to the devotee. If this energy is directed to the different parts of the body, the entire body will be consecrated. This process can also be used for healing any imbalances in the body of oneself or of another. Similarly, the tantric practice of prana vidya involves awakening the energy within oneself through mantras and meditation and then directing it throughout the body.

The reference to the grinding stone here lends an intimacy to Shakti and Shiva that is soul stirring. It is a common tradition for the bridegroom to place the bride's foot on a grinding stone at the time of marriage and repeat mantras, so that she becomes stable like a rock in her household life. Shiva too must have placed Parvati's foot on a grinding stone at the time of their marriage!

89. Meditation on the wish-fulfilling feet of Devi

नखैर्नाकस्त्रीणां करकमलसंकोचशशिभिः
तरुणां दिव्यानां हसत इव ते चण्डि चरणौ ।
फलानि स्वःस्थेभ्यः किसलयकराग्रेण ददतां
दरिद्रेभ्यो भद्रां श्रियमनिशमह्नाय ददतौ ॥ ८९ ॥

nakhair-naakastreenaam kara-kamala-sankocha-shashibhih
taroonaam divyaanaam hasata iva te chandi charanau;
phalaani svahsthebhyah kisalaya-kara-agrena dadataam
daridrebhyo bhadraam shriyam-anisham-ahnaaya dadatau. (89)

te nakhaih shashibhih: thy moon-shaped toe nails; *kara kamala sankocha*: that shame the lotus-like palms; *naakastreenaam*: of heavenly damsels; *divyaanaam taroonaam hasata iva*: seem to mock at the celestial trees; *te charanau*: thy feet; *chandi*: oh! chandi; *phalaani*: desired gifts; *svah thebhyah*: to the devas; *kisalaya kara agrena*: tender branches; *dadataam*: which bestow; *daridrebhya*: to the poor and humble devotees; *bhadraam shriyam*: abundant wealth; *anisham*: always; *ahnaaya*: and quickly; *dadatau*: offer

Translation
O Chandi! Thy feet with moon-like toe nails, which shame the lotus-like palms of adoring heavenly damsels, quickly shower abundant wealth on the poor and humble devotees, seeming to mock the celestial (wish-yielding) trees, whose tender branches bestow desired gifts only to the devas.

Commentary
The feet of Shakti are a source of immense grace for the devotee, who can attain whatever he wishes through their worship. The *kalpavriksha*, or wish-yielding trees, are nothing in comparison to Shakti's feet that bestow abundant wealth on the humble and simple devotees. The wish-yielding trees bestow gifts only upon the devas who are in heaven, but Shakti grants gifts to the mortals.

Heaven and hell exist within, and so does the kalpavriksha, wish-yielding tree. Even the devatas reside in different parts of one's body, including the brain. However, one must be able to awaken the devatas and experience that state of mind, which is considered divine, where adoring, heavenly damsels abound. Then the kalpavriksha will grant all of one's wishes, but even then one will not be so fortunate as the poor and humble devotees of Shakti on whom her feet shower abundant wealth.

The kalpavriksha is actually a state of mind. This same mind that is forever distracted, dissipated, greedy, desirous and ambitious attains such intensity as it grows in awareness that it can achieve whatever it is set upon. But Shakti's grace is for all, even those who are not so evolved and have not attained the divine state of heaven. Even the simple fools who are still at a lower level of awareness can avail themselves of Devi's abundant grace if they worship her feet.

In this mantra, Sankara addresses Devi as Chandi, the terrible one, who is dark hued like Kali, the destroyer of time. Kali is invoked to transcend name and form, time and space, indriyas and mind. She devours everything and blesses the aspirant to enter the zone of timelessness or eternity, which is the abode of Tripura Sundari. Without obeisance to Kali and an encounter with this terrible force, which annihilates the ego principle, one simply cannot enter that level of experience. Kali scrutinizes the authenticity and qualification of the person who seeks to enter the state of timelessness. Once the selection has been made, Kali directs the aspirant on the right path, in the right direction, through the aid of the *dasa mahavidyas*, who are agents and manifestations of the supreme Shakti and act at her behest.

90. Meditation on Devi as Saraswati

कदा काले मातः कथय कलितालक्त करसं
पिबेयं विद्यार्थी तव चरणनिर्नेजनजलम् ।
प्रकृत्या मूकानामपि च कविताकारणतया
यदाधत्ते वाणीमुखकमलताम्बूलरसताम् ॥९०॥

kadaa kaale maatah kathaya kalitaalaktakarasam
pibeyam vidyarthee tava charana-nirnejana-jalam;
prakrityaa mookaanaam api cha kavitaa-kaaranatayaa
yadaadhatte vaani-mukha-kamala-taamboola-rasataam. (90)

kadaa kale: when; *maatah*: oh! mother; *kathaya*: tell me; *kalita aalaktakarasam*: lac-painted; *pibeyam*: will I imbibe; *vidyarthee*: I, seeker of knowledge; *tava*: thy; *charana nirnejana jalam*: water with which thy (lac-painted) feet have been washed; *prakrityaa mookaanaam api cha*: even in a naturally dumb person; *kavitaa kaaranatayaa*: that can generate poetic genius; *yadaa dhatte*: when will I let flow; *vaani*: speech symbolic of Saraswati; *mukha kamala taamboola rasataam*: the chewed betel leaf juice from the mouth of saraswati

Translation
O Mother! Tell me when will I, a seeker of knowledge, (have the privilege of) imbibing the (red-tinted) water in which Thy lac-painted feet have been washed, which can generate poetic genius, even in a naturally dumb person? When will I let the poetic speech flow, as the chewed betel leaf juice from the mouth of Saraswati?

Commentary
Here, Sankara prays for the grace of Shakti. As a seeker of knowledge, he asks for poetic genius, so that the speech simply flows out of his mouth as great poetry. This mantra also means that he has been healed! In this sense, *Saundarya Lahari* is also a testimony to the fact that Devi had answered his prayer.

A great poet possesses eloquence of thought and expression, and a superior mind. He is able to give philosophical attention to everything he fixes his mind upon, from a flower to the toenail of a beautiful woman. A great poet can make an ordinary object appear sublime. He can stir the heart and soul, and can conquer the minds of people with an idea.

However, the greatest of poets can also give birth to a spiritual awareness. Sankara was able to do that through his poem, *Saundarya Lahari*, which can generate a spiritual awakening in those who read it and confer all sorts of boons. Even before he wrote *Saundarya Lahari*, Sankara was already recognized for his powerful thoughts and ability to sway the minds of those he came in contact with. Even today, his compilations of stotras are still chanted with utmost faith and devotion throughout India.

The stotras of Sankaracharya are considered superior to most others, yet he fervently prays in this mantra for Devi's poetic grace. Speaking in the first person, he implores Devi to tell him when great poetry will flow from his mouth, as the chewed betel leaf juice flows from the mouth of Saraswati. That is the beauty of his expression and also a sure sign that he was a true jnani, because the more jnana permeates one's being, the more one begins to realize that one knows nothing. The true jnani is the most humble person because he realizes that he is a mere speck of dust in front of that almighty and absolute reality that is satyam shivam sundaram.

Sankara was a man with a mission. He had vowed to re-establish dharma and to restore faith in the divinity that exists within, and the universality and abiding nature of the atman. Thus it was natural that he should ask Devi for this boon, so that he would be successful in his mission. He needed to present his ideas to the people in such a way that they would develop a firm belief in what he was saying. He felt this was vital in order to stop the social and spiritual degeneration of his time.

From this mantra, the devotee also learns that if a great saint and siddha like Sankara could ask Devi for this boon, then he too should not have the least reserve in worshipping Devi and seeking her favour so that she may fulfil his desires.

91. Meditation on Devi's graceful gait

पदन्यासक्रीडापरिचयमिवारब्धुमनसः
चरन्तस्ते खेलं भवनकलहंसा न जहति ।
स्वविक्षेपे शिक्षां सुभगमणिमञ्जीररणितः
छलादाचक्षाणं चरणकमलं चारुचरिते ॥९१॥

*pada-nyaasa-kreedaa-parichayam-iva-arabdhumanasah
charantas-te khelam bhavana-kalahamsaa na jahati;
svavikshepe shikshaam subhaga-mani-manjeera-ranitah
chhalaad-aachakshaanam charanakamalam chaarucharite.* (91)

pada nyaasa kreedaa parichayam: learn from thy gait; *iva*: like; *arabdhumanasah*: in their effort to; *charantah*: their own defective gaits; *te*: thy; *khelam*: thy pursuit; *bhavana kalahamsaa*: swans in thy household; *na jahati*: do not abandon; *sva vikshepe*: movement of her own; *shikshaam*: instructions; *subhaga mani manjeera ranitah chhalaat*: in the guise of the tinkling sound of the anklets on them; *aachakshaanam iva*: seem to give; *charanakamalam*: thy lotus feet; *chaarucharite*: oh! goddess of graceful gait

Translation

O Goddess of graceful gait! The royal swans in Thy household never abandon their pursuit of Thee in their effort to learn from Thy gait in order to correct their own defective ways of walking. Thy lotus feet have movement of their own and seem to give instructions to them through the tinkling sounds of Thy anklets.

Commentary

Swans are known for their grace. They glide so effortlessly through the water with their necks tall and straight, emanating peace and tranquillity. However, they do not walk gracefully as their feet are large, flat and clumsy outside of water. Therefore, the beautiful swans which live in the royal mansion of Devi are forever following her to observe her grace and poise as she walks, so that they can correct their own defective gaits.

The feet of Devi are a source of grace and knowledge to all beings, whether mortals, heavenly damsels or royal swans. This is the importance of Devi's feet in worship. By worshipping her feet, the devotee worships the entire body of Devi, because all the organs of the body are connected to pranic points in the feet.

92. Meditation on Devi Tripura Sundari

गतास्ते मञ्चत्वं द्रुहिणहरिरुद्रेश्वरभृतः
शिवः स्वच्छच्छायाघटितकपटप्रच्छदपटः ।
त्वदीयानां भासां प्रतिफलनरागारुणतया
शरीरी शृङ्गारो रस इव दृशां दोग्धि कुतुकम् ॥९२॥

*gataaste manchatvam druhina-hari-rudreshvara-bhritah
shivah svachchhach-chhaayaa-ghatita-kapata-prachchhada-pata;
tvadeeyaanaam bhaasaam pratiphalana-raagaa-runatayaa
shareeree shringaaro rasa iva drishaam dogdhi-kutukam. (92)*

gataah: have taken; *te manchatvam*: shape of the legs of thy bed; *druhina hari rudreshvara bhrita*: thy servants brahma, vishnu, rudra and ishvara; *shivah*: shiva; *svachchhach chhaayaa ghatita kapata prachchhada pata*: formed himself into thy bedspread with his lustrous whiteness; *tvadeeyaanaam bhaasaam*: thy glory; *pratiphalana raagaa runatayaa*: reflecting thy crimson colour; *shareeree shringaara rasa iva*: thereby becoming the embodiment of the erotic emotion; *drishaam*: for the eyes; *dogdhi-kutukam*: and making thee happy

Translation
Thy servants Brahma, Vishnu, Rudra and Ishwara have taken the shape of the four legs of Thy bed. Shiva has formed himself into Thy bedspread with his lustrous whiteness reflecting Thy crimson glory, thereby becoming the embodiment of erotic emotions for the eyes, and making Thee happy.

Commentary
The supreme Shakti forever reclines above sahasrara on a bed supported by four legs, which are Brahma, the creator; Vishnu, the preserver; Rudra, the destroyer; and Ishwara, the indestructible element that resides in all. Brahma, Vishnu, Rudra and Ishwara are purushas endowed with authority. In order to be close to Devi, they

have transformed themselves into the four legs of her bed upon which she is seated. The mattress of her bed is formed by Sadashiva and the bedcover by Shiva. In the human body, these four legs of Devi's bed represent the chakras from mooladhara to anahata. Vishuddhi is the mattress, corresponding to Sadashiva, and ajna the bedcover, corresponding to Shiva on whom Devi, as the awakened kundalini, is seated.

The concept of Shakta darshan in which Shakti is the highest of all, above the devatas and even Shiva, is clearly revealed in this mantra. All the principles of creation, preservation and destruction as well as the indestructible seed within each of them are absorbed into Shakti and remain as archetypes, awaiting creation. Shiva is the luckiest of them all on account of being her husband. He is a shuddha tattwa and, therefore, remains in close proximity to Shakti. They complement each other, his lustrous white brilliance setting off her crimson radiance. He, the embodiment of eroticism, and she, the embodiment of beauty!

93. Meditation on Aruna Shakti

अराला केशेषु प्रकृतिसरला मन्दहसिते
शिरीषाभा चित्ते दृषदिव कठोरा कुचतटे ।
भृशं तन्वी मध्ये पृथुरपि वरारोहविषये
जगत्त्रातुं शंभोर्जयति करुणा काचिदरुणा ॥ ९३ ॥

*araalaa kesheshu prakriti-saralaa mandahasite
shireeshaabhaa chitte drishadiva kathoraa kuchatate;
bhrisham tanvee madhye prithu-rapi varaaroha-vishaye
jagat-traatum shambhor-jayati karuna kaachid-arunaa. (93)*

araalaa kesheshu: with curly hair; *prakriti saralaa*: (that is) artless; *manda hasite*: with smile; *shireeshaabhaa*: soft as the shirisha flower; *chitte*: with heart; *drishat iva kathoraa*: tight and hard as a grinding stone; *kuchatate*: with breasts; *bhrisham tanvee*: extremely slender; *madhye*: waist; *prithu*: generous in size; *rapi varaaroha vishaye*: breasts and hips; *jagat traatum*: to protect the universe; *shambhoh*: shiva's; *jayati*: shines; *karuna*: compassionately; *kaachit*: indescribable; *arunaa*: arunaa

Translation
With curly hair and artless smile, with heart soft as the shirisha flower, with breasts tight and hard as a grinding stone, waist extremely slender, breasts and hips generous in size, the indescribable Aruna Shakti, the grace of Shiva, shines compassionately for the protection of the universe.

Commentary
Each day that heralds the birth of the rising sun, which grants life, sustenance and nourishment to creation, is termed *arunodaya*. In the same way, the birth of the rising grace of Tripura Sundari, whom Sankara has invoked within himself, is known as *Aruna Shakti*. This form of Tripura Sundari will confer life on him and rejuvenate him. Sankara has a vision of Aruna Shakti in mantras 16 and 18 too. This indicates a very heightened state of meditation as Shakti in

this form denotes a highly creative and life-giving force that is unmatched.

This mantra describes the most graceful and benevolent form of Tripura Sundari. She is the creator, protector and destroyer of this universe. She protects each and everything through her different agencies, who are all rooted in her. She is the indescribable Aruna Shakti that shines compassionately, always sustaining and protecting the universe. Everyone is alive because of her. She radiates truth, beauty and auspiciousness.

Aruna is the name of Shakti that is identical with the grace of Shiva. The golden radiance of Aruna Shakti is on account of the gunas in total balance. Aruna Shakti of golden hue revealing herself to Sankara is what stands between him and the Supreme Truth or Tripura Sundari, which is also described in *Ishavasya Upanishad* (mantra 15):

> *Hiranmayena paatrena satyasyaa pihitam mukham*
> The face of truth is covered by a golden vessel.

The golden rays of Aruna Shakti are so dense that they cover the vision of Tripura Sundari, who is the most sublime and supreme experience of truth, auspiciousness and beauty, *satyam, shivam, sundaram*. Her rays, which are derived from the supreme source that she is concealing, spread out towards the universe at the behest of that supreme power, Tripura Sundari, the highest Shakti.

94. Meditation on the reflection of Shakti in the sun

समानीतः पद्भ्यां मणिमुकुरतामम्बरमणिः
भयादास्यादन्तःस्तिमितकिरणश्रेणिमसृणः ।
दधाति त्वद्वक्त्रप्रतिफलनमश्रान्तविकचं
निरातङ्कं चंद्रान्निजहृदयपंङ्केरुहमिव ॥ ९४ ॥

*samaaneetah padbhyaam mani-mukurataam-ambara-manih
bhayaad-aasyaad-antah stimita-kirana-shreni-masrinah;
dadhaati tvadvaktra-pratiphalanam-ashraanta-vikacham
niraatankam chandraan-nijahridaya-pankeruham-iva.* (94)

samaaneetah: is included in, has assembled; *padbhyaam*: (your) two feet; *mani*: gem; *mukurataam*: mirror, looking glass; *ambara-manih*: wanderer in the sky (sun); *bhayaat-aasyaat-antah*: and from fear of this end; *stimita*: gets wonderstruck, limited or dazzled; *kirana-shreni masrinah*: limitless rows of rays; *dadhaati*: gives; *tvat vaktra*: your face; *pratiphalanam*: reflected image; *ashraanta*: tranquil; *vikacham*: blown, expanded, open, spread about scattered over; *niraatankam*: free from blemish; *chandraan*: like the moon; *nija hridaya*: one's own heart; *pankeruham-iva*: like the lotus

Translation
The sun, having assembled Thy two feet in the jewel looking glass (of its rays), becomes wonderstruck by the limitless rays that the reflected image of Thy face gives off. From fear of that, he (withdraws Thy image) into his own heart lotus, where it appears full blown, tranquil, open, expanded, spread out and free of blemish, like the moon.

Commentary
Beautiful poetical allegory is depicted in this verse. The sun represents prana shakti, which transmits life energy through its rays. The sun is a reservoir of prana shakti, but it needs to replenish itself all the time. Therefore, the sun is naturally a worshipper of Shakti whom he keeps at

the nucleus of his core, the heart lotus. This heart lotus is forever blooming due to Shakti's grace, so the sun has no need to worry on account of the moon, who is his rival for the grace of Shakti.

The period before dawn, when the sun is about to come up, is highly charged because the prana emitted by the sun is very intense and pure. During that period Shakti hands out prana through the medium of the sun for about two hours. At that time the sun becomes a messenger of the supreme Shakti, doling out prana to the entire creation. The aspirant can avail himself of this by arising early and meditating on Devi, who is the source of prana.

Kamadeva is present in the form of agni, symbolic of erotic desire, in mantra 86, when Shiva and Shakti have transcended name and form. In the same way, Surya, the sun, is present at this heightened stage of experience to withdraw the image of Shakti's rays into himself and, as this mantra suggests, is wonderstruck at the limitless number of rays that Shakti projects. Shakti is then reflected in the inner core or heart lotus of the sun, where she appears expansive, tranquil, in full bloom and free from blemish, like the moon.

The sun here stands for prana shakti, and the process described is the involution of prana back to its source, so that the meditator can experience the glory of the highest and most supreme Shakti.

95. Meditation on Devi in her mansion

कलङ्कः कस्तूरी रजनिकरबिम्बं जलमयं
कलाभिः कर्पूरैर्मरकतकरण्डं निबिडितम् ।
अतस्त्वद्भोगेन प्रतिदिनमिदं रिक्तकुहरं
विधिर्भूयो भूयो निबिडयति नूनं तव कृते ॥९५॥

*kalankah kastooree rajani-kara-bimbam jalamayam
kalaabhih karpoorair-marakatakarandam nibiditam;
atas-tvadbhogena pratidinam-idam-riktakuharam
vidhir-bhooyo bhooyo nibidayati noonam tava krite.* (95)

kalankah: dark mark on the moon; *kastooree*: is musk; *rajani kara bimbam*: moon; *jalamayam*: is watery (with rosewater); *kalaabhih karpooraih*: with pieces of camphor; *marakata karandam*: is an emerald cup; *nibiditam*: filled; *atah*: hence; *tvat bhogena*: by thy using them; *pratidinam*: every day; *idam*: this (cup); *rikta kuharam*: become empty; *vidhih*: brahma; *bhooya bhooya*: again and again; *nibidayati*: fills it up; *noonam*: certainly; *tava krite*: for thee

Translation
The dark mark on the moon is musk. The moon's watery disc is an emerald cup filled with pieces of camphor (the small projections on the moon). When the contents of this cup are exhausted by Thy using them, Brahma certainly fills it up every day for Thee.

Commentary
This mantra once again emphasizes Shakti's supremacy. The dark spots on the moon are musk, which she applies as fragrance. The moon is her emerald cup in which she keeps the camphor that she uses to wave as lights. Brahma is forever in her service to replace whatever she uses whenever her cup empties. Brahma is the creator assigned by Shakti. Whenever anything is depleted, he rushes to create more in order to replenish what has been exhausted. He does all

this in the service of Shakti, for he is ever at her command to fulfil her tasks.

After asserting the role of the sun in withdrawing the prana shakti back to its source, the presence of the moon is highlighted here as Sankara is about to enter the highest dimension of experience. These three cosmic counterparts, agni, surya and soma, which represent the highest Shakti and journey with her in the process of evolution and involution, are the last of her companions before the final appearance of the Supreme Beauty, Tripura Sundari. They have been by her side at each stage of her manifestation, carrying out their ordained duties.

At this final stage too they are by her side to aid her in the final amalgamation of matter into spirit. Only when she withdraws these three cosmic forces, which here represent iccha shakti, kriya shakti and jnana shakti, will she involute into her supreme self, Tripura Sundari, for Sankara to behold.

96. Meditation on the most supreme Tripura Sundari in her inner apartment

पुरारातेरन्तः पुरमसि ततस्त्वच्चरणयोः
सपर्यामर्यादा तरलकरणानामसुलभा ।
तथाप्येते नीताः शतमखमुखाः सिद्धिमतुलां
तव द्वारोपान्तस्थितिभिरणिमाद्याभिरमराः ॥९६॥

*puraaraater-antah puramasi tatas-tvachcharanayoh
saparyaa-maryaadaa tarala-karanaanaam-asulabhaa;
tathaapy-ete neetaah shatamakhamukhaah siddhim-atulaam
tava dvaaropaanta sthitibhir-animaadyaabhir-amaraah.* (96)

puraaraateh: (thou, the consort) of the destroyer of cities (shiva); *antah puram asi*: reside in the inner apartments; *tatah*: hence; *tvat charanayoh*: thy feet; *saparyaa maryaadaa*: privilege of worshipping; *tarala karanaanaam*: for the fickle-minded; *asulabhaa*: is not easy; *tathaapi*: is well-known; *ete shatamakhamukhaah amaraah*: devas like indra; *neetaah*: attained; *siddhim*: perfection; *atulaam*: unparalleled; *tava*: thy; *dvaaropaanta sthitibhih*: who are thy gatekeepers; *animaadyaabhih*: anima and other psychic powers

Translation
Thou, the Consort of Shiva, the destroyer of the cities, resides in the inner apartment. Hence, the privilege of worshipping Thy feet is not easy for the fickle-minded. It is well known that the devas, like Indra, who are Thy gatekeepers, have attained unparalleled siddhis or powers of perfection, such as anima and others.

Commentary
This mantra describes the supreme Shakti, who is most difficult to experience. The fickle-minded can never hope to reach the inner recesses where she resides. Even the gods, such as Indra, who have attained the eight siddhis through their unparalleled austerities, are only her gatekeepers.

Now the experience of the highest Shakti is drawing near. In fact, Sankara is at the door of her inner apartment. Only those who qualify can go beyond what lies behind these closed doors. The Goddess leaves her siddhis and other powers belonging to the worldly planes outside these doors. Those who run after these powers can never hope to cross the threshold of her inner residence. These powers were only intended to entice devotees towards higher experience, but those who get caught up in the mire of attachment and cannot rise above them are left waiting outside. Sankara does not belong to this category; thus the highest darshan is ensured for him.

This mantra is also a word of caution to those seeking gratification at the lower mundane level, who wish to exploit the goddess for their selfish ends, which are rooted in *bhoga*, or enjoyment. The Goddess diplomatically leaves them behind and enters her inner chamber where she resides with her Lord, Shiva. This indicates that Devi is available to all at the lower level, but she is very selective about whom she bestows her vision upon at the level of higher experience. As the Bible says: "It is easier for a camel to pass through the eye of a needle than for the worldly to enter the gates of heaven." This entry is reserved for those who are established in the highest ideals of *tyaga*, renunciation, and *vairagya*, dispassion, as was the case of Sankara.

97. Meditation on the unattainable Shakti above sahasrara

कलत्रं वैधात्रं कति कति भजन्ते न कवयः
श्रियो देव्याः को वा न भवति पतिः कैरपि धनैः ।
महादेवं हित्वा तव सति सतीनामचरमे
कुचाभ्यामासंगः कुरवकतरोरप्यसुलभः ॥ ९७ ॥

kalatram vaidhaatram kati kati bhajante na kavayah
shriyo devyaah ko vaa na bhavati patih kairapi dhanaih;
mahaadevam hitvaa tava sati sateenaama-charame
kuchaabhyaam-aasangah kuravaka-tarorapy-asulabhah. (97)

kalatram vaidhaatram: saraswati, the wife of brahma; *kati kati*: how numerous; *bhajante na*: have courted and attained; *kavayah*: are the poets; *shriya devyaah*: of lakshmi; *ka vaa*: anyone; *na bhavati patih*: fails to become the lord; *kairapi dhanaih* with some wealth; *mahaadevam hitvaa*: besides shiva; *tava*: thy; *sati*: oh! embodiment of chastity; *sateenaama charame*: oh! the foremost of chaste ones; *kuchaabhyaam aasangah*: embrace of thy breasts; *kuravaka taror api*: not even the kuravaka tree; *asulabhah*: none has had

Translation

O Sati! How numerous are the poets who have courted and attained Saraswati! Who with some wealth fails to become the lord of Lakshmi! But, O foremost of chaste ones! None besides Shiva, not even the kuravaka tree, has had the embrace of Thy breasts.

Commentary

Even Saraswati and Lakshmi, who are Devi's very own embodiments, are easily attainable. Saraswati has been won by innumerable poets, and so too those with some wealth have attained Lakshmi. But the highest Shakti has been embraced by no one except Shiva, because she is pure, *shuddha* tattwa without any trace of maya. In that state Shakti is *mayatita* and *gunatita*, beyond maya and the gunas. This mantra establishes the purity of Shakti that Sankara is beholding, a vision that is granted only to Shiva. Shakti allowed Sankara this vision, for he was Shiva incarnate.

98. Meditation on Tripura Sundari

स्वदेहोद्भूताभिर्घृणिभिरणिमाद्याभिरभितो
निषेव्यां नित्ये त्वामहमिति सदा भावयति यः ।
किमाश्चर्यं तस्य त्रिनयनसमृद्धिं तृणयतो
महासंवर्ताग्निर्विरचयति नीराजनविधिम् ॥ ९८ ॥

*svadehodbhootaabhir-ghrinibhir-animaadyaabhir-abhito
nishevyaam nitye tvaam-ahamiti sadaa bhaavayati yah;
kimaashcharyam tasya trinayana-samriddhim trinayato
mahaa-samvartaagnir-virachayati neeraajana-vidhim.* (98)

svadeha udbhootaabhih: emanating from thy body; *ghrinibhih*: (are) rays; *animaadyaabhih*: divine powers like anima and others; *abhita*: (who) art surrounded; *nishevyaam*: (and) served by; *nitye*: (oh) eternal mother; *tvaam*: thee; *aham iti*: feeling of identification; *sadaa*: always; *bhaavayati*: meditations (on thee); *yah*: a devotee; *kim aashcharyam*: no wonder; *tasya*: him; *trinayana samriddhim*: the glory of the three-eyed shiva; *trinayata*: far above; *mahaa samvartaagnih*: flames of dissolution; *virachayati*: do; *neeraajana vidhim*: adoration by waving lighted camphor

Translation
O Eternal Mother! By always identifying in meditation with Thee, who art surrounded and served by the divine powers like anima and others, which are the rays emanating from Thy body, a devotee attains glories far above even those of the three-eyed Shiva. No wonder the flames of the cosmic dissolution prove only to be the waving of camphor lights in Thy adoration.

Commentary
The devotee has to caution himself from being diverted by siddhis. The tantric texts identify them as eight in number: i) *anima*, ability to reduce oneself; ii) *mahima*, to expand oneself; iii) *laghima*, to become light; iv) *garima*, to

become heavy, v) *prapti*, to move at will, vi) *prakashya*, to enjoy whatever one desires; vii) *varitva*, to exert influence on others; and viii) *isitva*, to gain absolute control. These eight siddhis are extremely powerful and can easily sway the devotee who is not established in discernment or dispassion.

These siddhis are the rays emanating from the lotus feet of Shakti which fall on the aspirant as grace, but should never be mistaken for the ultimate experience. The devotee must always identify with the supreme Shakti in totality and not just with her limited powers. In doing so, he attains greatness that surpasses even the glory of Shiva, the destroyer of the universe. For such a devotee, the flames that arise at the time of *pralaya*, or dissolution, are but the waving of camphor lights in adoration of Shakti, who has the power to consume even Shiva, the destroyer.

Trinayana samriddhim refers to the glory of the three-eyed Shiva. However, it also alludes to the richness of experience generated by the equipoise of the three forces: ida pingala and sushumna, and the three aspects of Devi's body: *agni*, *surya* and *chandra*, fire, sun and moon. The devotee who identifies with Shakti in totality begins to find siddhis irrelevant. As he surpasses their influence, he attains greatness that is far beyond that of even Shiva. In other words, he enters *samadhi*, or union with Tripura Sundari. In samadhi there is no duality; the idea of individuality is transcended and the meditator and object of meditation become one. The devotee merges into Shakti and attains glories that are beyond imagination.

In this mantra, Sankara makes it very clear that the state of union between Shakti and Shiva, which other schools of tantra consider to be final and absolute, is not final according to Samaya tantra. He speaks of a richness of experience that far exceeds the level of other divinities and lies beyond their union. *Trinayana samriddhim* refers not only to the three-eyed Shiva, but to an experience which is beyond ida, pingala and sushumna, as well as the sun, moon and fire.

Samaya tantra advocates the unified field theory, which has become the discovery of modern science as well. In this theory the individual experiences himself as no different from the rest of creation. He sees an intense field of energy flowing from one object to another at different levels of frequency. By intensifying one's own field of energy and converging it at sahasrara, the highest point of human existence, one is able to penetrate this level and go still higher to get a whiff of the divine chakras that are beyond sahasrara.

Once the kundalini pierces ajna chakra, it begins to have the sights and smells of sahasrara. In the same way, once the kundalini unites with Shiva at sahasrara, the individual beholds the higher *lokas*, or planes of existence, which bring him in contact with a power that is higher than Shiva-Shakti. That power is Tripura Sundari, whom Sankara was beholding. In other words, he was having the highest darshan.

99. Meditation on the inconceivable and limitless power of Devi

गिरामाहुर्देवीं द्रुहिणगृहिणीमागमविदो
हरेः पत्नीं पद्मां हरसहचरीमद्रितनयाम् ।
तुरीया कापि त्वं दुरधिगमनिः सीममहिमा
महामाया विश्वं भ्रमयसि परब्रह्ममहिषि ॥९९॥

giraam-aahur-deveem druhinagrihineem-aagamavido
hareh patneem padmaam harasahachareem-adritanayaam;
tureeyaa kaapi tvam duradhigamanih seemamahimaa
mahaamaayaa vishvam bhramayasi parabrahmamahishi. (99)

giraam deveem: as the goddess of learning, saraswati; *aahuh*: describe thee; *druhina grihineem*: wife of brahma; *aagamavido*: scholars, who are learned in the scriptures; *hareh patneem*: wife of hari; *padmaam*: as lakshmi; *hara sahachareem*: wife of hara (shiva); *adritanayaam*: as the daughter of the mountain; *tureeyaa kaapi*: art the indefinable fourth power; *tvam*: thou; *duradhigamanih seema mahimaa*: having inconceivable and limitless glory; *mahaamaayaa*: mahamaya; *vishvam bhramayasi*: world who amazes; *parabrahmamahishi*: oh! consort of parabrahman

Translation
O Consort of Parabrahman! The scholars who are learned in the scriptures describe Thee as the goddess of learning, Saraswati, the wife of Brahma; the lotus-born Lakshmi, the wife of Vishnu; and also the daughter of the mountain, the wife of Shiva. However, Thou art Mahamaya, the indefinable fourth power, having inconceivable and limitless glory, who revolves the wheel of this world.

Commentary
In this mantra Sankara makes it clear that the Shakti he has invoked is the highest, most supreme Tripura Sundari whom he regards as the fourth shakti or power, having

inconceivable and unlimited possibilities and potential. She is not Saraswati or Lakshmi or Parvati; nor is she Brahma, Vishnu or Mahesh. She is a unique, higher power that supersedes them all. It is she who operates as Mahamaya keeping everyone under her spell and forever enamoured of her processes of creation.

Tureeyaa kaapi denotes that this fourth power is the experience of the fourth and highest dimension of awareness, known as *turiya*, which is akin to the highest state of samadhi. There the meditator and the object of meditation become one and enter the dimension of unified awareness. However, this experience is only available to those who observe and respect the laws of this great power. There are sure and certain laws that govern this experience and any violation of these laws results in a reaction which can be detrimental to one's very existence. Thus one must approach her with utmost devotion and with extreme caution to avoid any violation of her inherent laws to ensure success of Her worship.

100. Meditation on the full form of Devi

समुद्भूतस्थूलस्तनभरमुरश्चारुहसितं
कटाक्षे कंदर्पाः कतिचन कदम्बद्युतिवपुः ।
हरस्य त्वद्भ्रान्तिं मनसि जनयन्ति स्म विमला
भवत्या ये भक्ताः परिणतिरमीषामियमुमे ॥ १०० ॥

samudbhoota-sthoola-stanabharam-urash-chaaruhasitam
kataakshe kandarpaah katichana kadamba-dyuti-vapuh;
harasya tvad-bhraantim manasi janayanti sma vimalaa
bhavatyaa ye bhaktaah parinatir-ameeshaam-iyam-ume. (100)

samudbhootah: emerging from; *sthoola*: big; *stana bharam*: heavy and full breasts; *urah*: waist; *chaaru hasitam*: smiling countenance; *kataakshe*: bewitching, inviting glances; *kandarpaah*: kamadeva, love lust, inflamer of even a god; *katichana*: several; *kadamba*: blossoming kadamba tree; *dyuti*: splendour, brightness, majesty, dignity; *vapuh*: body; *harasya*: of hara i.e. shiva; *tvat*: your; *bhraantim*: agitation; *manasi*: in the mind; *janayanti*: groups of people; *sma vimalaa*: spotslessly pure; *bhavatyaa*: of your (in respectful terms); *ye*: this; *bhaktaah*: devotees; *parinatih*: is changed or transformed into; *ameeshaam*: object of worldly enjoyment, luxury; *iyam-ume*: this, oh! uma

Translation

O Uma! This waist, emerging from large, heavy and full breasts, smiling countenance, bewitching glances like several Kamadevas, body with the splendour of a flowering kadamba tree, all these together create agitation in the mind of Hara (Shiva) and other people, as if Thou, who art spotlessly pure, art transformed into an object of worldly enjoyment for Thy devotees.

Commentary

In this mantra, that pure and spotless fourth power, which is nameless and formless, transforms into the beautiful

Uma, who is described here with slender waist, full breasts, beautiful smile and bewitching side glances that can compare to a thousand Kamadevas. Thus Uma creates agitation, *spandan*, vibration, and movement in Shiva, stirring the hearts of devotees, who emerge as a result of the spandan created by Shakti.

A faultless devotee is one who loves Devi with a pure heart and sees the hand of Devi in everything he does. One who forever meditates on Devi in this manner becomes like her. Whatever one meditates upon with intensity, one eventually becomes. There is a saying: *bhramar keet nyaya*, which describes an ordinary insect that is dragged into the nest of a wasp. As the insect is imprisoned in that nest, it looks only at the wasp with one-pointed vision. In a little while it too becomes a wasp, and then breaks free from the nest to catch another prey to convert into a wasp.

Faith and strong belief coupled with the innocence of a child are the basis of darshan of Shakti. This darshan leads to the experience of truth, beauty and auspiciousness, *satyam, shivam, sundaram*. With this experience the devotee himself becomes pure, beautiful and radiant. The devotee who worships her in this manner attains her slender frame, with well developed chest and breasts, a charming smile and a bewitching glance. Even Shiva will be attracted to such a devotee whom Devi favours so much. That devotee becomes just like Devi, and Shiva thus becomes confused.

101. Meditation on Tripura Sundari blessing her devotee

सरस्वत्या लक्ष्म्या विधिहरिसपत्नो विहरते
रतेः पातिव्रत्यं शिथिलयति रम्येण वपुषा ।
चिरं जीवन्नेव क्षपितपशुपाशव्यतिकरः
परब्रह्माभिख्यं रसयति रसं त्वद्भजनवान् ॥१०१॥

*sarasvatyaa lakshmyaa vidhiharisapatno viharate
rateh paativratyam shithilayati ramyena vapushaa;
chiram jeevanneva kshapita-pashupaasha-vyatikarah
parabrahmaabhikhyam rasayati rasam tvadbhajanavaan.* (101)

tvat bhajanavaan: thy devotee; *sarasvatyaa lakshmyaa*: with sarasvati and lakshmi; *vidhiharisapatna*: arousing jealousy of their consorts; *viharate*: sports; *rateh paativratyam*: rati's chastity; *shithilayati*: violates; *ramyena vapushaa*: rati's chastity; *chiram jeevanneva*: he enjoys long life; *kshapita pashupaasha vyatikarah*: freed from bondage of birth and death; *parabrahmaabhikhyam rasam*: essence of supreme bliss; *rasayati*: enjoys

Translation

(O Mother!) Thy devotee sports with Saraswati and Lakshmi, thus arousing the jealousy of their consorts, Brahma and Vishnu. (By his charm) he attracts the attention of Rati (the wife of Kamadeva) and thus violates her chastity. Freed from the bondage of birth and ignorance, he lives a long life and enjoys the essence of supreme bliss.

Commentary

That supreme Shakti can bestow all kinds of boons. Her devotee acquires immense knowledge and unlimited wealth. His body becomes so charming that he attracts beautiful women who are the embodiments of Rati. He lives a long life, enjoying all worldly or material bliss. At the same time he is freed from the bondage of birth and death and enjoys supreme bliss.

102. Meditation on Devi's hidden treasures

निधे नित्यस्मेरे निरवधिगुणे नीतिनिपुणे
निराघाटज्ञाने नियमपरचित्तैकनिलये ।
नियत्या निर्मुक्ते निखिलनिगमान्तस्तुतपदे
निरातङ्के नित्ये निगमय ममापि स्तुतिमिमाम् ॥१०२॥

*nidhe nityasmere niravadhigune neeti-nipune
niraaghaatagyaane niyama-parachittaika-nilaye;
niyatyaa nirmukte nikhila nigama-anta-stutapade
niraatanke nitye nigamaya mamaapi stutim-imaam.* (102)

nidhe: reservoir, store, treasure; *nityasmere*: always smiling; *niravadhigune*: one whose virtues are limitless; *neeti*: decorum, propriety, statesmanship; *nipune*: expert; *niraa ghaatagyaane*: unbound wisdom, knowledge; *niyama*: rules; *parachittaika*: whose minds do not deviate from; *nilaye*: bounty; storehouse; collection; *niyatyaa*: self-restraint, self-command or obligation; *nirmukte*: free from; *nikhila*: whole gamut of; *nigama anta*: end of the tantras, upanishads; *stutapade*: object of praise of; *niraatanke*: free from fear, ailment; *nitye*: always, ever; *nigamaya*: always approve; *mama api*: mine also; *stutim imaam*: this praise

Translation
O Hidden Treasure! Whose virtues are limitless, ever smiling and blissful, of excellent decorum, unlimited fountain of wisdom, ever abiding in the minds of those who do not deviate from the rules of self-restraint, free from conventions, whose feet are glorified by all the Upanishads, eternal and fearless, pray approve this hymn of mine (Thy humble devotee) in praise of Thee.

Commentary
The word *nidhe* has been translated by many enlightened rishis, like Yajnavalkya and Manu, as the 'hidden wealth of the universe'. This is a most apt description of Shakti,

because she is the wealth of this universe, without whom all would be not only destitute, but non-existent. The use of this word also implies that one who realizes Parashakti realizes the hidden, unmanifest supreme reality.

The word *nityasmere* indicates 'supreme bliss', which is a result of constant awareness of the supreme Shakti. A devotee of Sri Vidya is always in a state of *ananda*, bliss, and this permeates his immediate environment; his home becomes an abode of happiness and auspiciousness.

The word *niravadhiguna* indicates that the supreme Shakti always remains in an elevated state of awareness in which the gunas of sattwa, rajas and tamas are totally balanced. Being very proficient in balancing the gunas, Shakti grants the devotee that experience or level of mind that is in perfect equipoise. The word *nitinipune* refers to Shakti's proficiency in running the intricate affairs of the world with wisdom and clarity, which she grants her devotee.

The word *niraghatagyana* means 'clarity of mind' that Shakti grants the devotee, allowing him to understand things at once. The phrase *niyamaparachitaika nilaye* implies that Shakti resides in the minds of those devotees who follow the disciplines of her Sri Vidya upasana with regularity. To them She grants victory over the seven *bhumikas*, or levels of mind.

The word *nityata* means 'victory over death'. This does not mean that one's body will never die, but that one's spirit or atman will never die. One who is established in the atman becomes immortal like Devi. *Nikhila nigama* means that which the Tantras sing the praises of. *Niratanke nitye* is Devi's 'eternal state of ananda' attained by worshippers of Sri Vidya.

103. Meditation on Devi as the source of this hymn

प्रदीपज्वालाभिर्दिवसकरनीराजनविधिः
सुधासूत चन्द्रोपलजललवैरर्घ्यरचना ।
स्वकीयैरम्भोभिः सलिलनिधिसौहित्यकरणं
त्वदीयाभिर्वाग्भिस्तव जननि वाचां स्तुतिरियम् ॥१०३॥

*pradeepa-jvaalaabhir-divasakara-neeraajana-vidhih
sudhaasootesh-chandr-opala-jalalavair-arghya-rachanaa;
svakeeyair-ambhobhih salilanidhi-sauhitya-karanam
tvadeeyaabhir-vaagbhis-tava janani vaachaam stutiriyam.* (103)

pradeepa jvaalaabhih: with the flame of a lamp; *divasakara neeraajana vidhih*: offering niranjana to the sun; *sudhaasooteh*: to the nectar oozing moon; *chandra upala jalalavaih*: with the water oozing out of the moonstone; *arghya rachanaa*: offering 'arghya'; *svakeeyaih ambhobhih*: with its own water; *salilanidhi sauhitya karanam*: offering water to the ocean; *tvadeeyaabhih*: (in the same way) that are thine own; *vaagbhih*: with words; *tava*: thee; *janani vaachaam*: oh! source of all learning; *stutih iyam*: this hymn (is addressed to thee)

Translation
O Source of all learning! Just as performing the flame waving ritual to the sun is only offering his own light to him; offering arghya to the moon with the water that oozes out of the moon-stone is only to give back what belongs to the moon, and making water-offering to the ocean is to return what belongs to it, so this hymn addressed to Thee is composed of words that are already Thine.

Commentary
Sankara had performed *avahana* or invocation of the supreme Shakti within himself. Shakti awakened within to restore and rejuvenate him. At that time, the hymn that he composed was not in his words, but the words of Shakti,

speaking through him. As Sankara was a highly learned person as well as a siddha, naturally the outcome was the unparalleled verses of *Saundarya Lahari*. But one should never forget that these are the words of an awakened Shakti, so they are very potent and sacred.

Thus, as Shakti is speaking through him, Sankara says that this hymn of his is like addressing something to her which is already hers. Sankara takes no credit for this magnificent work and gives all the credit to Shakti, as she is everywhere, even in the words he is writing. By chanting these mantras, one can avail oneself of the benevolence of Shakti which Sankara had invoked.

Prayer to Shiva, the beloved of Shakti

नमस्ते नमस्ते विभोविश्वमूर्ते
नमस्ते नमस्ते चिदानन्दमूर्ते
नमस्ते नमस्ते तपोयोगगम्य
नमस्ते नमस्ते श्रुतिज्ञानगम्य

namaste namaste vibhovishamoorte
namaste namaste chidaanandamoorte
namaste namaste tapoyogagamya
namaste namaste shrutijnanagamya

namaste: salutations; *namaste*: salutations; *vibhovishamoorte*: to the dazzling and supreme embodiment of the cosmos; *namaste*: salutations; *namaste*: salutations; *chidaanandamoorte*: to the one who is the embodiment of the supreme bliss and consciousness; *namaste*: salutations; *namaste*: salutations; *tapoyogagamya*: to the one who is the final destination of all the austerities and yoga; *namaste*: salutations; *namaste*: salutations; *shrutijnanagamya*: to the one who is the final cherished fruit of the knowledge obtained from all the shrutis (divine sounds or mantras)

Translation
Salutations and prostrations to the dazzling and supreme embodiment of the cosmos, who is the personification of supreme bliss and consciousness, and also the final destination of all the austerities and yoga. Salutations and prostrations to the One who is the ultimate cherished fruit of the knowledge obtained from all the shrutis.

Commentary
This befitting invocation or prayer to Shiva at the end of *Saundarya Lahari* is not a part of *Saundarya Lahari*, but is chanted at the end of the hymn in the Satyananda tradition to please Shakti, as she is most delighted and happy when Shiva is remembered, for she loves him unabashedly. In fact,

her favourite occupation is to repeat the name of Shiva and whisper his mantra. She does it all the time. As Parvati, she repeated his name for at least a thousand years in order to attain him. As a devotee of the Supreme Shakti the upasaka of *Saundarya Lahari* should do the same at the end of each path in order to please her and obtain her grace, for Shakti and Shiva are one and the same, forever united, complete and homogenous.

Prayoga for Saundarya Lahari

The following Prayoga has been recorded by the tradition. The contribution of the author in this Prayoga is the mandala meditation which she considers to be the highlight of *Saundarya Lahari*. It is the mandala that confers grace and also inner vision. Some of the purposes have been amended wherever it was felt necessary.

	Inscribed on	No. of days	No. of japas per day	Food offering	Mandala meditation	Purpose
Mantra 1: क						
	a) Coloured flour with a ghee lamp in front	12	1000	Coconut, jaggery, ghee, tri-madhura	On Shiva and Shakti	Accomplishment of desired objects
	b) Gold plate; worship facing east	12	1000	Sweet cake		Prosperity; overcoming obstacles
Mantra 2: ह्रीं						
	Gold plate; worship facing north	55	1000	Milk gruel	On Sri Devi's feet	Mastery over matter
Mantra 3: श्री						
	a) Gold plate; worship facing north-east	54	2000	Black gram cake	On Devi in the mudra of granting what you desire	Knowledge; all that one can desire
	b) " "	15	1000	" "		Wealth and knowledge

	Inscribed on	No. of days	No. of japas per day	Food offering	Mandala meditation	Purpose
Mantra 4:	a) Silver plate; worship facing east	16	1000	Turmeric pongal with red gram dal	On Devi's full form in abhaya mudra (mudra of fearlessness & vara mudra (mudra of granting boons)	Dominion over an empire; happiness in this life and hereafter
	b) Gold plate	36	3000	"	"	Immunity from sickness and antidote for all diseases; protection from poverty
Mantra 5:	Copper plate; worship facing east	8	2000	Jaggery gruel and pongal with green gram dal	On Devi's full form radiating light	To win others and turn everything in one's favour; protection and progress
Mantra 6:	Gold plate; worship facing east	21	500	21 pieces of sugarcane	On the divine and irresistible form of Devi	Fertility and development of procreative power

	Inscribed on	No. of days	No. of japas per day	Food offering	Mandala meditation	Purpose
Mantra 7: (yantra image)	Gold plate or holy ashes; worship facing east	12	1000	Milk gruel and cooked rice	On the chaturbhuja roopa of Devi, a kanya with four hands holding a bow, arrows, noose and goad	Protection from danger
Mantra 8: (yantra image)	Red sandal paste; worship with red flowers	12	1200	Black pepper	On Devi at her abode made of gems, reclining on a bed of Shiva, covered with a bedspread of Paramashiva	Release from prison; success in enterprise; release from bonds of samsara
Mantra 9: (yantra image)	Gold plate, besmeared with civet	45	1000	Milk gruel	On the chakras forming a pathway for kundalini's ascent	Mastery over elements; return of loved ones from foreign countries

	Inscribed on	No. of days	No. of japas per day	Food offering	Mandala meditation	Purpose
Mantra 10:	Gold plate, mounted on red silk cord; to be tied around waist	6	1000	Fruit	On the beautiful form of Devi seated on the lap of Shiva in close embrace	Virility; purification of body
Mantra 11:	Gold plate or butter; butter to be eaten after japa	81	1000	Jaggery, gruel cakes and mahanaivedya	On Sri Chakra	Removal of sterility; to beget progeny
Mantra 12:	Vessel full of water; to be drunk after pooja	45	1000	Honey	On the beautiful form of Devi	Electric eloquence and poesy

	Inscribed on	No. of days	No. of japas per day	Food offering	Mandala meditation	Purpose
Mantra 13:	Gold plate or lead sheet; to be worn as a talisman around the neck after japa	6	1000	Tri-madhura or cooked rice	On the compassionate form of Devi	Power to attract others
Mantra 14:	Gold plate	45	1000	Milk gruel cakes and cooked rice	On the primeval form of Devi as Prakriti, the cosmic nature	Safeguard from famine, plague and pestilence
Mantra 15:	Gold plate as talisman; water to be drunk after japa	45	1000	Honey, fruit and refined sugar	On Devi speaking	Poetic imagination, knowledge and enlightenment

	Inscribed on	No. of days	No. of japas per day	Food offering	Mandala meditation	Purpose
Mantra 16:	Gold plate	35	1000	Honey	On the beautiful form of Devi bathed in the light of the sun, moon and fire	Master of temporal and transcendental knowledge
Mantra 17:	Gold plate	45	1000	Honey, fruit, milk sugar and sugar candy	On Devi placing her hand on your head	Comprehensive knowledge of all arts and sciences
Mantra 18:	Gold plate, sandal flower, saffron or turmeric	45	1000	Milk gruel and paan supari	On Devi in bhairavi mudra	Power to infatuate others; mastery of arts such as painting

	Inscribed on	No. of days	No. of japas per day	Food offering	Mandala meditation	Purpose
Mantra 19:	Gold plate; holy ashes, sandal, kumkum or swayambhu flower	25	1000	Milk, honey and fruit	On the bewitching glance of Devi	Develop the power of attraction
Mantra 20:	a) Holy ashes or water	45	2000	...	On Devi's mandala	Fascinating snakes
	b) " "	"	1000	...		Antidote against poison
Mantra 21:	Gold, silver or copper plate	45	1000	Fruit, honey and jaggery	On Devi's glistening body in the form of lightning	Winning over each and everyone, even those who dislike you

	Inscribed on	No. of days	No. of japas per day	Food offering	Mandala meditation	Purpose
Mantra 22:	Gold plate; to be worn as a talisman; worship on the bank of a or sacred river holy place	45	1000	Honey, tri-madhura, curds, milk and spiced rice of various kinds	On Devi sitting on a beautiful throne like an empress, listening to the prayers of her worshippers	Attainment of all worldly desires; increasing prosperity; acquisition of empires
Mantra 23:	Gold plate; to be worshipped in the house	30	1000	Milk gruel	On the Ardhanarishwara (half woman and half man) form of Shakti	Release from debt; release from danger
Mantra 24:	Gold plate; to be worn as a talisman	30	1000	Honey, black gram cake and sweetened sesame	On Kali	Immunity from danger and removal of afflictions

	Inscribed on	No. of days	No. of japas per day	Food offering	Mandala meditation	Purpose
Mantra 25:	Gold plate	45	1000	Honey	On Devi being worshipped	Highest place of honour and dignity in the world is secured; advancement in professional career
Mantra 26:	a) Gold plate (with name of the quarry)	6 new moon days	1000	...	On the form of Devi	All round success
	b) Gold plate	6	1000	Jaggery gruel		Winning over those who dislike you and gaining power
Mantra 27:	Gold or other plate	45	1000	Jaggery gruel	On the form of Devi	Attainment of atmajnana (self-realization) and vision of the divine

	Inscribed on	No. of days	No. of japas per day	Food offering	Mandala meditation	Purpose
Mantra 28:	Gold plate or tatanka; to be worn as a talisman	45	1000	Tri-madhura, milk gruel and paan supari	On the exquisite form of Devi decorated with flowers	Protection against untimely, unnatural death; attainment of all ends
Mantra 29:	Gold plate; to be worn on the wrist	45	1000	Honey and black gram cake	On Devi bedecked like a bride	Taming of wild natures; turning enemies into good friends; removal of all ailments
Mantra 30:	Gold plate; after worship the plate should be worn on the head	96	1000	Honey, tri-madhura, paan supari	On Devi seated regally amidst her divine attendants	Acquisition of unlimited powers

	Inscribed on	No. of days	No. of japas per day	Food offering	Mandala meditation	Purpose
Mantra 31:	Gold plate; to be held in the hand	45	1000	Honey and milk	On sound emanating from the form of Devi	Power to captivate all, especially kings, and gain all round prosperity
Mantra 32:	a) Gold plate	45	1000	Curd, rice and black gram cake	On Devi as mantra, in the form of Sri Yantra in the heart centre	Accomplishment in alchemy and other sciences
	b) Gold plate; to be fixed to the place of business	45	1000	Sweet pongal		Success in business
Mantra 33:	Gold plate; to be placed in a box made of antelope horn and buried	45	1000	A coin; to be held in the closed hand while japa is performed	On Devi as mantra, in the form of Sri Yantra at the eyebrow centre	Acquisition of wealth and multiplying of riches

	Inscribed on	No. of days	No. of japas per day	Food offering	Mandala meditation	Purpose
Mantra 34:						
	Gold plate	45	1000	a) Honey	On Shiva-Shakti in maithuna	Blooming of genius
	Gold plate	45	1000	b) Pepper powdered and mixed with ghee		Remedy for rheumatism; freedom from all doubts
Mantra 35:						
	Gold plate; to be worn as a talisman	45	1000	Sugar, honey, milk and milk gruel	On the nirakara Shakti	Remedy for consumption and immunity from wasting diseases
Mantra 36:						
	a) Gold plate	45	1000	Honey and black gram cake	On Shiva-Shakti at ajna	Alleviation of incurable disease
	b) Water in a vessel	45	1000	Cooked rice mixed with pepper		" "

	Inscribed on	No. of days	No. of japas per day	Food offering	Mandala meditation	Purpose
Mantra 37:	Gold plate or vessel of water	45	5000	Fruit, coconut and jaggery gruel	On Shiva-Shakti at vishuddhi	Release from effects of possession; protection from harmful influences
		45	1000	Black gram sweet cakes and milk gruel		Antidote for all diseases
Mantra 38:	a) Gold plate	45	1000	11 black gram cakes, coconut and paan supari	On Shiva-Shakti at anahata	Remedy for infantile disease
	b) Gold plate and vessel of water	4	4000	" "		Drink the mesmerized water for immunity from all diseases
Mantra 39:	Gold or silver plate	12	108	Milk, milk gruel and honey or pongal	On Shiva-Shakti at swadhisthana	Avoidance of bad dreams

	Inscribed on	No. of days	No. of japas per day	Food offering	Mandala meditation	Purpose
Mantra 40:	Gold plate; to be placed under pillow or on the head	45	1000	Honey, milk, gruel, paan supari	On Shiva-Shakti at manipura	Foreseeing the future through dreams
Mantra 41:	Gold plate; to be worn as talisman; or writing the letters on salt (same salt to be used for 30 days and administered as medicine)	30	4000	Honey	On Shiva-Shakti at mooladhara	Remedy for digestive ailments
Mantra 42:	Gold plate or kuruvai rice flour mixed with onam powder	45	1000	Refined sugar (the rice flour to be taken after japa)	On the crown of Devi	Protection against infectious diseases

	Inscribed on	No. of days	No. of japas per day	Food offering	Mandala meditation	Purpose
Mantra 43: श्री	Gold plate; to be worn as a talisman in the form of a ring	45	1000	Honey	On the locks of Devi's hair	Success, popularity and removal of all diseases
Mantra 44: क्ली	Gold plate; also 12 in saffron powder or turmeric; to be marked on the forehead		1000	Jaggery gruel and honey	On the parting line of Devi's hair	Fascination; alleviation of suffering and hysteria
Mantra 45: स स स	Gold plate	45	1000	Tri-madhura and honey	On Devi's smile	Fortune-telling and ability to foretell events

	Inscribed on	No. of days	No. of japas per day	Food offering	Mandala meditation	Purpose
Mantra 46:	Gold plate; to be worn as a talisman	45	1000	Milk gruel and honey	On Devi's forehead	Return of husband, progeny
Mantra 47:	Gold plate; to be worn on the crest; or holy ashes	25	1000	Coconut, fruit and honey	On the captivating eyes of Devi	Power to attract the person you love
Mantra 48:	Gold plate	45	1000	Spiced rice of various kinds, fruit and honey	On the three eyes of Devi	Counteracting adverse planetary influence

	Inscribed on	No. of days	No. of japas per day	Food offering	Mandala meditation	Purpose
Mantra 49:	Turmeric powder; after japa turmeric should be charred and mixed with sesame oil and used as a collyrium	10	1000	Pongal and honey	On the glory of Devi's eyes	Discovery of hidden treasure and immense wealth
Mantra 50:	Gold plate, water or butter; to be taken after japa	5	1000	Refined sugar, sugar candy, jaggery, honey, fruit and coconut	On the allure of Devi's eyes	Immunity from infectious diseases such as smallpox
Mantra 51:	Gold plate or sandal paste; with mark on the forehead	45	1000	Black gram cake and honey	On Devi's glance	Power to gain tremendous popularity; bestowal of desires

	Inscribed on	No. of days	No. of japas per day	Food offering	Mandala meditation	Purpose
Mantra 52:	Gold plate or holy ashes	45	1000	Sesame, rice and milk gruel	On Devi's seductive look	Remedy for eye and ear diseases
Mantra 53:	Gold plate or on the floor with a lamp burning beside; if flame is bright, good omen; if dim, bad omen	45	1000	Sweet cake, black gram cake and milk gruel	On Tri Devi, Kali, Lakshmi and Durga	Fulfilment of all wishes
Mantra 54:	Gold plate or medicinal herb; water in a vessel	45	1000	Jaggery gruel	On the convergence of Devi's three eyes	Remedy for gynaecological diseases

	Inscribed on	No. of days	No. of japas per day	Food offering	Mandala meditation	Purpose
Mantra 55:	Gold plate or myrobalan	45	2500	Fruit, milk, gruel, honey and paan supari	On Devi Aparna's eyes	Remedy for diseases of men such as hydrocele; victory over enemies
Mantra 56:	Gold plate	45	20,000	Honey	On Devi's unblinking eyes	Opening of fetters; release from bondage or prison
Mantra 57:	Gold plate	45	1000	Milk gruel and honey	On Devi's compasionate eyes	Attainment of all round prosperity

	Inscribed on	No. of days	No. of japas per day	Food offering	Mandala meditation	Purpose
Mantra 58:	a) Gold plate; to be worn along with ear ornament	5	1000	...	On the sideways glance of Devi	To fascinate another, e.g. the boy you love
	b) Kumkum; to be marked on the forehead after japa	45	1000	Honey		Royal favour; popularity; freedom from disease and suffering
Mantra 59:	Gold plate or turmeric	45	1000	Sugar pongal and honey	On the erotic face of Devi	Power to fascinate the person you love; overcome an adversary
Mantra 60:	Gold plate	8	12,000	Sugar, honey and milk gruel	On Devi's sweet speech	Acquisition of all knowledge
		45	1000			

	Inscribed on	No. of days	No. of japas per day	Food offering	Mandala meditation	Purpose
Mantra 61: (triangle with क्लीं)	Gold plate or necklace; to be worn as a jewel by women	8	12,000	Coconut, fruit and honey	On Devi's nose	Fascinating a person you love; success in all tasks undertaken; development of inner experience
Mantra 62: (ह ह ह)	Gold plate; to be placed under pillow after japa	8	1000	Black gram cake and honey	On the redness of Devi's lips	Good sleep for insomniacs
Mantra 63: (क्लीं)	Gold plate; to be worn around the waist	30	30,000	Coconut	On Devi's sweet smile	Command over others; ready obedience

	Inscribed on	No. of days	No. of japas per day	Food offering	Mandala meditation	Purpose
Mantra 64:	Kumkum or gold plate; to be worn as a nose screw	18	10,000	Jaggery gruel and honey	On the redness of Devi's tongue	Power to charm everyone; frees a woman of all diseases; remedy for infections
Mantra 65:	Gold plate; also worship of Sri Chakra with red flower and incense	45	1000	Honey	On Devi's worship by the Devas	All round success; achievement of dharma, artha, kama and moksha
Mantra 66:	a) Gold plate	45	1000	Jaggery gruel and honey	On the sweetness of Devi's voice	Proficiency in music
	b) Holy ashes	3	5000	"		Protection against ill health

	Inscribed on	No. of days	No. of japas per day	Food offering	Mandala meditation	Purpose
Mantra 67:	Gold plate; to be worshipped by the couple jointly	45	1000	Honey, milk gruel and paan supari	On Devi's matchless chin	Development of deep bonds of love between husband and wife
Mantra 68:	Kumkum; also worship of Sri Chakra	45	1000	Honey and paan supari	On Devi's graceful neck	Power to captivate rulers; purification of samskaras and removal of obstacles
Mantra 69:	Gold plate	45	1000	Honey	On the three strands at Devi's throat	Success in all undertakings

	Inscribed on	No. of days	No. of japas per day	Food offering	Mandala meditation	Purpose
Mantra 70:	Gold plate	45	1000	Coconut and honey	On Devi's protective arms	Power to fascinate and attract people
Mantra 71:	Gold plate; japa should be performed seated under a banyan tree	45	12,000	Honey	On the splendour of Devi's hands	Command over other dimensions of existence
Mantra 72:	Gold plate or walking stick	45	1000	Honey	On Devi's overflowing	Freedom from fear, especially of the breasts

	Inscribed on	No. of days	No. of japas per day	Food offering	Mandala meditation	Purpose
Mantra 73:	Gold plate or water; to be drunk or sprinkled after japa	7	1000	Honey and milk	On the nectar of Devi's breasts	Fertility and motherhood
Mantra 74:	Gold plate in front of Devi	3	108	Milk gruel and honey	On the pearl necklace adorning Devi's breasts	Enhanced reputation and unlimited fame
Mantra 75:	Gold plate	3	12,000	Fruit and honey	On Devi's breast milk	Skill in poetry; blossoming of creativity and genius

	Inscribed on	No. of days	No. of japas per day	Food offering	Mandala meditation	Purpose
Mantra 76: (yantra)	Gold plate	10	1000	Coconut, fruit, honey and curd rice	On the navel of Devi	Power to fascinate people and acquire great power
Mantra 77: (yantra)	Charcoal of the red lotus flower mixed with ghee (yantra and stanza); worn as a mark on the forehead after japa	10	1000	Honey and fruit	On Devi's slender waist	Royal favour; advancement in career
Mantra 78: (yantra)	Red sandal paste mixed with rose water and civet; to be worn as a mark on the forehead after japa	45	108	Honey and black gram cake	On the glory of Devi's yoni	Royal favour; success in all endeavours

	Inscribed on	No. of days	No. of japas per day	Food offering	Mandala meditation	Purpose
Mantra 79:	Gold plate; to be worn after japa is completed	45	1000	Honey and milk gruel	On Devi before giving birth to creation	Power to create an illusion and win others
Mantra 80:	Gold plate; to be worn after japa is completed	45	1000	Honey	On Devi giving birth to creation	To acquire deftness and skill
Mantra 81:	Gold plate; worship facing east	16	1000	Honey, jaggery gruel and black gram cake	On Devi's expansive hips	Immunity from accidents, especially those related to fire

	Inscribed on	No. of days	No. of japas per day	Food offering	Mandala meditation	Purpose
Mantra 82:	Bhurja leaf; a pair of wooden sandals; a log of asvakarna tree under the bark	45	1000	Coconut, fruit and honey	On Devi's thighs and knees	Immunity from accidents, especially those related to water and drowning
Mantra 83:	Gold plate; worshipped with red cotton flower	12	1000	Jaggery gruel and honey	On Devi's thighs and toenails	Control over powerful forces such as wild and strong animals or even an entire army
Mantra 84:	Gold plate	365	1000	Milk gruel, spiced rice of various kinds and honey	On the feet of Devi	Acquisition of great mental and spiritual power

	Inscribed on	No. of days	No. of japas per day	Food offering	Mandala meditation	Purpose
Mantra 85:	Gold plate; using flowers of eight different colours for worship	12	1000	Milk gruel, jaggery drink and fruit	On Devi in the mudra of granting happiness	Power to remove evil spirits
Mantra 86:	Gold plate with a pot of water; to be used for bathing after worship	21	1000	Milk gruel, coconut and honey	On the kick of Devi's lotus foot	Drive away evil spirits
Mantra 87:	Ashes from a crematorium; sandal	16	1000	Milk gruel, honey, fruit and coconut	On the lotus of Devi's feet	Control over snakes

	Inscribed on	No. of days	No. of japas per day	Food offering	Mandala meditation	Purpose
Mantra 88: (triangle with क क क क)	Gold or silver plate	180	1000	Jaggery gruel, fruit and coconut	On the feet of Devi	Control over animals
Mantra 89: (triangle with ह्रीं)	Gold plate or holy ashes	30	1000	Jaggery gruel and honey	On the wish-fulfilling feet of Devi	Alleviation of all disease
Mantra 90: (rectangle with ह्रां ह्रीं ह्रूं ह्रैं)	Gold plate	30	1000	Milk gruel and honey	On Devi as Saraswati	Counteracting influence of black magic; bestowal of all desires

	Inscribed on	No. of days	No. of japas per day	Food offering	Mandala meditation	Purpose
Mantra 91:	Gold plate (yantra and stanza)	25	1000	Milk gruel	On Devi's graceful gait	Acquisition of land, property and wealth
Mantra 92:	Gold plate or holy ashes	30	4000	Spiced rice of various kinds, milk, milk gruel and paan supari	On Devi Tripura Sundari	Bestowal of a kingdom; warding off evil spirits
Mantra 93:	Gold plate	25 45	2000 1000	Honey	On Aruna Shakti	Accomplishment of desires; endowment of women with power of conception

	Inscribed on	No. of days	No. of japas per day	Food offering	Mandala meditation	Purpose
Mantra 94:	Gold plate; worship facing east	45	2000	Sweet milk rice	On the reflection of Shakti in the sun	Rejuvenation and restoration of health
Mantra 95:	Gold plate	45	2000	Pongal, coconut and fruit	On Devi in her mansion	Gratification of desires
Mantra 96:	Gold plate; cover yantra with sesame oil during japa and apply to body	3	108	Sesame rice and jaggery	On the most supreme Tripura Sundari in her inner apartment	Healing of wounds

	Inscribed on	No. of days	No. of japas per day	Food offering	Mandala meditation	Purpose
Mantra 97:	Piece of white arka wood with turmeric; to be marked on forehead	10	1000	Honey and milk gruel	On the unattainable Shakti above sahasrara	Strong physical health
Mantra 98:	Gold or copper plate	8	1000	Cooked rice and honey	On Tripura Sundari	Physical strength, virility and sexual happiness
Mantra 99:	Gold plate	30	1000	Almond milk	On the inconceivable and limitless power of Devi	Immense beauty and acquisition of siddhis

	Inscribed on	No. of days	No. of japas per day	Food offering	Mandala meditation	Purpose
Mantra 100:	Gold plate or holy ashes	30	1000	Honey	On the full form of Devi	Virility and fertility after riddance of disease; power to conceive
Mantra 101:	Gold plate	15	1000	Tri-madhura, black gram cake and fruit	On Tripura Sundari blessing her devotee	Valour
Mantra 102:	Gold plate	15	1000	Fruit and milk with ladoo	On Devi's hidden treasures	Health and comforts

Mantra 103:

Inscribed on	No. of days	No. of japas per day	Food offering	Mandala meditation	Purpose
Gold plate	16	1000	Fruit and coconut	On Devi as the source of this hymn	Accomplishment of desired objects

Appendices

Appendix A

Sanskrit Text

सौन्दर्यलहरी

१. शिवः शक्त्या युक्तो यदि भवति शक्तः प्रभवितुं
न चेदेवं देवो न खलु कुशलः स्पन्दितुमपि ।
अतस्त्वामाराध्यां हरिहरविरिञ्चादिभिरपि
प्रणन्तुं स्तोतुं वा कथमकृतपुण्यः प्रभवति ॥

२. तनीयांसं पांसुं तव चरणपङ्केरुहभवं
विरिञ्चिः संचिन्वन् विरचयति लोकानविकलम् ।
वहत्येनं शौरिः कथमपि सहस्रेण शिरसां
हरः संक्षुद्यैनं भजति भसितोद्धूलनविधिम् ॥

३. अविद्यानामन्तस्तिमिरमिहिरोद्दीपनकरी
जडानां चैतन्यस्तबकमकरन्दस्रुतिझरी ।
दरिद्राणां चिन्तामणिगुणनिका जन्मजलधौ
निमग्नानां दंष्ट्रा मुररिपुवराहस्य भवति ॥

४. त्वदन्यः पाणिभ्यामभयवरदो दैवतगण-
स्त्वमेका नैवासि प्रकटितवराभीत्यभिनया ।
भयात्रातुं दातुं फलमपि च वाञ्छासमधिकं
शरण्ये लोकानां तव हि चरणावेव निपुणौ ॥

५. हरिस्त्वामाराध्य प्रणतजनसौभाग्यजननीं
पुरा नारी भूत्वा पुररिपुमपि क्षोभमनयत् ।
स्मरोऽपि त्वां नत्वा रतिनयनलेह्येन वपुषा
मुनीनामप्यन्तः प्रभवति हि मोहाय महताम् ॥

६. धनुः पौष्पं मौर्वी मधुकरमयी पञ्च-विशिखाः
वसन्तः सामन्तो मलयमरुदायोधनरथः ।
तथाप्येकः सर्वं हिमगिरिसुते कामपि कृपाम्
अपाङ्गात्ते लब्ध्वा जगदिदमनङ्गो विजयते ॥

७. क्वणत्काञ्चीदामा करिकलभकुम्भस्तनभरा
परिक्षीणा मध्ये परिणतशरच्चन्द्रवदना ।
धनुर्बाणान् पाशं सृणिमपि दधाना करतलैः
पुरस्तादास्तां नः पुरमथितुराहोपुरुषिका ॥

८. सुधासिन्धोर्मध्ये सुरविटपिवाटीपरिवृते
मणिद्वीपे नीपोपवनवति चिन्तामणिगृहे ।
शिवाकारे मञ्चे परमशिवपर्यङ्कनिलयां
भजन्ति त्वां धन्याः कतिचन चिदानन्दलहरीम् ॥

९. महीं मूलाधारे कमपि मणिपूरे हुतवहं
स्थितं स्वाधिष्ठाने हृदि मरुतमाकाशमुपरि ।
मनोऽपि भ्रूमध्ये सकलमपि भित्वा कुलपथं
सहस्रारे पद्मे सह रहसि पत्या विहरसे ॥

१०. सुधाधारासारैश्चरणयुगलान्तर्विगलितैः
प्रपञ्चं सिञ्चन्ती पुनरपि रसाम्नायमहसः ।
अवाप्य स्वां भूमिं भुजगनिभमध्युष्टवलयं
स्वमात्मानं कृत्वा स्वपिषि कुलकुण्डे कुहरिणि ॥

११. चतुर्भिः श्रीकण्ठैः शिवयुवतिभिः पञ्चभिरपि
प्रभिन्नाभिः शंभोर्नवभिरपि मूलप्रकृतिभिः ।
त्रयश्चत्वारिंशद्वसुदलकलाश्रत्रिवलय-
त्रिरेखाभिः सार्धं तव चरणकोणाः परिणताः ॥

१२. त्वदीयं सौन्दर्यं तुहिनगिरिकन्ये तुलयितुं
कवीन्द्राः कल्पन्ते कथमपि विरिञ्चिप्रभृतयः ।
यदालोक्यौत्सुक्यादमरललना यान्ति मनसा
तपोभिर्दुष्प्रापामपि गिरिशसायुज्यपदवीम् ॥

१३. नरं वर्षीयांसं नयनविरसं नर्मसु जडं
    तवापाङ्गालोके पतितमनुधावन्ति शतशः ।
    गलद्वेणीबन्धाः कुचकलशविस्रस्तसिचया
    हठात् त्रुट्यत्कांच्यो विगलितदुकूला युवतयः ॥

१४. क्षितौ षट्पंचाशत् द्विसमधिकपञ्चाशदुदके
    हुताशे द्वाषष्टिश्चतुरधिकपंचाशदनिले ।
    दिवि द्विःषट्त्रिंशन्मनसि च चतुःषष्टिरिति ये
    मयूखास्तेषामप्युपरि तव पादाम्बुजयुगम् ॥

१५. शरज्ज्योत्स्नाशुभ्रां शशियुतजटाजूटमुकुटां
    वरत्रासत्राणस्फटिकघुटिकापुस्तककराम् ।
    सकृन्न त्वां न त्वा कथमिव सतां संनिदधते
    मधुक्षीरद्राक्षामधुरिमधुरीणा भणितयः ॥

१६. कवीन्द्राणां चेतः कमलवनबालातपरुचिं
    भजन्ते ये सन्तः कतिचिदरुणामेव भवतीम् ।
    विरिञ्चिप्रेयस्यास्तरलतरशृङ्गारलहरी-
    गभीराभिर्वाग्भिर्विदधति सभाराञ्जनममी ॥

१७. सवित्रीभिर्वाचां शशिमणिशिलाभङ्गरुचिभिः
    वशिन्याद्याभिस्त्वां सह जननि संचिन्तयति यः ।
    स कर्ता काव्यानां भवति महतां भङ्गिसुभगैः
    वचोभिर्वाग्देवीवदनकमलामोदमधुरैः ॥

१८. तनुच्छायाभिस्ते तरुणतरणिश्रीसरणिभिः
    दिवं सर्वामुर्वीमरुणिमनिमग्नां स्मरति यः ।
    भवन्त्यस्य त्रस्यद्वनहरिणशालीननयनाः
    सहोर्वश्याः वश्याः कति कति न गीर्वाणगणिकाः ॥

१९. मुखं बिन्दुं कृत्वा कुचयुगमधस्तस्य तदधो
    हकारार्धं ध्यायेद्वरमहिषि ते मन्मथकलाम् ।
    स सद्यः संक्षोभं नयति वनिता इत्यतिलघु
    त्रिलोकीमप्याशु भ्रमयति रवीन्दुस्तनयुगाम् ॥

२०. किरन्तीमङ्गेभ्यः किरणनिकुरुम्बामृतरसं
हृदि त्वामाधत्ते हिमकरशिलामूर्तिमिव यः ।
स सर्पाणां दर्पं शमयति शकुन्ताधिप इव
ज्वरप्लुष्टान् दृष्ट्या सुखयति सुधासारसिरया ॥

२१. तटिल्लेखातन्वीं तपनशशिवैश्वानरमयीं
निषण्णां षण्णामप्युपरि कमलानां तव कलाम् ।
महापद्माटव्यां मृदितमलमायेन मनसा
महान्तः पश्यन्तो दधति परमाह्लादलहरीम् ॥

२२. भवानि त्वं दासे मयि वितर दृष्टिं सकरुणाम्
इति स्तोतुं वांछन् कथयति भवानि त्वमिति यः ।
तदैव त्वं तस्मै दिशसि निजसायुज्यपदवीं
मुकुन्दब्रह्मेन्द्रस्फुटमुकुटनीराजितपदाम् ॥

२३. त्वया हृत्वा वामं वपुरपरितृप्तेन मनसा
शरीरार्धं शंभोरपरमिति शङ्के हृतमभूत् ।
तथा हि त्वद्रूपं सकलमरुणाभं त्रिनयनं
कुचाभ्यामानम्रं कुटिलशशिचूडालमुकुटम् ॥

२४. जगत्सूते धाता हरिरवति रुद्रः क्षपयते
तिरस्कुर्वन्नेतत्स्वमपि वपुरीशस्तिरयति ।
सदापूर्वः सर्वं तदिदमनुगृह्णाति च शिवः
तवाज्ञामालम्ब्य क्षणचलितयोर्भ्रूलतिकयोः ॥

२५. त्रयाणां देवानां त्रिगुणजनितानामपि शिवे
भवेत् पूजा पूजा तव चरणयोर्या विरचिता ।
तथा हि त्वत्पादोद्वहनमणिपीठस्य निकटे
स्थिता ह्येते शश्वन्मुकुलितकरोत्तंसमुकुटाः ॥

२६. विरिन्चिः पंचत्वं व्रजति हरिराप्नोति विरतिं
विनाशं कीनाशो भजति धनदो याति निधनम् ।
वितन्द्रा माहेन्द्री विततिरपि संमीलति दृशां
महासंहारेऽस्मिन् विहरति सति त्वत्पतिरसौ ॥

२७. जपो जल्पः शिल्पं सकलमपि मुद्राविरचनं
गतिः प्रादक्षिण्यं भ्रमणमशनाद्याहुतिविधिः ।
प्रणामः संवेशः सुखमखिलमात्मार्पणदृशा
सपर्यापर्यायस्तव भवतु यन्मे विलसितम् ॥

२८. ददाने दीनेभ्यः श्रियमनिशमाशानुसदृशीम्
अमन्दं सौन्दर्यप्रकरमकरन्दं विकिरति ।
तवास्मिन् मन्दारस्तबकसुभगे यातु चरणे
निमज्जन् मज्जीवः करणचरणैः षट्चरणताम् ॥

२९. सुधामप्यास्वाद्य प्रतिभयजरामृत्युहरिणीं
विपद्यन्ते विश्वे विधिशतमखाद्या दिविषदः ।
करालं यत् क्ष्वेलं कबलितवतः कालकलना
न शंभोस्तन्मूलं जननि तव ताटङ्कमहिमा ॥

३०. किरीटं वैरिञ्चं परिहर पुरः कैटभभिदः
कठोरे कोटीरे स्खलसि जहि जम्भारिमुकुटम् ।
प्रणम्रेष्वेतेषु प्रसभमुपयातस्य भवनं
भवस्याभ्युत्थाने तव परिजनोक्तिर्विजयते ॥

३१. चतुःषष्ट्या तन्त्रैः सकलमभिसंधाय भुवनं
स्थितस्तत्तत्सिद्धिप्रसभपरतंत्रैः पशुपतिः ।
पुनस्त्वन्निर्बन्धादखिलपुरुषार्थैकघटना-
स्वतंत्रं ते तंत्रं क्षितितलमवातीतरदिदम् ॥

३२. शिवः शक्तिः कामः क्षितिरथ रविः शीतकिरण
स्मरो हंसः शक्रस्तदनु च परामारहरयः ।
अमी हृल्लेखाभिस्तिसृभिरवसानेषु घटिता
भजन्ते वर्णास्ते तव जननि नामावयवताम् ॥

३३. स्मरं योनिं लक्ष्मीं त्रितयमिदमाद्ये तव मनो-
निधायैके नित्ये निरवधिमहाभोगरसिकाः ।
जपन्ति त्वां चिन्तामणिगुणनिबद्धाक्षवलयाः
शिवाग्नौ जुह्वन्तः सुरभिघृतधाराहुतिशतैः ॥

३४. शरीरं त्वं शंभो शशिमिहिरवक्षोरुहयुगं
तवात्मानं मन्ये भगवति नवात्मानमनघम् ।
अतः शेषः शेषीत्ययमुभयसाधारणतया
स्थितः संबंधो वां समरसपरानन्दपरयोः ॥

३५. मनस्त्वं व्योम त्वं मरुदसि मरुत्सारथिरसि
त्वमापस्त्वं भूमिस्त्वयि परिणतायां न हि परम् ।
त्वमेव स्वात्मानं परिणमयितुं विश्ववपुषा
चिदानन्दाकारं हरमहिषि भावेन बिभृषे ॥

३६. तवाज्ञाचक्रस्थं तपनशशिकोटिद्युतिधरं
परं शंभुं वन्दे परिमिलितपार्श्वं परचिता ।
यमाराध्यन् भक्त्या रविशशिशुचीनामविषये
निरालोके लोके निवसति हि भालोकभवने ॥

३७. विशुद्धौ ते शुद्धस्फटिकविशदं व्योमजनकं
शिवं सेवे देवीमपि शिवसमानव्यसनिनीम् ।
ययोः कान्त्या यान्त्या शशिकिरणसारूप्यसरणिं
विधूतान्तर्ध्वान्ता विलसति चकोरीव जगती ॥

३८. समुन्मीलत् संवित् कमलमकरन्दैकरसिकं
भजे हंसद्वन्द्वं किमपि महतां मानसचरम् ।
यदालापादष्टादशगुणितविद्यापरिणतिः
यदादत्ते दोषाद् गुणमखिलमद्भ्यः पय इव ॥

३९. तव स्वाधिष्ठाने हुतवहमधिष्ठाय निरतं
तमीडे संवर्तं जननि महतीं तां च समयाम् ।
यदालोके लोकान् दहति महति क्रोधकलिले
दयार्द्रा या दृष्टिः शिशिरमुपचारं रचयति ॥

४०. तटित्वन्तं शक्त्या तिमिरपरिवृत्तिस्फुरणया
स्फुरन्नानारत्नाभरणपरिणद्धेन्द्रधनुषम् ।
तव श्यामं मेघं कमपि मणिपूरैकशरणं
निषेवे वर्षन्तं हरमिहिरतप्तं त्रिभुवनम् ॥

४१. तवाधारे मूले सह समयया लास्यपरया
नवात्मानं वन्दे नवरसमहाताण्डवनटम् ।
उभाभ्यामेताभ्यामुदयविधिमुद्दिश्य दयया
सनाथाभ्यां जज्ञे जनक-जननी-मज्जगदिदम् ॥

४२. गतैर्माणिक्यत्वं गगनमणिभिः सान्द्रघटितं
किरीटं ते हैमं हिमगिरिसुते कीर्तयति यः ।
स नीडेयच्छायाच्छुरणशबलं चन्द्रशकलं
धनुःशौनासीरं किमिदमिति बध्नाति धिषणाम् ॥

४३. धुनोतु ध्वान्तं नस्तुलितदलितेन्दीवरवनं
घनं स्निग्धं श्लक्ष्णं चिकुरनिकुरुम्बं तव शिवे ।
यदीयं सौरभ्यं सहजमुपलब्धुं सुमनसो
वसन्त्यस्मिन्मन्ये बलमथनवाटीविटपिनाम् ॥

४४. वहन्ती सिन्दूरं प्रबलकबरीभारतिमिर-
द्विषां बृन्दैर्बन्दीकृतमिव नवीनार्ककिरणम् ।
तनोतु क्षेमं नस्तव वदनसौन्दर्यलहरी
परीवाहस्रोतः सरणिरिव सीमन्तसरणिः ॥

४५. अरालैः स्वाभाव्यादलिकुलहसश्रीभिरलकैः
परीतं ते वक्त्रं परिहसति पंकेरुहरुचिम् ।
दरस्मेरे यस्मिन् दशनरुचिकिञ्जल्करुचिरे
सुगन्धौ माद्यन्ति स्मरमथनचक्षुर्मधुलिहः ॥

४६. ललाटं लावण्यद्युतिविमलमाभाति तव यत्
द्वितीयं तन्मन्ये मुकुटघटितं चन्द्रशकलम् ।
विपर्यासन्यासादुभयकृतसंधानमयितः
सुधालेपस्फूर्तिः परिणमति राकाहिमकरः ॥

४७. भ्रुवौ भुग्ने किंचिद्भुवनभयभङ्गव्यसनिनि
त्वदीये नेत्राभ्यां मधुकररुचिभ्यां धृतगुणे ।
धनुर्मन्ये सव्येतरकरगृहीतं रतिपतेः
प्रकोष्ठे मुष्टौ च स्थगयति निगूढान्तरमुमे ॥

४८. अहः सूते सव्यं तव नयनमर्कात्मकतया
त्रियामा वामं ते सृजति रजनीनायकममुम् ।
तृतीया दृष्टिस्ते दरदलितहेमाम्बुजरुचिः
समाधत्ते संध्यां दिवसनिशयोरन्तरचरीम् ॥

४९. विशाला कल्याणी स्फुटरुचिरयोध्या कुवलयैः
कृपाधारा धारा किमपि मधुरा भोगवतिका ।
अवन्ती दृष्टिस्ते बहुनगरविस्तारविजया
ध्रुवं तत्तन्नाम्नव्यवहरणयोग्या विजयते ॥

५०. कवीनां संदर्भस्तबकमकरन्दैकभरितं
कटाक्षव्याक्षेपभ्रमरकलभौ कर्णयुगलम् ।
अमुञ्चन्तौ दृष्ट्वा तव नवरसास्वादतरलौ
असूयासंसर्गादलिकनयनं किंचिदरुणम् ॥

५१. शिवे शृङ्गारार्द्रा तदितरमुखे कुत्सनपरा
सरोषा गङ्गायां गिरिशनयने विस्मयवती ।
हराहिभ्यो भीता सरसिरुहसौभाग्यजननी
सखीषु स्मेरा ते मयि जयति दृष्टिः सकरुणा ॥

५२. गते कर्णाभ्यर्णं गरुत इव पक्ष्माणि दधती
पुरां भेत्तुश्चित्तप्रशमरसविद्रावणफले ।
इमे नेत्रे गोत्राधरपतिकुलोत्तंसकलिके
तवाकर्णाकृष्टस्मरशरविलासं कलयतः ॥

५३. विभक्तं त्रैवर्ण्यं व्यतिकरितनीलाम्बुजतया
विभाति त्वन्नेत्रत्रितयमिदमीशानदयिते ।
पुनः स्रष्टुं देवान् द्रुहिणहरिरुद्रानुपरतान्
रजः सत्त्वं बिभ्रत्तम इति गुणानां त्रयमिव ॥

५४. पवित्रीकर्तुं नः पशुपतिपराधीनहृदये
दयामित्रैर्नेत्रैररुणधवलश्यामरुचिभिः ।
नदः शोणो गङ्गा तपनतनयेति ध्रुवममुं
त्रयाणां तीर्थानामुपनयसि संभेदमनघे ॥

५५. तवापर्णे कर्णेजपनयनपैशुन्यचकिता
निलीयन्ते तोये नियतमनिमेषाः शफरिकाः ।
इयं च श्रीर्बद्धच्छदपुटकवाटं कुवलयं
जहाति प्रत्यूषे निशि च विघटय्य प्रविशति ॥

५६. निमेषोन्मेषाभ्यां प्रलयमुदयं याति जगती
तवेत्याहुःसन्तो धरणिधरराजन्यतनये ।
त्वदुन्मेषाज्जातं जगदिदमशेषं प्रलयतः
परित्रातुं शङ्के परिहृतनिमेषास्तव दृशः ॥

५७. दृषा द्राधीयस्या दरदलितनीलोत्पलरुचा
दवीयांसं दीनं स्नपय कृपया मामपि शिवे ।
अनेनायं धन्यो भवति न च ते हानिरियता
वने वा हर्म्ये वा समकरनिपातो हिमकरः ॥

५८. अरालं ते पालीयुगलमगराजन्यतनये
न केषामाधत्ते कुसुमशरकोदण्डकुतुकम् ।
तिरश्चीनो यत्र श्रवणपथमुल्लङ्घ्य विलसत्
अपाङ्गव्यासङ्गो दिशति शरसंधानधिषणाम् ॥

५९. स्फुरद्गण्डाभोगप्रतिफलितताटङ्कयुगलं
चतुश्चक्रं मन्ये तव मुखमिदं मन्मथरथम् ।
यमारुह्य द्रुह्यत्यवनिरथमर्केन्दुचरणं
महावीरो मारः प्रमथपतये सज्जितवते ॥

६०. सरस्वत्याः सूक्तीरमृतलहरीकौशलहरीः
पिबन्त्याः शर्वाणि श्रवणचुलुकाभ्यामविरलम् ।
चमत्कारश्लाघाचलितशिरसः कुण्डलगणो
झणत्कारैस्तारैः प्रतिवचनमाचष्ट इव ते ॥

६१. असौ नासावंशस्तुहिनगिरिवंशध्वजपटि
त्वदीयो नेदीयः फलतु फलमस्माकमुचितम् ।
वहत्यन्तर्मुक्ताः शिशिरतरनिःश्वासघटिताः
समृद्ध्या यस्तासां बहिरपि च मुक्तामणिधरः ॥

471

६२. प्रकृत्या रक्तायास्तव सुदति दन्तच्छदरुचेः
प्रवक्ष्ये सादृश्यं जनयतु फलं विद्रुमलता ।
क्व बिम्बं दृग्बिम्बप्रतिफलनरागादरुणितं
तुलामध्यारोढुं क थमिव न लज्जेत कलया ॥

६३. स्मितज्योत्स्नाजालं तव वदनचन्द्रस्य पिबतां
चकोराणामासीदतिरसतया चञ्चुजडिमा ।
अतस्ते शीतांशोरमृतलहरीमम्लरुचयः
पिबन्ति स्वच्छन्दं निशि निशि भृशं काञ्जिकधिया ॥

६४. अविश्रान्तं पत्युर्गुणगणकथाम्रेडनजडा
जवापुष्पच्छाया तव जननि जिह्वा जयति सा ।
यदग्रासीनायाः स्फटिकदृषदच्छच्छविमयी
सरस्वत्या मूर्तिः परिणमति माणिक्यवपुषा ॥

६५. रणे जित्वा दैत्यानपहृतशिरस्त्रैः कवचिभिः
निवृत्तैश्चण्डांशत्रिपुरहरनिर्माल्यविमुखैः ।
विरिञ्चीन्द्रोपेन्द्रैः शशिशिशिरकर्पूरधवला
विलिप्यन्ते मातस्तव वदनताम्बूलशकलाः ॥

६६. विपंज्या गायन्ती विविधमपदानं पशुपतेः
त्वयारब्धे वक्तुं स्खलितवचसा साधुवचने ।
तदीयैर्माधुर्यैरपलपिततन्त्रीकलरवां
निजां वीणां वाणी निचुलयति चोलेन निभृतम् ॥

६७. कराग्रेण स्पृष्टं तुहिनगिरिणा वत्सलतया
गिरीशेनोदस्तं मुहुरधरपानाकुलतया ।
करग्राह्यं शंभोर्मुखमुकुरवृन्तं गिरिसुते
कथंकारं ब्रूमस्तव चिबुकमौपम्यरहितम् ॥

६८. भुजाश्लेषान्नित्यं पुरदमयितुः कण्टकवती
तव ग्रीवा धत्ते मुखकमलनालश्रियमियम् ।
स्वतःश्वेता कालागरुबहुलजम्बालमलिना
मृणालीलालित्यं वहति यदहो हारलतिका ॥

६९. गले रेखास्तिस्रो गतिगमकगीतैकनिपुणे
विवाहव्यानद्धत्रिगुणगुणसंख्याप्रतिभुवः ।
विराजन्ते नानाविधमधुररागाकरभुवां
त्रयाणां ग्रामाणां स्थितिनियमसीमान इव ते ॥

७०. मृणालीमृद्वीनां तव भुजलतानां चतसृणां
चतुर्भिः सौंदर्यं सरसिजभवः स्तौति वदनैः ।
नखेभ्यः संत्रस्यन् प्रथममदनादन्धकरिपोः
चतुर्णां वक्त्राणां सममभयहस्तार्पणधिया ॥

७१. नखानामुद्द्योतैर्नवनलिनरागं विहसतां
कराणां ते कांतिं कथय कथयामः कथमुमे ।
कयाचिद्वा साम्यं भजतु विधया हन्त कमलं
यदि क्रीडल्लक्ष्मीचरणतललाक्षारुणदलम् ॥

७२. समं देवि स्कन्दद्विपवदनपीतं स्तनयुगं
तवेदं नः खेदं हरतु सततं प्रस्नुतमुखम् ।
यदालोक्याशङ्काकुलितहृदयो हासजनकः
स्वकुम्भौ हेरम्बः परिमृशति हस्तेन झटिति ॥

७३. अमू ते वक्षोजावमृतरससमाणिक्यकुतुपौ
न संदेहस्पन्दो नगपतिपताके मनसि नः ।
पिबन्तौ तौ यस्मादविदितवधूसङ्गमरसौ
कुमारावद्यापि द्विरदवदनक्रौञ्चदमनौ ॥

७४. वहत्यम्ब स्तम्बेरमदनुजकुम्भप्रकृतिभिः
समारब्धां मुक्तामणिभिरमलां हारलतिकाम् ।
कुचाभोगो बिम्बाधररुचिभिरन्तः शबलितां
प्रतापव्यामिश्रां पुरविजयिनः कीर्तिमिव ते ॥

७५. तवः स्तन्यं मन्ये तुहिनगिरिकन्ये हृदयतः
पयः पारावारः परिवहति सारस्वत इव ।
दयावत्या दत्तं द्रविडशिशुरास्वाद्य तव यत्
कवीनां प्रौढानामजनि कमनीयः कवयिता ॥

७६. हरक्रोधज्वलावलिभिरवलीढेन वपुषा
गभीरे ते नाभीसरसि कृतसङ्गो मनसिजः ।
समुत्तस्थौ तस्मादचलतनये धूमलतिका
जनस्तां जानीते तव जननि रोमावलिरिति ॥

७७. यदेतत्कालिन्दीतनुतरतरङ्गाकृति शिवे
कृशे मध्ये किंचिज्जननि तव तद्भाति सुधियाम् ।
विमर्दादन्योन्यं कुचकलशयोरन्तरगतं
तनूभूतं व्योम प्रविशदिव नाभिं कुहरिणीम् ॥

७८. स्थिरो गंगावर्तः स्तनमुकुलरोमावलिलता
निजावालं कुण्डं कुसुमशरतेजोहुतभुजः ।
रतेर्लीलागारं किमपि तव नाभि गिरिसुते
बिलद्वारं सिद्धेर्गिरिशनयनानां विजयते ॥

७९. निसर्गक्षीणस्य स्तनतटभरेण क्लमजुषो
नमन्मूर्तेर्नाभौ वलिषु शनकैस्त्रुट्यत इव ।
चिरं ते मध्यस्य त्रुटिततटिनीतीरतरुणा
समावस्थास्थेम्नो भवतु कुशलं शैलतनये ॥

८०. कुचौ सद्यः स्विद्यत्तटघटितकूर्पासभिदुरौ
कषन्तौ दोर्मूले कनककलशाभौ कलयता ।
तव त्रातुं भङ्गादुदरमवलग्नं तनुभुवा
त्रिधा नद्धं देवि त्रिवलिलवलीवल्लिभिरिव ॥

८१. गुरुत्वं विस्तारं क्षितिधरपतिः पार्वति निजान्
नितम्बादाच्छिद्य त्वयि हरणरूपेण निदधे ।
अतस्ते विस्तीर्णो गुरुरयमशेषां वसुमतीं
नितम्बप्राग्भारः स्थगयति लघुत्वं नयति च ॥

८२. करीन्द्राणां शुण्डान् कनककदलीकाण्डपटलीम्
उभाभ्यामूरुभ्यामुभयमपि निर्जित्य भवति ।
सुवृत्ताभ्यां पत्युः प्रणतिकठिनाभ्यां गिरिसुते
विजिग्ये जानुभ्यां विबुधकरिकुम्भद्वयमति ॥

८३. पराजेतुं रुद्रं द्विगुणशरगर्भौ गिरिसुते
निषङ्गौ जङ्घे ते विषमविशिखो बाढमकृत ।
यदग्रे लक्ष्यन्ते दशशरफलाः पादयुगली-
नखाग्रच्छद्मानः सुरमुकुटशाणौघनिशिताः ॥

८४. श्रुतीनां मूर्धानो दधति तव यौ शेखरतया
ममाप्येतौ मातः शिरसि दयया धेहि चरणौ ।
ययोः पाद्यं पाथः पशुपतिजटाजूटतटिनी
ययोर्लाक्षालक्ष्मीररुणहरिचूडामणिरुचिः ॥

८५. नमोवाकं ब्रूमो नयनरमणीयाय पदयोः
तवास्मै द्वन्द्वाय स्फुटरुचिरसालक्तकवते ।
असूयत्यत्यन्तं यदभिहननाय स्पृहयते
पशूनामीशानः प्रमदवनकङ्केलितरवे ॥

८६. मृषा कृत्वा गोत्रस्खलनमथ वैलक्ष्यनमितं
ललाटे भर्तारं चरणकमले ताडयति ते ।
चिरादन्तःशल्यं दहनकृतमुन्मीलितवता
तुलाकोटिक्वाणैः किलिकिलितमीशानरिपुणा ॥

८७. हिमानीहन्तव्यं हिमगिरितटाक्रान्तिचतुरौ
निशायां निद्राणं निशि च परभागे च विशदौ ।
परं लक्ष्मीपात्रं श्रियमतिसृजन्तौ समयिनां
सरोजं त्वत्पादौ जननि जयतश्चित्रमिह किम् ॥

८८. पदं ते कान्तीनां प्रपदमपदं देवि विपदां
कथं नीतं सद्भिः कठिनकमठीखर्परतुलाम् ।
कथं वा हस्ताभ्यामुपयमनकाले पुरभिदा
यदादाय न्यस्तं दृषदि दयमानेन मनसा ॥

८९. नखैर्नाकस्त्रीणां करकमलसंकोचशशिभिः
तरूणां दिव्यानां हसत इव ते चण्डि चरणौ ।
फलानि स्वःस्थेभ्यः किसलयकराग्रेण ददतां
दरिद्रेभ्यो भद्रां श्रियमनिशमह्नाय ददतौ ॥

475

९०. कदा काले मातः कथय कलितालक्त करसं
पिबेयं विद्यार्थी तव चरणनिर्णेजनजलम् ।
प्रकृत्या मूकानामपि च कविताकारणतया
यदाधत्ते वाणीमुखकमलताम्बूलरसताम् ॥

९१. पदन्यासक्रीडापरिचयमिवारब्धुमनसः
चरन्तस्ते खेलं भवनकलहंसा न जहति ।
स्वविक्षेपे शिक्षां सुभगमणिमञ्जीररणितः
छलादाचक्षाणं चरणकमलं चारुचरित ॥

९२. गतास्ते मञ्चत्वं द्रुहिणहरिरुद्रेश्वरभृतः
शिवः स्वच्छच्छायाघटितकपटप्रच्छदपटः ।
त्वदीयानां भासां प्रतिफलनरागारुणतया
शरीरी शृङ्गारो रस इव दृशां दोग्धि कुतुकम् ॥

९३. अराला केशेषु प्रकृतिसरला मन्दहसिते
शिरीषाभा चित्ते दृषदिव क्षोरा कुचतटे ।
भृशं तन्वी मध्ये पृथुरपि वरारोहविषये
जगत्त्रातुं शंभोर्जयति करुणा काचिदरुणा ॥

९४. समानीतः पद्भ्यां मणिमुकुरताम्बरमणिः
भयादास्यादन्तःस्तिमितकिरणश्रेणिमसृणः ।
दधाति त्वद्वक्त्रप्रतिफलनमश्रान्तविकचं
निरातङ्कं चंद्रान्निजहृदयपंङ्केरुहमिव ॥

९५. कलङ्कः कस्तूरी रजनिकरबिम्बं जलमयं
कलाभिः कर्पूरैर्मरकतकरण्डं निबिडितम् ।
अतस्त्वद्भोगेन प्रतिदिनमिदं रिक्तकुहरं
विधिर्भूयो भूयो निबिडयति नूनं तव कृते ॥

९६. पुरारातेरन्तः पुरमसि ततस्त्वच्चरणयोः
सपर्यामर्यादा तरलकरणानामसुलभा ।
तथाप्येते नीताः शतमखमुखाः सिद्धिमतुलां
तव द्वारोपान्तस्थितिभिरणिमाद्याभिरमराः ॥

९७. कलत्रं वैधात्रं कति कति भजन्ते न कवयः
श्रियो देव्याः को वा न भवति पतिः कैरपि धनैः ।
महादेवं हित्वा तव सति सतीनामचरमे
कुचाभ्यामासङ्गः कुरवकतरोरप्यसुलभः ॥

९८. स्वदेहोद्भूताभिर्घृणिभिरणिमाद्याभिरभितो
निषेव्यां नित्ये त्वामहमिति सदा भावयति यः ।
किमाश्चर्यं तस्य त्रिनयनसमृद्धिं तृणयतो
महासंवर्ताग्निर्विरचयति नीराजनविधिम् ॥

९९. गिरामाहुर्देवीं द्रुहिणगृहिणीमागमविदो
हरेः पत्नीं पद्मां हरसहचरीमद्रितनयाम् ।
तुरीया कापि त्वं दुरधिगमनिःसीममहिमा
महामाया विश्वं भ्रमयसि परब्रह्ममहिषि ॥

१००. समुद्भूतस्थूलस्तनभरमुरश्चारुहसितं
कटाक्षे कंदर्पाः कतिचन कदम्बद्युतिवपुः ।
हरस्य त्वद्भ्रान्तिं मनसि जनयन्ति स्म विमला
भवत्या ये भक्ताः परिणतिरमीषामियमुमे ॥

१०१. सरस्वत्या लक्ष्म्या विधिहरिसपत्नो विहरते
रतेः पातिव्रत्यं शिथिलयति रम्येण वपुषा ।
चिरं जीवन्नेव क्षपितपशुपाशव्यतिकरः
परब्रह्माभिख्यं रसयति रसं त्वद्भजनवान् ॥

१०२. निधे नित्यस्मेरे निरवधिगुणे नीतिनिपुणे
निराघाटज्ञाने नियमपरचित्तैकनिलये ।
नियत्या निर्मुक्ते निखिलनिगमान्तस्तुतपदे
निरातङ्के नित्ये निगमय ममापि स्तुतिमिमाम् ॥

१०३. प्रदीपज्वालाभिर्दिवसकरनीराजनविधिः
सुधासूतेश्चन्द्रोपलजललवैरर्घ्यरचना ।
स्वकीयैरम्भोभिः सलिलनिधिसौहित्यकरणं
त्वदीयाभिर्वाग्भिस्तव जननि वाचां स्तुतिरियम् ॥

Appendix B

Translation

Saundarya Lahari

1. Shiva, the divine one, when united with Shakti is endowed with the power to create, protect and destroy the universe; otherwise, he is unable even to stir. How can one who has not acquired great merit be capable of worshipping Thee, who art praised and worshipped by Hari (Vishnu), Hara (Shiva) and Virinchi (Brahma), and even by the eternal Vedas?

2. Collecting the minute particles of dust from Thy lotus feet, Virinchi (Brahma) creates this universe. Shauri (Vishnu) holds this entire universe on his thousand heads, thus sustaining it with great difficulty, and Hara (Shiva) reduces it to ashes and besmears his body with it.

3. For the ignorant (the dust of Thy feet) is the island of shelter where the luminous sunrise (of spiritual illumination) dawns, driving away the overcast darkness (of ignorance). For the dull-witted it becomes clusters of flowers from which the nectar of awareness gushes forth. For the destitute it is a necklace of wish-yielding gems. And for those immersed in the ocean of samsara, it becomes their uplifter, like the tusk of Vishnu (which raised the earth from submergence) when he incarnated as Varaha, the cosmic boar.

4. Excepting Thou, all other deities grant protection and boons by hand gestures (mudras). Thou alone art not given to such demonstrations of bestowing boons and shelter. Instead, Thy two feet alone are capable of providing protection from fear, the shelter of the universe and granting more than could ever be desired.

5. Long ago, adoring Thee who bestows prosperity on all Thy devotees, Vishnu, could become an (enticing) female and stir passion even in Shiva. Even Kamadeva, the god of love, having bowed before Thee (in devotion) has become such an attractive personality to his consort Rati and is thus capable of inciting great passion, even in the minds of sages.

6. O Daughter of the snow clad mountain, having obtained some little favour by Thy sideways glance, Kamadeva, even though bodiless, is able to conquer the world with a bow of flowers, a bowstring made of honey bees, only five arrows in his sheath, the southern breeze as his war chariot and the spring season as his assistant.

7. Slender waist, girdled with jingling bells, frame slightly bent by the weight of full breasts, like the lobes of a baby elephant, face blooming like the autumnal full moon, Thou who art the pride of Shiva. Please manifest Thy presence before us, holding all these, bow, arrows, noose and goad, in your hands.

8. In the midst of the ocean of nectar, surrounded by gardens of kalpaka trees, on an island of precious gems, encircled by groves of nipa or kadamba trees, in a mansion made of chintamani gems, reclining on a mattress that is the supreme Shiva placed on a couch that is Shiva, fortunate are the few who worship Thee (like this), for they experience ripples of bliss in their consciousness.

9. As earth and also water in mooladhara, (Thou art) established in swadhisthana, as fire in manipura, as air in the heart (anahata), and above as ether and also mind in bhrumadhya, between the eyebrows (ajna), also the entire path of kundalini, piercing which Thou sporteth with Thy consort in the solitude of sahasrara padma, the thousand-petalled lotus.

10. With streams of nectar gushing from Thy feet, irrigating the five elements again from the region of illumination (sahasrara), Thou returnest to Thy home via the six chakras. Converting Thyself into the individual self, or jivatman, Thou sleepest in the deep pit of Thy own home, like a serpent of three and a half coils.

11. The four triangles that enclose the supreme energy and also the five shakti triangles form the nine basic triangles of the root manifestations (of Shakti). Then there are the eight-petalled and sixteen-petalled lotuses, three surrounding circles and three lines. Distinct from Shiva, these angles which house Thee become Thy mansion of forty-three triangles.

12. O Daughter of the snow clad mountain, Brahma and other greatest of poets, even after taking great pains, are not capable of comparing Thy beauty, which being eager to glimpse, they mentally try through penance to attain that most difficult state of absorption in Shiva with the hope that they will behold Thy effulgent and undying youth and beauty.

13. If Thy gracious sideways glance should fall on anyone, even a decrepit, ugly old man with dead (erotic) sensibilities, he will be hastily followed by hundreds of young women with their hair unbound, their robes slipping down, their girdles undone, and their rounded breasts exposed due to the loosening of their upper cloth.

14. The rays: fifty-six in earth, fifty-two in water, sixty-two in fire, fifty four in air, seventy-two in ether and sixty-four in mind, emanate from Thy two lotus feet, which rest above.

15. How can words excelling the sweetness of honey, milk and grapes not flow from the good men who have prostrated before Thee, who are fair and spotless as the autumnal moon, who wears the crescent moon in her locks, whose two hands are in the gesture of granting shelter and boons, and the other two hands holding a crystal rosary and a book.

16. O Aruna, Thou crimson-gold hued goddess, who art like the rays of the rising sun on the pure minds of gifted poets (helping their poesy to burst forth). Those who adore Thee become capable of delighting the minds of good people with the majestic flow of words that surge like waves of erotic emotions, emanating from the youthful Saraswati (the goddess of speech).

17. O Mother, whoever meditates on Thee as Vasini and other devis, who are the source of speech and whose radiance resembles the lustre of freshly cut moonstone, can become the writer of poetical works as delightful and interesting as those of the great authors, and emitting words sweet with the fragrance of Saraswati's mouth.

18. How can the many heavenly damsels and celestial courtesans, like Urvashi, with bashful eyes like those of timid deer in the forest, not become fascinated by a person who meditates on the beauty of Thy form, like the early rays of the rising sun, which bathes the heaven and earth in a crimson radiance.

19. O Consort of Hara, whoever meditates on Thy face in the bindu, with Thy twin breasts below it, and the half akshara *'ha'* also below, Kamadeva evokes a string of emotions by

which he becomes identified with Thee in meditation, and thus can quickly stir the mind of any woman. To instantly fascinate anyone is indeed a trifle for him who meditates on Thee as Triloki (the ruler of the three worlds) with the sun and moon as breasts.

20. Whoever meditates in the heart on Thee as an idol sculpted of moonstone and on the nectar flowing from the rays sent forth from Thy body, like Garuda himself, humbles the pride of snakes and with mere looks cures the fever of the nectar-showering nadi.

21. The noble aspirants with minds free from the impurities of maya (such as illusion and ignorance) are filled with thrills of spiritual bliss by (the vision of) Thy lightning-like body with its manifestations of sun, moon and fire, located above the six lotuses as Thy rays in the core of the sahasrara lotus.

22. O Bhavani, do Thou have pity and bestow Thy glance on me, Thy servant. Whoever is desirous of Thee, prays thus, even before he starts uttering your name. Thou instantly bestow on him oneness with Thyself, at whose feet divinities like Mukunda (Vishnu), Brahma, Indra (and others) perform the ceremony with lighted lamp.

23. Thou, having appropriated the left side of his body as Ardhanarishwara, Thy mind was not satisfied, I suspect, and hast invaded Shambhu's right half as well, because of which Thy form (that shines in my heart) is totally crimson in hue and slightly bent by the weight of Thy two breasts, having three eyes and the crescent moon adorning Thy crown.

24. Brahma creates the universe, Hari protects it, and Rudra destroys it. Then Isha absorbs these deities (which include the entire universe in involution) into himself, and all of

them disappear into Sadashiva. Only a mandate from Thee through a single movement of Thy creeper-like brows confers Thy blessings (to spur them into activity again).

25. O Auspicious One, the worship done at Thy feet becomes the worship of the three illumined ones (Brahma, Vishnu and Shiva), who have their origin in Thy three gunas (rajas, sattwa and tamas). (They require no special worship) because they are ever waiting by the side of the diamond foot-stool that bears Thy feet, with their joined palms held above their crowned heads (in salutation to Thee).

26. Virinchi (Brahma) is reduced into the elements; Hari (Vishnu) meets his end; Kinasha (Yama, the god of death) himself dies; Kubera (the god of wealth) meets with destruction, and Indra with all his followers closes his eyes in the face of death. O Sati! Thy consort Shiva alone is sporting in such a state of dissolution as this.

27. May my prattle be the utterance of Thy mantra; my hand movements, the gestures (mudras) of Thy worship; my walking, Thy circumambulation; my eating and drinking, oblations to Thee; the stretching of my limbs, prostration to Thee; all my enjoyments, the various offerings made during Thy worship. Thus may all my actions become acts of self-dedication performed in the worship of Thee.

28. May my life become beautiful as a bunch of flowers on Thy feet, dripping with the honey of splendour, bestowing abundant wealth that is always desired upon Thy poor devotees, with its six sensory organs (including the mind) forever drowned at those feet, like a six-legged honey bee.

29. Even after consuming the nectar that confers immunity from frightful old age and death, the divine beings like Brahma and Indra perish finally at the time of cosmic dissolution. O Mother, if (Thy consort) Shiva is not

destroyed by time, despite having swallowed the dreadful poison, it is because of the greatness of Thy ear ornaments.

30. Even while Brahma, Vishnu and Indra are prostrated before Thee, still at the unannounced arrival of Shiva at Thy abode, Thou springest up (in such a hurry to receive Him that) Thy attendants (have to caution Thee), crying out, "Take care of the crown of Brahma, avoid tumbling over the heavy diadem of Vishnu, and beware of the crest of Indra."

31. Pashupati (Shiva) at first remained satisfied after giving to the world the sixty-four tantras (which expound practices), conferring only one or other of the various psychic powers and worldly fulfilments. Later, at Thy insistence, he revealed this, Thy own tantra, to the world, independent of all the others, and capable of conferring the four aspirations of men: artha, kama, dharma and moksha.

32. O Mother! (the syllables) *Ka, Ee, Ai* and *La* indicated by Shiva, Shakti, Kama and Earth; *Ha, Sa, Ka* and *La* denoted by Ravi (sun), Sheetakirana (moon), Smara (Kamadeva) and Hamsa (swan); and then *Sa, Ka* and *La* denoted by Para (Brahma), Mara (Kamadeva) and Hari (Vishnu), form the mantra of Thy name when joined with the syllable *Hreem* at the end of each of the three groups.

33. O Eternal One! Some connoisseurs of the highest enjoyment do japa of Thee adorned with the rosary of chintamani gems, adding the syllables of Kamaraja (*Kleem*), Bhuvaneshwari (*Hreem*) and Sri (*Shreem*) at the beginning of Thy mantra. (Thus do they) worship Thee with the oblations of countless streams of ghee from Surabhi (the celestial cow) in the purified fire of Shiva (i.e. Shakti established as the trikona in the anahata chakra).

34. O Bhagavati! I realize Thy body as Shambhu's with the sun and the moon as Thy two breasts. This relationship

exists in common between you. Thy pure atma, having nine principal and accessory manifestations (is thus the atma of the entire universe, which is none other than Shiva). Hence Thou art equipoised as transcendent bliss and consciousness.

35. O Consort of Shiva! Thou art mind; Thou art ether; Thou art air; Thou art fire, water and earth too. When Thou hast transformed Thyself into the form of the universe in this way, there is nothing beyond what is not included in Thee. This form of Consciousness and Bliss that Thou assumest rules in the form of Shiva's consort.

36. I salute the supreme Shambhu, residing in Thy ajna chakra, resplendent as millions of suns and moons together, whose left side is integrated with the supreme consciousness (Thyself), who adores Thee with devotion, and lives in that effulgent mansion (where Thou reside), which is outside the reach of sun, moon and fire, and beyond the grasp of the world.

37. I meditate in Thy vishuddhi chakra, on Shiva and Devi, who is equal to Shiva in all respects, the creator of ether, shining like pure crystal. By the radiance emanating from Shiva-Shakti, resembling moonlight, the universe enveloped in the darkness of ignorance rejoices, like the chakori bird bathing in the rays of the moon.

38. (O Mother!) I adore the pair of swans (Shiva-Shakti), who delight in the honey of the full-blown lotus of knowledge (anahata chakra), and who swim in the minds of the great. From their mutual conversation the eighteen arts have emerged. They separate good from evil, like (swans separate) milk from water.

39. O Mother! I worship him, who is always invoking the fire in Thy swadhisthana, as Samvarta, the lord of the fire of

dissolution. I adore Thee, great Samaya (his potent power). When the angry looks of the great (Samvarta) burn up the universe, Thy glance drenched with compassion renders a cooling treatment.

40. I worship that unique and indescribable dark-blue rain cloud which abides ever in manipura with the lightning form of Shakti, dispelling darkness, and the rainbow formed by her dazzling gem-decked ornaments, sending showers upon the universe burnt by the sun of Rudra.

41. I venerate Navatmana, who is engaged in the mahatandava dance, expressing the nine emotions, in the company of Samaya, who is dancing the lasya in Thy mooladhara chakra. In you both, this universe has come to have a father and a mother, who have come together graciously for its regeneration.

42. O Daughter of the snow-clad mountain! The golden crown on Thy head is densely bedecked with precious gems that glitter like the stars attaining a ruby colour. The poet who praises it is likely to have the impression that the crescent moon on Thy crown is a rainbow, because of the multicolour sheen of the inlaid gems.

43. O Consort of Shiva! May Thy dense, soft and shining braid of locks, resembling a forest of full-blown, blue lotus flowers, remove the darkness of ignorance (in our hearts). I presume that the heavenly flowers of Indra's garden have taken a place in these locks to absorb a little of their natural fragrance.

44. May we be blessed by the streak of vermilion (adorning Thy parting line) that appears like the rays of the rising sun, imprisoned as it were by the darkness of the thick locks of Thy hair. The thin band formed by the middle parting line of Thy hair appears to be a canal for carrying the overflowing flood of beauty of Thy face.

45. Naturally, Thy face surrounded by curly forelocks, beautiful like a swarm of honey bees, ridicules the beauty of lotus flowers. The slight smile on Thy face, rendered charming by the brilliance of bud-like teeth, emits a fragrance that gives great pleasure to the bees that are the eyes of Shiva, the destroyer of Kamadeva (the God of love).

46. I think Thy forehead, shining with the pure brilliance of its youthful beauty, is the second (crescent moon in addition to) the crescent moon already attached to Thy crown. (As the upper is) inverted (both crescent moons) appear to be joined together by the nectar dripping from them and form the autumnal full moon.

47. O Uma, who art bent on dispelling the fears of the world! I consider Thy slightly raised eyebrows to be the bow of Kamadeva, Thy eyes shining like bees as the bowstring held in the forearm of Kamadeva, whose clenched fist hides Thy middle portion.

48. Thy right eye, being of the nature of the sun, gives birth to the day. Thy left eye, being of the nature of the moon, causes night, and Thy third eye, resembling a golden lotus slightly in bloom, causes the twilight in between day and night.

49. Thine eyes are glorious, surpassing all the great cities in their uniqueness: wide, auspicious, undefeated even by the blue lotuses, shedding a continuous flow of grace, subtly sweet, bestowing enjoyment and offering protection to the world. Thy glance is fit to be referred to by their respective behaviour.

50. The two honey bees of Thy long eyes are constantly hovering about Thy ears, imbibing the honey dripping from the flower bunch of the nine poetic emotions poured into them by the poet-devotees (singing hymns of Thee).

Seeing this good fortune of Thy two eyes, Thy third eye in the forehead looks slightly red out of jealousy.

51. (O Mother!) Thy glance at Shiva is softened by love; at others (it is characterized) with that (feeling) of dislike; at Ganga with that of anger; on hearing of the heroic exploits of Shiva, with that of wonder; at the great serpents forming the ornaments of Shiva, with that of dread; at the sight of Thy comrades, with that of a smile; and at me, Thy devotee, with that of compassion. Moreover, Thy glance has the red-tinged loveliness of a lotus flower, indicating courage and heroism.

52. O Devi, who art the bud on the crest of the mountain king's dynasty! Thy two eyes which extend up to the ears, with eyelashes resembling the feathery wings (attached to arrows), engaged in disturbing the tranquillity of the mind of Shiva, look like the arrows of Kamadeva, aimed and draw up to the ear.

53. O Consort of Isha (Maheshwara)! The lustrous beauty of Thy three eyes shines with three distinct colours (red, white and black) when beautified with collyrium, like the three gunas: rajas, sattwa and tamas, which Thou assumest with a view to reviving Brahma, Vishnu and Rudra, after their dissolution (during the pralaya) and start them once again on creative activity.

54. O Goddess, who has surrendered her heart only to Pashupati (Shiva)! (It seems certain that) with Thy compassionate eyes, having the three colours of red, white and black, Thou presentest to us the confluence of the holy rivers, Shone, Ganga and Yamuna, to sanctify ourselves by immersing in them.

55. O Aparna! The female fish hide themselves in water surely without blinking, being afraid of the telltale activities of

Thy eyes. Sri, the goddess of beauty, also abandons the closed petals of the blue lily during the day (in order to reside in Thy lotus-like eyes) and returns again at night to the open blue lily.

56. O Daughter of the mountain king! The sages have said that the world is dissolved and created with the closing and opening of Thine eyes. I suspect that Thou dost not blink, but keepest Thine eyes always open to prevent this universe that has sprung up at the opening of Thine eyes from going into dissolution.

57. O Shive, Auspicious One! Grace me also, being far removed from Thee and miserable, with Thy far-reaching and compassionate look, beautiful like the slightly blooming blue lotus. By this I shall feel blessed, while to Thee it involves no loss. The rays of the moon do fall on the palace and on the wilderness alike.

58. O Daughter of the mountain king! The curved space between Thy eyes and ears creates the feeling of Kamadeva's beautiful bow. The length of Thy side-glances cast through them, reaching beyond the ears, creates the impression of an arrow mounted on a bowstring.

59. I fancy that Thy face, having two ear ornaments that reflect on Thy glistening cheeks, is verily the four-wheeled chariot of Manmatha, the god of love. Seated in this chariot of Thy face, he inflicts pangs on the Lord of Pramathas (Shiva), who is fully equipped and ready (to fight back) with the earth for a chariot, whose wheels are the sun and moon.

60. O Consort of Shiva! Saraswati continuously imbibing Thy sweet speech that humbles the sweetness of nectar, through the cups of Thine ears, is seen to reply in the affirmative by shaking her head, congratulating Thee by the loud clanging Omkara of her ear ornaments.

61. O Flag Bearer of the race of the snowy mountain! May Thy bamboo-like nose ridge quickly bestow the appropriate fruits on us. The moon cooled breath of Thy left nostril pushes out pearls from inside in such abundance that one pearl can be seen outside as Thy nasal pendant.

62. O Goddess with beautiful teeth! I shall say the names of that which have a likeness to the splendour of Thy naturally red parted lips. (I am afraid I shall have to wait until) the coral creeper produces a fruit (which is redder than the bimba fruit). Will not even the bimba fruit feel a little ashamed to be compared with the redness of Thy lips, since it is the mere reflection of Thy lips that has made the bimba fruit so red.

63. The chakora birds have developed insensitivity of the tongue by drinking the extreme sweetness of the luminous light of Thy smile on Thy moon-like face. For this reason every night they drink as much as they want of the waves of nectar from the moon to obtain some sour taste under the impression that it is gruel (that will relieve the insensitivity of their tongues).

64. O Mother! Glory to Thy tongue that defies the lustrous redness of the hibiscus flower and is constantly engaged in articulating the glories of Thy consort. (The redness of Thy tongue is so intense that) the white crystal-like complexion of Saraswati, the goddess of speech who dwells on the tip, changes into the colour of a ruby.

65. O Mother! Rejecting the remains of the offerings made to Shiva, as those are the share of Chanda, celestials like Brahma, Indra and Vishnu, after their victory over the asuras, (come to Thee) clad in armour with their head dress removed (to receive as Thy gracious gift) the betel leaf rolls from Thy mouth with white camphor pure as the moon and chew them until they melt away.

66. While Saraswati sings with her vina, extolling the glorious deeds of Pashupati (Shiva), Thou beginest to express words of appreciation, nodding Thy head. The sweetness of Thy voice (however seems to ridicule) the soft melody of her musical instrument, and hence Saraswati silently covers the vina with its cloth.

67. O Daughter of the mountain! How can I describe the matchless beauty of Thy chin, which is touched with affection by Thy father Himavan, the mountain king, and lifted again and again by Thy consort Shiva with the intensity of his desire to kiss Thy lips, and which forms the handle of the mirror of Thy face for Shambhu to hold and view.

68. Thy neck, always thrilled by the embrace of the destroyer of cities (Shiva), displays the gracefulness of the lotus-stalk. Below this neck with the naturally white garland (of pearls), darkened by the application of agaru paste, presents the charm of the fibrous root of the lotus.

69. O Mistress of the musical modes, modulations and songs! The three lines on Thy throat, indicating the number of strings in the auspicious cord fastened at the time of Thy wedding, shine like boundaries demarcating the three musical scales which form the source of the various melodies of musical notes.

70. Brahma, being afraid of the fingernails of Shiva due to the earlier mishap (when he nipped off his fifth head), is now praising the loveliness of Thy creeper-like four arms, smooth like the lotus stalk, with his remaining four heads simultaneously hoping that Thou might give him protection.

71. O Uma! How can we describe the splendour of Thy hands, lit up with the radiance of Thy nails, which surpasses the brightness of the morning's lotus blooms? Alas, the lotus

can perhaps attain some similarity (with Thy hands), if its redness is enhanced by contact with the red dye on the feet of goddess Lakshmi, who sports in it.

72. O Devi! May Thy pair of breasts from which milk is overflowing, suckled simultaneously by both Skanda and Ganesha, always expel our sorrows. Suddenly, with suspicion in his heart, Ganesha feels with his hands to see whether the pair of frontal globes of his elephant face are there (or whether they have become Thy breasts before his eyes), thus causing great amusement (to his parents).

73. O Mountain King's flag of victory! We have no doubt at all in our mind that these two breasts of Thine are jars of ruby filled with nectar, because by drinking their contents, Thy two sons, Kumara and Vinayaka, (have remained) young boys to this day, not having known the pleasure of the company of women.

74. O Ambe! The expanse of Thy breasts bears a creeper-like necklace made of pure pearls obtained from the frontal globe of Gajasura, variegated from within by the brilliance of Thy bimba-like lips, as if it were the confluence of the fame (white) and the valour (red) of Thy consort Shiva, the destroyer of the cities.

75. O Daughter of the mountain king! I remember Thy breast, the milk ocean emerging as poetic inspiration from Thy heart, graciously given to the Dravidian child (Sankara) by which, due to drinking it, among great composers, he became a noted poet.

76. O Devi, daughter of the mountain! When the flames of Shiva's wrath consumed the body of Manmatha (Kama-deva), he took refuge in the deep lake of Thy navel from which arose a creeper-like column of smoke, which people describe, Mother, as the line of Thy hair below the navel.

77. O Shive, auspicious mother! Thy slender middle region, which appears to devotees like the subtle ripples of the river Kalindi, being compressed as the ether in between Thy bulging breasts, is forced into the cavity of Thy navel.

78. O Daughter of the mountain! Glory to Thy navel, (which is like) a steady whirlpool on the surface of the river Ganga. The wet soil-bed for the creeper of Thy navel hair bears the two flower buds of Thy breasts. The gentle depression (of Thy yoni) is the sacrificial pit, wherein resides the fire of the prowess of Kamadeva, which is also the pleasure house of his wife, Rati, opening the cave for yogic success to the eyes of Shiva.

79. O Ornament of womankind! May Thy naturally slender waist, labouring under the weight of Thy breasts and therefore slightly bent and threatening to break under that weight, whose precarious stability is like that of a tree on a cracking river bank, be safe, O Daughter of the mountain!

80. O Devi! The three folds in Thy middle region look like three strands of lavali creeper wound by Kamadeva for support to prevent Thy middle region from breaking under the weight of Thy quickly perspiring breasts, bright as golden pots, touching Thy armpits and bursting the brassiere covering them.

81. O Parvati! Thy father, the mountain king, has presented to Thee as dowry (at the time of Thy marriage), the heaviness and expansiveness cut from his flanks. For this reason Thy stupendous hips, extensive and heavy, cover this entire earth and thus lighten its weight.

82. O Daughter of the mountain! The beauty of Thy thighs surpasses both the trunks of lordly elephants and also the stems of golden coloured banana trees. O Devi, observer of

all ordained duties! Thy perfectly rounded knees, hardened by repeated prostrations to Thy consort, rival the frontal lobes of the heavenly elephant, Airavata.

83. O Parvati, daughter of the mountain! Surely, in order to conquer Rudra, Kamadeva has converted Thy two thighs into quivers to store therein double the number of arrows. For at the end of Thy feet are seen ten crescent-shaped arrow heads under the guise of Thy toenails, sharpened on the whetstone of the crowns of prostrating divinities.

84. O Mother! Be pleased to place Thy two feet, which the Upanishads, the crown of the Vedas, wear as the crest jewel, on my head too. River Ganga, who resides in the matted locks of Shiva, offers them water in worship, and their bright red dye gives a crimson brilliance to the jewels on the diadem of Vishnu.

85. Salutations to Thy feet, a delight to the eyes, because of the brilliance of the lac dye applied to them! Thy consort, Pashupati, desiring to be kicked by those feet, is jealous of the kankeli (ashoka) tree in Thy pleasure garden.

86. When Thou suddenly kicked at the forehead of Thy husband with Thy lotus foot, as He bent His head in shame for calling Thee inadvertently by the name of another woman, His enemy Kamadeva got an opportunity in the form of the tinkling of Thy anklets to get rid of the long-standing rumour about Shiva consuming him in the fire of his anger.

87. O Mother! The lotus flower of Thy feet, which always remain on the snow mountains (of the Himalayas), blooming day and night, and bestowing grace on devotees, is undoubtedly far superior to the common lotus flower, which perishes in snow, closes at night and is dependent for its prosperity upon Lakshmi, the goddess of wealth, whose blessings on devotees are quite temporary.

88. O Devi! How can the great poets equate Thy feet, which are the seat of fame and beyond the reach of mishaps, to the hardened shell of the tortoise? And how did Thy consort Shiva, the destroyer of cities, in spite of all his tenderness towards Thee, place Thy foot on the grinding stone with his two hands during Thy marriage ceremony?

89. O Chandi! Thy feet with moon-like toe nails, which shame the lotus-like palms of adoring heavenly damsels, quickly shower abundant wealth on the poor and humble devotees, seeming to mock the celestial (wish-yielding) trees, whose tender branches bestow desired gifts only to the devas.

90. O Mother! Tell me when will I, a seeker of knowledge, (have the privilege of) imbibing the (red-tinted) water in which Thy lac-painted feet have been washed, which can generate poetic genius, even in a naturally dumb person? When will I let the poetic speech flow, as the chewed betel leaf juice from the mouth of Saraswati?

91. O Goddess of graceful gait! The royal swans in Thy household never abandon their pursuit of Thee in their effort to learn from Thy gait in order to correct their own defective ways of walking. Thy lotus feet have movement of their own and seem to give instructions to them through the tinkling sounds of Thy anklets.

92. Thy servants Brahma, Vishnu, Rudra and Ishwara have taken the shape of the four legs of Thy bed. Shiva has formed himself into Thy bedspread with his lustrous whiteness reflecting Thy crimson glory, thereby becoming the embodiment of erotic emotions for the eyes, and making Thee happy.

93. With curly hair and artless smile, with heart soft as the shirisha flower, with breasts tight and hard as a grinding stone, waist extremely slender, breasts and hips generous

in size, the indescribable Aruna Shakti, the grace of Shiva, shines compassionately for the protection of the universe.

94. The sun, having assembled Thy two feet in the jewel looking glass (of its rays), becomes wonderstruck by the limitless rays that the reflected image of Thy face gives off. From fear of that, he (withdraws Thy image) into his own heart lotus, where it appears full blown, tranquil, open, expanded, spread out and free of blemish, like the moon.

95. The dark mark on the moon is musk. The moon's watery disc is an emerald cup filled with pieces of camphor (the small projections on the moon). When the contents of this cup are exhausted by Thy using them, Brahma certainly fills it up every day for Thee.

96. Thou, the Consort of Shiva, the destroyer of the cities, resides in the inner apartment. Hence, the privilege of worshipping Thy feet is not easy for the fickle-minded. It is well known that the devas, like Indra, who are Thy gatekeepers, have attained unparalleled siddhis or powers of perfection, such as anima and others.

97. O Sati! How numerous are the poets who have courted and attained Saraswati! Who with some wealth fails to become the lord of Lakshmi! But, O foremost of chaste ones! None besides Shiva, not even the kuravaka tree, has had the embrace of Thy breasts.

98. O Eternal Mother! By always identifying in meditation with Thee, who art surrounded and served by the divine powers like anima and others, which are the rays emanating from Thy body, a devotee attains glories far above even those of the three-eyed Shiva. No wonder the flames of the cosmic dissolution prove only to be the waving of camphor lights in Thy adoration.

99. O Consort of Parabrahman! The scholars who are learned in the scriptures describe Thee as the goddess of learning, Saraswati, the wife of Brahma; the lotus-born Lakshmi, the wife of Vishnu; and also the daughter of the mountain, the wife of Shiva. However, Thou art Mahamaya, the indefinable fourth power, having inconceivable and limitless glory, who revolves the wheel of this world.

100. O Uma! This waist, emerging from large, heavy and full breasts, smiling countenance, bewitching glances like several Kamadevas, body with the splendour of a flowering kadamba tree, all these together create agitation in the mind of Hara (Shiva) and other people, as if Thou, who art spotlessly pure, art transformed into an object of worldly enjoyment for Thy devotees.

101. (O Mother!) Thy devotee sports with Saraswati and Lakshmi, thus arousing the jealousy of their consorts, Brahma and Vishnu. (By his charm) he attracts the attention of Rati (the wife of Kamadeva) and thus violates her chastity. Freed from the bondage of birth and ignorance, he lives a long life and enjoys the essence of supreme bliss.

102. O Hidden Treasure! Whose virtues are limitless, ever smiling and blissful, of excellent decorum, unlimited fountain of wisdom, ever abiding in the minds of those who do not deviate from the rules of self-restraint, free from conventions, whose feet are glorified by all the Upanishads, eternal and fearless, pray approve this hymn of mine (Thy humble devotee) in praise of Thee.

103. O Source of all learning! Just as performing the flame waving ritual to the sun is only offering his own light to him; offering arghya to the moon with the water that oozes out of the moon-stone is only to give back what belongs to the moon, and making water-offering to the ocean is to return what belongs to it, so this hymn addressed to Thee is composed of words that are already Thine.

Glossary

Abhaya – freedom from fear
Abhyasa – constant, uninterrupted practice
Adhara shakti – energy which supports
Adhishthatri devi – established deity
Adi – first
Advaita bhava – experience of oneness with the supreme atman
Agamas – sixty-four tantric texts
Agni – fire
Aham – I; 'I am'
Ahamkara – sense of I-ness
Ahuti – oblation
Aishwarya – divine glory
Akasha – space
Akshara – indestructible sounds
Amrita varsha – drenching of one's entire being with nectar, indicative of spiritual awakening
Amrita – nectar of immortality
Amsha avataras – partial manifestations
Anadi – eternal
Ananda – unending bliss
Annamaya kosha – food or material body
Antar yaag – inner worship
Antaratman – inner self
Anu – atomic
Anubhava – direct perception and cognition
Anusthana – intensive practice of mantra meditation

Apara – limited
Apara prakriti – manifest nature
Aparokshanubhuti – direct perception of truth
Apas – water
Aradhana – worship
Ardhanarishwara – form of Shiva-Shakti, which is half male and half female
Ashtami – eighth day of the moon, particularly auspicious for Devi worship
Ashirvada – blessing, benediction
Ashuddha – impure
Atman – Self, soul or inner consciousness
Atma vishwas – belief in the self; self-confidence
Avahan – invocation
Avatara – descent of a manifestation of God to the mortal plane
Avyakta – unmanifest creation
Bahir yaag – external worship
Bhagavati – name of Devi, the supreme goddess
Bhashya – commentary
Bhava – inner feeling or attitude
Bhoga – worldly enjoyment
Bhu loka – worldly plane of gross objects
Bhupura – square surrounding a yantra, which represents the earth element that contains the diagram and all that it represents
Bhuta jaya – victory over the elements
Bija mantra – seed sound
Bindu – point or nucleus
Brahma granthi – psychic lock at mooladhara
Brahmaloka – plane of Brahma
Brahmamuhurta – time of day between 4.00 and 6.00 am prescribed for sadhana
Brahman – ever-expanding consciousness
Brahmanda – macrocosmos
Brahmastra – missile of the potency of Brahma
Buddhi – heightened intellect
Chakra bhedana – piercing of the chakras when the kundalini ascends to sahasrara

Chandi – the terrible one, who is dark-hued like Kali, the destroyer of time
Charana amrita – life-giving nectar of the feet
Chetana – consciousness; conscious
Chidananda – blissful consciousness
Chinmayi – pure awareness
Chitshakti – energy of consciousness
Chitta – individual consciousness
Daitya – demon
Darshan – direct cognition; inner experience
Dasa mahavidyas – ten agents and manifestations of the supreme Shakti that act at her behest
Deva – illumined being, deity, god
Devi – Mother goddess; luminous nature of spirit in its female aspect
Devi bhakti – devotion to the Mother goddess
Devi vigraha – yantra of the cosmic mother
Dharana – one-pointed concentration
Dhvani – sound vibration
Dhyana – meditation
Drashta – seer or witnessing aspect of consciousness
Drishti – vision
Dvaita bhava – duality and limited experience
Dwesha – repulsion
Ekagrata – one-pointed concentration
Granthi – psychic knot
Grihastha – householder; second of the four ashramas or stages of life according to ancient vedic tradition
Guna – quality of nature
Hara – epithet of Shiva
Hari – epithet of Vishnu
Hiranyagarbha – the golden egg or womb of creation
Hridayapeetha – centre of Shakti at Deoghar where her heart fell
Iccha shakti – power of desire or will
Ida nadi – channel of lunar, mental energy
Idam – this; 'I do'
Jada – inert, dormant matter
Jagrat – waking state of consciousness

Japa – continuous repetition of mantra
Jivatman – individual, embodied soul
Jnana – discriminating knowledge
Jnana shakti – power of discriminating knowledge
Jnanendriyas – five sensory organs
Jyoti – light
Kaamkala kut – meditation on Devi's body from the neck to the waist, which confers fulfilment of all one may desire
Kaamkala mantra – combination of sounds which ensure happiness in this life and moksha in the life beyond
Kala – rays; arts
Kali – consumer of time
Kalpavriksha – wish-fulfilling tree
Kama – root of desire
Kama-bija mantra – source of the Sri Chakra mantra
Kanchuka – veil of maya which limits and restricts consciousness
Karana – causal state of consciousness
Karma – action; residual impression
Karmendriyas – five organs of action
Kaula marga – path of tantra; vama marga and dakshina marga, the left hand and right hand path, are a part of this path
Kaya kalpa – rejuvenation of the body
Klesha – inherent source of all pain and suffering: avidya (ignorance), asmita (ego), raga (attraction), dwesha (repulsion) and abhinivesha (fear of death)
Kriya shakti – power of action
Krodha – anger, hatred
Kshipta – mental state of dissipation
Kundalini – embodied spiritual force; evolutionary potential related to consciousness
Likhit japa – writing of sacred mantras or hymns
Lingam – source, causal form of Shiva
Loka – worlds or planes of consciousness which the awareness passes through
Madhukari – nectar-producing ray
Mahadeva – great god
Mahakaal – form of Shiva who absorbs the universe into its source at the time of pralaya

Mahashakti – great energy
Mahavakya – great utterance or statement
Maithuna – fusion of male and female energies; physical union
Mandala – sacred circle or wheel; three-dimensional form, such as a murti or image
Manidvipa – island of jewels; abode of Parashakti
Manmatha – churning the mind
Mantra – special syllable, word or group of words used for meditation; sound vibration of intense frequency
Matri bhava – motherly feeling
Matrika – original sound syllables; storehouses of energy
Matrika shakti – supreme energy as sound
Mayatita – equipoise of the three gunas
Moha – delusion
Moksha – liberation
Moodha – dull and inert mental state
Mudras – gestures
Mukti – liberation
Nada – subtle, inner sound
Nadi – flow
Nakshatras – planets
Navaratri – anusthana of nine nights
Nirakara – without form
Nirbhasa shakti – absolute power
Nirguna – without guna
Nirguna upasana – formless worship
Nirodhika – subtle chakra above ajna
Niruddha – state of total control of mind
Nirvikalpa – transcendence
Nyasa – tantric practice in which mantras are systematically placed at specific centres and parts of the body
Omkara – mantra or sound of Aum
Pancha mahabhutas – five great elements: prithvi (earth), apas (water), agni (fire), vayu (air) and akasha (ether)
Panchagni tapas – austerity of sitting amidst five fires
Panchakshari – fifteen-syllabled mantra, as in Sri Vidya
Parabrahman – supreme consciousness
Paramananda – highest bliss

Paramanu – basic particle or energy unit
Paramatman – supreme soul
Paramtattwa – Mahashakti
Para prakriti – supreme nature
Parashakti – supreme power
Paravidya – transcendental knowledge
Parikrama – circumambulation
Parkaya pravesh – to enter the body of another
Pasupatastra – missiles of the potency of Shiva
Peetha – seat or place where sacred energy is enshrined
Pindanda – microcosmos
Pingala nadi – channel of physical, solar energy
Pooja – worship
Poorna avatara – total manifestation of the godhead
Poornima – full moon
Prajna – intuitive knowledge
Prakasha – effulgent illumination
Prakriti – cosmic nature; the manifest Shakti
Pralaya – destruction, dissolution
Prana pratishtha – invocation of energy into a mandala or yantra
Pranava – Aum
Pratyaya – mental object or image
Puranas – 18 ancient texts containing the earliest mythology of the tantric and vedic traditions
Purusha – cosmic consciousness
Purushartha – four essential requisites of life: artha, kama, dharma and moksha
Raga – attraction
Rajas – force of dynamism, movement
Rasa – feeling or emotion
Rashis – astrological formations
Riddhi – immense wealth and glamour
Rudra abhisheka – ceremony performed for Shiva in which milk and other substances are offered to the shivalingam
Rudra granthi – psychic lock at ajna chakra
Sadakhya tattwa – seed form of creation
Sadakhyakala – transcendental form of Shakti
Sadhaka – established practitioner

Saguna upasana – worship with form
Sahasrara padma – thousand petalled lotus at the crown of the head
Sakara – with form
Sakshi – witnessing consciousness
Sakshi bhava – observer or knower state of awareness
Salokya – coexistence with God
Samadhi – transcendental state of meditation; total oneness or absorption in the object of meditation
Samaya tantra – school of tantra which advocates highest experience where the individual realizes the divinity within; basis of Saundarya Lahari
Samipya – in close proximity to God
Sammohana shakti – force of attraction
Sampradaya – tradition
Samput – capsule containing the heart and soul of the worship
Samskaras – impressions, archetypes
Samudra manthana – churning of the ocean when the devas and demons were in pursuit of amrita
Sankalpa – resolve, willpower
Sannyasin – renunciate
Santosha – deep contentment
Sanyama – simultaneous dharana, dhyana and samadhi on the gross, subtle, and causal dimensions of the tattwas
Sapta dhatus – seven physical elements
Sapta loka – seven planes of existence: bhuh, bhuvah, suvah, maha, jana, tapah and satya, as well as the seven nether worlds: atala, vitala, sutala, rasatala, talatala, mahatala and patala
Sarupya – having the same form as God
Satchidananda – truth, knowledge and bliss of the inner self
Sattwa – force of luminosity, purity and balance
Satya loka – highest plane of truth and bliss
Saubhagya – happily married state
Sayujya – state of total union
Sesha – serpent on whom Vishnu reclines in the midst of the waters
Shakta darshana – philosophy related with Shakti as the creator

Shakta tantra – tradition which emphasizes Shakti as the creatrix; three main paths are: Kaula, Mishrit, and Samaya

Shakti – primal energy; manifest consciousness; power, potential; the female aspect of creation and divinity worshipped by the Shakta tradition

Shaktikut – meditation on Devi's body from the waist down, which gives the ability to fulfil one's goals

Shaktiman – holder of Shakti; an epithet of Shiva

Shaktipat – direct transference of energy to the disciple or devotee

Shaktipeethas – 64 centres of Shakti created when the different parts of Sati Devi's body fell on earth after she immolated herself at the Daksha yajna and her body was dismembered by Shiva

Shaktopasana – worship of Shakti

Shaktyatmaka – nature of Shakti

Shastrartha – intellectual debate on the scriptures

Shiva – 'auspicious one'; eternal, transcendental consciousness; counterpart of Shakti

Shivalingam – oval symbol of Shiva's causal form; form of subtle consciousness

Shivaloka – plane of Shiva

Shivaratri – night of Shiva; darkest night of the year

Shivatmaka – nature of Shiva

Shodashi – 'sixteen'; here it refers to the sixteen-lettered mantra of Sri Vidya

Shoonya – void

Shraddha – faith, reverence

Shringara – beautification

Shruti – revealed sounds or knowledge heard in a higher state of consciousness

Shuddha tattwa – pure element

Siddhapeetha – awakened shrine

Siddhi – accomplishment, perfection and power

Sloka – verse of praise

Smashan – burial or cremation ground

Soma – life-giving nectar

Spandan – underlying vibration of all existence

Sphota – bursting forth (of sound)

Sri – auspiciousness; name of Devi
Sri Yantra – geometrical diagram containing 43 triangles; complete symbol of creation, as it houses the entire energy of the microcosmos and reveals the connection with the macrocosmos; represents the eternal seat of Shiva and Shakti
Srishti – creation, manifest universe
Sthiti – maintenance
Sthoola – gross state of consciousness
Stuti – song praising God
Sukshma sharira – subtle body
Sundaram – beauty
Sushupti – deep sleep state of consciousness
Swapna – dreaming state of consciousness
Swayambhu linga – smoky lingam at mooladhara
Tamas – quality of stability or inertia
Tantra – process of expansion of mind and liberation of energy and consciousness from matter
Tapobhoomi – place of sadhana and austerity
Tarka – logic
Tattwa – element
Tattwajnana – experience of the transcendental nature
Tattwatita – beyond the tattwas or elements
Tejas – effulgence
Trataka – one-pointed gazing on a chosen object
Trigunatita – beyond the influence of the three gunas; experience of the inner eye, consisting of pure, unadulterated consciousness
Trigunatmika – comprised of the three gunas
Trimurti – the united form of Brahma, Vishnu and Shiva, representing the trinity of creation, preservation and destruction
Tripura – three cities; one who gains victory over the three states of consciousness: jagrat (waking), swapna (dreaming) and sushupti (deep sleep)
Tripura Sundari – the ultimate beauty inherent in the three worlds; the experience that lies beyond the three states of consciousness; the devi of the Sri Yantra
Turiya – superconscious or transcendental state of consciousness
Tyaga – renunciation
Upasaka – worshipper

Upasana – worship
Vaagbhav kut – meditation on Devi's body from the crown to the neck, which confers wisdom, learning and skill in the arts
Vairagya – non-attachment, dispassion
Vaishvanara – first dimension of universal consciousness, whose sphere is the waking state where the consciousness is associated with physical matter
Vak siddhi – power of speech
Vasanas – deep-rooted desires
Vayu – wind, prana
Vedana – inward feeling
Vibhooti – spiritual glory, accomplishment of yoga
Videha – unembodied
Vidya – inner knowledge, higher knowledge; the goddess Durga
Vigraha – a mandala or image which when concentrated upon through mantras or devotion becomes the being itself
Vikshipta – mental state of fluctuation between dissipation and one-pointedness
Vimarsha – awareness
Virat – universal form
Virinchi – Brahma
Vishnu granthi – psychic lock in anahata
Vishnuloka – plane of Vishnu
Vishwa – universe
Vishwas – belief
Vyakta – manifest creation
Yajna – sacrificial ceremony in which the cosmic energy is invoked, worshipped and displayed within a particular time frame
Yantra – geometrical diagram
Yogagni – fire created through yogic powers
Yoni – womb of creation
Yonipeetha – centre of Shakti at Kamakhya, where her yoni fell; the most sacred shrine of Shakti

Index

Adi Guru Sankara 2–7
Advaita 4, 6–8, 10, 13, 25–28, 86, 383–384
Ajna 28, 78, 83,182, 222, 223, 233–235, 259, 286
Akasha 237, 252–253, 355
Amrita 29, 138, 232, 237, 241, 263
Anahata 28, 222, 239–242, 259, 285, 347
Ananda Lahari 4, 12, 68, 253
Antar yaag 66, 68, 69, 75, 76,
Ardhanarishwara 29, 187–189
Atman 24–25, 28, 41, 43, 153, 222, 224, 383, 417
Aum 35, 82, 303, 328–329
Auspiciousness 18, 19, 26, 30, 166
Awareness 163–164, 182, 185, 218, 219, 222, 234, 235, 241, 253, 254, 392; unified 412

Bahir yaag 66, 68, 75–76,
Beauty 18–27, 121, 123, 124, 147–150, 195, 253, 257, 327, 346–348, 353, 365
Bindu 73, 80–81, 87, 128, 143–145, 156, 172, 222, 233, 367
Bliss 12–13, 30, 128, 129, 140, 195, 225, 232–235, 253, 369, 417
Brahma 190, 191, 197, 209, 331–333, 402

Chakras 12, 38, 40, 49, 72, 70, 74, 75, 76, 77, 80, 81, 133, 157, 182, 192, 235, 237, 238, 246, 249, 253, 353, 397, 410
Compassion 100, 244, 285, 286, 399
Consciousness 28, 45, 50–57, 93–96, 99, 103, 123, 126, 134, 139, 217, 223, 228, 229, 232–235, 237, 270, 303
Creation 1, 14, 20–21, 24–27, 34, 42, 64, 72, 80, 84, 85, 87, 88, 94, 104, 112, 136, 156, 190, 191, 193, 195, 197, 219, 224, 225, 229, 250, 292, 338, 347, 362, 356–357, 365, 367, 397, 410, 412

Darshan 10, 16, 18, 19, 28, 41, 43, 49, 62, 71, 75 82, 83, 50, 152, 166, 168, 169, 178, 179, 182, 185, 223, 253, 257, 259, 386, 405, 407, 410, 414
Dasa mahavidyas 54–56, 57–59
Desire 110–113, 114, 121, 173–175, 197, 246, 264, 301, 346–348, 353, 365, 372
Devi's grace 8–9; manifestation 10, 13; names 32; Sankara's experience 7; Sankara's invocation 3–4; supreme godhead 7; worship 31, 32, 254
Durga 45; chanting of names 74
Dvaita 6, 10, 13–14, 18, 25–28, 383–384

Emotions 27–28, 51, 94, 174, 261, 272, 274–278, 280, 297–299, 346,
Energy 9, 28–30, 38, 47, 48, 50–56, 60, 65, 66, 69, 93–96, 99–100, 117, 146, 177, 182, 188, 218, 221, 228, 229, 232–235, 237, 244, 245, 250, 257, 298, 315, 339, 351, 363, 388, 400, 410
Eroticism 162–164, 117–118, 174, 298–299, 301, 339, 382

Faith 140, 186, 266, 286, 414
Fear 266–268
Feet 102–111, 137–138, 155, 157, 194, 380, 381, 389, 395

Ganesha 338–340, 342, 344
God 1–2, 11, 14, 21, 61, 210–211, 232, 253
Grace 8, 9, 22, 26, 90, 129, 140, 150, 164, 168, 205, 247, 295, 380, 389, 392
Granthis 27, 28, 70, 135, 157, 158, 218
Gunas 26, 85, 191, 195, 217, 218, 281–283, 371, 399, 407, 417
Guru 69, 76, 79, 89, 179, 218, 222, 383

Haadi vidya 77, 78, 220–223
Healing 12–13, 205, 256, 304, 362, 388, 391

Iccha shakti 85, 128, 197, 217, 282, 348, 403
Ida 28, 29, 49, 65, 158, 188, 234

Indriyas 83, 138, 139, 235, 388
Invocation 129, 250, 268; Satyananda tradition 420–421

Jnana 97, 152, 154, 182, 226, 247, 392; shakti 85, 128, 197, 282, 403

Kaadi vidya 77, 78, 220–223
Kaamkala kut 217, 218, 264
Kalas 80–83, 84, 89, 128, 155–159, 166, 172, 182, 184, 225, 226, 233–235, 234, 235, 241, 246, 264, 288, 380
Kali 45, 46, 59, 390
Kalpavriksha 389–390
Kamadeva 115, 119–120, 171, 172, 173, 174, 261–262, 266, 268, 280, 300–301, 346, 352, 359, 360, 365, 373, 382, 401
Kaula marga 65, 76, 77, 221
Kayakalpa 151–154
Kriya shakti 85, 128, 197, 217, 282, 403
Kulapatha 221, 241, 232, 233, 247
Kundalini 12, 13, 31, 68, 70, 71–75, 78, 80, 81, 84, 88, 133–140, 142, 209, 210, 221, 222, 226, 244, 250, 369

Lakshmi 45, 334–335, 386
Liberation 26–27, 74, 98, 112–113, 129, 151–153

Maithuna 49, 223, 226, 231–235, 237–238, 239–242, 386
Mandala 9, 10, 12, 27, 30, 31, 32, 33, 40, 41, 43–53, 75, 86, 90, 125, 176, 219, 256, 362–363

Mantra 9–13, 16, 17, 19, 26, 30, 31, 32, 33–37, 61, 74, 75, 78, 89, 109, 132, 160, 216, 219, 222, 255, 256
Maya 180–183
Mind 8, 10, 16–18, 26, 27, 35, 39, 43, 44, 51, 52, 53, 56, 68, 69, 73, 83, 89, 90, 99, 108, 130, 133, 138, 139, 155, 157, 158, 163, 172, 173, 177, 180, 203, 222, 228, 237, 261, 268, 274, 292, 309, 346, 353, 359, 383, 386, 390, 392, 417
Mishrit marga 65, 76, 77
Mooladhara 27, 132, 221, 369
Moon 79–80, 83, 88, 89, 182, 217, 263–265, 402

Nada 34, 72–73, 78, 80, 81, 128, 156, 160, 223, 303, 307, 329–330
Navaratri 234–235
Nyasa 362

Pancha mahabhutas 104
Panchadasakshari mantra 216–219, 222–223, 226
Paramatma 4, 26, 240–241, 262
Parvati 31, 42, 54, 85, 97, 210, 254, 280, 289, 291–292, 301, 305–306, 315, 335–336, 388, 421
Peethanyasa 60–61
Pingala 28–29, 49, 65, 158, 188, 234
Prana 81–82, 264, 309–311, 319–320, 343–344, 395, 400–401
Prana shakti 116–117
Pranava (see Aum)

Prayer 43, 185; Sankara's prayer 391–393
Protection 51, 161, 332–333, 399
Purification 36, 45, 153, 222, 339

Reverence 71, 98–99, 102, 115, 123, 257, 332
Rudra 190, 191, 244

Sadashiva 191, 192, 197
Sahasrara 28, 65, 69, 76, 80, 83, 128, 134, 139, 140, 148, 163, 182, 183, 184, 192, 218, 222, 226, 232–235, 237, 231, 253–254, 259, 362, 382, 386, 410
Samadhi 14, 28, 327, 327, 359, 409, 412
Samaya 194, 225, 244, 246, 249; marga 65, 76, 77; tantra 49, 61, 65, 67–68, 76, 77, 82, 125, 163, 200, 210, 219, 226, 237, 243, 247, 256, 409–410
Sammohana shakti 115–121
Saraswati 302–303, 315, 321–323, 331–332
Sat Chandi Mahayajna 8–10
Sati 54–55, 59, 60, 97, 113, 291–293
Shakti 14–18, 42, 50, 54–60, 65–77, 83–87, 89–90, 108–109, 126–136, 184, 193–195, 200–201, 205, 227–230, 253, 272–273, 385
Shakti kut 217, 218, 264
Shaktipeetha 59, 61, 211–214, 343
Shiva 204–205, 209–211, 261
Shivam (see auspiciousness)

Shiva-Shakti 29, 40, 72, 85, 86, 93–101,129–130, 136, 138, 139, 145, 148, 160, 188, 189, 215, 218, 223, 225, 226, 230, 324–325, 327, 343, 388, 409, 421; ajna 231–235; anahata 239–242; manipura 246–248; mooladhara 249–250; swadhisthana 243–245; vishuddhi 236–238
Shodashi 72, 78, 79, 82, 89, 99, 188, 191, 194, 222, 226, 241, 264, 265; mantra 218, 219
Siddhis 153, 166–170, 295, 405, 408–409, 185
Sixty-four tantras 210–212
Sound 32, 33–36, 72–73, 74, 80, 81, 84, 94, 128, 132–133, 145, 146, 156, 160, 165, 182, 215, 241, 242, 303, 307, 328, 375
Spandan 96–98, 104, 131, 156, 303, 366–367
Sri Chakra 73, 76, 78, 87, 141–146, 218; worship of 219, 221, 223
Sri Vidya 87, 100, 172, 221, 417; upasana 3, 75–80, 253
Sri Yantra 39–41, 78, 87, 87–89, 215, 225
Sun 167–168, 182, 217, 398, 400–401
Saundarya Lahari sadhana 89–90
Supreme consciousness 14, 19, 152–153, 204, 226, 253, 254, 284, 382
Surrender 179, 184, 201, 203, 253, 284–285, 289, 297, 306
Sushumna 28–29, 49, 65, 140, 158, 188, 234, 237

Swami Satyananda 60, 112, 137, 149, 137, 178, 183, 194, 286, 289; worship of Devi 8–10

Tantra 26, 28, 30–33, 63, 64, 69–72, 359
Tattwas 24, 77, 80, 86, 104, 132–134, 142, 155–157, 169, 192, 197, 198, 200, 212, 229, 235, 242, 355, 369, 374, 382, 397
Third eye 270, 275, 285, 360
Transformation 151–154, 244
Tripura Sundari 3, 31, 57, 56, 76–79, 82, 83, 86, 134, 143, 145, 148, 152, 154, 189, 197, 212, 217, 218, 223, 225, 264, 265, 384, 383, 386, 390, 398 399, 403, 409, 411
Truth 18, 19, 25, 26, 30
Turiya 78, 172, 173, 218, 265, 303, 327, 386, 412

Uma 334–336, 413–414

Vaagbhav kut 217, 264
Vak siddhi 159–164, 165, 166, 302
Vama marga 49, 61, 65
Vishnu 29, 108–109, 115, 190, 191, 197, 207
Vishuddhi 236–238
Visualization 40–41, 125, 128, 186, 218, 257, 259

Yantra 10, 12, 30, 31, 32, 33, 37, 39, 40, 75, 78, 87, 88, 89, 141–146, 219, 256
Yoni 24–25, 94, 226